Ethnic Autonomy—
Comparative
Dynamics
(Pergamon Policy Studies—40)

Pergamon Policy Studies on Ethnic Issues

Ra'anan ETHNIC RESURGENCE IN MODERN DEMOCRATIC STATES

Related Titles

Hall BLACK SEPARATISM AND SOCIAL REALITY: RHETORIC AND REASON

Power MIGRANT WORKERS IN WESTERN EUROPE AND THE UNITED STATES

Allworth ETHNIC RUSSIA IN THE USSR

McCagg & Silver SOVIET ASIAN ETHNIC FRONTIERS

PERGAMON
POLICY
STUDIES

ON ETHNIC ISSUES

Ethnic Autonomy— Comparative Dynamics

The Americas, Europe and the Developing World

Edited by
Raymond L. Hall

Pergamon Press
NEW YORK • OXFORD • TORONTO • SYDNEY • FRANKFURT • PARIS

Pergamon Press Offices:

U.S.A.   Pergamon Press Inc., Maxwell House, Fairview Park, Elmsford, New York 10523, U.S.A.

U.K.   Pergamon Press Ltd., Headington Hill Hall, Oxford OX3 0BW, England

CANADA   Pergamon of Canada, Ltd., 150 Consumers Road, Willowdale, Ontario M2J, 1P9, Canada

AUSTRALIA   Pergamon Press (Aust) Pty. Ltd., P O Box 544, Potts Point, NSW 2011, Australia

FRANCE   Pergamon Press SARL, 24 rue des Ecoles, 75240 Paris, Cedex 05, France

FEDERAL REPUBLIC Pergamon Press GmbH, 6242 Kronberg/Taunus,
OF GERMANY   Pferdstrasse 1, Federal Republic of Germany

Library of Congress Cataloging in Publication Data

Main entry under title:

Ethnic autonomy.

    (Pergamon policy studies)
    Includes bibliographies and index.
    1. Autonomy. 2. Ethnicity. I. Hall, Raymond L.
JC327.E74 1979   323.1   79-10115
ISBN 0-08-023683-9
ISBN 0-08-023682-0 pbk.

Printed in the United States of America

To Anna Kristine

Contents

CONTENTS

Preface

There is a paucity of works on the comparative study of social movements, and particularly comparative ethnic movements, from an international perspective. Although there are works concerned with ethnic dynamics from a comparative perspective, they focus in the main on international politics, development, resource competition, and other aspects of ethnic intergroup conflict. Centered as they are on what might be defined as residual elements or by-products of ethnic relations and conflict, they do not bring the relationship between ethnicity and movements for self-determination into a clear focus. Hence, this volume took another approach, one that is unique in that it deals with ethnic behavior as it relates specifically to a wide variety of movements for self-determination. We refer to these movements under the general heading of <u>ethnic autonomy</u>, but they include nationalist, secessionist, irredentist, schismatic, and separatist movements.

The inspiration for this volume emerged from my - and the contributors - interest in social change resulting from large-scale ethnic movements. Specifically, the recent development of movements for ethnic autonomy around the world, combined with my long interest in ethnic separatism, prompted me to undertake a survey of its emergence and development. After a fairly close examination of a few of these movements, however, it became apparent that my work on ethnic autonomy in the United States would not serve as the best model for treating it elsewhere. It also became apparent that it was not feasible for one individual to study each one of these movements and formulate a framework for analyzing them. Thus, after two or three years of searching out particularly well-qualified specialists, I obtained, through coercion in some cases, their agreement to contribute.

My introduction attempts to put the volume in perspective

by first calling attention to the multiplicity of ethnic movements for autonomy around the world, and then focusing on
specific cases to be treated. Although ethnic autonomy movements stem from many causes, it should be fruitful to examine
the cases covered in this volume by using a limited set of
variables, which appear to be prominent in all such movements - culture, economics, ethnicity, geography, history,
language patterns of domination, and religion. These variables
seem to be prominent "explainers" and "causers" of movements
for ethnic autonomy, but none of the contributors has been
obligated to utilize them.

   After the papers were written, the contributors held a
symposium at Dartmouth College's Minary Conference Center.
We agreed that the ultimate purpose of this volume should be
to provide extensive information about the important and
complex topic of ethnicity and ethnic movements, as well as to
facilitate more rigorous thought, analysis, and research
regarding them. The outcome is a volume of original contributions by experts on ethnic movements in various parts of
the world. Their viewpoints are disparate, and therefore make
no claim to a thorough-going coherence. The book is a series
of case studies of movements for ethnic autonomy in an international perspective.

   Neither do we claim comprehensiveness. Because ethnic
movements are found in all parts of the world, only some of
them can be treated meaningfully in a single volume. We have
selected more than a dozen significant cases. Taking a multi-
disciplinary/interdisciplinary approach, this book should be
highly useful to sociologists, political scientists, anthropologists, psychologists, historians, and indeed, anyone interested
in ethnic dynamics and social movements around the world.

THE ORGANIZATION OF THE BOOK

   Part I begins with a general discussion of some attri-
butional and subjective dimensions of ethnic identification. It
then highlights one of the variables associated with ethnic
identity - language - in terms of its role in various kinds of
movements for ethnic autonomy. In sum, Part I serves as a
conceptual overview of ethnic dynamics, and sets the stage for
the case studies that follow.

   Part II focuses on aspects of ethnic autonomy in North
America. The problems of blacks, Native Americans, Indians,
and Chicanos, in the United States are explored as well as the
separatist dimensions of efforts by French-speaking Quebec to
separate from English-speaking Canada.

   Part III traces ethnic autonomy in Europe, Scotland,
Northern Ireland, Spain, France, and the Soviet Union are

examined as they attempt to deal with various ethnic group efforts to bring about autonomy.

Part IV considers ethnic autonomy in the developing world. It begins with the premise that ethnic dynamics in the Third World are patterned after those in the developed world. Ethiopia, Uganda, West Africa, and India are included in this section.

Part V synthesizes and puts the common elements of the case studies into perspective.

Finally, a word regarding comparative studies. Most social scientists aspire to universal generalizations in their work. However, most comparative social science ultimately suffers from culture-bound constructs and, worse, ethnocentrism. Part of the problem is theoretical. Comparative theory that attempts to leap the sea of national boundaries by leveling social, political, and economic systems often is swept away by the strong current of culture-bound and ethnocentric constructs. To avoid this pitfall, it would be wise to pay serious attention to the importance of observing and analyzing social phenomena within the context of specific social systems. Although the task of comparative theorizing is difficult for a variety of reasons, the occurrence of similar behavior in different states is sufficient reason for attempting to reduce the similarities to their lowest common theoretical denominator. We believe that ethnic autonomy is a good example of action that can be placed in a framework of analysis where it can be treated from a relatively culture-free perspective. Although we utilize culture-bound constructs, we use only ones that have been tested in different settings; and, by placing the case studies in global perspective, we hope to enhance a universal understanding of ethnic autonomy.

Acknowledgments

Gene Lyons, Stanley H. Udy Jr., and Richard W. Sterling, all of Dartmouth College, and Willie B. Lamouse-Smith of the University of Maryland, Baltimore County have our gratitude for their contributions to a successful symposium. The Sociology Department's secretary, Patricia Bromley, also contributed skilled assistance in making the symposium a success. Thanks again to Pat Bromley and to Ann Kulesza for typing portions of the manuscript.

Very special help was received from Gene Lyons, Joseph Curran, William W. "Bill" Cook, David T. Lindgren, Richard W. Sterling, and Jere Daniell.

I am also grateful to the Kel Smith Fund of Dartmouth College for the generous financial underwriting of the Symposium on Ethnic Autonomy at Dartmouth's Minary Conference Center. Thanks go as well to the Sociology Department and the Urban Studies Program, of Dartmouth College. This generosity enabled the editor and the contributors to have three days of sophisticated, elegant, and lively presentations and discussions, thus contributing to a unique and, I hope, seminal work on ethnic autonomy.

Many, many thanks to Terry Tarun Hall for indexing the book.

I am grateful to my wife Terry and to my daughter Anna for the comfort they provided while I was trying to do all the necessary things to complete this volume. They illuminate my life's path.

Introduction

The vast majority of the world's population lives in
ethnically-heterogeneous states.(1) Ethnic diversity means
ethnic differences, and these differences too often contain a
potential for intergroup conflict. Because conflict usually
emerges from a specific kind of relationship between two or
more parties who believe they have incompatible goals, conflict
can erupt over any number of differences among diverse
groups in a shared social environment. Ethnic discord constitutes the most widespread, protracted, and violent form of
intergroup conflict throughout the modern world. Because the
state is the dominant structure in the international system,
and because social and political relationships exist within its
bounds, it is ultimately responsible for resolving or coping
with ethnic differences that can contribute to ethnic conflict.

However, ethnic conflict often transcends the boundaries
of individual states. International concerns arise when latent
or manifest ethnic conflict in one state has implications for
ethnic counterparts in other states. For example, the ethnic
composition of a delegation representing a heterogeneous state
in an international organization may be of concern to ethnic
groups of other states. This situation has possible ramifications for the foreign policy of particular states as well as
international organizations, and thus becomes an international
issue. Moreover, the militant manifestation of ethnicity in one
state may serve as a catalyst for others, causing the mobilization of ethnic cohorts or sympathizers beyond its boundaries.
In sum, ethnic diversity can be one of the most powerful of
sociopolitical forces that influence the balance of power within
heterogeneous states and it can have potential international
implications.

Although ethnic heterogeneity in modern states stands in
vivid contrast to a time when most groups lived in autonomous

and mostly homogeneous social environments, in the past other forms of large-scale political organization also incorporated diverse peoples into shared social environments as the consequence of territorial expansion. The band, the chiefdom, the peasant society, the empire, and the state, nation, or nation-state(2) represent the incorporation, consolidation, and organization of larger territorial units and, consequently, more diverse groups. Hence, it is important to differentiate between the old and the new heterogeneity.

OLD HETEROGENEITY

Prior to the emergence of the modern state, the empire represented the largest of many kinds of political units. (The Roman Empire may be used as a reference point in the following discussion.) Because of its sheer size, it inevitably incorporated diverse peoples; yet size also allowed these diverse groups to remain in essentially homogeneous social environments. This homogeneity was facilitated by the division of empires into several units, each administered by officers representing the emperor. Because the imperial system - or any other political system -centered on the expropriation of resources from the hinterland, the basic responsibility of the imperial officer and his staff in the hinterland usually was to collect tribute to be passed on to the imperial center. Except in cities, the outcome of this process of resource expropriation did not necessitate significant population shifts, and thus groups were able to maintain their ethnic homogeneity.

Distance, as well as imperial preoccupation with collecting tribute, was a significant factor in the maintenance of ethnic homogeneity. In general, there was a direct relationship between the location of the imperial center and its ability, or will, to dominate effectively each ethnic group within its domain: the further away from the center of control an ethnic group lived, the more likely it was to maintain its pre-imperial mode of existence. Indeed, groups so situated probably had only a vague awareness of imperial law and order; their own group norms retained primacy.

There is a further areal implication. Although it was easy to claim vast reaches of territory as part of an imperial domain, consolidating and maintaining hegemony over the domain for a long period of time proved difficult. This was not only because the initial efforts regarding expropriation were unsuccessful, but also because it became increasingly difficult to maintain hegemony over, or gain allegiance from, those groups in the imperial periphery; and imperial centers tended to keep expanding their periphery.

As the periphery expanded, additional diverse groups

were incorporated. Eventually, the cost, in terms of both logistics and manpower, of coercing allegiance from groups in an overextended empire amounted to about the same as the worth of goods expropriated from it. Hence, simple economics dictated that either the number of tribute collectors, or the size of the imperial domain itself, or both be reduced. In either case, emphasis was placed on controlling territory closer to the center. An important result of shrinking the size of the imperial domain was the elimination of outside pressure on diverse groups to share a social environment with other groups. With the elimination or significant diminution of external pressure to share heterogeneous political structures, ethnic groups in the periphery continued to exist according to the dictates of their homogenous social environments. It was not until a new kind of political and social system emerged that the old heterogeneity - essentially one in name only - gave way to the new.

THE NEW HETEROGENEITY

The new heterogeneity first emerged when the imperial system gave way to the monarchically-dominated (nation) state. "L'etat c'est moi," Louis XIV's famous dictum, epitomizes this form of nation-state. The emergence of the (nation) state in Europe was a prerequisite for European colonialism and imperialism around the world. One of the significant outcomes of European incursion was that colonial territory was organized in much the same way as the European (nation) state. In most cases, the impact of European organization on non-European peoples and territory enlarged the scale of indigenous social and political units, and thus incorporated diverse peoples into a larger political union. Consequently, autonomous ethnic groups became, in most cases, "national minorities."(3) This heterogeneity was a new experience to those ethnically-diverse groups, who found themselves pitted against one another in new and different forms of competition. In order to facilitate control of resources, imperialism and technological and commercial developments necessitated the organization of territory and people(s) in new ways. Except in large urban settings, the new mode of state organization could no longer tolerate ethnic preference for homogeneity, which might stand in the way of the "progress of expropriation" or the development of the (nation) state.

The Democratic Idea

While most European states and their colonies experienced the emergence of a new form of state organization hostile to ethnic minorities, the emergence and development of democracy and democratic ideas - especially in the United States - tended to deny the importance of ethnicity. The new loyalty was no longer to the tribe and the religion, but to the "ideology of the common good." This common good was based on the idea that diverse peoples could be brought together in a new heterogeneous social system where the state, rather than ethnicity, was paramount. The intent of this arrangement was to dilute or subordinate the potency of ethnicity vis-a-vis social values; small-scale, simple, homogeneous, ethnic social systems characterized by submission to the group or "mechanical solidarity" were to be elevated to complex, large-scale systems with "organic solidarity" symbolized by the state.

"Organic solidarity" suggests a complex division of labor based on a social bond favoring individual freedom within a context of mutual interdependence, and with state-defined goals superseding those of ethnic groups. Therefore, states tend to define their goals in universal terms in order to minimize ethnic diversity. However, because ethnicity and ethnic identity signify group cohesion centered on traditions, symbols, and psychological phenomena not shared by others with whom the group is in contact, ethnic behavior usually is based on particular definitions of situations motivated by group self-interest. Consequently, when state-defined and imposed values and goals conflict with ethnic values and goals, the disaffected ethnic groups usually persist in pursuing ethnic rather than state goals. Nevertheless, when ethnic and state goals clash, compromise can sometimes avert conflict. In sum, although the "new" heterogeneity fostered by the state was designed to minimize ethnic conflict and facilitate the acceptance of ethnic differences, ethnic conflict is still the rule rather than the exception in most heterogeneous societies.

Urbanization and Urbanism

Despite the general belief that ethnic oppression and inequality have their roots in rural areas, the most developed and ardent expression and organization of social action based on ethnic autonomy is found in cities. On the one hand, it is ironic that separatism and conflict are urban-based, for cities are generally regarded as heterogeneous; but on the other, it must be remembered that precursors of modern urban centers emerged and developed as places where trade and commerce involving diverse individuals and groups could be expedited.

Trade and commerce are business transactions that divide urban residents horizontally along class lines during the daytime, but at night they are for the most part divided vertically along ethnic lines.

Despite the fact that modern cities are more heterogeneous in all respects than rural areas, ethnic and kinship ties remain important elements of individual and group homogeneity. Hence, the city provides a pattern of social organization in which ethnically-aggrieved groups may seize the opportunity to engage in collective efforts to aggrandize their position. However, state domination is usually not threatened in these situations; they are local problems. As a consequence of this feature, it is not coincidental that New York, Chicago, Montreal, Lima, London, Belfast, Madrid, Paris and Addis Ababa are but a few of the many urban centers where active, ethnically-based movements are located. It is important to note the particular contexts of ethnic autonomy in the individual contributions to this volume.

ETHNIC AUTONOMY

There are many reasons why ethnic conflict is so widespread. One is the tendency of groups to reject imposed social and political arrangements that place them in disadvantageous positions. The most prevalent response of an ethnic group to alleged and real state-imposed disabilities is to seek autonomy. Behavior oriented to the establishment of ethnic autonomy may be regarded as a collective effort to create political and social arrangements based on the ethnic groups' own traditions, values and Weltanschauungen. These arrangements may differ from and oppose those defined by the state or by other groups in the wider social system.

Having placed activity directed toward ethnic autonomy in this general context, attention can be focused on the varieties of ethnic group behavior. Some authorities treat ethnic behavior geared to secure autonomy under the general heading of nationalism. However, there are several such kinds of ethnic autonomy, and care must be taken to relate only specific kinds of ethnic autonomy to nationalism.

Nationalism

Nationalism conventionally means united and systematic political action by people or states to achieve or maintain self-determination in the international order. Nationalism may also be a state's instrument for bringing about far-reaching changes within a society. It follows that if ethnic action

within a state is based on the idea of imperium in imperio, it
may be properly labeled ethnic nationalism. However, ethnic
efforts to seek autonomy outside the bounds of specific states
with a view toward establishing a state centered on ethnicity
may also be regarded as ethnic nationalism or separatism.
This form of ethnic nationalism may have regional, religious,
and varied political implications, as in the creation of Israel
and Pakistan. In short, nationalism is too broad a concept to
illuminate the complex dynamics of ethnic action within states.

Secessionism

Secession is generally associated with a region that severs
its ties to a union. The American Civil War, the Nigerian
Civil War, and the crisis of 1965 in Uganda, were all the
result of secession. However, whether the secession is
ethnically-based depends upon the ethnic composition of the
regional breaking away.

Irredentism

Irredentism advocates the recovery of land or territory
once held by a state, or the annexation of a geographic area
historically or culturally related to it. Irredentism played a
significant role in the post-World War I developments that led
to the outbreak of World War II: Mussolini's call for "Italia
irredenta" and Hitler's "mission" to unite all German-speaking
peoples are examples of the power of irredentist sentiments.
Irredentist sentiments currently thrive in the troubled Middle
East, where Arabs and Jews press historical and cultural
claims to the same territory.
Ethnic irredentism obtains when a specific ethnic group in
one state proposes to, or actually does, occupy land in the
legal possession of another state because of historical or cultural claims to the territory. Ethnic irredentism and ethnic
secessionism are both based on historical and cultural claims.

Separatism

Separatism is yet another form of ethnic autonomy; it is
frequently applied - especially by historians and political
scientists - to movements seeking complete political independence from an existing state. Applying the term
separatism to such movements does not clearly differentiate it
from nationalism and its subcategories, such as secessionism or
irredentism. Nevertheless, there is a clear-cut difference:
nationalism involves social action geared to bring about national

self-determination or large-scale social change within a state;
separatism tends to emerge as an expression of a group's
dissatisfaction with its lack of meaningful control over material
and status resources. Unlike nationalism, separatism usually
does not seek pervasive change in the international system.
Rather, it is confined to ethnic action geared to enhance
cultural, linguistic, religious, geographical, and economic
autonomy within specific states. In this sense, separatism is a
subcategory of nationalism insofar as it promotes ethnic autonomy within states, as opposed to the establishment or maintenance of national self-determination. Most of the case
studies in this volume treat various kinds of ethnic autonomy
within states. Nevertheless, there are ethnic groups that
accept inclusion in an existing state, yet seek autonomy and,
in addition, participate in action with their counterparts in
other states to establish a separate state based on ethnicity.
Separatist Basque and Somali ethnic groups, for example, are
not confined to Spain or Somalia; they are also present in
France and Ethiopia, respectively, seeking to establish a
sovereign nation based on their own ethnicity. Neither
nationalism nor separatism describes adequately the dynamics
of cases where separatism shades into nationalism, and care
must be taken to distinguish between them. Clearly, then,
analysis, description, and explanation of ethnic behavior aimed
at autonomy necessitate paying special attention to such
dynamics, especially because separatist movements often
operate like nationalist movements, and have similar
implications.
        Separatism is nonetheless the most frequent form of ethnic
action aimed at complete withdrawal from state-imposed sociopolitical arrangements. Because movements for ethnic autonomy occur so frequently throughout the world, often manifesting themselves similarly in different states, they are
amenable to comparative treatment. Such treatment illuminates
the common features of - as well as the distinct differences
among - the many varieties of ethnic autonomy extant in the
contemporary world.

Ethnic Autonomy Covered in This Work

        The drive for ethnic autonomy is present in almost all
heterogeneous societies in the modern world, and takes many
forms. Its pervasiveness imposes limits on how many examples
can be treated in one volume. This work, indicated in Table
I.1, focuses on just a few of the many examples in the international system. The strength of a case study approach lies
in its capacity to provide the specific setting within which
attention can be focused. Case studies do not have the
perspective necessary to permit generalization about different

Table I.1. Ethnic Autonomy Treated in This Volume

Continent	State	Ethnic Groups in Conflict
North America	The United States	blacks, whites Native Americans (Indians) Chicano
	Canada	French, English
South America	Peru	Indians vs. Europeans
Western Europe	France	Basques Catalonians etc.
	Spain	Basques, Spanish
	Northern Ireland	Catholics, Protestants
	Scotland	Scottish, English
Eastern Europe	USSR	Asians, Slavs, etc.
Asia	India	Hindi, Pakistani, etc.
Africa	Uganda	Ankole vs. Bairu
	West Africa	Multiple Groups in 17 States
	Ethiopia	Amhara, Somalis, etc.

sociocultural and political settings; generalizing from one or two case studies may, in fact, provide only enough detail to explain the social reality of the phenomenon in those limited settings. Moreover, treating a number of case studies from the perspective of a theory derived from only one environment may distort reality in all cases.

The case studies in this volume are, therefore, presented in a global context. That is, an attempt has been made to compensate for the shortcomings of the approach by using a macroscopic framework. Such a broad framework allows us to place the phenomenon under study in a fairly comprehensive context, while simultaneouly utilizing the microscopic strength of the case study approach. Many of the shortcomings of comparative inquiry can be avoided by combining the two approaches, illuminating those features common to autonomy movements and their specific variations by continent, nation, region, and ethnic group.

VARIABLES SELECTED FOR THE ANALYSIS OF SEPARATISM

Conditions under which a movement for autonomy may emerge and develop vary from nation to nation and involve multiple causes; even in a nation where several groups exhibit autonomy-oriented behavior, the behavior may stem from several causes. For example, Native American, Chicano, and black autonomy oriented behavior involve racial oppression, economic exploitation, and cultural and linguistic differences. Hence, it appears that it is a difficult enough task to analyze and explain autonomic behavior in one nation without attempting comparative analysis; behavior in one nation may have little or nothing to do with such behavior in another. However, surface appearances and observations are almost always misleading. Consider separatist behavior by French Canadians, Basques in France, and Walloons in Belgium; in each of these cases, language differences play an important role in the separatist dynamics. It is possible, therefore, through the use of specific variables to account for common features in autonomy behavior in various nations.

However desirable it might be to classify all the possible causes of an event, social science methodology has yet to develop tools to deal effectively with a large number of variables. In the words of Neil Smelser, the alternative is to "reduce the number of conditions, to isolate one condition from another, and thereby make precise the role of each condition, both singularly and in combination with other conditions [by imposing] some sort of organization on the conditions." Table I.2 is an alphabetical list with generalized definitions of microvariables representing a reduced number of many possible ones frequently discussed in the analysis of ethnic autonomy. Each variable should be regarded as an indicator of differences between or among diverse ethnic groups in a shared sociopolitical environment.(4) They are used as variables to explore how they may be associated with ethnic behavior aimed at autonomy.

Table I.2.   Microvariables Selected to Explain Group
Differences and to Account for Ethnic Autonomy
in a Shared Social and Political Environment
(in Alphabetical Order)

The Microvariables

CULTURE: Attitudes, beliefs, norms, values, aesthetics, and lifestyles of a group or nation; its knowledge, actions, and material objects.

ECONOMY: Systematic organization, production, management, and distribution of material and status values.

ETHNICITY: Characteristics of internally- and externally-defined groups who behave and are regarded as a distinctive social entity.

GEOGRAPHY: Territory and boundary identified with or designated to specific ethnic-cultural or national groups; spatial limits of a political entity.

HISTORY: The construction or reconstruction of a nation's past from an ethnic perspective; the differences among ethnic groups' pasts in relationship to a national history, especially between superordinate and subordinate groups.

LANGUAGE: Oral/written communication of a group's systematized values, beliefs, norms, and knowledge among its members.

PATTERNS OF   Legitimate and illegitimate superordination;
DOMINATION: techniques and mechanisms of gaining and perpetuating superordination; to exercise transcendent authority in a social system or possess veto power in it.

RELIGION: Attitudes and behavior caused by a group's belief in its relationship with the supernatural.

The first response to the list of variables should be that they pose a serious problem of multicolinearity; culture, ethnicity, and economy all have an historical aspect; religion and language are included in culture; patterns of domination may be largely economic. However, considering that the variables were selected to identify those that were present most frequently when and wherever ethnic autonomy occurred, the culture variables are used separately, as well as in an analytical scheme. Understanding ethnic autonomy usually requires that each variable be distinguishable individually, even while it simultaneously interacts with others.(5) Hence, it is important to pay special attention to the generalized definitions of each variable and to note their phenomenological implications.

All the contributors to this volume share the view that domination and the patterns in which it is achieved are the most important variables associated with ethnic action aimed at autonomy. Patterns of domination heads the list because it is the term used to describe various forms of control and domination; it is synonymous with power – the antithesis of powerlessness. The other seven variables in themselves are neutral; they become active agents only insofar as they interact with patterns of domination. That is, there is little evidence to suggest that differences among diverse people in a shared social environment cause conflict in the absence of patterns of domination. For example, despite the existence of multiple ethnic groups in Switzerland, the absence of the use of differences in ethnicity, religion, culture, language, and geography as mechanisms of control has resulted in minimum conflict. The misuse of power, the desire to dominate, the urge to control, the creation of "us" against "them" dichotomies where one or more variables are used to bring about the hegemony of one group over another – that is what fosters conflict.

Take the following examples: Although religion appears to be the most potent cause of conflict in Northern Ireland, the conflict is basically the product of the use or abuse of religion by combined external - England - and internal - Protestant majority - forces as a pattern of domination. Linguistic differences in Canada in themselves were neutral until the Quebecois objected to English being the sole language of business, commerce, and finance; language then came to be regarded as a pattern of domination.

Shared social environments, characterized by widely diverse heterogeneity, are more likely to produce ethnic autonomy because of the high probability that one or more ethnic groups will utilize the differences associated with heterogeneity to dominate another group. In the final analysis, whether an ethnic group will seek autonomy is closely linked to the question of superordination or subordination, which ultimately involves the phenomenon of power. What are some of the various dimensions of power as it relates to ethnic group relations?

Power

The quest for autonomy by ethnic groups always involves power; the degree to which power is possessed or lacking is related to superordination or subordination. The possession of power carries with it the option of utilizing a range of patterns of domination. Power should not be regarded in zero-sum terms of whether one has it or not. There are many historical examples of groups in slave societies that seemingly lacked power, but who were able, perhaps in concert with external factors, to transform gradually their powerless positions. Although it is not our purpose to elaborate on the theoretical and methodological issues surrounding the question of power, it should be clear that we regard the usual definition of power - "A's ability to get B to do something he would not otherwise have done" - as merely a provocative statement to trigger discussion regarding the many dimensions of power.

Although coercion is ultimately the basis of all power, the exercise of power in intergroup relations can seldom be equated with "your money or your life" situations. Power is real or imagined influence, persuasion, exchange, and resources. Patterns of domination include several aspects of power, including physical coercion and other forms of negative sanctions. However, I believe that the power involved in patterns of domination follows Blau's broad definition of power (1964, p. 115), "all kinds of influence between ... groups, including those exercised in exchange transactions, where one induces others to accede to his wishes by rewarding them for doing so." Dominant groups not only coerce others into subordination, as whites do blacks in South Africa, but also maintain their dominant position by arranging rewards in a hierarchical system favoring instrumental groups, such as that found in the United States.

Instrumentality may or may not focus on color. In South Africa privilege is hierarchically distributed, with white groups occupying the most privileged position in the system and blacks the least. In the United States, however, Japanese and Chinese are relatively free to exhibit the same achievement-oriented values as those of dominant whites; therefore, they experience little discrimination compared to that felt by other non-white groups. Remaining vestiges of anti-Semitism and religious differences notwithstanding, Jews in the United States are accorded almost equal privilege with the dominant white Anglo-Saxon Protestants. Theoretically neutral, power may be activated and employed in the interest of either dominant or subordinate forces, although this is rare in the latter case. Dominant elements may subordinate others through the use of one or more variables in any number of combinations: economic inequality, the imposition of or restriction on the use of a particular language, or restricting subordinate groups to unfavorable geographic locations. Native Americans in the United States were forced to live on "reservations" in the most desolate parts of the country; blacks tend to occupy the increasingly-desolated central cities; in Soviet Central Asia, ethnic groups of Asian descent are being pushed out of potentially-rich agricultural regions.

Any of the selected variables is capable of becoming a mechanism through which power can be exerted. Religion, geography, language, and economics are all potential mechanisms of domination, as can be evidenced in Northern Ireland, the Soviet Union, Canada, and the United States, respectively. Although the above four may be used as independent variables in relation to ethnic autonomy, the culture, history, and ethnicity are seen as dependent variables in the relationship. In other words, if an ethnic group did not define itself as culturally different by emphasizing its historical difference from other groups, it is improbable that the group itself or external elements would or could use the independent variables in any pattern of domination. Of course, the group could be subordinated if it were to be externally defined as different in other respects. In short, there are many ways in which the selected variables could be seen and treated in the conceptualization and analysis of ethnic autonomy.

SUMMARY

The state tends to create diffuse national values from diverse groups' norms, values, and traditions, with a view toward establishing unity to carry out state, as opposed to ethnic, goals; in the process important specific ethnic values, sentiments, and aspirations are distorted. As a consequence of state action, ethnic groups often seek ethnic homogeneity through autonomy in order to control, materially and psychologically, their own destinies. The state is the dominant sociopolitical entity in the modern world, despite its relatively recent emergence and "unnatural" organization of ethnic diversity. It is therefore important to explore the many motives impelling ethnic groups to seek autonomy within or outside the state's shared social environment. Selecting several variables to highlight important elements of ethnicity, an attempt was made to explore some of the parameters of ethnic autonomy-oriented action as a way of introducing, in

general terms, the case studies. As you read the cases, keep
the selected variables in mind; in one way or another, they
crop up in every case. Again, our intention is both to highlight specific features of ethnic autonomy in individual state
settings and to place them in global perspective.

NOTES

1. "A sample of 132 states shows that only 12 (9.1%) can be
    considered ethnic-free. Twenty-five states (18.9%) are
    comprised by an ethnic group that represents more than
    90% of the state's aggregate population; in another 25
    states the largest ethnic group accounts for possibly
    75-89% of the population. However, in 31 states (23.5%)
    of the total) the significant ethnic group constitutes only
    50-74% of the population; and in 3 states (29.5%) the
    largest group does not account for half the state's popu-
    lation. It has been estimated that in 53 states (or 40.2%)
    the population is comprised into five or more significant
    ethnic groups." Abdul A. Said and Luiz R. Simmons
    (eds.), Ethnicity in an International Context (Brunswick,
    New Jersey: Transaction Books, 1976), p. 10.
2. Throughout this volume the terms state, nation, and
    nation-state will be used by contributors in different
    ways. Some believe that the three terms should not be
    defined as descriptive terms for societies; they argue that
    "nation" should be recognized as a particular subcategory
    of "state." Further, some argue that "nation-state" is
    too vague and nebulous to be useful in empirical research.
3. "The term national minorities came into use in Europe to
    describe the particular social position of some people in
    relation to the rest of the population. In European
    countries with a long history, people with a certain
    cultural background frequently had ancient attachment to
    a given piece of land. They were known as a nationality
    group, and the land they occupied bore their name. But
    [often] ... small groups of people found themselves
    within political boundaries in which the majority group
    was of a different nationality. That is, the territories
    covered by political nations ceased to be exactly the same
    as the territories inhabited by the historical nationality
    groups." Arnold M. Rose and Caroline B. Rose,
    Minority Problems (2nd ed.; New York: Harper and Row,
    1972), p. 2.
4. I label them microvariables instead of macrovariables,
    despite their comprehensibility, because they are treated
    as descriptors of specific aspects of the macro inter-
    national system.

5. The use of nonrecursive models, such as systems dynamics with its multiple feedback loops, would more clearly highlight the importance of interaction among these microvariables in the analysis of ethnic autonomy.

BIBLIOGRAPHY

Ake, Claude. A Theory of Political Integration. Homewood, Ill.: The Dorsey Press, 1967.

Barth, Fredrik (ed.). Ethnic Groups and Boundaries. Boston: Little, Brown, 1969.

Basham, Richard. Urban Anthropology: The Cross-Cultural Study of Complex Societies. Palo Alto, Cal.: Mayfield, 1978.

Bennett, Lerone, Jr. Before the Mayflower: A History of the Negro in America. Baltimore: Penguin Books, 1966.

Blau, Peter. Exchange and Power in Social Life. New York: John Wiley, 1964.

Chaput, Marcel. Why I Am Separatist. Toronto: Ryerson Press, 1961.

Despres, Leo. Ethnicity and Resource Competition. The Hague: Mouton, 1975.

DeVos, George and Lola Romanucci-Ross (eds.). Ethnic Identity: Cultural Continuities and Change. Palo Alto, Cal.: Mayfield, 1975.

Eisenstadt, S. N. The Political Systems of Empires. New York: The Free Press, 1963.

Enloe, Cynthia H. Ethnic Conflict and Political Development. Boston: Little, Brown, 1973.

Etzioni, Amitai. Political Unification: A Comparative Study of Leaders and Forces. New York: Holt, Rinehart and Winston, 1965.

Gelfand, Donald E. and Russell D. Lee (eds.). Ethnic Conflict and Power: A Cross-National Perspective. New York: John Wiley, 1973.

Jordan, Winthrop D. White over Black: American Attitudes Toward the Negro, 1550-1812. Baltimore: Penguin Books, 1969.

Mason, Philip. Patterns of Dominance. New York: Oxford University Press, 1970.

Rose, Arnold M. and Caroline B. Minority Problems. 2nd ed., New York: Harper and Row, 1972.

Said, Abdul and Luiz R. Simmons (eds.). Ethnicity in an International Context. New Brunswick, N.J.: Transaction Books, 1976.

_____. Ethnicity and U.S. Foreign Policy. New York: Praeger, 1977.

Smelser, Neil J. "The Methodology of Comparative Analysis," in Donald P. Warwick and Samuel Osherson (eds.). Comparative Research Methods. Englewood Cliffs, N.J.: Prentice-Hall, 1973, pp. 42-86.

Sterling, Richard W. Macropolitics: International Relations in a Global Society. New York: Alfred A. Knopf, 1974.

Tilly, Charles (ed.). The Formation of National States in Western Europe. Princeton, N.J.: Princeton University Press, 1975.

Vallieres, Pierre. White Niggers of America. Montreal and Toronto: McClelland and Steward, 1971.

I

Conceptual Overviews of Ethnicity and Ethnic Dynamics

Introduction

Ethnic identity is the result of membership in a specific group based on a number of criteria, including culture, history, language, religion, and geographic location. In addition, ethnic identification tends to evoke a sense of loyalty to, and oneness with, a particular group, thereby creating a feeling of security. Hence, individuals and groups in all societies - developed or developing, democratic or totalitarian, open or closed - tend to base their definitions and interpretations of social reality on their ethnicity.

The three chapters that follow, discussions of ethnicity and ethnic autonomy from a comparative perspective, are by sociologist Bernard E. Segal, anthropologist Hoyt S. Alverson, and symbolic interactionists/sociologists Edward Sagarin and James Moneymaker. These chapters serve as generalized overviews of the specific case studies in Parts II, III, and IV; they emphasize the importance of viewing ethnic autonomy in a comparative perspective.

Segal is chiefly concerned with the dynamic relationship among ethnicity, stratification, and politics. He argues that, although modern states have developed in spite of ethnicity, the modernization of the Third World may be impeded because of it, particularly if development is predicated on the state being the only power center to regulate the political economy. He then compares and contrasts some features of ethnicity's relation to politics and stratification, suggesting that ethnicity can be manipulated by both objective and subjective actors in their own interest. In the last analysis, the importance of ethnic identity in the contemporary world - in both developed and developing societies - is of no less significance today than in the past.

Since ethnicity is the basis of ethnic movements for autonomy, the paper by Alverson points up yet another com-

3

parative dimension. While Segal emphasized some of the af-
fective dimensions of ethnicity, stressing the importance of
solidarity stemming from a common location and subjective
identification, Alverson has addressed the question of why
ethnic distinctions emerge in a given cultural-geographic area.
Barth's view, in Ethnic Groups and Boundaries, is "that the
emergence of group boundness, even among populations which
share much culture and history in common, is occasioned by
ecological and economic exigency ... [Moreover], that ethnic
groups cum boundaries can cross them electively." Those who
oppose Barth's utilitarian explanation of ethnicity argue that
ethnicity does not arise and persist because it is adaptive; it
persists despite sometimes devastating ecological and social
costs to the group. The key question then is, "Why are
commitments to heritage and origin maintained when in terms of
other utilitarian values such continued commitment is
debilitating?"

Alverson posits that one fruitful way of dealing with the
contradiction between these two views of ethnicity is to ask
questions relating to the individual group member. For
example: "To what extent is ethnic corporateness and ethnic
identity a voluntary, utilitarian action? Is the individual free
to choose what part of his personality to cede to the group's
typification of him? To what extent does he retain the power
to withdraw that concession, negating it in favor of another
commitment elsewhere?" Answers to these questions, Alverson
suggests, depends upon whether the social scientist answers
them from a verstehen or positivist perspective.

There are but a few monolingual states. Sagarin and
Moneymaker address one of the significant variables, language,
in a wide range of ethnic autonomy movements around the
world, including some not dealt with in the case studies in this
volume. Polylingualism takes on a variety of forms: different
languages are spoken by peoples in different parts of the same
country, as in Canada and Switzerland; an imported lingua
franca is accompanied by numerous local languages, as in
Africa; dispersed pockets of peoples speak a language that
differs from the official one, as in the United States; an
official tongue and a somewhat related vulgate or patois coexist
among different peoples for different purposes, as in Haiti;
and language can set people apart and become a symbolic
rallying point for national identity, as it has with the
Basques, the Welsh, and the Irish.

Sagarin and Moneymaker assert that "in all these and
other situations, linguistic distinction is seen as augmenting
such other social identifiers as religion, common ancestry, and
shared culture." In a world of national and international
tensions, language is power: it is the power to rally people to
a cause and to apply pressure for a greater share of goods,
wealth, and recognition. A common language alone will not

bind people, but without such a common language, their bonds are weakened.   Finally, they observe that "separatists will seek to exploit this issue, and their opponents will seek to defuse it, either by concessions or by linguistic and other forms of subordination."

1 Ethnicity: Where the Present Is the Past

Bernard E. Segal

This paper looks at some of the relations among ethnicity, stratification, and politics. Although ethnicity is a far older basis of social organization than either the nation-state or systems of rank based more on classes and less on status groups, it does not lose its salience as these other forms develop around it. Instead, structural change transforms and frequently strengthens it, making it either a firmer obstacle to, or a more pliant instrument for, the dissemination and consolidation of systems of centralized co-ordination and control. Such systems, after all, do not have to be applied equitably in order to be effective; no matter how complex contemporary economic and political systems are run, they must be at least somewhat effective if they are to function at all.

Two items may be taken as given, although with the caveat that their specific manifestations vary. First, one of the most common ways in which centralized control systems turn out to be inequitable is by using ethnic lines to demarcate how much is demanded of, and how much is offered to, those people who are defined as "different"; second, and more generally, ethnicity impedes the spread of universalistic treatment of people simply by its presence as a more or less distinctive complex of culture and individuals within the body of a larger society. At practically any given moment, some ethnic thrust somewhere will be devoted to winning equal treatment for all. Nevertheless, it is important to understand that such an initiative and aim would not be necessary were it not for the previous existence of an ethnically-patterned departure from universalism.

Even so, most ethnically diverse societies - and most contemporary societies are ethnically diverse, as Hall's chapter on ethnic autonomy points out - manage to hang together despite the inequities associated with their internal differences. In large measure, this is simply because the ethnically-subordinate people have nowhere else to go and little hope of creating societies of their own. Aside from the overturning of colonial regimes (an important ethnic matter in its own right, but worthy of a detailed consideration that cannot be given here), examples of successful, politically-complete attainments of ethnic autonomy are rare. Pakistan and Bangladesh spring to mind as such examples; yet, because Pakistan emerged as part of the agreement ending British rule over the entire Indian subcontinent, Bangladesh is the only true case of the pair. The peaceful separation of Singapore from Malaysia, is another.

After World War I, the possibly misguided efforts of Woodrow Wilson helped to form European states out of what earlier had been no more than provinces striving for ethnic autonomy. The same war, and the transparently imperialist designs of oil-thirsty Western nations, led to similar outcomes in parts of the Middle East. A great international cataclysm that shook loose the peripheries of the Austro-Hungarian and Ottoman Empires, and cut off a portion of what had been the Czarist realm as well, obscured the origins of those new states. They, plus the few similar cases that have occurred elsewhere in more recent history, seem obvious testimony to what a great capacity for coalescence modern states appear to have when compared to the lumbering relics of an earlier era. Once established, modern states maintain their juridical and territorial integrity, except for a few instances where some quite small ones, such as Tibet and Latvia, have been overwhelmed and incorporated into their larger neighbors. Still, the general rule seems to hold: states hang together, despite the movements of populations across boundaries and the inclinations of patriotic chauvinists, devoted irredentists, and stubborn ethnic autonomists to deny that borders are valid. Some argue, for instance, that the American Southwest is more Mexican than American; this contention has been based on geography, the length of a particular people's attachment to the land, and, at one time, on population composition. Others assert that the Ogaden is more Somali than Ethiopian; the Basque regions are not Spain; or people so geographically distant as Algerians and Saudis are nonetheless brothers.

Borders do exist. However, the people who argue that ethnicity either does or ought to override them are not to be dismissed, for social facts are often nothing more than what a large enough number of people say they are. With so many people in so many different places insisting that ethnicity can ignore borders, we are forced to take their words seriously. When we do, we become more judicious in evaluating statements about the permanence and inalterability of ethnically-diverse states. How can their coalescence be anything but tenuous

when there are so many counter-movements at work? Can an
irredentist movement initiated from abroad get more foreign
support than a central government trying to preserve its space
and exerts its control over all its people. (Somali irredentists
almost won in the Ogaden, but they got less foreign support
than the Ethiopians.) Is a central state strong enough to
maintain control over one of its own dissident groups, or
flexible enough to grant it partial self-direction? (Even with
considerable Syrian support, Lebanon is too weak to control its
Christian population, which itself is strengthened by its
receipt of Israeli aid; in contrast, both India and Nigeria now
have ethno-federalist arrangements different from those they
had at the dawn of their independence.) Are there restraints
on the use of force against ethnic dissidents? (In Nigeria,
restraints were weak; the result was a civil war won by a
central government that, despite its victory, has since had to
continue conceding to ethnic demands. It seems quite doubtful, however, whether Canada would be willing to risk blood if
Quebec decided to secede peacefully, or whether England,
even if pushed far more than it is now, would be prepared to
make another Ireland of Scotland.)
      Why is there ethnic dissidence? The range of com-
binations of different motivating grievances is more extensive
than the variety of different ethnic groups themselves. We
choose, therefore, to emphasize just one general point:
ethnicity brings together ideal and material interests, fusing
them with sentiment and adorning them with rationalizations
that appear just. Movements for ethnic autonomy usually arise
when a group of people, feeling themselves bound together in
origin and destiny, either decides it no longer needs swallow a
soup too thin, or wishes to withdraw from a union calling upon
it to share a richer stew. The first point is too obvious to
need any clarification by example. As for the second, there
are Scottish separatists whose stew pot smells of oil, and
Katangese whose pot heats up quite quickly because it is made
of copper.
      It is probably safe to say that, in any empirical instance,
the unfolding of the immanent design of any form of political
or economic system is wrinkled by the interaction of polity and
economy. By way of summarizing, we argue for little more
than a one-step extension in the appreciation of empirical
complexity. Ethnicity further complicates the interaction of
political and economic processes. Sometimes ethnicity magnifies
the effects of these processes by providing a basis for excluding one group from property ownership or elite positions
in order to enhance the relative advantage of another. At
other times, ethnicity diminishes these effects by withholding
loyalty or co-operation and blocking government attempts to
keep an ethnic labor force or region under control. Either
way, whether as conductor or resistor of other institutional

currents, ethnicity matters.

To understand why it does, we need to be clear about what it is. Ethnicity has three essential components. First, a combination of factors from among phenotype, faith, language, origin, or population concentration in a given region, clustered over time and passed from generation to generation, must serve to demarcate a given collectivity. Note that these criteria are not economic. Although they may have important economic effects, and although the members of an ethnic group may disproportionately occupy a particular class position, ethnicity is not to be confused with class. Furthermore, whatever may be the combination of the factors thus far noted, if that combination is all that a collectivity's members have in common, they are merely part of a category, and not yet an ethnic group.

Second, therefore, the members of the collectivity must also share a sense of solidarity, a common subjective identification focused around the factors mentioned above, that serves as centerpoint and expression of their sentimental attachment to one another. There is no ethnicity without community; moreover, this community has to involve shared loyalties that surpass what Max Weber once called "the feeling of the actors that they belong together." Again, economic factors may strengthen or may help to awaken this fellow-feeling, but they are not a substitute for it. In the matter of ethnicity, the question is never one of association for seeking economic revindication or perpetuating advantage alone, but rather of how people band together, and around what rallying points, to further such aims.

The third essential component of ethnicity is that a purported ethnic group must be in contact with another in the same society. Differences between the two allow the members of each to view members of the other as outsiders. Indeed, the subjective sense of ethnicity always depends on this interaction. Moreover, the larger context of the setting where inter-group contacts are played out shapes the ways ethnic organization takes place. If a given group with its own culture occupies its territory exclusively and without contact with outsiders, or, if the contact which it does have with others takes place only across juridically-defined boundaries such as those which make a society coterminous with a state, then the group might be called something like a tribe on the one hand or a nation on the other, although neither term is satisfactory; but it is not ethnic.

Ethnicity, then, is objective and subjective, involving the fact and the sense of membership in a group in contact with another in the same society where each has at least a partially unique normative culture resting upon, reflecting, and sustaining its notions of its own origins and history. Whether that group is numerically preponderant or not, whether it is superordinate or subordinate, whenever a member of the group takes its standards into account and uses them as criteria to assess his own judgments or performances or those of others, he is ethnically-oriented. Although ethnically-oriented actions may be pragmatic, instrumentally-useful, and rational in the technical sense, they are never completely so; the cues and devices that sustain ethnicity are always "given," and are, therefore, somewhat arbitrary. That is because ethnicity is not invented anew with each generation, but is instead a transmitted cultural product depending on shared definitions that do not have to be more than tangentially related to fact. These definitions, expressed in sentiment, myth, stereotype and rationalization, passed on orally or in writing, sometimes as lore and other times as history, serve as instruments through which ethnicity is perpetuated.

It is precisely because ethnicity calls for distinct patterns of loyalty and solidarity passed on through differential socialization that it makes complete universalization impossible. A serious problem in any ethnically-diverse society is deciding in what ways ethnic groups should be left free to live by their own standards, or, alternatively, in what ways they ought to live by a common code. Generally, however, the problem never arises in quite that form. More usual is the subordination of some ethnic groups to others, with weaker groups limited either by having to adapt themselves to what is held to be the common core culture, or by discrimination. That is, a set of specific isolating regulations not of their own choosing is applied to them and not to others. Furthermore, even the most equitable attempts to apply identical standards to different groups are reinterpreted once they pass ethnic boundaries.

Despite ethnicity's tendency to be perpetuated, it is not constant. When its assignment or assumption is categorical, one is, or is not, an "X" or a "Y"; but under other circumstances, depending on the criteria used to make the judgement, one may be only more or less an "X" or a "Y." The criteria may shift, along with the emphases placed on some of them; and the rigidity with which any or all of the criteria are applied may also change. A more important corollary of these rather obvious points is that ethnicity itself may take on new forms and new meanings as a response to changes in its contextual circumstances. For example, through means as different as totalitarian control or an institutionalized process that promises acceptance and mobility after assimilation, ethnicity's impact and staying power may markedly diminish.

The spread of centralized economics and politics, the hallmark of structural modernization, may not lead to either the totalitarian or the absorptive outcome. Instead, as it brings people together from groups that have not been intimately associated, thereby heightening competition and com-

parison among them, it may also heighten the sense of ethnic
identity. Furthermore, to the extent that centralized economics helps create similar mass problems of income and employment at the same time as centralized politics makes the
state responsible for resolving them, ethnicity becomes an
obvious locus of interest-group activity. The concern over
group identity for its own sake is then mixed in varying
proportions with concerns over maintaining the group as an
instrument for accomplishing other ends. Modernization can
also promote ethnicity because it occurs against a backdrop of
pre-existent ethnic differences in wealth, rank, and power.
These past conditions affect the process of newer, changing
ones. Thus, although partial cultural coalescence between
previously more-distinct ethnic blocs is common, it is likely to
be temporary and shallow, composed primarily of similar surface responses to the stimuli of general - but not equally
shared - institutional arrangements. (Where there are
factories, work organizations set the pace, hours, and
schedules, and these are more likely to be equal than the pay;
where there is suffrage, minorities can vote but cannot outvote
majorites; where there are mass media, there are approved and
more questionable stereotypes. The number of examples could
be extended enormously.) If these circumstances persist,
and if superordinate groups can no longer hold subordinate
ones in check, then the groups will tend to conflict sooner or
later. Perhaps they will split, just as the common poles of two
magnets can be brought only so close before they repel each
other.

BIBLIOGRAPHY

Davis, F. James. Minority-Dominant Relations. Arlington
Heights, Ill.: AHM Publishing, 1978.

Gerth, Hans and C. Wright Mills. From Max Weber. New
York: Oxford, 1946.

Gordon, Milton M. Human Nature, Class, and Ethnicity.
New York: Oxford, 1978.

Shibutani, Tamotsu and Kian M. Kwan. Ethnic Stratification.
New York: Macmillan, 1965.

2 The Roots of Time: A Comment on Utilitarian and Primordial Sentiments in Ethnic Identification*

Hoyt S. Alverson

In the view of many scholars, perhaps most notably Frederik Barth (1969, p. 10), ethnic groups arise and persist by virtue of "boundary creation and maintenance," social processes that members of the group consciously and actively participate in and help to determine. Barth posits the concept of ethnicity to account for the presumptive fact that groups persist through time in some integral, corporate fashion independently of, and in spite of, changes in the culture and institutions which the group circumscribes spatially and temporally. Said differently, ethnicity is that dimension of corporate identity that exists independently of any repertoire of customs, beliefs, or institutions; because these are contingent and ever changing, they cannot account for group continuity and persistence. For a group to <u>have</u> a history and tradition, it must consist in some essential element <u>prior</u> to that history and tradition. This essential element <u>is</u> ethnicity, which at the individual level constitutes a pivotal role that affects all other roles the individual may play.

In Barth's view, the social insignia or markers of the ethnic group are not necessarily elaborate, pervasive, or frequently observed in the group's social life. Typically, in fact, the maintenance of ethnic boundaries is accomplished by signs, icons, totems, and other markings of limited scale, their only function being to distinguish the group in question from other ethnic groups that bound it spatially or temporally.

*Material support for undertaking preparation of portions of this paper has been provided by the National Endowment for the Humanities and by the Ford Foundation in grants made to Yale-Wesleyan Southern African Research Program.

Why is it that ethnic distinctions and divisions emerge in a given cultural/geographic area? In Barth's view, the emergence of group boundedness, even among populations which share much culture and history in common, is occasioned by ecological and economic exigency. Microecologic specialization, often including environmental demands to limit the size and/or rate of change in population, requires an imposition or restriction on the movement of people among ecologic niches and, by extension, among economically-specialized activities. Ethnic divisions emerge frequently in situations where people, quite similar in culture and/or quite similar in their modes of production, increase their likelihood of survival by restricting communication, interaction, and the flow of people over a given eco-zone. This encourages economic specialization, and is often attended by exchange of the products of their respective specialized productive activities. For this reason, strong, persistent ethnic boundedness does not frequently entail significant cultural differences among groups. Cultural schisms are seldom bases for keeping people living in discrete groups; it is, rather, the adaptiveness of discreteness itself, coupled with the demographic or economic implications this discreteness usually entails, that is sufficient to maintain ethnic boundaries.

Barth's view of ethnicity purportedly accounts for the continuity and discreteness of groups over time, yet it bestows on ethnicity an historical, or temporal, aspect in a contingent sense only. That is, ethnic groups are said to persist only insofar as the particular discreteness or boundedness is ecologically "adaptive." Groups do not persist by dint of cultural momentum or inertia, but by dint of adaptation to selective pressures of natural and cultural environments.

This notion, "adaptive," requires some comment. According to Barth and others, the adaptation of ethnic groups to their environments takes place through individuals' conscious, purposive, rational decisions to remain within the group or to "opt out." Barth imputes to ethnic-group members an individualistic calculus of utility resembling cost-benefits analysis. Specifically, he avers (1969, p. 25) that personal standards of excellence and achievement, if not served by continuing membership in one group, will motivate an individual to seek membership in another group. At least this process will go on if circumstances, such as a caste-like racial proscription or political tyranny, do not make the costs of trying to "pass" too high.

In purely formal terms, Barth's account would seem to bestow the categorization of "ethnic group" on such diverse social forms as lineages, feudal estates, utopian communities, and even business firms. It is not clear to this writer why almost any group, totemically differentiated from other groups and capable of providing a high percentage of its own material

requisites for existence, could not be defined as an "ethnic
group." Indeed, in many regards Barth's discussion of ethnic
boundedness parallels Levi-Strauss' discussion of "totemism,"
in that both elucidate schematisms for creating a semantic and
social network of oppositions among corporate groups.

In keeping with Barth's thesis, several scholars have
argued that leaders can consciously create boundaries for
ethnic groups, whose members may then cross them electively.
Bates (1973) and Uchendu (1975) echo Barth's claims in their
discussions of ethnic autonomy in post-independence Africa.
According to Bates, the urban bourgeoisie, especially those
involved in politics, can be seen as manufacturers of ethnicity.
Ethnic incorporation of a population can be an effective
strategem for urban elites in their quest for political power
and influence. Political leaders often strive to inculcate in
rural peoples a sense of ethnic identity in opposition to competing groups, and to press by means of these groups their
claims for distribution of the national largesse. Ethnicity in
many parts of Africa, according to these and like-minded
scholars, requires no long tradition of such corporateness, no
a priori or axiomatic belief in a heritage and a commitment to
it. Rather, this sense of ethnic corporateness can be op-
portunistically created, as local leaders cope with social forces
unleashed by colonialism and its aftermath in nominal political
independence. Thus, ethnicity is a consequence of nation
building, not its precursor.

Quite opposed in spirit to the work of Barth, Uchendu,
and Bates is that of scholars such as DeVos (1975) and
Devereaux (1975). For them and kindred thinkers, ethnicity
is not seen as a force that arises because it is "adaptive," but
as one that persists despite sometimes devastating ecological
and social costs to the group. DeVos asks directly why ethnic
groups persist despite severe individual and collective disadvantages to continued ethnic corporateness. Why are commitments to heritage and origin maintained when, in terms of
other utilitarian values, such continued commitment is
debilitating?

The answer, according to DeVos, lies in the surmise that
ethnicity is not based in boundary maintenance with "selective"
advantage, but is rather an essential orientation to the past,
to collective origin. Celebrated in rituals, narratives, and
histories, ethnicity is the sense of belonging, the submersion
of the self in something that transcends self, the "we-ness" of
heritage and ancestry. Such a view of ethnicity suggests its
existential import. Indeed, Devereaux argues that ethnic
boundaries follow as a consequence of commitment to, and
identity with, the group. Boundaries are a means of preserving the self-identity, not an end in themselves. In this
view, whatever benefit exists in belonging to a group results
from the individual's commitment to the group, not from the

resources the group provides the individual. Membership in itself is the reason for belonging. Hence, an individual can deny or abandon this ethnic identity only at great psychic cost, for it lies at the core of self-identity.

Because the disparity in the conceptions of ethnicity offered by those such as Barth on the one hand and Devereaux on the other is so great, it would appear that either entirely different phenomena are being described by a single term, or the accounts are in substantial contradiction. Assuming the latter, perhaps the most important conflict lies in the discrepancy between what Barth, Bates, and Uchendu claim ethnic identity means to the individual and that which DeVos and Devereaux claim it means to him. This conflict can be phrased as a set of questions. To what extent is ethnic corporateness and ethnic identity a voluntary, utilitarian action, a result of consciousness and reason, an individual's decision to belong? Conversely, to what extent is ethnic corporateness and ethnic identity an involuntary, primordial commitment and belief, an unfalsifiable or undeniable condition? Is an individual free to choose what part of his personality to cede to the group's typification of him as member? To what extent does he retain the power to withdraw that concession, negating it in favor of another commitment elsewhere?

A resolution of this seeming paradox in the fundamental conceptualization of ethnicity is necessarily a preliminary to any subsequent attempts to describe empirically the conditions which foster or attenuate ethnic boundaries and ethnic separatism. One of the forces sustaining this state of affairs lies in the ethnic provenance of social scientists themselves. Social scientists, like all others, have axes to grind, axes that cannot always be set forth as purely formal, epistemologic arguments. Specifically, it can be claimed that those social scientists who are members of the ethnic group under investigation approach their study in the main by means of definitions and methodologies which presuppose the factuality and validity of the ethnic group's consciousness-of-itself and consciousness-in-itself as an ethnic group. For example, Jewish American, black American, and Native American social scientists typically explicate the persistence of ethnic identity in their respective reference groups by arguments predicated upon the value, if not the veracity of, "insiders" conditions of consciousness. This method and its variants are called verstehen, "phenomenology," or "ethno-methodology."

Opposed to this "school" are those social scientists who are typically not seen by themselves or by others as belonging to the ethnic group whose existence is being investigated. These scientists, in the main, adopt positivist suppositions and methodologies in attempts to explicate ethnicity. Because positivism demands that the scientists be an "objective" spectator of the phenomenon being investigated, there will follow a requirement that "insiders" knowledge be treated as simply an object of inquiry; hence, its meaning must be other than that claimed for it by the "insiders", who never see their knowledge as an object of inquiry. Positivist scholars account for the consciousness of ethnicity and group persistence by positing a schematism that has general applicability to all instances of ethnic consciousness, but is not understood by non-scientists. Rational utilitarianism and the material of Darwinist or Marxist scholars fall into this category.

These two different approaches have a discrepant view of the meaning and significance of "roots," origins, heritage, tradition, and commitment. The "verstehen" scholars typically suppose the veracity and factuality of these metaphors or ethnic identity and identification. Indeed, some, wittingly or not, even celebrate them. Positivist scholars argue that these metaphors of identity are, at best, resources which work efficaciously in individual decision making, or in group survival over short periods of time. In general, however, they are seen as manifestations of chauvinism, "false consciousness," and the handiwork of clever leaders, or as the results of oppressive labeling and typification by dominant "outside" groups.

Of course, a scholar could attempt to meld these two strands of thought. However, melding has not been a popular course, and so most writing reflects the clear dominance of one or the other approach. This paper cannot attempt a review of the massive literature that is required to demonstrate by specific instances the general applicability of the commentary offered here. Rather, it is hoped that the salience of the point raised here will be manifest in the case studies presented here.

BIBLIOGRAPHY

Barth, Fredrik. Ethnic Groups and Boundaries. Boston: Little, Brown, 1969.

Bates, Robert. Ethnicity in Contemporary Africa. Eastern African Studies, Volume XIV, 19, 1973.

Devereaux, George. "Ethnic Identity: Its Logical Foundations," Ethnic Identity: Cultural Continuities and Change, George DeVos and Lola Romanucci-Ross (eds.) Palo Alto, Calif.: Mayfield, 1975.

DeVos, George. "Ethnic Pluralism: Conflict and Accomodation," Ethnic Identity, op. cit.

Uchendu, Victor C. "The Dilemma of Ethnicity and Polity Primacy in Black Africa," Ethnic Identity, op. cit.

3 Language and Nationalist, Separatist, and Secessionist Movements*

Edward Sagarin
James Moneymaker

It would appear that the rise of nationalism, a social force motivating tens of millions of people, can be isolated as one of the major movements in the history of the twentieth century. It is not that nationalism had ever died, but it had receded, manifesting augmentations and diminutions during the last two millennia.

However, the nationalist fervor which swept through the Western world, especially Europe, during the mid-years of the nineteenth century was directed primarily, although not exclusively toward unification of previously-divided groups. People sought to unite where before they had been bound to one another only in the loosest fashion. Although breakaway or separatist nationalism was manifest in the Balkans, Ireland, and various other parts of the world, the major thrust of nationalist fervor in the nineteenth century was toward national unity. In the independent areas on the peninsula that was to become Italy, enthusiasm for the movement was expressed in its very name: it was called a revival or rebirth, risorgimento.(1)

Twentieth century nationalism, particularly after World War II, has had the opposite aim: to create and recreate, to emphasize and at times invent - although invention was seldom necessary - any feature that could distinguish one group from another, and that could logically result in separation between the two.

That both of these thrusts, one toward unity where before there had been distinction, and the other in the opposite direction, should be expressions of nationalism is an

irony that is not at all inexplicable. One need only think of
nationalism as a strong movement toward identification of large
groups of people with others having similar traits, and, by
extension, a lack of identification with those of the human
species who do not have those particular traits. From this,
one can isolate two strands that are actually quite similar:
people wanted to be part of a nation-state with others like
themselves, and to separate from the nation-state with which
they could not identify. The first strand is encompassed by
those speaking similar languages, racially alike and living on
contiguous territories, who sought strength through merger:
Germany and Italy are the prime examples. The second stage
emerged in the wake of the anti-colonial and liberationist
movements following World War II, when peoples sought independence for themselves rather than interdependence with
others.

LANGUAGE AND NATIONALISM

The role of language in nationalism was emphasized by
Max Boehm (1933), who called it the most important factor in
modern nationalism. Although some of what Boehm wrote
requires modification, his discussion of language and nationalism can serve as a point of departure for the present
discussion:

The concept of a mother tongue has made language
the source from which springs all intellectual and
spiritual existence. The mother tongue represents
the most suitable expression of spiritual individuality .... A people not only transmits the store of
all its memories through the vocabulary of its
language, but in syntax, word sound and rhythm it
finds the most faithful expression of its temperament
and general emotional life. The rare cases wherein
a people has retained its individuality despite the
loss of its language do not disprove the conviction
of a people or national group that they are defend-
ing in language the very cornerstone of their
national existence. The encouragement of dialect is
somewhat analogous to the regionalist cult of the
local homeland. Its exaggeration leads to a dissolution of the nation into smaller component parts,
which may remain independent for a longer or
shorter period and thus jeopardize the greater
national idea. The development of a linguistic
pluralism, such as the Afrikaans as opposed to the
Dutch, the American to the English, the Penn-

sylvania Dutch or Luxembourgian to High German,
is a symptom which reveals, even outside the realm
of language, divisions and separations from earlier
and more comprehensive social groups (1933, p.
235).

Nonetheless, there have been, and in some instances still
are, autonomist and secessionist movements in which language
distinction is completely absent, as in the movement toward
autonomy in modern Scotland. It can be argued, however,
that this is a factor restraining Scottish Nationalists from
becoming secessionists rather than autonomists. Elsewhere,
language is present only symbolically, as part of a tradition;
in Wales, despite street signs and some television and radio
broadcasting in Welsh, few aspire to a return to a Welsh-
speaking society (Trudgill, 1974, p. 135).
    In most nationalist-separatist movements, however,
language is a major factor, and often a major issue of contention between groups in conflict. In irredentist movements,
which aim to liberate unredeemed territory (terra irredenta),
language is almost invariably a factor, along with ethnic unity
and division of power and resources, in determining whether
the people identify with one nation-state over another that is
outside their own national boundary. Thus, the unification of
Italian-speaking areas into one nation left certain territories
inhabited by speakers of Italian outside the new national
boundaries: some remained part of Austria; Corsica belonged
to France; and still another area of Italian speakers remained a
Swiss canton (Francis, 1976, p. 80).

Monolingual and Polylingual Nations

    Pure monolingual nation-states are few in number and
small in size and power in the modern world. Nevertheless,
the degree to which they are mono- or polylingual can differ
considerably, and a few generalizations and illustrative examples can serve as a framework to note patterns, mosaics, and
gradations.
    Jamaica, Cuba, Luxembourg, and Portugal are examples of
one-language nations; of these two are island nations, former
colonies where no indigenous language was able to survive. If
one conceptualizes Luxembourgian and German as one language, then the inhabitants of the two countries live adjacent
to others speaking the same tongue. Although, Cuba is
geographically close to numerous other Spanish-speaking
nations, the possibility of a movement toward merger is remote
because of insularity, racial and political considerations, the
presence of the United States, and the considerable number of
adjacent Spanish-speaking nations whose peoples have their

own identities.

Essentially monolingual countries, both in the number of people speaking one language and its official and dominant position in the nation, differ from polylingual countries in that the boundary lines of a political-territorial nature have not been drawn to coincide with the linguistic-nationalist groups. Albanian is the sole language of almost the entire population of that country, except for a sector where Greek is spoken (Zavalani, 1969); parts of Finland are inhabited by Swedish-speaking people, and the people of Lapland have languages unrelated to Finnish; large numbers of Albanian-speaking people constitute a regional majority, in a sector of Yugoslavia. Greeks in Albania do not have a proportional share of power and resources and feel themselves to be the out-group; whereas the Swedes in Finland, although not controlling the seat of power, have more than a proportional share of the wealth and completely lack any sense of social inferiority.

Federations in which large segments of the population speak different languages, recognize the sense that the national government and its institutions are bilingual or polylingual. Switzerland and Belgium illustrate this pattern, while Canada is making some moves in this direction. Switzerland officially recognizes four languages: German and French are spoken by large numbers of people; Italian, by a smaller sector of the population; and Romansch is the tongue of less than 100,000 Swiss. Except for Romansch, the languages of Switzerland are spoken by people who have a language-identity with neighbors in other nations, yet separatist and irredentist movements are almost unknown. In Belgium, French and Flemish (a version of Dutch) are each spoken by approximately half of the population, and bilingualism is officially recognized. Belgium, however, has had nationalist-irredentist and anti-federationist movements.

There are similar federations where bilingualism is artificially imposed on the nation as a whole. The major example is Canada - English was dominant there until recent upheavals in French-speaking Quebec brought about considerable change.

There are also federations in which one language has unquestioned hegemony, even though the people speak different languages in various parts of the political unit. Holland is such a nation: Dutch is dominant, and Frisian is spoken in a northern sector and on islands off the coast. Denmark is similar to Holland, with Faeroese spoken in outlying island areas. The Soviet Union, where sizable territories are occupied by people who speak Ukranian, Esthonian, Latvian, Armenian, Georgian, and probably 150 to 200 other languages, nevertheless gives official and unofficial recognition to Russian. Although the USSR completely supresses secessionist and serious autonomist movements, local languages are discouraged rather than suppressed. Should Georgian, Armenian, and other languages become associated with anti-Communist or anti-Russian movements, there might well be an effort to impose Russian as the language of the country. However, the co-optation of a language movement directed by local leaders of the Communist Party of the Soviet Union is a much more likely scenario.

There are also federations in which the lingua franca, as well as the official language of urban centers, international relations, and higher education, is an imported, formerly colonial tongue. India can serve as an example, although English in India does not have quite the undisputed position as an official language as French, English and Portuguese have in the black-controlled African nations south of the Sahara. The Indian example is extremely complex; there is a dominant official indigenous language, a colonial language whose official position has been recognized, and several hundred different, mutually unintelligible tongues that are spoken by people who have a strong linguistic-identity loyalty, and who often cannot speak another language (Brass, 1974). According to a 1961 census, there were 1652 mother tongues in India; in such a situation, the colonial language emerges as the medium of discourse both within the country and internationally. The competition among diverse languages can be gleaned from the wording of the official statement by the Ministry of Information in New Delhi: "The Official Languages Act, 1963, as amended, lays down that English may continue to be used in addition to Hindi as the official language of India, for all official purposes of the Union for which it was being used immediately before 26 January 1965 and also for the transaction of business in Parliament" (India, 1974, p. 23). Although an effort was made to divide India into ethnic-linguistic-religious states, this left unresolved what Brass (1974, p. 23) referred to as "the status and rights of minority language speakers and minority religions." Brass continues:

> The demarcation of the boundaries of the Indian states has nowhere neatly divided and compart-mentalized the segmented groups of Indian society. Every state has both linguistic and religious minor-ity groups.... All the Hindi-speaking states contain significant linguistic and religious minorities, whose numbers are themselves in dispute.

Although some countries have an indisputable dominant and official language, they also have dispersed groups speaking other tongues. In the United States, Spanish is spoken by a considerable proportion of the population in Miami, parts of Texas and Southern California, and sections of New York, in addition to being the mother tongue of the Puerto Ricans. However, these Spanish-speaking people identify with one another only in language, not nationality: they are Cuban-Americans, Mexican-Americans or Chicanos, and Puerto Ricans or Puerto Rican-Americans in New York, they have come to be called New Yoricans. In addition, there are scattered American Indian-speaking groups in the United States; although they have some sense of identity with one another, they speak entirely different Indian languages. There are also Eskimo-speaking populaces in Alaska and the Aleutian Islands. When Guatemala and several other Latin American countries are examined, it is found that large parts of the populace speak only an Indian language, while in the urban centers and on an official level, Spanish is spoken - or Portuguese, in Brazil.

Some nations have an official language while most of their people speak a "vulgate," a version of the official language that is simplified, different, and not usually intelligible to one who has not lived in the country and knows only its official tongue. French is the official language of Haiti, but Haitian-Creole is used for everyday speech by most persons. This form of bilingualism differs from that of Holland, Belgium, and Canada, where some of the people speak one language, and some another. Although a United States Department of State Fact Book (1970, pp. 284-288) reports that ten percent of the Haitians speak French and ninety percent Creole, most scholars would say that the entire population is able to communicate, albeit with difficulty, in both languages. Some Haitians go back and forth from one language to the other with ease; and which one is used depends on social class, familiarity, and the nature of the setting.

There are nation-states in which local variations of what might be described as the dominant or official language differ considerably in either a graduated or an abrupt manner. Thus, Mandarin, Cantonese, and several others are called "Chinese," but speakers of one of the Chinese languages cannot be understood by speakers of another. However, the Chinese can communicate rather well by script because of the use of ideographs that are almost identical in all the Chinese languages. The regional languages of China differ from those of Switzerland, for example, in that all the tongues are closely related to one another.

Then, there are essentially monolingual nations in which "other-speaking" groups have tended to lose their language, but not necessarily their identity. The languages of the groups survive in folklore, in rural areas where the intercourse with the outside world is limited, and in university courses. They also serve as symbol and rallying point for those who seek to further a feeling of identity and disassociation for political-nationalistic aims. Different as they are in other respects, Breton is an example of such a language in France, and Sicilian in Italy.

It might appear that there is no pattern at all, with so many different types of language-nationality-society relationships. Numerous nations fall into one of these groups but with exceptions, or fall into two or more of them. The above is not meant to be a typology, but only a rough framework in which to see the backgrounds of mono- and polylingualism, and against which the relationship of language to separatism and nationalism can be understood.(2)

Language and Territory

Language, like race, is immediately distinguishable. Although racial differences often create fear of intermingling, stereotyping, hatred and antagonism between groups, and ethnocentric feelings of inferiority and superiority, racially-different groups have possibilities for greater cooperation if they are not linguistically separate. Where the competition between ethnic and racial groups is diminished, a population of marginal people might grow, but linguistic marginals would be unlikely.

When the inhabitants of a territorially-bounded group share a common language, forces converge to make it likely that ethnic nationalistic identity will endure. Fishman (1968, p. 3) describes this phenomenon in terms of the "principle of co-territoriality," in which "one and the same population usually controls several fully systematic varieties (whether registers, dialects, or languages) and these varieties may come to influence each other quite systematically as well (emphasis in original)."

The socioeconomic structure largely determines the extent of geographic mobility in a country. Industrialization and urbanization further mobility, an agricultural economy restrains it. Should there be little geographic mobility, and hence relatively little in- or out-migration from the language identity group, the group remains intact both as a separate people and as one distinguished by its language. With few outsiders coming in, the populace is not exposed to another language, and can well survive without learning it; with few insiders leaving, the language does not lose its base. In such a situation, the language does not tend to become "contaminated." However, contamination also depends upon whether the language is suppressed by a political power center, and whether it has a similarity to the official or neighboring one. There has been a high level of immigration and emigration within the Soviet republics, resulting in a "disproportionate index of language maintenance" (Lewis,1972). In effect various populations with different identities and languages have contaminated Russian as the mother tongue.

Geographic isolation is usually synonymous with nonmobility because opportunities for social and technological advancement are generally not found in isolated areas. Although geographic isolation has declined in the modern world, the extent of this decline has been exaggerated. There are few outposts that cannot be reached easily and quickly, but there are many that are not reached often. For example, one can go from Helsinki to the Lapp-speaking areas of Finland in a brief time, but few people make the journey. Islands in the Adriatic and Aegean, not far from the coasts of Yugoslavia and Greece, receive mail and supplies - and tourists - perhaps once a week (Whiteley, 1971). The Basque population in both France and Spain was traditionally a geographically-isolated one. Today, however, trains run often and highways carry automobile traffic. But when travel to an fro was difficult, slow, and infrequent, the territorial integrity of the Basques remained intact. The same was true, to some extent, of the Frisians in the Netherlands and the Faeroese in Denmark.

With little mobility, there is going to be little exogamy. Peoples speaking different languages are unlikely to court and mate; sexual interaction among them is likely to be limited to prostitution. The language thus remains intact intergenerationally because it is the native tongue of both parents, and the one spoken either exclusively or primarily in the area where they live.

Race and religion act against exogamy, but possibly not as powerfully as language. When language distinction is added to either race or religion, the possibilities for exogamy are further reduced, and the distinct nationality does not tend to become dispersed into a larger society or nation-state.

Language as Nationalist Symbol

A nationalist movement often uses language as a symbolic rallying point, very much as it would a flag, a slogan, or a mythological figure. The use or disuse of one language or another in naming cities, rivers, mountains, writes Boehm (1933), "leads to the growth of definite national claims, of either a cultural or political character, which assume a popular symbolical significance." An example of this can be seen in the renaming of many of the former colonial lands in Africa; at the time of this writing, black forces in Africa plan to discard the name Rhodesia in favor of Zimbabwe.

In international diplomacy, language as symbol is often evident. The Vietnamese refused to negotiate with the French in the French language, although their leadership was undoubtedly fluent in French; to use both languages, whatever difficulties this might entail, was an expression that they were meeting as equals. International diplomats who are known to speak English with great fluency often come to Washington with interpreters and insist on speaking only in the language of their own country.

The language-separatist movements may rally around the language as recognition of a heritage, although its use may be diminishing and any hope for widespread revival may be unrealistic. This may be true of the Welsh and the Basques; it is certainly true of the Breton nationalists (New York Times, 1978a). Where, however, the language remains widely spoken among the people, as it does in Soviet Armenia, Soviet Georgia, and Catalonia, there is demand for official recognition in political meetings and local significance; and schools, printers, employers, and the religious are asked to use the regional language. In Ireland, by contrast, the prime demand was for separation from England because of national identification as Irish, but even the most ardent Irish revolutionaries no longer aspire to replace English with Irish as the national tongue.

In short, language is not an essential for a nationalist movement. People can have identities other than those of their neighbors while speaking the same language. However, language offers a symbol and a mechanism for the homogenization of a people, and for the distinction of such a people from others around them. Given this distinction, essential features conducive to the growth of autonomist and separatist movements are present.

The Colonial Experience

Language plays a peculiar and ironic role in the independence, autonomist, and secessionist movements of erstwhile colonial peoples; this is exemplified in many of the new African nations. Almost all of Africa south of the Sahara, with the exception of Liberia, had been colonies until rather recently. Furthermore, the old colonies and the new nations were not ethnically-homogeneous: they were federations of multilingual tribes. These tribes are relatively isolated from one another, and only in the slightest and most tenuous sense can one find similarities in language between one people and a nearby group. The lines of demarcation are strong. What are you? I am a Kikuyu. I am an Ibo. This means that I belong to that group of people speaking a particular language, worshipping in one manner, and living in a given valley or between two rivers.(3)

In Africa, where it is estimated that 2000 separate languages are spoken, language is an essential ingredient of ethnic identity, and is usually coterminous with the boundaries that are drawn around religion and other identifiers. Seldom do two tribes speak the same language and usually they do not even speak similar ones; and if a single group were to use more than one language, it would not constitute one tribe. Few tribal members are bilingual, save for an elite that has gone abroad and been educated, or those who have gone to the cities and become urbanized. When there is bilingualism, it usually does not consist of two tribal languages, but rather one tribal tongue and a lingua franca or the colonial language. Intertribal relations are minimal.

Under these circumstances, two simultaneous phenomena seem to have emerged in the new African nations: some have accepted the colonial language, once the hated symbol of a colonial master, as the official tongue as well as the lingua franca; and in others, one tribe has emerged as politically dominant, but has not imposed that tribal language on the rest of the country.

It is estimated that Ethiopia has more than forty different tribes, with perhaps as many local languages. Nigeria has no politically-neutral language because the region is divided into three separate areas, each with its own language - Hausa, Yoruba, and Ibo (Francis, 1976, pp. 316-317). The only example of what might be termed a native African tongue that has survived as the dominant language of a country could be Swahili, which emerged as a result of the influence of Arab traders on indigenous tongues. Predominantly found in East Africa, it is nonetheless used to a limited extent throughout the continent. In Tanzania and Kenya, Swahili is considered as a culturally-transmitted tradition of speech, and is used in education, politics, and legal transactions (Fraenkel, 1967, pp. 186-189; Pei, 1958, pp. 20-23; Whiteley, 1971, pp. 185-186).

The African scene has other complexities. Some of the languages are tonal, where the meaning imputed to a given sound depends upon the pitch with which it is spoken, and few have been reduced to writing. They have an oral history, a folklore, and mythology, but no written literature. Furthermore, the tribes need the languages not merely to survive as separate entities, but for the people to survive at all. As Peter Berger (1976, p. 7) reminds us, language is words, and words

describe the realities of human life. But words also have the power to create and shape realities. The words of the strong carry more weight than the words of the weak. Indeed, very often the weak describe themselves in the words coined by the strong. Over the last two centuries or more the strong have been the technologically advanced nations of the West. As they improved their military, political and economic power over most of the world, they also improved the power of their words.

With the anticipated development of writing systems in the tribal languages, there is a movement toward compulsory education in these tongues. This may increase ethnic solidarity and movements toward dissociation. It is unlikely, however, that secession will be for the purpose of preserving linguistic integrity; rather, language will serve as a unifying force if power struggles of a political and economic nature should result in the development of autonomist, secessionist, and separatist movements.

Bilingualism as a Defusing Response

National political leaders who want to retain their territories and power through federationism or assimilation can anticipate separatist movements and react in a variety of ways, ranging from the permissive to the repressive. An effort can be made to suppress the local language and muffle the identity. This was attempted in Spain against the Basques and proved a failure. In-group cohesion grew with out-group hostility, as sociologists might have predicted. In the south of France, by contrast, as in Provence, the regional-national consciousness is displayed in literary and antiquarian interests, but rarely in separatist tendencies (Francis, 1976, pp. 102-108).

Languages can be given recognition in their respective territories with efforts to encourage schooling, publications, religious ceremonies, and political and economic affairs in the local tongue. This is difficult for a nation-state to effectuate, and the success of Switzerland is unique. Switzerland is a relatively prosperous country that has lived in peace with its neighbors for several hundred years. There are few enticements to secession. The people are highly literate, and knowledge of at least two languages is probably more prevalent than in any other country of the world, (except for special situations, as in Haiti). The cantons making up Switzerland have a great deal of autonomy, and there appear to be few economic or political advantages to separatism around which the people could be rallied. It is not surprising, then, that Switzerland has been called the one multilingual European country where political and cultural language problems are solved by the application of individual liberty and democratic federalism (Kohn, 1956). According to Kerr (1974), trends in the political expression of the Swiss show that, as far as linguistic divisions are concerned, the major underlying source of internal peace is the occurrence of conflicts or wars among neighboring countries. The German-speaking Alamanns tend to have a stronger sense of Swiss identity than do the French-speaking Romands who have a stronger identification with their language. The shift in the identity of the Romands over the years is partly explained by the two successive generations of people who experienced a war in which France and Germany were enemies. With little or no challenge to the national Swiss identity, young people born after World War II became more involved in a search for what they termed "personal identity."

Nevertheless, some people are not optimistic about linguistic federationism, even in Switzerland. They cite a slow but steady mobilization toward centralization by the federal authorities. This has prompted a renewal of linguistic identification among the Romands and smaller minorities, who feel that they are losing ground to the technological and industrial interests centered among the Alamanns. As the anticentralist groups lose their collective bargaining power vis-a-vis the federal state, the risk of linguistic conflict in Switzerland increases. It would not be a conflict over language, however, but a power struggle between groups distinguished from one another primarily by language.

In most countries, a single language becomes dominant when people in other ethnic groups perceive that there is a flow of power, authority, and wealth to the persons speaking the major tongue of the land. Polylingualism without inequality presents intrinsic difficulties. In many of the regions and constituent republics of the Soviet Union, children in school are taught in one of the approximately 200 languages that are recognized, and newspapers and official documents are printed in those tongues (New York Times, 1978b). Nevertheless, there are fewer books published in Georgian, Armenian, or Ukranian than in Russian. A student from one of the outlying areas wanting to enter a major university would travel to Moscow, Leningrad, or another large urban center where the language is Russian. Polylingual duplication of all facilities is difficult. Yet, without such duplication, the potential for secession remains omnipresent, although in the Soviet Union, as in most other countries, it is vigorously suppressed.

Linguistic interdependence is usually one-sided rather than mutual. The Georgians and Ukranians depend on Russian, not the reverse. A special form of linguistic interdependence would be a delicate balance between bilingualism and linguistic integrity. Perhaps the linguistic-ethnic identity movement could be handled by attempting to make all parts of the nation-state bi-, tri-, or polylingual. The official dominant language could be brought to the potential secessionist territory, and the secessionists' language to the remainder of the country. Such linguistic balance might defuse secession, by demonstrating a de jure equality.

Probably no country had tied this so carefully, and with so many misgivings, as Canada. Canada is divided into ten provinces, in nine of which English is the dominant language; a few scattered groups speak one of the Eskimo or Amerindian tongues, or an immigrant language. In one province, Quebec,

French is dominant. In the French Canadians' struggle for a greater share of power in the nation and their own province, language became a major issue. Quebec separatism is an example of regional-subcultural separatism; a minority community became increasingly alienated from the larger political unit, and language was utilized to accentuate the cleavage and to enhance the power of the Quebecois.

Political efforts to solve this situation have exacerbated both sides. From 1867 to 1960, stability in Canada was maintained through accommodations designed specifically to co-opt minority elites. During the late 1960s, under the guidance of Pierre Trudeau, a bicultural-bilingual program was initiated for the entire nation. Nevertheless, projections show that there will be few French-speaking persons in Canada outside of Quebec in the years ahead, leading to a cynical attitude toward the "bi and bi" movement.(4)

The problems of separation have gone far beyond language, bilingualism, and biculturism in Quebec. Language was the catalyst, the centripetal force to rally persons to a given identity, the symbol to distinguish some people from others, and it carried a distinction fraught with numerous inequities of power and wealth.

Isolation and Alienation, Social and Territorial

One of the correlates of secessionism is territorial integrity of the people identifying with one another. Although the territorial integrity of a linguistically-unified group that is distinct in language from others in the nation does not necessarily lead to autonomist and secessionist movements, without it such a group could not have autonomy as its aim. A linguistically-dispersed group, no matter how strong the other correlates of ethnic and national identity, is not likely to aim for separatism. It might seek greater recognition of its language, as the Spanish-speaking have done in the United States. One of the most renowned instances of dispersion, that of the Jews, did not involve a linguistically-united group, but one united by religion, ancestry, and common bonds of defense against widespread persecution.

In the Soviet Union, territorial integrity is generally coterminous with linguistic distinction, but autonomy movements are given little opportunity to develop. On the one hand they are co-opted by the official Soviet policy toward national cultural pluralism; and, on the other, anything going beyond such pluralism is considered anti-Soviet and meets ruthless repression, as do other forms of dissent generally tolerated in many democratic countries. However, it is not unusual for the "free world" or the Third World to take stringent measures to suppress secessionists who are considered traitorous and

beyond the levels of tolerance of a nation-state. Such repressive measures are not generally taken against autonomists
and devolutionists, a factor to be recalled when one considers
the stance of Downing Street toward Scottish and Welsh
nationalism.

The Biafran experience is a recent example of a civil war
for secession that was not exacerbated by any linguistic
problem. The Biafrans, a group having a single national
identity and occupying one territory within a federation,
perceived themselves as victims of economic and political
inequality in Nigeria.

Although language differences do not usually generate the
same degree of hostility and fear as differences in race,
religion, and national identity, they are always a contributory
factor. People tend to be suspicious when they hear others
speaking a language that they do not understand. During the
First World War, the sentiment against the German language
was so strong in the United States that many colleges discontinued teaching it, despite the extraordinarily important
place it held in the world of science.

Many people mimic those whose tongues they do not
understand. They hear words as grunts, and tones as
childish singsong. Recall the "Ugh" which studded con-
versations of American Indians in the movies of the 1930s.

This is not a serious problem for a linguistically-
integrated territorial nationality, where only the stranger or a
government functionary from the center of power is likely to
be present. However, when minority-language persons drift to
an urban area, they are likely to be disparaged as much for
their speech as for their customs, religion, rituals, and
racially-characterizing appearance. Regional modes of speech,
accents, and special terms and phrases associated with ethnicity and social class distinguish them from those who speak
the "true," official, or "correct" version. An alleged inferiority is imputed to people by virtue of their ignorance of
methods of speech which "everbody" is capable of mastering.

It is unlikely that gestures, cues, nonverbal communication, and body language can bridge a gap of this sort. Important as such forms of communication are, particularly in
giving insights to observers and social scientists, they are
limited in scope, often lack specificity, have greater significance on the unconscious than conscious level, and do not
have shared meanings in different nationalities; oral communication is complemented and supplemented, but not replaced. Linguistic difference is the impediment to social interaction. Without such interaction, there is little potential for
nonverbal "discussion"; a wink or a smile can initiate a
one-to-one interaction, but cannot sustain it.

Social Structure and the Foundations for
Linguistic Separatism

With so wide a range of complex relationships among language, religion, physical traits, ancestry, and other identifiers, and secessionist and autonomist movements of various aspirations, strengths, and potentials, one can do little more than draw some tentative conclusions concerning the role of language in this intricate picture.

Linguistic identity groups are more likely to remain intact in an agricultural than in an industrial economy because of the lack of geographic mobility and the intergenerational continuity of language in a monolingual community. To the extent that industrialization and urbanization appear to be the dominant movements of the twentieth century, one might be led to expect the diminution and dispersion of language groups. However, industrialization has been reversed in areas such as Cambodia, and tribal groups in Africa remain relatively isolated from the industrializing and modernizing sectors of their nations.

The movement toward autonomy and separatism is an international phenomenon, supranational in roots and scope. It has been aggrandized by anti-colonialism and the development of new, independent nation-states. To countervail secessionist drives, the new nationalism seeks international strength through federations of different language movements.

National and international demographic factors influence whether a language-nationality group is autonomist, secessionist, or irredentist, or remains in a culturally-pluralistic federation. If irredentist, such movements can arise from the neighboring states rather than from within; but whether the neighboring state will be "subversive" depends upon diplomatic, military, and other aspects of relative power. Following the Nazi accession to power in 1933 in Germany annexation movements of German-fascist origin arose wherever German was spoken in Central Europe, with the exception of Switzerland. In Canada, the French-speaking populace cannot unite with France for many reasons, the most apparent being geographic, but it conceivably might look to becoming part of an international community of French-speaking nations. The Greeks in Albania might aspire to unity with Greece, although differences between the political systems of the two nations, and the strong suppression of separatists in Albania would appear to negate this possibility. Also for political reasons, the Albanians in Yugoslavia are unlikely to aspire to unite with Albania (Stavrou, 1975). The Scots are more autonomist- than secessionist-oriented because of geographic-demographic, linguistic, and economic factors - a land border continuous with England, the disappearance of a Celtic tongue and the expectation that the Scottish people can, by greater home rule, obtain a larger share of the wealth in England's sagging economy.

The specific forms of the industrial and/or agricultural economies, whether capitalist or communist or the combination thereof that appears to be emerging in various areas of the Third World, are not significant factors in determining the survival or decline of the language, or the role of language as symbol for rallying the people toward association or dissociation. Although secession may be more vigorously suppressed in communist nations, Basque, Puerto Rican, and Moroccan separatists were repressed by Spain, the United States, and France, respectively; and the history of the British, Dutch, Portuguese, and other empires is there for all to read.

Linguistic distinction is a major factor in differentiating some peoples from others, but is not an absolute requirement for such distinction. It augments religious, racial, and perceived ancestral differences.

Whether a separate language of a nationality group is likely to survive intergenerationally is dependent upon the answers to many questions: What is the absolute and relative size of the group, its demography? Is it geographically isolated from others? What is its mobility in terms of frequency of physical contact with others? Do its leaders perceive economic advantages or losses from separatism? Is the language taught in the schools as a primary tongue, and how universal and compulsory is education? Is political power shared? To what degree, if any, is the language repressed?

A language can diminish in its daily utilization, and become little more than a cultural fossil, while it continues to be a symbolic rallying point for the ethnic group. One can say that the aims are not linguistic, but linguistic aims can be superimposed on nationalistic ones. We believe, along this line, that Fishman (1968, p. 7) overstates the case when he declares that "the ideologization of languages, which enables them to play desired roles in symbolic mobilization and unification, also leads to the development of these languages per se into fitting instruments of government, technology, and High Culture."

The technology generally acts to reduce linguistic differences by increasing geographic mobility and ease of communication between localities and groups. However, the new technology may be augmenting linguistic differences by reducing numerous languages to writing systems, thereby making education in the lingua franca or the dominant language less necessary than it had been.

The recognition of the minority group language, on a local and to some extent on a national scale, serves to diminish secessionist drives, but entails many difficulties in the functioning of the complex institutions of a culturally-pluralistic nation.

Modern communication, particularly television, and wide-spread literacy will probably diminish the survival potential for many language groups and increase bilingualism. Residents will become fluent in the major language or the linga franca, and, at the same time, the old language can be carefully used by political leaders of the dominant group to make concessions, offer programs and newspapers, and develop a sense of cultural pluralism rather than dissociation.

The coalescence of national versions of the same language into one single tongue has probably not run its course. A force that reduces regional nationalist identity in favor of identification with the nation-state as a whole, it is facilitated by technology. However, it cannot take place except where contiguous languages have strong similarities and are derived from the same language family, and where there is a gradual rather than a discontinuous development from one language group to another.

Although language is a factor in feeding nationalism, nationalist movements find other factors when linguistic distinction is absent. In such instances, language is often used as a symbol. However, efforts to revive a language that is rarely spoken and impose it on a newly independent country such as Ireland have met with little success. The one example of such success is the use of Hebrew in Israel; this was made possible by a group of unique factors: immigrants speaking different tongues needed a common language in which to communicate, and there was a strong desire on the part of the central power group to develop the concept of the Jews as a nation in addition to be a religious group.

Language groups will not move toward secession when they see marked economic and possible political advantages in staying in the state in which they constitute a minority. Instead, they will tend to use their minority status to obtain concessions for more jobs, social welfare programs, and aid to education - including bilingualism.

Language as symbol can be satisfied at times by changes in names; some black Americans have taken on African-like names. A former colonial tongue can become a symbol only where national disidentity with the imperialist-colonial power is so complete that it is unthreatened, and where the international, economic, and other advantages to continued use of the colonial tongue are evident and beyond dispute.

Language as a factor in a power struggle can seldom be satisfied merely by recognition of the equality of the minor language because the demands go beyond the use of the language itself. Official bilingualism is more the handle around which demands are made than an end in itself.

Autonomist movements can survive without language distinction, and language distinction without autonomist movements; in the first instance, these can be explained in terms of major differences in race, social treatment, and power within a country, and in the second, by equal treatment or by perceived and believed advantages to continued affiliation.

IN CONCLUSION: A FEW WORDS ON POWER

To summarize the many disparate strands in this essay, we would conclude that language is power. It is the key issue in the struggle for power in Quebec, and is utilized by both sides in the fight over the redistribution of power. It is useful, if not indispensable, in rallying people in power struggles, although the aims, goals, and motives may be unrelated to language itself. An autonomist movement can develop its campaign for power without aspirations for a separate language, as it has in Scotland; but the movement that is inspired by language identity has a symbolic power built into it.

It is not so much that the struggles for power will result in the revival, strengthening, and continuity of the language, but rather that the presence of language, whether in current usage or as an historical symbol, strengthens a people in power struggles.

NOTES

(1) The term _risorgimento_ is derived from _risorgere_ which means "to rise again." For a discussion, see Francis (1976, pp. 79-82).
(2) A "tighter set of typologies is developed by Kloss (1968), although some of his descriptions seem to employ jargon unnecessarily, and some types that he creates are not as useful as others.
(3) Van den Berghe (1968) refers to the political movement based on ethnicity as nationalism (e.g., Kikuyu nationalism or Yoruba nationalism). See also Turner (1972).
(4) For studies of the rise of Quebec nationalism, see McRoberts and Posgate (1976), McRae (1974), Pious (1973), Meisel (1974), and Henripin (1974), a few informative pieces in a very large body of literature.

BIBLIOGRAPHY

Berger, Peter L. _Pyramids of Sacrifice: Political Ethics and Social Change_. New York: Doubleday-Anchor, 1976.

Boehm, Max Hildebert. "Nationalism," Encyclopaedia of the Social Sciences, Vol. 11. New York: Macmillan, 1933.

Brass, Paul R. Language, Religion and Politics in North India. London: Cambridge University Press, 1974.

Fishman, Joshua A., Charles A. Ferguson, and Jyotirindra Das Gupta (eds.). Language Problems of Developing Nations. New York: John Wiley, 1968.

_____. "Sociolinguics and the Language Problems of the Developing Countries." ibid., pp. 3-16.

Fraenkel, Gerd. Languages of the World. Boston: Ginn, 1967.

Francis, E.K. Interethnic Relations: An Essay in Sociological Theory. New York: Elsevier, 1976.

Henripin, Jacques. L'immigration et le desequilibre linguistique. Ottawa: Main d'oeuvre et Immigration, 1974.

India: A Reference Annual. Research and Reference Division, Ministry of Information and Broadcasting. New Delhi: Government of India Press, 1974.

Kerr, Henry, H., Jr. Switzerland: Social Cleavages and Partisan Conflict. Beverly Hills, Cal.: Sage Publications, 1974.

Kloss, Heinz. "Notes Concerning a Language-Nation Typology," in Fishman et al., pp. 69-86.

Kohn, Hans. Nationalism and Liberty: The Swiss Example. New York: Macmillan, 1956.

Lewis, E. Glyn. Multilingualism in the Soviet Union. The Hague: Mouton, 1972.

McRae, Kenneth (ed.). Consociational Democracy: Political Accommodation in Segmented Societies. Toronto: McClelland & Stewart, 1974.

McRoberts, Kenneth, and Dale Posgate. Quebec: Social Change and Political Crisis. Toronto: McClelland & Stewart, 1976.

Meisel, John. Cleavages, Parties, and Values in Canada. Beverly Hills, Cal.: Sage Publications, 1974.

New York Times. (a) "Bretons attack the glory of France." July 2, 1978.

_____. (b) "Georgian and Armenian pride lead to conflicts with Moscow." June 26, 1978.

Pei, Mario. One Language for the World. New York: Devin-Adair, 1958.

Pious, Richard. "Canada and the Crisis of Quebec," Journal of International Affairs, 27(1) (1973), pp. 53-55.

Stavrou, Nikolaos A. "Unity, Brotherhood and Manipulation: Language and Minorities in Yugoslavia," Society, 12(2) (1975), pp. 75-78.

Trudgill, Peter. Sociolinguistics: An Introduction. New York: Penguin, 1974.

Turner, Thomas. "Congo-Kinshasa: Indigenous Cultures and Political Institutions," in Victor A. Olorunsola (ed.), The Politics of Cultural Sub-Nationalism in Africa. New York: Doubleday: 1972.

United States Department of State. Fact Book of the Countries of the World. New York: Crown, 1970.

Van den Berghe. "Language and 'Nationalism' in South Africa," in Fishman et al., pp. 215-224.

Whiteley, W.H. Language Use and Social Change. London: Oxford University Press, 1971.

Zavalani, T. "Albanian Nationalism," in Peter F. Sugar and Ivo J. Lederer (eds.). Nationalism in Eastern Europe. Seattle: University of Washington Press, 1969.

II
Racial and Ethnic Autonomy in North America

Introduction

The concept of pluralism in broad context implies that in order to avert or minimize ethnic conflict, a social system characterized by diverse ethnicity should be constructed on its ethnic heterogeneity. The state must, therefore, create a set of diffuse values in order to establish national identity and loyalty based on a consensus of minimum values, as opposed to maximum adherence to ethnic values. The state's basic task, then, is to synthesize from the diverse groups a set of diffuse values and ideals that can be shared by all in a meaningful way. Each group, consequently, can retain its own ethnic distinctiveness, while simultaneously accepting diverse values and ideals common to all groups comprising the ethnically-heterogeneous social system. And state leadership can assume the authority to maintain law and order and implement national and foreign policy based on a pluralistic value consensus.

Both the United States and Canada possess ethnically-diverse groups, and both countries espouse a policy of ethnic pluralism. In addition, both countries combine pluralism and democratic ideals to accommodate ethnic diversity. Furthermore, the concept of democratic pluralism emphasizes not only the social dimensions of peaceful ethnic coexistence, but the necessity for diverse groups to participate in the political process. If politics at the national level embodies each group's sociocultural, economic, and aesthetic interests, than participation enables all ethnic groups to pursue their own well-being and that of the state with a minimum conflict of interest.

Although the ideal is to distribute power evenly among diverse groups, the fact is that some ethnic groups are more powerful than others. In both countries specific groups dominate power: in the United States, white Americans control the bulk of power; in Canada, those of English stock are in control of most of it. Color and race in the United States, and language in Canada, are the areas of contention.

In the United States, the black civil rights movements of the 1960s not only activated black consciousness, but prompted white ethnic groups of European origin to reassess the cost of giving up their Old World culture and values for "the American Way." However, it is much easier for white ethnic groups, even those who hold on to Old World traditions, to accept American values, in that the whole of the complex of American values and life styles is merely the sum total of the many ethnic groups of European origins. Although some white ethnic groups may raise questions regarding how their values fit into the American system, most have judged that the benefits of simmering in the broth of the American melting pot far outweigh the cost of being burned in their own ethnic fire.

The primary reason for the minimum of ethnic conflict among groups of European origin stems from the fact that the political system operates in the best interests of the white majority; therefore, conflict among them is regulated through the political process. Avowedly separatist Hutterites, Mormons, and Amish groups are permitted to live autonomously with their religious beliefs within the sociopolitical framework of democratic pluralism; these groups have carved out autonomous territories in Pennsylvania, Utah, and Ohio. Cities, especially old northeastern ones, also tend to be ethnically-divided, allowing individuals who are particularly sensitive to their ethnicity to reside in a neighborhood with members of their own group. Despite the myriad problems associated with ethnic diversity, democratic pluralism has worked exceptionally well for the vast majority of white Americans.

In contrast, the history of white racism in the United States has had an exceptionally deleterious effect on the vast majority of black Americans. White prejudice, discrimination, and exclusion have promoted and maintained black inequality from the time blacks disembarked from slave ships to the civil rights demands of recent times. Only the most unregenerate racists would argue that contemporary black inequality in the United States cannot be explained in part by the long history of white racism. There is a vast body of literature dealing with the past and present "Negro" problem in American society; the bulk of it deals with various aspects of the sociopolitical, economic, and historical dimensions of race relations. The paper by Cook focuses on some of the sociocultural dynamics of the black experience from the perspective of selected black American writers.

The choice of a literary piece rather than a specifically sociopolitical one stems from an awareness that one of the most important - yet neglected - sources for gaining insight into the inner dimensions of social movements is through the analysis of fiction and nonfiction works by ethnic writers. Authors who identify with a particular movement bring insight into a complex phenomenon, and provide a rich data source for those who utilize ethnomethodological approaches. Cook has selected various liberation or self-determination themes by selected black writers stemming from the liberation movement of the 1960s.

In spite of the clear and desirable variations in genre, philosophy, political and social ideology, and structure among these writers, there are at least two common concerns: (1) black Americans are part of a culture that is separate from, and superior to, that of Euro-America, and the surrender of this culture for the dubious benefits of assimilation or integration would mean a loss of identity; (2) black Americans possess a rich and expressive language, and a variety of verbal and linguistic forms which should form the basis for a renaissance in black literature. Emphasis on these two themes, however, is not to suggest that political and ideological views, theories of a homeland in North America or Africa, and the adoption of non-European languages are absent from the opinions articulated by some of these writers. Political and artistic leadership may be, and often are, incarnate in the same individual - vide Imamu Amiri Baraka aka LeRoi Jones. For many of these artists, the first line of battle is on the cultural front; cultural separatism must either precede or accompany political liberation.

The black liberation movement of the 1960s inspired other groups to protect their subordinate positions. Native Americans and Mexican American Chicanos are two of those that generated social movements geared to bring about autonomy. Both groups have been the victims of cultural, linguistic, and racial prejudice by the dominant society. Blacks have struggled against oppression from the very beginning of their forced residence in the New World in the sixteenth century, but the native inhabitants of North America - labeled "Indians" as a result of navigational disorientation - have been victimized by Euro-Americans even longer.

Any rudimentary understanding of the contemporary mood, activity, and goals of the Native American people in the United States requires a knowledge of the historical dynamics of their relations with whites. The selection by Dorris, himself a Native American, explores various aspects of this relationship. He observes that "from the very beginning, [whites] have consistently assumed that their particular brands of social organization, religion, language, and lifestyles would prove so compelling, so magnetic, that all indigenous alternatives would, almost as an act of nature, give way. This belief, engendered by millennia of European isolation from the rest of the world, and reinforced by apparent competitive success, was grounded in two basic - and short-sighted - hypotheses: (1) all inhabitants of the New World constituted in fact but a single ethnic community; and (2) human culture was

universally and teleologically evolutionary, with Western
Civilization forever holding 'most advanced' status." He observes further that Native Americans, in the main, have never
been "submerged in, or even a subset of the Euro-American
world. They are not ... separatist for they have never been
a part of a larger multi-ethnic matrix"; they steadfastly maintain "their right to be distinct, to be plural, to be un-
American."

The bases for Chicano autonomy are probably more
complex than those for blacks and Native Americans because
the racial, cultural, and language factors are composite. A
mixture of native groups of pre-Columbian Mexico led to the
Aztecs, whose blood was then mixed with that of their Spanish
conquerors. Finally, as Mexicans emigrated to North America
they commingled with various northern European strains. Culturally, these origins are all evident as a Mexican cultural mix
with the United States industrial culture. Linguistically, the
Chicano may or may not speak Spanish; in either case, he
usually speaks English. The Chicano may be a recent Mexican
immigrant or a descendant of sixteenth-century settlers.
Although most Chicanos feel that they belong in the United
States, they also feel some ties to Mexico.

Maria Kleitz explores aspects of the complexity of Chicano
identity before tackling the still-more-difficult task of dealing
with the social and political dynamics of the Chicano movement
in American society. This movement has forged a common
identity, enabling Chicanos to put aside intragroup conflict
and adopt a militant stand toward the larger oppressive
society. The movement shows signs of maturation by its
effective use of frustration as a unifying tool to mobilize
political action and economic bargaining power in the drive for
autonomy and a working relationship with the larger society.

George Theriault focuses on the conflict between the
French- and English-speaking groups in Canada. Unlike the
United States, where race, color, and culture are significant
factors contributing to conflict; language and culture, accompanied by economic and political factors, play significant roles
in Canadian unrest. Just as the historical dynamics of Euro-
American versus Native American are highlighted, the historical forces behind the French-English rift in Canada are
explored. Theriault observes that "the struggle between the
English and French for sovereignty over territory and resources on the North American continent dates back to the
early seventeenth century. The issue of control emerged with
the earliest exploration and first settlement. In examining
Quebec separatism in retrospect and prospect, our goal is to
understand the circumstances, influences, and turns of events
that have nourished and maintained the identity of the French
people; after nearly four centuries, they have the vigor,
determination, and courage to run up the flag over their

Quebec stronghold, man the political ramparts, and fling down the gauntlet to the Anglo-Saxon host, some 220 million strong, besetting them on all sides."

ME ON THE SUBLIME

The critic pulpits
"Learn your craft!
Check out the job the masters' poets used to do."
And since I had made up my mind to get it on
I went back all the way to Greece and Rome
The cradles of the original high.
I even read Satyricon where
Petronius peeped my card.
No kinda way could I write lines that breathed.
(That was a kick)
No poetry, Eumopul says,
Is founded on colloquial speech
Debased and corrupted in the street.
He almost made me drop the library book.
(The man went on to pull my coat.)
Its beauty is both formal and internal
Its texture bees intrinsic
Yes indeed.
Heavy language to threaten me
Across so many centuries.
But niggers always did their solo thing
Too dumb to know there was no way ...
With their black gods
Some made the middle passage whole,
Then in the face of all good sense
They sang and danced and cut the fool
And made a church of cotton fields.

                                William W. Cook

4 Swim: Cultural Separatism in Contemporary Black Literature
William W. Cook

There is a tradition in our land as old as Roger Williams and the Pilgrims. It takes the term New World with literal seriousness. America, it declares, shall be the New Jerusalem, the kingdom of Heaven brought from within each man to earth, and expressed in the forms of our American society. The deepest aesthetic creators of America have been partisans, indeed hierophants, of this tradition. This great tradition, with its demand that men, here on Earth, within an American social structure, work out the relevation of God, is often present only as a river flowing underground, nourishing but unseen.(1)

So stated Waldo Frank in "Hart Crane." He continues this thought in the introduction to The Bridge:

This tradition rose in the Mediterranean world with the will of Egypt, Israel and Greece, to recreate the individual and the group in the image of values called divine. The same will established catholic Europe, and when it failed (producing nonetheless what came to be the national European cultures), the great tradition survived. It survived in the Europe of the Renaissance, Reformation, Revolution. With the Puritans, it was formally transplanted to the North American Seaboard ... the great tradition, unbroken from Hermes Trismegistus and Moses, does not die.(2)

There is an underground river not dealt with in Frank's brief article or in his more extended treatment of the great

tradition in the introduction to Crane's The Bridge. That
river is the separatist stream of black American literature; it
is a stream that runs counter to the great tradition and its
determination to work out the revelation of God within an
American social structure. It is a tradition which defines its
sources not as the Greaco-Roman ones described by Frank,
but rather as African and Afro-American. Although this
tradition only became apparent to the general public during
the black power movement of the 1960s, it dates back to the
black writers and orators of the nineteenth century.

When Leopold Senghor was inducted into the Black
Academy of Arts and Letters in 1971, Imamu Amiri Baraka
(Leroi Jones) wrote to C. Eric Lincoln that the effect of the
honor was to "glorify Mr. Sanghor's contributions to the arts,
without taking into consideration his total presence in the
world; that is, as a politician and the would-be leader of a
country ...I cannot see how you can justify honoring Senghor,
which is at the same time the honoring of neo-colonialism and
slavish commitment to European ideas. And to try to separate
art from life by giving this award to Senghor in the midst of
his degeneracy is in itself European because the African artist
knows that art and life are the same."(3)   Baraka's letter
points up two elements of that branch of Afro-American
literature which, because it defines itself in ways that are
counter to the great tradition, can be called separatist. It is
a literature which is not committed to European ideas or forms;
and it is a literature which insists on judging artistic worth
not solely on the basis of technique and form, but also on its
political and social relationship to liberation efforts. Art for
art's sake is an anathema to its adherents.

Although separatist elements can be found in Black
writing since its inception in the United States, the most
coherent analyses of what came to be known as the Black
Aesthetic began in the 1960s. Early in her career Gwendolyn
Brooks wrote a moving "integration" poem:

Grant me that I am human, that I hurt
That I can cry.
Not that I now ask alms, in shame gone hollow.
Nor cringe outside the loud and sumptuous gate.
Admit me to our mutual estate.

Open my rooms, let in the light and air.
Reserve my service at the human feast,
And let the joy continue.(4)

By the time In The Mecca was published, however, she was
not nearly so convinced of the value of being admitted to an
estate held in common with white America; the river of
American culture must be rechannelled if it is to be a stream

in which black Americans will wish to bathe:

> My people, black and black, revile the River.
> Say that the River turns, and turn the River.(5)

The cry for understanding and a recognition of humanity that are heard in the first selection by Brooks are a reflection of the division that DuBois sees in black Americans:

> It is a peculiar sensation, this double consciousness, this sense of always looking at one's self through the eyes of others, of measuring one's soul by the tape of a world that looks on in amused contempt and pity. One ever feels his two-ness - an American, a Negro; two souls two thoughts, two unreconciled strivings; two warring ideals in one dark body, whose dogged strength alone keeps it from being torn asunder. The history of the American Negro is the history of this strife, this longing to attain self-conscious manhood, to merge his double self into a better and truer self. In this merging he wishes neither of the older selves to be lost. He does not wish to Africanize America, for America has too much to teach the world and Africa; he does not wish to bleach his Negro blood in a flood of white Americanism, for he believes ... that Negro blood has yet a message for the world. He simply wishes to make it possible for a man to be both a Negro and an American without being cursed and spit upon by his fellows, without losing the opportunity of self-development.(6)

This division is healed in Larry Neal's black liberation chant: "This is the death of the white lie that our ancestors prophesied. This is the death of the double consciousness."(7) However, that healing takes forms different from those DuBois envisioned. The healing takes place not because the river of black consciousness joins the stream of the great tradition, but because black men and women come to grips with, understand, and finally accept the separateness and the superiority of the black experience; and this experience has its roots in Africa and Afro-America, not in the great tradition described by Waldo Frank. It is an experience which Don L. Lee defines in his introduction to Black Spirits: The writer/artist must avoid "imitating the dirtiness of the European consciousness," must realize that "there are more similarities, between a Harlem and a Zimbabwe, than differences."(8) The white culture so long admired is to be seen for what it is. In 1917, DuBois saw World War I not as an instance of "Europe gone mad;" "not aberration nor insanity,"

but "the real soul of white culture - back of all culture -
stripped and visible today."(9) So too do his heirs in the
1960s and 1970s see little in American and European culture
worth emulating or joining.

> To write black poetry is an act of survival, of
> regeneration, of love. Black writers do not write
> for white people and refuse to be judged by them.
> They write for black people and they write about
> their blackness, and out of their blackness, re-
> jecting anyone and anything that stands in the way
> of self-knowledge and self-celebration.(10)

That the revolution is clearly cultural as well as political is
central to this analysis by Stephen Henderson.

> This rejection of white values and standards is one
> of the most powerful aspects of the black revo-
> lution. It appears in fiction, in drama, in poetry,
> and in criticism, both literary and social, when
> such distinctions are admitted. It is directed not
> only at whites but at negroes too, who have re-
> jected their blackness or have never been fully
> aware of it.(11)

That integration or assimilation with white America is to be
avoided is equally evident.

> What the black revolution seeks is not integration
> into American society as it now stands. A few
> years ago the slogan was, "Not integration but
> transformation." That, of course, is just a mild
> way of saying what has been said in other terms;
> and what has been said is that this society as we
> know it must be destroyed and another erected in
> its place.(12)

The very concept of black power according to Henderson
implies a kind of society which differs from the one in which
we now live. It implies not transformation but revolutionary
change.
     To return to the definition of separatist black literature
implicit in Baraka's letter, we cite yet another source, Ron
Karenga. Karenga may be called one of the major theoreticians
of the black aesthetic, for other major spokesmen - Neal,
Baraka, King, Gayle - draw freely from his statements of
theory. According to Karenga, the truly revolutionary black
art is functional and useful, not merely decorative. It must
be collective, for "individualism is a luxury that we cannot afford." Black art must "commit us to revolution and

change ... For all our art must contribute to revolutionary change and if it does not, it is invalid." It must "expose the enemy, praise the people, and support the revolution."(13) This is an art no longer torn by the double consciousness of DuBois.

> [The artists] are fully aware of the dual nature of their heritage, and of the subtleties and complex- ities; but they are even more aware of the terrible reality of their outsidedness, of their political and economic powerlessness, and of the desperate need for unity. And they have been convinced over and over again, by the irrefutable facts of history and by the cold intransigence of the privileged white majority, that the road to solidarity and strength leads inevitably through reclamation and indoctrina- tion of black arts and culture.(14)

There has been some disagreement as to ideology - some of the writers espouse Marxist-Leninist politics and others rejecting them as simply another European dodge - and tech- nique - some members of the Black Aesthetics movement argue strongly for a social-realist approach to art while other black writers demand the freedom to experiment with form and structure. Nevertheless, there are, if one ignores some of the pamphleteering, strong ties binding the writers who have emerged since the black power movement. They are all con- cerned with reexamining history in the light of their recognition of a heritage that cannot be understood in the setting of the great tradition. One of the goals of this re- examination is to discover, extol, and analyze heroes whom the mainstream historian has ignored or maligned. According to Addison Gayle, Jr., John Oliver Killens, spiritual father of the new novelists, is concerned with reordering the historical record of American participation in World War II, and, in particular, the experience of that war as it was felt by black Americans. Killens' hero comes to realize that there are two wars being waged: the first, and least important one, for it is a sham, is the war against the Japanese; the second is the war between black and white Americans, which finally erupts in all its vehemence in Australia. The black soldiers have always been a part of this second war but their awareness of it and their part in it comes only after a series of disillusion- ments. They find that protesting their treatment in Georgia only results in their being transferred to California, and finally being shipped overseas to the Philippines. The changes of locale are changes of locale and nothing more; the reality of racial hatred and unfair treatment are with them everywhere they go. Killens' hero is a man who, after becoming aware of the reality of war in American society, takes his place in the ranks with his brothers.

Black writers before Killens have struggled with the question of black American participation in America's wars, as have many writers who followed him. This question is central to Yerby's "Health Card," to John A. Williams' Captain Blackman, to many of Langston Hughes' Simple stories, to Ellison's "Flying Home," and to many other works by black Americans.

The reexamination of history attempts to set the record straight by pointing out black heroes and the nature of true heroism. Davidson's El Hajj Malik, a dramatization of The Autobiography of Malcolm X, presents the life and the struggle of that hero as exemplary of the experience of all black Americans. His play is not only a record of the development of a hero, but also an examination of those elements of black American life that support - and those that hinder - true revolution. It extols not the life of the black middle class and its aspirations to membership in the mainstream culture of America, but rather those black Americans who live in the America which has been invisible to many artists claiming to record the experience of the race.

One of the most impressive of the histories is the recently-published Motion of History, in which Baraka moves from the Civil Rights Movement back through the history of revolution in America. Nathaniel Bacon, Nat Turner, Harriet Tubman, Denmark Vesey, Gabriel Prosser, and John Brown are among the early revolutionaries who are placed in the stream of American rebellion against racism and capitalism. The blurring of the lines which separate them from revolutionaries of the twentieth century has as its purpose the denial of substantive change in America, and leads to the final and inevitable conclusion that their failed revolutions could be attributed in part to betrayal from within, underestimation of the power and craft of the enemy, and their own ideological weaknesses. The symbol of a black and a white man with their heads through a screen on which many of the events of the play are projected is a telling concretization of the attitude of many black Americans. They are surrounded by history and revolutionary struggle, but understand this not in the least. They are still victims of the divisions created by their masters, divisions created for the sole purpose of keeping them fighting each other rather than attacking their true oppressors. Motion of History differs in this respect from an earlier Baraka work, the much-anthologized Dutchman. In the latter, Clay struggles toward manhood and an awareness of his position vis a vis Lula, a white American; but he is destroyed as a result of this awareness and his revelation to her concerning his feelings about America. Baraka himself describes the characters and their roles as follows:

> But I will say this, if the girl (or the boy) in that play has to "represent" anything, I mean if she must be symbolic in the way demented academicians use the term, she does not exist at all. She is not meant to be a symbol - nor is Clay - but a real person, a real thing, in a real world. She does not represent anything - she is one. And perhaps that thing is America, or at least its spirit. You remember America don't you, where they have unsolved murders happening before your eyes on television. How crazy, extreme, neurotic, does that sound? Lula, for all her alleged insanity, just barely reflects the insanity of this hideous place. And Clay is a young boy trying desperately to become a man. <u>Dutchman</u> is about the difficulty of becoming a man in America. It is very difficult, to be sure, if you are black, but I think it is now much harder to become one if you're white. In fact, you will find very few white American males with the slightest knowledge of what manhood involves. They are too busy running the world, or running from it.(15)

<u>The Motion of History</u> ends with the newly-radicalized comrades "cheering and surging forward ... Richie and Lenny among them." They, unlike Clay, have profited from studying Marx, Lenin, and Stalin, in addition to reexamining the early heroes of the revolution in America. Armed with this awareness, they transcend the artificial boundaries that separate black and white workers and move toward revolution and the final re-making of America. A major difference between <u>The Motion of History</u> and <u>Dutchman</u>, is the attitude toward white America, and toward <u>Marx</u> and Lenin. In "A Black Value System," published in 1969, Baraka made the following statement:

> When we say 'revolution' we mean the restoration of our national sovereignty as a people, a people, at this point, equipped to set new paths for the development of man. We mean the freeing of our-selves from the bondage of another, alien, people. We are not warring upon our own society among ourselves. These pigs are no kin to us. We are trying to destroy a foreign oppressor. It is not 'revolution' but <u>National Liberation</u>.(16)

Capitalism is not the solution: "When you speak of capitalism you speak of the European mind. We do not want to be Europeans. No, not of any persuasion." The "any per-suasion" here clearly includes major spokesmen of the left. Responding to the statement that blacks such as J. A. Rogers

should be studying Marx, Engels, and Lafargue, Baraka asks
why this should be so. "Are not Marx, Engels and Lafargue
just another list of 'great' men ... but great white men, or at
least white men thought great by one particular group of white
men?" The solution is to be found not in these Europeans,
but in a Black value system: "If you cannot have faith in
blackness, in the black mind and the black man to find a way
out of this slavery, you are full of despair, or else emotionally
committed to white people." Baraka argues that blacks must
conceive of themselves as a separate nation and not as part of
America: "Nationalism must be the basis for our entire lives
... contribute to the building of a Nation. That is our purpose, Nationalism or direction. Black is our identity." If this
nation building is to take place, there must be constructed a
system of values different from that of America.

> If you do not consciously create a new value
> system, one that is quite different from the rest of
> crazy America's - you will be exactly what crazy
> America is and die the way she dies.(17)

That value system "is African, because we are African, no
matter that we have been trapped in the West these few
hundred years." It is a system which "at each level is a
contrast to Euro-American morality, because first it is based
on teachings that are superior to the practiced morality of
Euro-American civilization." The Euro-American value system
"has always been detrimental to black people."(18)
     In Leroi Jones' The Dutchman Clay's long speech on the
relationship between black culture and a hatred of whites
comes from an awareness of the superiority of that culture and
its origins in suffering and deprivation. He is determined to
destroy whites and their sterile European legacy. Ishmael
Reed travels a similar route. The very form of many of his
novels is a repudiation of "culture." He adopts the format
not of Dostoevsky, Melville, Tolstoy, James, or Hemingway,
but, rather, turns to the Yellow Back adventure novels, to
the whodunit detective story, to the cowboy movie, to the
radio thriller, and to the slave narrative for his structure.
Not only does he deny the superiority of the establishment's
literature, but he also attacks the very institutions on which
the establishment is based. The Judeo-Christian tradition and
its repressive and anti-life variations in America are satirized
in The Freelance Pallbearers when Reed's hero, in his attempt
to succeed in America, joins the Nazarene Apprentices. The
Atonist conspiracy which Reed traces back to Ikhnaton and Set
is alive and well in America, appearing not only in religious
forms, but in political and artistic forms as well. Opposed to
this is a tradition that is not only superior but older. While
the Atonist is dour and serious, the Jes Grew Carrier is full
of life and music. The Wallflower Order, in keeping with its
Atonist philosophy is opposed to the natural:

> The headquarters of the Wallflower Order. You
> have nothing real up here. Everything is poly-
> urethane, polystyrene, Lucite, Plexiglas, acrylite,
> Mylar, Teflon, phenolic, polycarbonate. A gal-
> limaufry of synthetic materials. Wood you hate.
> Nothing to remind you of the Human Seed. The
> aesthetic is thin flat turgid dull grey bland like a
> yawn. Neat. Clean, accurate, and precise. The
> Atonists got rid of their spirit 1000s of years ago
> with Him. The flesh is next. Plastic will soon
> prevail over flesh and bones.(19)

This philosophy is the product of a religious sense which is
the antithesis of the natural religions of Africa and North
American Indians.

> LaBas could understand the certain North American
> Indian tribe reputed to have punished a man for
> lacking a sense of humor. For LaBas anyone who
> couldn't titter a bit was not Afro but most likely a
> Christian connoting blood, death, and impaled
> emaciated Jew in excruciation. Nowhere is there an
> account or portrait of Christ laughing. Like the
> Marxists who secularized his doctrine, he is always
> stern, serious and as gloomy as a prison guard.
> Never does I see him laughing until tears appear in
> his eyes like the roly-poly squint-eyed Buddha
> guffawing with arms upraised or certain African
> loas, Orishas.(20)

It is this philosophy of life and the art and culture which is
derived from it that Reed in all his novels, Chester Himes in
Pinktoes, Charles Wright in The Messenger and The Wig,
Douglas Turner Ward in Day of Absence, Ossie Davis in Purlie
Victorious, and a host of other black satirists hold up to
ridicule. It represents a cultural sterility that characterizes
not only white America, but also those black groups which
aspire to membership in the decadence called mainstream
culture.

Reexamination of history and cultural warfare are not the
only tasks with which the separatist artist busies him/herself.
It is equally important that the work of art, if it is to be the
liberating force which it aspires to be, point toward positive
unity and the destruction of those attitudes and customs which
stand in the way of positive identity. Although Ellison can
hardly be called a separatist, his Invisible Man is the odyssey
of a black protagonist who must come to some definition of
himself in the face of a series of external and destructive
characterizations of his identity and role. He must create "the
uncreated features of his face." Ellison holds that, "Our task

is that of making ourselves individuals. The conscience of a
race is the gift of its individuals who see, evaluate, record
... We create the race by creating ourselves and then to our
great astonishment we will have created something far more important: We will have created a culture."(21)   Although
Karenga, Neal, Gayle, and Baraka would have trouble with
Ellison's insistence on individuality as the first step, the ends
which he seeks are similar to theirs: all desire the creation of
a culture and a conscience, and all agree that the black man
in the streets should repudiate the white line and have his
own lifestyle.   An artist whose name is anathema to the
separatists is Charles Gordone, Jr. Nevertheless, he works at
themes which are not alien to the separatist tradition. In No
Place to Be Somebody, he derides the victims of Charley Fever
who compete by using the same disgraceful tools as white
Americans. The March on Washington, the high hopes of the
Civil Rights Movement, and integration are the subjects of two
of Gabriel's most savage poem/satires.
       Paul Carter Harrison is another artist concerned with
negative attitudes and values. The Great MacDaddy exposes
the evils of drug addiction, and praises the mythic figure who
frees black America from its depredations; this play and his
The Drama of Nommo: Black Theater in the African Continuum
point to still another aspect of the separatist movement in
black American literature: Writers are determined to find
alternatives to Anglo-European models for their work, and
some find these alternatives in African literary forms and
rituals. In his introduction to the latter work, Harrison makes
clear his opposition to the Western aesthetic:

> The black artist, particularly in the theater, at-
> tempts to rationalize his own powers in an op-
> pressive force field, and does so by adoring the
> protective, unassuming cloak of Western aesthetics.
> Upon initiation into such a cultural mode, owing to
> the fact that his own community has not been able
> to authenticate him, the sum total of the black
> artist's existence becomes defined for him: his
> contribution, purged of its spiritual intensity,
> becomes locked into a socio-grammatic scale of
> reality.(22)

Such a writer becomes concerned not with the spirit or the
function of art within a culture, but rather with art as a
construction of images and symbols that bear little or no
relationship to the experience and spiritual life of a community, or to its customs and needs. He writes for a
privileged class rather than for the masses. Art which aspires
to teach and to hold up those values which are a part of
Afro-America must be based on forms which are peculiar to

Afro-America, and which are readily recognizable to its people. These forms, Harrison argues, are African in origin. Like Reed, Harrison is interested in exploiting them:

> Most black dramatists do possess the power of vision and the sincerity of consanguinity to communicate the ethos of black life. However, they are often misled into believing that their minds must necessarily be committed to the logic of the Babylonian mode which, supposedly, holds all the answers to universality; the development of native traits, then, becomes perverted. These persons enter into a double standard which negates the validity of their natural sensibilities.(23)

A black church and black rituals can be likened to African models; these practices and values must become the basis of any true black literature. The artist must look to them as his source. Ishmael Reed puts it another way:

> Black writers have in the past written sonnets, iambic pentameter, ballads, every possible Western gentleman's form. They have been neo-classicists, Marxists, existentialists, and infected with every Western disease available. I have a joke I tell friends about a young black poet who relies upon another people's systems, and does not use his head. He wears sideburns and has seen every French film in New York. While dining at Schrafft's, he chokes to death on nut-covered ice cream and dies. He approaches the river Styx and pleads with Charon to ferry him across: "I don't care how often you've used me as a mythological allusion," Charon says. "You're still a nigger - swim!"

> One has to return to what some writers would call "dark heathenism" to find original tall tales, and yarns with the kind of originality that some modern writers use as found poetry - the enigmatic street rhymes of some of Ellison's minor characters, or the dozens. I call this new-hoodooism; a spur to originality.(24)

Any reader who examines Reed's novels and poems will recognize the use to which he puts street rhymes and "dozens." He sounds on the gods of Western culture in "Bad Man of the Guest Professor," and his clear purpose is warfare:

> The   Afro-American   artist   is   similar   to   the
> Necromancer   (a   word   whose   etymology   is   revealing
> in   itself!)   He   is   a   conjuror   who   works   JuJu   upon
> his   oppressors;   a   witch   doctor   who   frees   his   fellow
> victims   from   the   psychic   attack   launched   by   demons
> of   the   outer   and   inner   world   ...   The   artist   is   the
> new   preacher,   the   prophet   of   the   modernist
> religion.(25)

African   religion   and   customs   and   new   world   variants   of
these   customs   and   religions   are   central   to   the   work   of   many
black   American   artists.   Toni   Morrison   chooses   a   traditional
Afro-American   folktale   of   flying   Africans   as   the   mythic   base   of
her   Song of Solomon.   Hel   Bennett's   novels   Wait Until The
Evening,   Lord of Dark Places,   and   Seventh Heaven   demonstrate
his   interest   in   African   and   Afro-American   religious   practices.
He   is   never   far   from   voodoo,   or   its   North   American   variant,
hoodoo.   African   and   Afro-American   ceremony   shape   the
theater   pieces   of   Melvin   Van   Peebles,   and   the   poetry   of
writers   as   varied   as   Ted   Joans   and   Henry   Dumas.
     The   reader   who   is   unfamiliar   with   verbal   rituals   of   black
America   is   often   unaware   of   their   presence   in   the   works   of
black   writers.   "Sounding,"   "signifying,"   and   "dozens"   are
games   of   ritual   insult   common   to   the   experience   of   most   black
Americans.   Rap   Brown,   Melvin   Van   Peebles,   Baraka,   and
many   others   speak   of   their   admiration   for   these   games.   They
are   central   to   a   great   deal   of   the   work   coming   out   of   black
America.   To   put   one's   enemy   in   the   dozens   is   to   work   JuJu
on   him;   the   goal   is   psychic   warfare.   This   is   the   tactic   which
Ellison's   protagonist   uses   with   Tobitt   during   the   confrontation
with   the   Brotherhood   committee.   Tobitt   is   destroyed   because
he   is   unaware   of   the   weapon   being   used   against   him   and   is
unable   to   defend   himself.   Dozens   and   sounding   are   common
verbal   strategies   in   Al   Young's   Sitting Pretty.   Young   de-
vastates   the   so-called   "street   poet"   by   sounding   on   his   method
and   style,   through   the   character   of   O.O.   Gabugah,   street   poet
extraordinaire   and   author   of   O.O's Greatest Hits.   Sidney
Poitier,   James   Brown,   and   Jack   Benney   are   among   the   victims
of   Baraka's   street   talk.   The   ultra-sophisticated   Negro   is
given   this   comeuppance   in   Don   L.   Lee's   -   now   Haki
Madhubuti   -   "But   He   Was   Cool."   These   writers,   using   a   black
tradition   that   may   have   its   roots   in   the   "halo"   of   the   Ewe
people   of   West   Africa,   use   humor   to   shame   the   erring   back   to
the   right   path,   to   render   the   enemy   powerless   by   holding   him
up   to   ridicule,   and   to   point   up   the   adversary's   ignorance   by
besting   him   in   a   contest   of   wit.
     The   master   of   these   forms   is   Ishmael   Reed,   whose   works
rely   on   the   aggressive   verbal   strategies   of   black   America   to
constitute   a   ritual   attack   on   the   culture   and   values   of   white
America   and   its   black   allies.   Note   the   way   in   which   Reed

reworks Ellison: He makes the deathbed sequence in Invisible Man blacker, but at the same time he sounds on the serious tone of Ellison's depiction of the scene. Ellison's protagonist describes the death of his grandfather:

> He was an odd old guy, my grandfather, but I am told I take after him. It was he who caused the trouble. On his deathbed he called my father to him and said, "Son, after I'm gone I want you to keep up the good fight. I never told you, but our life is a war and I have been a traitor all my born days, a spy in the enemy's country ever since I give up my gun back in the Reconstruction. Live with your head in the lion's mouth. I want you to overcome 'em with yesses, undermine 'em with grins, agree'em to death and destruction, let 'em swoller you till they vomit or bust wide open." They thought the old man had gone out of his mind. He had been the meekest of men. The younger children were rushed from the room, the shades were drawn and the flame of the lamp turned so low that it sputtered on the wick like the old man's breathing. "Learn it to the young'uns," he whispered fiercely; then he died.(26)

The death-bed scene in Reed's The Freelance Pallbearers echoes the Ellison scene. The sage advice comes, in this instance, from Harry Sam's mother, "a low down, filthy hobo infected with hoof-and-mouth disease. A five-o'clock shadowed junkie who died of diphtheria and an overdose of phenobarb."

> "Looka heah, Sam," his mother said before they lifted her into the basket and pulled the sheet over her empty pupils." It's a cruel, cruel world and you gots to be swift. Your father is a big fat stupid kabalsa who is doing one to five in Sing Sing for foolin' around with them blasted chickens. That is definitely not what's happening. If it hadn't been for those little pills, I would have gone out of my rat mind a long time ago. I have paid a lot of dues, son, and now I'm gonna pop off. But before I croak, I want to give you a little advice.
>
> Always be at the top of the heap. If you can't whup um with your fists, keek um. If you can't keek um, butt um. If you can't butt um and if you can't bite um, then gum the mothafukas to death. And one more thing, son," this purple-tongued

> gypsy said, taking a last swig of sterno and wiping
> her lips with a ragged sleeve. "Think twice before
> you speak 'cause the graveyard is full of peoples
> what talks too much."
>
> Sam never forgot the advice of this woman whose
> face looked like five miles of unpaved road.(27)

Not only is Reed sounding on Ellison, he is also, in the
tradition of the dozens, commenting on the heritage of the
Harry S. Truman figure in the novel. Political figures like
Truman, Hoover, L.B.J., Averall Harriman and, Nixon - note
D Hexorcism of Noxon d Awful - abound in the novels of
Reed, in company with Theda Doompussy Blackwell, Nancy
Spellman, Rev. Eclair Porkchop, Minnie the Moocher, Drag
Gibson, and Chief Showcase.
    Language different from that of the enemy becomes im-
portant. By language, Afro-Americans mean not only the
words themselves, but the context in which they are used, the
structures, gestures, and rituals surrounding the language.
It is no accident that black writers are abandoning the lan-
guage habits of the great tradition and seeking a language
that is a natural reflection of the world view of black America.
Smitherman's Talkin and Testifyin: The Language of Black
America attempts to describe and defend this "Africanized form
of English reflecting black America's linguistic-cultural African
heritage and the conditions of servitude, oppression and life in
America. Black language is Euro-American speech with an
Afro-American meaning, nuance, tone, and gesture. The
Black Idiom is used by 80-90 percent of American Blacks, at
least some of the time. It has allowed blacks to create a
culture of survival in an alien land, and as a by-product has
served to enrich the language of all Americans."(28)
Smitherman notes that black speech is not only language but
style.
    J. L. Dillard in Black English and in All-American English
also attempts to explain the separate branch of American
English called black English. He and Smitherman are among
those linguists who argue not for its classification as a dialect,
but for the recognition of black speech as a language with a
separate grammar and syntax. Writers who accept this definition choose to write in this language, and not in that of the
mainstream, believing that to falsify language is to falsify
experience. In "Expressive Language," Baraka argues that
"speech is the effective form of a culture." Because this is
so, and because speech is "the way one describes the natural
proposition of being alive" it "is much more crucial than even
most artists realize." To alter the speech of black Americans,
as our schools attempt to do, is to alter the culture of those
speakers and their relationship to it. "Being told to 'speak

proper,' meaning that you must become fluent with the jargon of power, is also a part of not 'speaking proper.' That is, the culture which desperately understands that it does not 'speak proper,' or is not fluent with the terms of social strength, also understands somewhere that its desire to gain such fluency is done at a terrifying risk. The bourgeois Negro accepts such risk as profit. But does close-ter mean the same thing as closer?"(29)

This attitude toward speech represents a radical departure from the attitude of James Weldon Johnson who, in his 1922 preface to The Book of American Negro Poetry, doubted that Negro "dialect" was a language suited to the expression of the range of human experiences or to the attempts of other black writers to "regularize" the speech of black America.

The separatist element in black American literature justifies treatment of that literature not as part of mainstream American literature, but as a critique of it and American society. Although one would not be justified in arguing that all the writers discussed here hope for political, cultural or even social separation from white America, it is clear that they conceive of themselves as part of a heritage that is either invisible to the mainstream, or undervalued by it. They are not interested in surrendering that heritage in hopes of acceptance. Rather, they seek to understand the unique character of that legacy and to communicate this understanding to their audiences. They are sure of the existence of two Americas, and they are not loath to take sides:

> cause there's only two parties in this country
> anti-nigger and pro-nigger
> most of the pro-niggers are now dead
> this second reconstruction is being aborted
> as was the first
> ....
> let's build a for real black thing
> called revolution
> known to revolutionists as
> love(30)

Clayton Riley in his introduction to A Black Quartet clearly distinguishes between the black theater of the 1960s and the theater which preceded it: The new black theater saw "blackness in all arenas as a new direction, the new/lost reality of ourselves as architects of our own sense of beauty, builders pledged to constructing disregarded collective dreams. Creating a mythology out of a consciousness durably shaped by a continuum of black experience. Awareness."(31) This new theater was "a theater moved by a commitment to a view of ourselves and the world inspired by those portions of our spirit which are informed by an acknowledged blackness. A

view of ourselves, for instance, no longer influenced by the
visions or nightmares white America possesses ... A new black
art emerges from an exploration beyond our skins (now
recognized as containing the beauty we once could never see)
and into remembrance of the currency implied by a life no one
else in this country has lived in quite the way we have."(32)
"Exploration" is the operative term here, exploration of history
and the discovery of heroes previously-neglected and ridiculed
through ignorance or malice, exploration of black culture in all
its ramifications and especially in its antagonistic relationship
to the Euro-American tradition, exploration of those people and
forces that threaten unity, exploration of our roots in the
African culture and its ceremonies.

Although it can be argued that the separatist impulse as
it appears in some writers in the later half of the twentieth
century is best defined as a desire for clear divisions between
black and white, the strongest impulse is toward coalition with
all those people committed to revolution. Whether the initial
point of attack is cultural uniqueness or political ideology, the
end - a restructuring of America - is the same. The goal,
according to Reed, is to "appreciably curtail Judeo-Christian
culture's domination of our senses ... What's ahead, I think,
is that this system is going to fall, probably through a bloodless coup. It's already a bloodless coup when the old whiskey
drinkers who run the country are stumbling around like
Frankenstein."(33) Reed sees a coalition emerging; his part in
forging this coalition can be seen in his close cooperation with
Asian-American and Native American writers and his use of
characters and imagery from the cultures which they
represent:

> What we're going to see emerge is a cooperative of
> autonomous groups who are going to come up with
> new ways of making America work, thus making the
> planet work. We're already seeing that the old
> religious institutions are dying and they die hard
> ...The seventies will belong to black people, In-
> dians, cosmic creatures and anybody else who wants
> to climb aboard.(34)

Baraka, in his introduction to The Motion of History and
Other Plays, emphasizes the shift in point of view that has
occurred in his work. His latest works focus "principally on
the conscious separation created between black and white
workers who are both exploited by the same enemy. The play
sets itself the task of exposing this treachery and sham, but
also of telling a part of this nation's history through its recurrent rebellions."(35) He describes himself as having moved
"from petty bourgeois radicalism, nationalism (and its low point
of bourgeois cultural nationalism) on through to finally grasp-

ing the science of revolution, Marxism-Leninism-Mao Tse-tung Thought." Baraka has moved away from separatism defined as a desirable division between the races to a concern with ideological revolution, from a concern with cultural nationalism and separate black political institutions to an anti-capitalist coalition of the exploited. The forces which exploit black Americans and deny them humanity are the same forces which deceive and abuse the white worker. The way to such a coalition is not the route so often traveled - denial of one's heritage - but one that leads to understanding and accepting that heritage.

> and what
> will we do
> > what should we do
> >
> > look into the eyes of
> > the blackest
> > child
> > and listen to the speech
> > the images (in
> > his eyes) make
> > and you will under-
> > stand
> > how simple in the
> > future
> > the complex present
> > is laughingly run down.(36)

The cosmic people of whom Reed speaks can be found in many of the cultures of the great tradition, and they become fit cadre in the revolution when they learn who they are and learn to love themselves and their heritage. This love leads naturally to acceptance:

> You can do what you want with your hair ... and you still won't like yourself. Your mind has to go natural while you straighten your soul ... the process got to be on the inside ... I mean we all in trouble ... terrible trouble, an we ain't in it in no bits, pieces, or sections. It's a common trouble, share and share alike, want to or not; the high and the low of us, the black and the yallar of us, the gas head and the natural bus, the Negro and the black man, the dungarees and the African robe, the fat black lady with the blow-hair, and the long brown lady in the wig. You and me and your mama and your stepgrandpa ... the Ph.D. and the high school dropout ... we in some terrible deep trouble .. and we in it together ... I am what I am ... but I do wanta be free ... and I'm gonna be ... by any means possible ... and you just better-black-believe-it.(37)

Addison Gayle, Jr. described the 1970s as "a Black cultural renaissance, in which for, perhaps the last time, Black Nationalist writers will be able to project - to Black people - a sense of our unique, separate cultural identity by resolving the dichotomy between art and function, thereby making art functional and relevant to the Black community."(38)   This is an art which will satisfy the requirements of Ron Karenga.   It is an art which will "remind us of our distaste for the enemy, our love for each other, and our commitment to the revolutionary struggle."(39)

NOTES

1. Waldo Frank, "Hart Crane" in Brom Weber, (ed.), The Complete Poems and Selected Letters and Prose of Hart Crane (Garden City: Anchor/Doubleday, 1966), pp. 269-270.

2. Waldo Frank, Introduction to The Bridge (New York: Liveright, 1970), pp. xvii-iii.

3. Imamu Amiri Baraka (LeRoi Jones) in Black World, October 1971, p. 61.

4. Gwendolyn Brooks, as quoted in Margaret J. Butcher, The Negro in American Culture (New York: Albert Knopf, 1956), p. 138.

5. Gwendolyn Brooks, In the Mecca (New York: Harper & Row, 1968), p. 49.

6. W. E. B. DuBois, Souls of Black Folks (Millwood, N.Y.: Kraus-Thomson, 1903), p. 3.

7. Larry Neal, "Any Day Now: Black Art and Black Liberation" in Woodie King and Earl Anthony (eds.), Black Poets and Prophets (New York: NAL, 1972), p. 164.

8. Don L. Lee, "Introduction to Black Spirits" (New York: Random House, 1972), p. xvii.

9. W. E. B. DuBois, "Of the Culture of White Folk," Meyer Weinberg (ed.), W. E. B. DuBois: A Reader (New York: Harper & Row, 1970), pp. 311-312.

10. Stephen E. Cook and Mercer Henderson, The Militant Black Writer (Madison: University of Wisconsin Press, 1969), p. 65.

11. Ibid., p. 75.

12. Ibid., p. 126.

13. Ron Karenga, "Black Art: Mute Matter Given Force and Function," in King and Anthony, Op. Cit., p. 175.

14. Addison Gayle, Jr., The Way of the New World (New York: Anchor/Doubleday, 1976), p. 316.

15. LeRoi Jones (Imamu Amiri Baraka), "LeRoi Jones Talking," Home (New York: William Morrow, 1966), p. 187-188.

16. Imamu Amiri Baraka (LeRoi Jones), "A Black Value System," in King and Anthony, Op. Cit., p. 141.
17. Ibid., p. 146.
18. Ibid., p. 140.
19. Ishmael Reed, Mumbo Jumbo (New York: Bantam, 1973), pp. 70-71.
20. Ibid., p. 110.
21. Ralph Ellison, Invisible Man (New York: Random House, 1972), p. 268.
22. Paul Carter Harrison, The Drama of Nommo: Black Theater in the African Continuum (New York: Grove Press, 1972), p. xv.
23. Ibid., p. xvii.
24. Ishmael Reed, Introduction to Nineteen Necromancers From Now (Garden City: Anchor/Doubleday, 1970), p. xvi.
25. Ibid., p. xvii.
26. Ellison op. cit., pp. 13-14.
27. Ishmael Reed, The Freelance Pallbearers (New York: Bantam, 1967), pp. 1-2.
28. Geneva Smitherman, Talkin and Testifyin: The Language of Black America (Boston: Houghton, Mifflin, 1977), pp. 2-3.
29. LeRoi Jones, "Expressive Language," in Home, p. 171.
30. Nikki Giovanni, Black Feeling, Black Talk, Black Judgment (New York: William Morrow, 1970), pp. 83-84.
31. Clayton Riley, Introduction to A Black Quartet, (New York: NAL, 1970), pp. vii-viii.
32. Ibid., p. x.
33. Ishmael Reed, "When State Magicians Fail," in John Bart Gerald and George Blecker eds., Survival Prose (Indianapolis: Bobbs-Merrill, 1971), p. 163.
34. Ibid., p. 163.
35. Imamu Amiri Baraka (LeRoi Jones), The Motion of History and Other Plays (New York: William Morrow, 1978), p. 13.
36. Imamu Amiri Baraka, "Move," in Black Spirits, p. 26.
37. Alice Childress, "The African Garden" in Alice Childress (ed.), Black Scenes, (Garden City,: Doubleday, 1971), pp. 143-144.
38. Addison Gayle, Jr., quoted in "Introduction to Black Spirits," p. xxviii.
39. Black Poets and Prophets, p. 179.

5 Twentieth-Century Indians: The Return of the Natives
Michael Dorris

With increasing persistence over the past 400 years, Native North American societies have been forced to define themselves relative to an invading foreign population. From the beginning, Europeans have consistently assumed that their particular brands of social organization, religion, language, and life-style would prove so compelling, so magnetic, that all indigenous alternatives would, almost as an act of nature, give way. (The term "European," as it is used in this essay, is an unavoidable generalization; not all Europeans shared exactly the same attitudes or beliefs. However, as this paper suggests, certain widespread concepts were predictably held in common and promulgated as a result of the particular circumstances of European cultural development.) This belief, engendered by millenia of European isolation from the rest of the world, and reenforced by apparent competitive success, was grounded in two basic - and short-sighted - hypotheses: (1) all inhabitants of the New World constituted in fact but a single ethnic community; and (2) human culture was universally and teleologically evolutionary, with Western Civilization forever holding "most advanced" status.

EUROPEAN WORLD VIEW

It is little wonder that fifteenth-century European explorers often didn't know where they were. For well over a 1,000 years their little home-continent had existed in a practical state of cultural deprivation and isolation. With only a few minor exceptions, virtually all its inhabitants spoke languages derived from a single linguistic family - Indo-European - and, thus, shared a meaningful and pervasive socio-cultural common denominator. Moreover, in the larger perspective, the continent's religious and philosophical divisions were little more than variations on a single theme. Although much was made of regional or doctrinal distinctions, virtually everyone from Baltic to Balkans to British Isles professed belief in the same single male divinity or, in the case of European Jewry, His father.

As side effects of this theological homogeny, Latin became a lingua franca for intellectuals from all regions, and the Mosaic code formed the basis for practically every ethical or legal system. The assumption that patriarchy and male dominance was the normal order of existence reigned supreme, from individual marriage contracts to the leadership hierarchy of emergent nation-states.

Prior to the fifteenth century, Europeans had little contact with populations dissimilar to themselves, certainly not enough to shake their entrenched sense of ethnocentrism. Relations with central or east Asia, or sub-Saharan Africa, were rare, and usually filtered through the Islamic societies occupying the southern and eastern shores of the Mediterranean. Although Arabs were regarded in certain respects as "exotic", they were, nevertheless, comprehensible; generally similar in terms of skin pigmentation, patriarchal orientation, and even religious derivation, they were appositives whose customs fell within the range of at least plausible behavior. The Arabs were ideal "heathens" because they tended to embrace the same values as the Europeans themselves - messianic monotheism, territorial conquest, the accumulation of material wealth. In so doing, they provided a societal contrast that helped to define and affirm the concept of Europe as the center of the world.

This comfortable smugness was very nearly shattered when the first few boatloads of Spanish and Portuguese sailors failed to topple off the edge of the world - located, predictably, just beyond the sight of Christiandom's shore - and blundered into a series of incredible "New Worlds." Verifying the existence of Africa and the Orient, each replete with undeniably non-European populations, was traumatic enough, but not altogether a surprise. Spices had been around for some time and they had to come from somewhere! But, when Christopher Columbus accidentally collided with the Western Hemisphere, the realities of global diversity and possibility were no longer avoidable.

If the basis of European cosmology was to remain intact, some method had to be found to expand the traditional understandings of the world so they could incorporate and absorb the unsurmised pluralism that existed outside the confines of Europe and the Mediterranean basin. The initial solution - one that is still used to "solve" many problems - was to define out of existence any data which might be disruptive. Via this

facile mechanism, non-Western peoples were quickly branded
"sub-human"; as such, their lands, goods, and even their
lives should logically be subject to the control of their more
"advanced" discoverers.

Unfortunately, this approach was a bit hard to maintain;
troublesome cultures uncooperatively refused to evaporate or
devolve. Non-European intelligence and industry were evident
in the cities, sophisticated agriculture, science, and art of
this New World. Regretfully, gracelessly, and on the advice
of the Pope himself, Europeans had to admit that, however
distasteful it might be, it appeared possible to be certifiably
human and yet not Caucasian.

However, this capitulation did not signify agreement with
the principle of cultural relativism. Almost nowhere was it
suggested that non-European peoples were the mental equals of
Europeans, or that their societies possessed any rights equivalent to those of European nations. On the contrary, the
White Man's Burden became the onerous task of persuading, by
all conceivable means of coercion, indigenous peoples to cast
away their traditional mores and beliefs and adopt . the
European model in all things.

To assist them in this stewardship, a variety of convenient and necessary attitudes were approved. Primary
among them were the absolute refusal to recognize anything of
value or worth in the indigenous society, and the assumption
that all resident Natives were the same. (The supposed "State
of Nature" in which some cultures were said to exist was
praised by some European observers, but this condition was
non-volitional and, therefore, not credited to the choice of any
Native population.) From this latter insistence emerged a
plethora of familiar misnomers and generalizations, from the
ubiquitous "Ethiope" of the nineteenth century, to the ever-
present "Indian," to the more unambiguously pejorative "wog,"
"redskin," or "savage." The ascription of such honorifics
infinitely alleviated the mental anguish a homogenized European
must necessarily have felt when faced with what must have
seemed a monstrously confusing, unexpected, and disorganized
world.

These non-European populations were regarded, in the
most positive sense, as "pre-European," or, said another way,
"pre-civilized." As such, they were unilaterally and pre-
sumptuously incorporated into a tidy European world view as
anonymous and somewhat obstreperous juveniles, retardees,
and incompetents. It was righteously expected that, when
apprised of the wonders of "civilization," they would summarily
accept this ignominious valuation of themselves and aspire
fervently to their self-betterment in accordance with the
European mode.

Distinctions were made according to status within a closed
and controlled culture-specific system, and not on the basis of

linguistic, historical, or societal diversity.

All "Indians" were, therefore, the same in their relative rank on a hypothetically-evolutionary scale. No amount of perfection within traditional cultural criteria was even minimally capable of provoking the smallest move in the direction of assimilation. Those populations which had the effrontery to resist or, worse, ignore these haloed principles so necessary to the preservation of European peace of mind were characterized as devils, fools, or incorrigibles, and were deemed worthy of either incarceration or a more permanent solution. Good Indians, after all, were dead ones.

EUROPEAN ADVANTAGES

Before examining the roots of Native American attitudes and reactions to transatlantic contact, an answer should be proposed to the underlying question: How was it that Europeans were able to impose themselves and their ideas so widely around the world, and particularly in the Americas? Three reasons predominate, each in and of itself foreordaining the speedy overthrow of Native America.

According to most archeological theories, human beings first entered the Western Hemisphere via a land bridge uniting Siberia and Alaska. This natural route, at times up to 300 miles in breadth, existed during the height of the Wisconsin glacial period 28,000 to 40,000 years ago. Although a few immigrants, primarily Eskimo and Aleut are said to have successfully managed a transpolar entry about 10,000 years ago, it seems clear that the vast majority of the proto-Native population has been in residence in North and South America - and cut off from further intercourse with "Old World" peoples - for at least 25,000 years.

It is well-documented that during that period successive waves of disease wreaked havoc among the populations of Europe, Asia, and Africa. Tuberculosis, plague, smallpox, diptheria, gonorrhea, typhus, cholera and a host of other maladies were rampant at various times. When an infection struck, the majority of a population would often succumb immediately. The only protection from contagion was the haphazard occurence of mutation in the genes, which gave some persons a "natural immunity" to a particular disease. They alone would survive the holocaust and, in so doing, would strengthen future generations by passing on the immunity to their descendants.

Thus, over time, the greater part of Eurasian and African populations was winnowed and regenerated by many strains of disease. To be sure, epidemics still occurred in the modern era, but with a decreasing likelihood that any known

contagion would prove lethal to a majority of the populace.
For some unknown and inexplicable reason, it is archeologically-verifiable that Western Hemisphere populations escaped exposure to literally all of these diseases before Columbus' voyage. As a result, the estimated 100 million people resident in North and South America - approximately 15 million of whom lived north of the Rio Grande - lacked precedent immunities, and lay wholly vulnerable to the multifarious bacteria inadvertently carried by European explorers, traders, and colonists.

The results of even the most cursory interactions were both scientifically inevitable and socially devastating. Old World diseases spread rapidly to all parts of the Hemisphere by way of traditional trade networks, and radically depopulated both continents. Some Native societies were all but wiped out in a matter of weeks; in a single summer, smallpox reduced the Assiniboine population from 40,000 to 2,500. Contemporary demographers estimate that often as many as 19 out of 20 people succumbed. Entire culture complexes, such as the urbanized "Mound Builder" or "Mississippian" civilization, were substantially obliterated by infection long before the first European crossed the Appalachians; no people were spared the effects of the contagions. By 1910, the U.S. census reported a Native American population of only about 200,000, hardly more than one percent of its probable aboriginal total.

The relatively few survivors - who themselves had an apparent set of natural immunities - were faced with additional and continuing traumas that were direct effects of the diseases. All indigenous societies faced situations of gross confusion and demoralization: social organization that was dependent upon extensive kinship systems was especially sensitive to drastic depopulation; individual cultures, confronted by illnesses whose symptoms were unfamiliar and unresponsive to traditionally-effective remedies, postulated extraordinary causes, ranging from the witchcraft of a malevolent neighbor to the end of the world itself; inter-tribal conflicts occurred, each side blaming the other for the spreading disaster; and large areas of once densely populated territory were left empty as the survivors of epidemics sought to quit habitats thought to harbor evil influences.

Severely depopulated, demoralized, and depressed, Native American societies were hardly in a physical or psychological position to defend their sovereignty against an invading, hale, and ever-expanding force of Europeans. Moreover, they were faced with a foe that had a military technology stimulated and perfected by centuries of inter-state warfare in Europe. Conflicts of multi-generational duration had spurred the development of both sophisticated methods and clearly-defined theories of waging war. "Victory" under the European system meant the recognized and acknowledged defeat of an enemy group, the annexation of that group's lands, and the right to suppress that group's population. It was expected that, under certain circumstances, members of particular classes were liable for enlistment or impressment into a standing army; they might then be compelled, either by overt sanction or by a more abstract appeal to "patriotism," to risk their lives at the bidding of an inaccessible and unelected head of state. Motivation for battle came largely from political rather than personal ambitions; decisions as to who the enemy was, where and for how long it was to be engaged, and what was to become of it afterwards, were normally made without reference to the wishes or goals of the individual combatant.

Native American societies, even at their healthiest, were historically ill-adapted and unprepared to successfully balance such a foe over any extended time, far from living up to their contemporary "warlike" stereotypes, they were by and large agriculturists or hunters with little experience in organized militancy. Most Native people lived in small, relatively self-sufficient communities. Their time was consumed with an abundancy of duties connected to the survival and perpetuation of their respective societies. It is almost a truism to state that the traditional small community, in whatever place and time it is situated, can ill-afford the human and economic expense of war-making. In an internally-dependent aggregation of people, the loss of a single productive individual has serious ramifications.

This is not to imply that no inter-group conflicts took place among Native Americans. On the contrary, some societies had long-term traditions of hostility and antipathy. However, virtually all Native American cultures sharply contrasted with their European analogues in the degree, frequency, and duration of actual aggressive international behavior. Few conflicts extended beyond a single battle or raid; rarely was one side clearly defeated by the other; almost never was territory lost or an entire population subjugated; and it was abnormal for a single community to be involved, to any extent, in more than a handful of belligerent encounters in the course of a year. Military technologies had, therefore, never developed to any real degree of efficiency; artifacts that were used as weapons more often served as implements for hunting or processing game animals.

Moreover, it seems doubtful whether any North American society was organized in a way which would permit a tribal leader to force anyone into a military undertaking. Chiefs were usually nothing more than the current experts at specific tasks and had no sanctioning power beyond the combined persuasiveness of their oratory and proven abilities. (Consequently, most indigenous cultures had a multiplicity of chiefs at any one time; there was often simultaneously a war chief, a peace chief, a rabbit-hunt chief, an antelope-hunt chief, and

so on.)   As a result, individuals decided whether to go into
battle for personal reasons, ranging from an effort to authen-
ticate a newly-adult status to a desire to acquire goods owned
by another tribe.   Indeed, on the Plains, stereotypically
infamous in American popular culture for its war-crazed
ambiance, the bravest and most status-producing act a warrior
could accomplish was to tag, not kill, an enemy and live to
sing the tale.   Inter-tribal conflicts were unarguably dangerous for the combatants, but neither the philosophy nor the
technology of battle was aimed primarily at the physical destruction - as opposed to the temporary embarrassment or
impoverishment - of the opposing side.

Consequently, in encounters between Europeans and
Native American groups, the European had a decided historical
and attitudinal advantage.   Although an individual battle could
go either way, European tenacity and perseverance, always
won the wars.   From a Native American perspective, this
refusal to modulate aggressive behavior to allow time for food
production, rest, and recuperation was unchivalrous and
unethical; but, increasingly sick and powerless, they were
hardly in a position to press their complaints.

Finally, in the arena of Old and New World contact there
existed an enormous dichotomy in terms of the degree of
cultural similarity existing within each set of opposing forces.
To be sure, various European groups competed with each other
for territory and expansion, but the French, British, and
Spanish were each a unified and mono-ethnic entity.   Even in
their mutual rapacity they shared certain key understandings
and connections; they could ultimately comprehend each other's
motivations and ambitions, and they were certainly undivided
in their fundamental assumptions of the cultural superiority of
the Christian tradition.   The eventual success of the English
set the stage for a truly monolithic Euro-American presence in
North America, one with the ability, determination, and as-
serted "right" to steamroll through any indigenous opposition.

Arrayed against this growing superpower was a tremen-
dously plural collection of tribes, alliances, bands, chiefdoms,
and agricultural and hunting communities.   A Native person
from almost any society could have, upon a day's walk,
realistically expected to encounter at least one, and possibly
more than one, other community whose inhabitants (a) spoke a
totally foreign and incomprehensible language that was often
derived from an altogether different linguistic stock, (b)
believed in a unique and foreign cosmological system in which
they played the leading role, (c) dressed in unfamiliar clothes,
(d) ate exotic foods, and (e) had a dissimilar form of political
organization, with variant age and sex roles.

While it is undeniable that the over 300 distinct cultures
resident in North America had learned to coexist in relative
harmony and mutual toleration, the social chasms which divided

them negated any possibility of an effective or durable alliance among them. On the one hand, out and out conditions of mistrust and antagonism, occasionally firmly entrenched in a mythic past, prohibited any sense of common purpose or identity between some groups; and on the other, the unreconcilable linguistic pluralism ensured that even neighboring tribes would find it impossible to communicate in any meaningful way. (Sign language was developed to facilitate trade among some groups, but, as its name implies, its repertoire was restricted to unabstract and one-dimensional transactions. It could hardly have served as a means of formulating life and death military alliances.) North America has been, throughout most of the past 20,000 years, among the most linguistically-diversified parts of the world. It harbors no less than seven distinct aboriginal language families, each at least as different from the other as from Indo-European, Bantu, or Malay; and each contains within it many mutually-unintelligible languages, most with a further subdivision of regional dialects.

Consequently, while the Euro-American experience in dealing with indigenous societies was, in a real and ever-growing sense, cumulative, the Native American knowledge of Europeans was not. Lessons learned from the frontier contact of one group usually either would not or could not be passed along to an adjacent people. Each Native society, therefore, was forced to calculate on its own the degree to which European mores deviated from the expected behavior of foreigners. By the time it was clear that old expectations and precedents did not apply, it was too late to resist for long the awesome strength and size of the invading force. Even such brilliant and promising pan-Native alliance schemes as those of Pontiac, Tecumseh, or Sitting Bull were doomed to be misunderstood, impossible to coordinate, and ultimately futile in preserving Native power.

From the moment the first European set foot on the North American continent, the outcome of the impending intercultural encounter was never in doubt. Those few Native Americans who survived the onslaught of European diseases had no real experience in the "art" of total warfare, and no possibility of mounting a unified defense. What is amazing is not that they lost their independence and territory, but that they have been able to maintain over time and in the face of incalculable opposition hundreds of pockets of ethnic tradition and solidarity, encompassing everything from religious systems to languages.

NATIVE AMERICAN WORLD VIEW

In the fifteenth, sixteenth and seventeenth centuries, a

Native American beholding his or her first European probably
had no portent of the disaster to come. To an eye trained in
the endless potentialities of plural world, the average Spaniard
or Swede would seem no more or less exotic than any number
of previously encountered domestic foreigners.   Their
languages, dress, and general demeanor appeared no more
barbarous than a score of surrounding or recorded tribes.
      Far from exhibiting fear of their early "discoverers,"
Native Americans frequently fed a starving boatload of them.
Contact with the representatives of extrinsic and unusual
human-like creatures was, if not a daily occurrence, little more
than an interesting and unalarming diversion.   And these
particular foreigners, although apparently singularly ill-
equipped to fend for themselves in matters of food or shelter,
did bring along with them some items of promising and curious
manufacture. One gleans from the earliest contact accounts
that most Native groups regarded Europeans with an attitude
of mixed benevolence, hilarity, and potential profit.
      In contrast to the casual reaction of Native Americans,
Europeans, as a consequence of their own history, perceived
this new contact as a cataclysmic and watershed occasion,
underscoring the incompatible and contradictory orientations of
the participants. The fact that Natives seemed not only un-
awed by the arrival of Europeans, but oblivious to its significance as well, caused Europeans to doubt their very
sanity.   Unlike the Moors, Native Americans seemed not to
take European concerns very seriously. Even in religion they
often proved disarmingly and misleadingly acquiescent, permitting missionaries to baptize at will, and then mildly and un-
dramatically demuring any abandonment of their own theologies. Native peoples gave every evidence of being indifferent
to the idea of emulating Europeans, but were, nevertheless,
quite willing to import, adapt, and utilize any number of
European products, from writing systems to steel knives.

                        REACTIONS TO CONTACT

      If the initial trends of contact, as they were com-
prehended by most Native groups, had prevailed, a continent
of distinct but connected cultures might well have expanded to
include Europeans. There appeared to be land and resources
enough for any amount of demographic growth, and the
benefits of cultural exchange and association seemed obvious.
However, such an arrangement was contingent upon the
willingness of Europeans to abandon visions of their own
human centrality, and to re-estimate old theories of structural
hierarchy. The "New World" might have been new - but not

that new.

Instead, Europeans and their descendants for the most part sought to deny, discredit, remove, destroy or, if all else failed, swallow up any discordant indigenous cultural systems. "Harmony," with the Europeans calling the tune, became the theme from earliest contact and it continues to the present day. The pre-existent variety of Native American societies, relative both to each other and toward other world states, has been consistently obscured and disallowed. Every effort has been made to almost existentially enclose the non-Western world into a European schema, and then to blame unwilling elements for being backward, ignorant, or without vision.

The ad initiam refusal of Europeans to call Native American societies by their own names is symptomatic of the wider issue of cultural domination. "Indian" is a blatant, know-nothing term which signifies only a negative status: "Indians" aren't Europeans or Africans, but the implied internal cohesion the single group name suggests an idea without a shred of real or supportive evidence. The only thing all "Indians" had in common was joint occupancy of half the earth. The term "non-Indian" is, therefore, just as descriptive and just as meaningless.

Mere fact, however, did not deter the creation and perpetuation of a set of multifaceted and self-serving European, and later American, policies based squarely on the principle that all Indians were the same. The imputation of a solitary ethnicity to several hundred heterogenous societies was accomplished for one purpose only: it suited the convenience, psychology, and bureaucracy of Euro-American management.

Even the standard vocabulary employed in referring to this fictional Indian underscores the extent to which Europeans viewed the world as their exclusive domain. Indians and their countries were "discovered" or "found," just as one might discover or find something of one's own that has been lost. Pseudo-academic speculations on Indians, origins identified them as a disjointed fragment of historical European or Mediterranean groups, be they errant Celts, Lost Tribes of Israel, or Phoenicians. Even the early proto-anthropologists studied Indian societies as throwbacks to, or stalled examples of, earlier stages of European cultural development. As such, indigenous cultures were labeled "primitive" or "unadvanced."

Arrested children stuck on an early evolutionary rung, Indians had no rights and nowhere to go but "up" toward a European model of civilization. Anything that moved them in this direction was "for their own good," and, hence, any and all means of removing their present culture and replacing it with suitable versions of "true culture" were deemed both ethical and pre-ordained by a watchful divinity.

EARLY ASSIMILATION ATTEMPTS

Federal Indian policy was, therefore, shaped from the beginning at least as much toward deculturation as acculturation. Nowhere is this intent more obvious than in Indian education as it has been designed and implemented by the American government over the years. The concept of the regional boarding school, long the darling of missionaries and bureaucrats alike, offered a double bonus: it detribalized children by intermingling students from a variety of societies in one institutional setting and, forcing them to speak only English, even among themselves, it removed children from direct parental or familial influence. While restrained in these palaces of the intellect, Native young people were systematically informed, both overtly in text and lecture and covertly in approved value-training and attitudes, that all things "Indian" were backward and embarrassing. Absent from their inflexible curricula were favorable, or even accurate, mentions of Native American histories or cultural achievements, and never was it suggested that a viable and worthwhile adult life might be lived outside the boundaries of the Puritan ethic.

These schools have always been notoriously substandard academically, poorly-funded, and staffed in large part by mediocre and racist teachers. They failed to provide even the most willing student with a minimally competitive education. They have, however, been quite successful in instilling shame, fear, and a sense of predestined failure in legions of their victims.

This message has been carried to the adult level and reenforced through a series of federal laws and programs that have operated without abatement over the past century. By the 1870s, virtually all survivors of the once-populous Native American nations were resettled, by internationally-recognized treaties, on hundreds of supposedly-sacrosanct reservations. These homelands, predictably located in areas deemed unsuitable for Euro-American habitation or exploitation, were defined by the U.S. Supreme Court as "domestic dependent nations," and were assured continuity "as long as the rivers run and the grasses grow." From a Native point of view, they constituted a last opportunity to keep unwanted Euro-Americans out and so preserve and develop one's own culture within. Poor though they might be, reservations at least theoretically offered the option of cultural pluralism and diversity-maintenance.

It is not surprising, therefore, that they have been unrelentingly assaulted by would-be assimilationists almost from the moment of their creation. It is arguable that many of the authors of Indian land policy fully expected that Native people would, with all due speed, either obligingly die out,

or emigrate from their own societies willingly and eagerly. To
encourage them on either course, reservations were maintained
at an unbearable level. They were hotbeds of disease, fiscal
corruption, unemployment, and gross poverty.

Nevertheless, the vast majority of Native Americans
seemed to prefer remaining in their own cultural milieu,
despite the imposed or incidental liabilities. When their
population began to increase dramatically, reservations - those
semi-sovereign, alien enclaves, that acted both as reminders of
past injustice and as ongoing threats to the myth of the
melting pot - seemed destined to become a permanent fixture in
the United States. As irrefutable evidence that at least some
poor, oppressed refugees declined to light their lamp beside
the Golden Door, they were perceived as an insult and an
irritant to an America in love with the idea of itself.

The perpetuation of Native American sovereignty was
intolerable even to those groups formally dedicated to
lamenting the "plight of the Redman." According to the
analysis of these benevolent associations, Native indifference
or antagonism to sharing the American dream could be attributed only to one or both of two causes: either Indians
didn't understand what they were missing by remaining
distinct; or else federal laws, treaties, and statutes conceived
and written in an earlier, less-expansive era, were impeding
their progress. Both assumptions rested confidently on a
belief in Native primitivism; as culturally immature children,
Natives could not be relied upon to know what was good for
themselves, and it was, therefore, the responsibility of their
"friends" to act as their trustees and dictate a wise and
proper course of action.

GOVERNMENTAL POLICIES

And dictate they did. Unmindful of Native American
protests that treaties were inviolable, advocacy organizations
began to lobby tirelessly for the abrogation of all laws
protecting, or even permitting, tribal continuity and integrity.
A coalition of missionary interests, in a rare act of ecumenical
cooperation, succeeded in parlaying a national paranoia over
the emergence of the Ghost Dance religion into a governmental
ban on the practice of virtually all forms of indigenous
worship.

Even more far-reaching and socially-disruptive was the
passage of the Dawes (or Allottment) Act in the late 1880s.
Under the provisions of this unilateral federal edict, all
reservations were to be abolished; in their place, each
qualifying Indian "head of household" would be allotted a small
amount of acreage to homestead, for which he would eventually

receive title. It was argued that such a reorganization would discourage the communal, collectivist tendencies of aboriginal culture and, by instilling an appreciation for the value of private property, achieve within a generation the successful and felicitous assimilation of all Native Americans.

The appeal of the Dawes strategy extended far beyond the ranks of "Indian friends"; through a series of provisions, it presaged the transmission, within the half century following its enactment, of almost half of all erstwhile reservation lands into the waiting hands of homesteaders, speculators, and the federal register. Meanwhile, the vast majority of Native people were not only left predictably unassimilated, but became even poorer and more disenfranchised than they had been during the reservation period.

Although the abysmal failure of allottment was officially admitted in the Meriam Report (1928), and although some small moves were made towards restoring a portion of the pre-Dawes status quo as part of the Indian Reorganization Act (1934), an uncannily similar proposal for Indian land disbursal popped up in the 1950s. Known ominously as "termination," this bright idea once again bewailed the continuing legal and social distinctions enjoyed by Native Americans and proposed that these remaining treaty rights and duties be bought off, once and for all time, by the federal government. Like an old refrain, it was insisted that the acquisition of private property, with its attendant attitudes of competition and greed, would propel heretofore recalcitrant Indians into the thick of the American system.

Two large reservations, Menominee and Klamath, and a substantial number of their inhabitants were sacrificed before the wholly-apparent liabilities and inequities of this policy were acknowledged, and all subsequently-scheduled terminations were cancelled. Less than 20 years later, and despite an official presidential repudiation of termination as an approved procedure, the Congress was at it again. The Alaska Native Claims Settlement Act (1971) differs from earlier rationalized land grabs only in its deferred impact and magnitude; for all practical purposes, it similarly promises to bring Native people into the fold by extinguishing their special status with irrefusable payoffs.

Native Americans were made United States citizens by a governmental decree issued in 1924. Prior to that time, they were not "persons" under the law and, therefore, could not defend their rights or their lands through appeal to the judicial system. Citizenship was supposedly bestowed as the reward of a grateful nation for the valorous performance of Indian volunteers in World War I; significantly, neither tribes nor Native individuals were asked if they wished to become citizens. The age-old European assumption that informed human aspiration and the current Western tradition are forever coincident prevailed. No sooner were Indians officially dubbed bona fide citizens of the Republic, however, than the by-now familiar argument began to be voiced; citizens should be equal under the law, and, therefore, all special status and privilege stemming from treaty provisions should be ipso facto voided. This battle cry, used by a non-Indian group calling itself the Interstate Congress for Equal Rights and Responsibilities, has been heard with particular vehemence in the late 1970s.

Government programs aimed at either homogenizing all reservation-based Indian people, or at flushing them out into the "greater society" have abounded during the twentieth century. Even the Indian Reorganization Act, a reform measure that attempted to rectify some of the difficulties brought about by allottment, contained the requirement that all tribes, regardless of individual historical precedent or contemporary preference, adopt the same leadership structure. It was stipulated that periodic elections be held for all political offices, and that the resultant councils constitute the only officially-recognized negotiating body for a tribe. Although this system was perfectly acceptable to some groups, it bred dissension and discord among others; and it eventually led, in several notable cases, to bifurcated and internally-competitive orders of social control, "traditional" on the one hand, and "progressive," or federally-sanctioned, on the other.

The Urban Relocation Program, initiated in the 1950s and still partially operative almost 30 years later, was based upon a premise that might be paraphrased, "If you can't take the reservations out of Indians, take the Indians out of reservations." Induced by offers of employment, training, and greater economic opportunity, some Native Americans agreed to quit their homes and be relocated in a selected urban center. In the most impoverished sections of such cities as Denver, Los Angeles, Phoenix, Chicago, Minneapolis, and Cleveland, "Indian" neighborhoods soon sprang up alongside Black, Samoan or Appalachian White ghettos, and the hardships and frustrations of reservation life were replaced by the anxieties and desperation of the city. Most relocatees possessed few marketable skills, and received only superficial "retraining." Therefore, they were faced with an unhappy choice: they could return defeated to the homes they had just optimistically left; or they could accept an insecure and ill-paying job at the lowest end of the employment scale.

Special stresses were in store for those who elected the latter course. On the reservation there had at least existed the solidarity of tribe, kin, and tradition as an antidote to poverty and economic deprivation. Native language, oral literature, and extended family served to preserve perspective and keep identity and culture intact. In the city, for the first time, the label "Indian" supplanted an individual's particular tribe as the primary identification group. (An anal-

ogous experience occurred for some, although with greater
transience, at the boarding school or while serving in the
armed forces.) Generalized "reservation culture," that
peculiar amalgam of bureaucratic horror story, cynicism, and
humor, became the common denominator and ethnic credential
for diverse peoples who found themselves, thanks to the same
federal scheme, in similar and unfamiliar circumstances.

The American city rarely welcomed these relocated Native
Americans. Incidence of arrest, degree of unemployment, and
other such statistics testify to the difficulties they experienced
as a result of history, racism, and the inability or unwilling-
ness of those in power to deal fairly with people from different
cultural traditions. In many cases, there were too few
contacts to maintain an individual tribal language or lifestyle,
and so they were replaced by a synthesized pan-Indian
image - a mixture of many indigenous traditions, "reservation
modern," and Hollywood stereotype.

UNVANISHING AMERICANS

It is unavoidable that at least some of the conceptions and
attitudes held by Euro-Americans about "Indians" would be
internalized over time by Native Americans themselves. Forced
into a situation where they had no control over media, history,
and education, Native Americans have for years been barraged
with ethnocentric and false information. Indian children are
expected to answer that Columbus discovered America on
standardized intelligence tests; they are not required to
know - and have often been actively discouraged from
knowing - anything about their own peoples, past or present.
Generations of Native American young people, together with
their non-Native fellow citizens, have been exposed to
thousands of feet of celluloid depicting sneaky, bad "redskins"
fighting ineffectually and "biting the dust" in great numbers
at the hands of true, blue-coated cavalry.

In the almost 500 since initial intercultural contact, Native
Americans have been systematically stripped of the outward
manifestations of their cultural distinctiveness by their con-
querers. The dominant Euro-American society has shamelessly
denied and disdained most of the artifacts and values once
esteemed by Native American nations. For substantial periods
of time, extending well into the modern era, it has literally
been a crime for Native Americans to speak in their own languages, to fashion their hair or their clothes in traditional
patterns, to practice and promulgate their beliefs, to eat
accustomed foods, or to enter formerly-respected professions.

At the same time, any degree of perfectly normal and
predictable cultural dynamics, change, or external borrowing -

elements common and essential to all societies throughout history - have been quickly and gleefully tagged as a sign of culture loss or disintegration. In order to remain acceptably and exotically "Indian," according to the rules enforced by United States attitudes and regulations, Native people must remain visibly and socially archaic. As long as the white expectations for Indian-ness" are fulfilled, Natives are identified as Indians.

And what are these conditions for ethnic validation? The stereotypes span the range from negative to positive, paradox notwithstanding. "Real" Indians are somehow simultaneously poor and proud, inarticulate and noble, savage and defeated, drunk and ecological. They are never, under any circumstances, aggressive, sharp, upwardly-mobile, or sophisticated. By popular definition, an Indian exhibiting any one of those normally-advantageous traits is instantly accused of having "lost" his or her culture and summarily forfeits all rights to consideration as a treaty partner. The international documents governing the relations between citizens of the United States and citizens of the many Native American nations were not written to self-destruct when and if Indian people chose to operate in a dynamic environment; but too often any assessment of Native American success, in European terms, has spelled their dissolution.

Native Americans, therefore, seem to be caught in a double bind; by affecting an almost mythic image, they are perceived by outsiders as being "genuine." This very representation, however, is grounded in an aura of powerlessness that automatically inhibits any effective assertion of real sovereignty, in spite of numerous legalistic guarantees to the contrary. On the other hand, by demonstrating clear parity of intelligence, resources, and ability, Native Americans risk the loss of all hard-won protection of sovereignty, such as special status and federal reservations, in the event of a Congressional reassessment. In the precarious area between these two poles, individual tribes must strive to carry on their own specific and unique culture complexes and avoid being lumped into the vast and ultimately meaningless category of "Indian."

Despite this collection of formidable obstacles to societal continuity and particularity, Native Americans have by and large managed to sustain a core of cultural pluralism. They remain legally, psychologically, and historically distinct both one from another, and each, on its own terms, from the dominant American society. Rarely is it possible to altogether differentiate a continuous society from its neighbor; acculturation is an on-going and often irresistible two-way street, and boundary crossings in the form of marriage, technology, and ideas are frequent. However, in the final analysis, Native American cultures have never viewed themselves as submerged in, or even a subset of, the Euro-American world. They are not, singly or collectively, "separatist" for they have never been a part of a larger multi-ethnic matrix. They did not join and then renege; they simply never joined. Even when deprived of every outward badge and banner of cultural autonomy, they have steadfastly hung on to that one reality which no amount of pressure or punishment could dislodge: their right to be distinct, to be plural, to be un-American.

BIBLIOGRAPHY

Bahr, Chadwick, Day. Native Americans Today. New York: Harper & Row, 1972.

Berkhofer, Robert F. The White Man's Indian. New York: Knopf, 1978.

Burnette, Robert. The Tortured Americans. Englewood Cliffs, N.J.: Prentice-Hall, 1971.

Cahn, S.S. (ed.). Our Brother's Keeper. New York: World Publishing, 1969.

Daniels, R. and Harry Kitano. American Racism. Englewood Cliffs, N.J.: Prentice-Hall, 1970.

Debo, Angie. A History of the Indians of the United States. Norman, Okla.: University of Oklahoma Press, 1965.

Deloria, Vine. Behind the Trail of Broken Treaties. New York: Dell Publishing Co., 1974.

_____. Custer Died for Your Sins. New York: Bantam Books, 1969.

_____. Of Utmost Good Faith. New York: Bantam Books, 1971.

Dorris, Michael A. Native Americans 500 Years After. New York: Crowell, 1975.

Forbes, Jack (ed.). The Indian in America's Past. Englewood Cliffs, N.J.: Prentice-Hall, 1964.

Jennings, Francis. The Invasion of America. Chapel Hill, N.C.: The University of North Carolina Press, 1975.

Josephy, Alvin. Red Power. New York: McGraw-Hill, 1970.

Levitan and Johnston. Indian Giving - Federal Program for Native Americans. Baltimore, Md.: John Hopkins University Press, 1975.

Marx, H.L. (ed.). The American Indian: A Rising Ethnic Force. New York: Wilson Co., 1973.

McNickle, D'Arcy. They Came Here First: The Epic of the American Indian. 1949; RPT. New York: Octagon, 1972.

Neils, Elane. Reservation to City: Indian Migration & Federal Relocation. Dept. of Geography, U. of Chicago, Research Paper #131, 1971.

Prucha, F.P. (ed.). Americanizing the American Indian. Howard University, 1973.

Rosen, Ken (ed.). The Man to Send Rain Clouds. New York: Viking, 1974.

Sanders, Ronald. Lost Tribes and Promised Lands. Boston: Little, Brown, 1978.

Spicer, H. (ed.). A Short History of the Indians of the United States. New York: Van Nostrand, 1969.

Spindler, George. Native North American Cultures: Four Cases. New York: Holt, Rinehart & Winston, 1977.

Steiner, Stan. The Vanishing White Man. New York: Harper & Row, 1976.

Sturtevant, William C. (ed.). Handbook of North American Indians. 20 Vols. Washington, D.C.: Smithsonian Institution, 1978.

Turner, Fred W. The Portable Native American Reader. New York: Viking, 1974.

Tyler, S.L. A History of Indian Policy. U.S. Dept. of Interior, 1973.

Vaudrin, Bill. Tanaina Tales From Alaska. Norman, Okla.: University of Oklahoma Press, 1969.

Waddell, J. and M. Watson. The American Indian in Urban Society. Boston: Little, Brown, 1971.

Walker, D.E. The Emergent Native American. Boston: Little, Brown, 1972.

Washburn, Wilcomb E. Red Man's Land, White Man's Law. New York: Scribner's, 1971.

Wax, Murray. Indian Americans. Englewood Cliffs, N.J.: Prentice-Hall 1970.

Welch, James. Winter in the Blood. New York: Bantam, 1974.

Yazzie, Ethalou. Navajo History. Many Farms, Ariz.: Navajo Community College Press.

ADDITIONAL BIBLIOGRAPHIES IN NATIVE
AMERICAN STUDIES

        . American Indian Reference Book. Alexandria, Va.:
Earth, 1976.

Byler, Mary G. American Indian Authors for Young Readers.
New York: Association on American Indian Affairs, 1973.

Cashman, Marc (ed.).   Bibliography of American Ethnology.
Rye, N.Y.: Todd, 1976.

Costo, Rupert (ed.).   Textbooks and the American Indian.
San Francisco: Indian Historian Press, 1976.

Hirschfelder, Arlene.   American Indian and Eskimo Authors:
A Comprehensive Bibliography.   New   York: Association of
American Indian Affairs, 1970.

Icolari, Dan, and Barry Klein (eds.). Reference Encyclopedia
of the American Indian. 2nd ed. 2 Vols. Rye, N.Y.: Todd,
1973-74.

Mudock, George and Timothy O'Leary.   Ethnographic Bibliography of North America.   5 Vols. New Haven: Human Relations Area Files Press, 1975.

Smith, Dwight (ed.).   Indians of the United States and
Canada: A Bibliography.   Santa Barbara, Cal.:   American
Bibliographical Center, 1974.

Stensland, Anna Lee.   Literature by and About the American
Indian: An Annotated Bibliography for Junior and Senior High
School Students.   Urbana, Ill.: National Council of Teachers of
English, 1973.

6 Chicano Identity: A Tree Growing from Many Roots*
Maria Kleitz

A prominent dentist, surnamed Lucero, was speaking to a group of Hispanic educators on his decision to run for political office: "I've gone about as far as most people go educationally and professionally. Still, whenever I hear a remark about my race or language or culture I feel the pain I've always felt, and still find myself on the defensive." Not all Chicanos are able to make such an admission. Some hide their pain by perpetuating the stereotype America has of the lazy, smiling, stupid wetback. Some, because of light hair and skin and lack of an accent, are able to hide the pain by changing their Martinez to Martin, their Jose to Joe, and by avoiding contact with Latinos. Many are reminded of the pain daily because they are trapped in the quicksand cycle of low income, low educational achievement, and poor job opportunities. It is a cycle of frustration that extends beyond economic life to what even professionally successful Chicanos feel, and that may be one clue to what unites Chicanos as a people: frustration.

Dr. Victor S. Clark, writing in the Bulletin of the Bureau of Labor in 1908, addressed the stereotype:

> The Mexican laborer is unambitious, listless, physically weak, irregular and indolent. On the other hand, he is docile, patient, usually orderly in camp, fairly intelligent under competent supervision, obedient and cheap. If he were active and ambitious, he would be less tractable and

---

*The author wishes to thank Tony and Mary Alvardo, Nadyne Gomez, Juan Montoya and Horacio Hernandez for their suggestions and encouragement.

> would cost more. His strongest point is his willing-
> ness to work for a low wage...Cotton picking suits
> the Mexican for several reasons: it requires nimble
> fingers rather than physical strength; in which he
> cannot compete with the white man or the Negro;
> it employs his whole family; he can follow it from
> place to place, living out of doors, which seems to
> suit the half-subdued nomadic instinct of a part of
> the Mexican race; it is a seasonal occupation,
> fitting in conveniently with the demands of labor
> and leisure in his own country.(1)

This racist rationalization, which attempted to establish as fact
something that was handy and desirable to those who reaped
financial gains from exploiting Mexican immigrants, shocking as
it is in the 1970s, unfortunately has an ongoing influence in
the thinking of many members of the mainstream society in the
United States; and the effect on the Chicano is frustration.

The term Chicano has by no means universal acceptance,
nor are its origins clear. It may have come in a derogatory
way from the Spanish word meaning little, chico. It may be a
bastardization of Mejicano (Mexican), in which the unvoiced
velar fricative "j" becomes "ch"; the Mechnicano Art Gallery is
a Chicano art gallery in California. It is probable that the
word Mejicano or Mexicano is a Spanish twisting of an Aztec
name which used a sound closer to the English "sh" than to
the Spanish "j" or "x," a sound which the Spanish mouth finds
difficult. Even the origin of the name Mexico is not agreed
upon by scholars. William H. Prescott, the eminent historian
who is often mistrusted by Chicanos, states that the great city
built by the Aztecs, "was called Tenochtitlan, in token of its
miraculous origin, though only known to Europeans by its
other name of Mexico, derived from their war-god, Mexitli."(2)
Indeed, Prescott's allusion to the name Tenochtitlan as be-
tokening a miraculous origin overlooks the widely-accepted
concept that Tenoch was one of the Aztecs - but not the only
one - who saw the prophesied eagle devouring a serpent as
the sign of the chosen location for the city. Tenoch also led
the Aztecs on the final miles of their centuries-long trek to
find a settling place, and gave his name to the city he
founded.

More acceptable to Chicano students is De Leon's explanation:

> In the early times while the Aztecs were still wan-
> dering, their high priest was delivered a message
> by their god, then known as Mixtli. Mixtli was
> later to be called Huitzilipochtli and Quetzalcoatl.
> This god Mixtli decreed that henceforth all people
> would be named Mexicans - in order that they be
> known as Mexicanos.(3)

It is probable that the "x" was pronounced somewhat like the English "sh" and that there was a glottal stop associated with the sound in juxtaposition with certain other sounds. The idea that the members of the tribe in question be known as The People, regardless of the fact that there were other human beings around, is common among native American legends. Part of the problem of origins is the translating of Nahuatl words into an inadequate European alphabet. The subject is of interest to Chicanos because it has to do with their heritage, and twisting of the probable truth by historians smacks of exploitation. It is of interest here because of the variety of explanations given for the term "Chicano," and the fervor with which the advocates of any one meaning or origin defend it. And, perhaps more importantly, although there is a strong refrain from many sources that emphasizes its original derogatory nature, the name Chicano has a growing positive connotation and respectability.

The term has feminine form: la Chicana has emerged recently as a personality somewhat at odds with her Chicano counterpart. Often the term is used with pride by young, active Spanish-surnamed people with militant tendencies. It has a connotation of anger, pride, racial identity, activism, and strength, which is highly attractive to some and repugnant to others. Those who resent the term are often older, conservative, economically-secure, or of non-Mexican Latin American origin; recently-naturalized citizens from South America resent being called Chicano, and Puerto Ricans usually identify as Puerto Rican rather than as Chicano. In response to Chicano student demands for representation on the faculty in the 1960s, a southern university hired a Guatemalan, who happened to be an albino and, therefore, lacked the required physical characteristics; the Chicano students did not identify him as Chicano, and did not accept his appointment even as tokenism.

For some, a Latino is anyone with origins in a Spanish-speaking country, a more extensive application than Chicano; some consider Hispano a calmer, more acceptable word than Chicano; and in some cases, Latino, Hispano, and Chicano are used interchangeably. A retired lady named Gonzales who denied any Indian blood and could trace her ancestry to Spain through the early settlers in northern New Mexico, refused to be called Chicano. Upon being called "Spanish-American," she declared, "I do not hyphenate myself. I am American." Thus, was with many an ethnic category, the term Chicano applies to anyone who thinks of himself as Chicano and is accepted by others as such.

Part of the difficulty in defining the term is the diversity of backgrounds and the mixed racial and cultural lines of Chicanos. The Mexicans who migrated north into Colorado, New Mexico, Texas, Arizona, and California, and whose de-

scendants have migrated to all the other states, were themselves a complex cultural and racial mixture. Long before the
Christian era, Indian peoples are believed to have crossed the
Bering Strait from Asia and migrated to what is now Mexico,
breaking up into related but distinct tribes. The last such
group to arrive in Mexico, the Aztecs, conquered many diverse
cultural groups of extensive tradition and highly-developed
culture; the Toltec, Olmec, Mayan, Mixtec, Zapotec, and
others were united under the Aztec empire. When the
Spanish conquistadores arrived in 1519, they found a rather
oppressive government controlling a rich and varied culture.

> The Spaniard was a composite himself when he
> arrived on these shores. Culturally, he was late
> Gothic, part Renaissance, and extensively Moorish
> ...linked to the Iberians, Phoenicians, Cartha-
> ginians, Romans, Greeks, and Visigoths.(4)

In settling Mexico, the Spanish brought very few women from
the homeland. Unlike the English and French colonizers of the
New World, the Spanish took Indian wives and established the
mestizo, the mixture of blood lines, in their first generation
here.
     Although the indigenous religion was systematically de-
stroyed and replaced by Christianity during the Spanish
conquest, many other aspects of the Indian culture were
espoused by the Spanish, such as local foods and Nahuatl
language elements, especially for New World plants and
animals. The blend from which modern Mexico grew retained
enough Indian identity to make the appearance of a vision of
the Virgin Mary with Indian features a vital element in the
spread of Christianity in the Western Hemisphere. Posing atop
a dark crescent moon, held by an angel and surrounded by
rays of light, this prayerful Virgen de Guadalupe is the
beloved patron saint of the New World and the Philippines;
indeed, she is frequently seen in the art of Spanish-speaking
America, including that of the Chicanos in the United States.
     The mixture of Indian and Spanish cultures also retained
some of the myths of the Aztecs as they wandered from their
obscure homeland, Aztlan, to establish Tenochtitlan, now
Mexico City. The eagle devouring a serpent, depicted on the
Modern Mexican flag and coins, was the sign to the Aztecs of
the chosen spot for their city. This eagle is a favorite
school art theme for the Chicano child, a symbol of pride and
identity; and it also evolved into the symbol for Cezar
Chavez's farm workers movement. The conjectural location of
Aztlan in modern New Mexico and Colorado now gives this
name a force as a rallying point for Chicano identity.
     During the three hundred years of Spanish rule, from
1519 to 1821, much of the European colonists' culture was

imposed and adopted, not only language and religion, but also styles of art and architecture, the political system, and technology of all sorts. In fact, the Spanish culture became the dominant force in Mexico, effectively submerging the indigenous culture during the first century of conquest. However, it was rediscovered when Spain was ousted.

In the history of the world, invaded peoples sometimes absorb and obliterate the invader, as China has often done; or the conqueror sometimes erases the conquered, as the northern Europeans attempted to do to the North American Indians. Mexican culture has a unique quality; by the time of the revolution of 1910, it had become a true blend of cultures, a fact that a growing sense of pride to Chicanos in their struggle against the dominance of the Anglo society in the United States.

The cultural blend has not always been accepted as something of which to be proud. Although some Mexicans are ashamed of their Indian heritage and Indian blood, there is a rising of contrasting feelings in Mexico that demonstrates great pride in an Aztec nose, black hair, Nahuatl words such as coyote, jaguar, chocolate, and in the relics of the pre-Hispanic culture that survived the calculated attempt by the Spanish to wipe out all traces of the heathen religion of the Aztecs. At one time, the only interest in pre-Columbian things came from European scholars: in this century, Guatemalan author Miguel Angel Asturias had to go to Paris to find the bible of his Mayan forebears, Popul Vuh; and his Spanish translation was made from French; and a book on the Quiche language of the Mayans was published in Paris in 1862, with some Spanish sections, but with some very important essays on pre-conquest culture in French.(5)

Rejection of one's background because of pressure from a dominant culture that considers it inferior may have been a tradition of sorts among Mexicans, and perhaps it was natural for some who moved north to reject Mexico and attempt total assimilation into the Anglo culture. Chicanos have a derogatory slang Spanish word meaning "sell-out" or "traitor" for those who do this. The mainstream cry, "They're in America, let them speak American," led to linguistic humiliation and educational inferiority because parents, who spoke only Spanish at home, forbade their children to speak Spanish. The public schools frequently have reinforced this rejection over the years, insisting on English and punishing the child who uttered a Spanish word. However, the tide is turning. Today there are Spanish-surnamed adults in the 25 to 50 year age bracket who, since the rise of Chicano pride in the 1970s, feel inferior because they speak no Spanish. Maintaining Spanish for a healthy self-image is one of the several aims of bilingual education in this decade.

There are several categories of Spanish-speaking people:

some, whose forebears were residents of the U.S. for centuries, have maintained their language because of isolation;
recent immigrants haven't yet learned English; and young
Chicanos learn and use Spanish for self-identity and self-
esteem. There are significant numbers of people in the
Southwest who trace their ancestry to the original settlers
from Spain via Mexico in the sixteenth and seventeenth centuries; they were cut off from the surrounding changing
culture, both Mexican and U.S., by geography and economics,
and to this day sixteenth century Spanish is spoken in pockets
of northern New Mexico. With increased interaction, this
linguistic relic has made itself felt through New Mexican
Chicanos, who persist in saying "naide," instead of the modern
Spanish "nadie," to the despair of Anglo teachers of academic
Spanish who do not accept the venerable antiquity of such
"mistakes."

Language alone tells only part of the story; an understanding of culture must accompany it. Among Chicanos,
there is growing reverence for this isolated cultural group,
more Spanish than Mexican, who maintained and nurtured Hispanic culture in the New World. The dignity and pride in the
Spanish heritage of the "backwater" towns in northern New
Mexico, particularly, is hailed by many writers. Sabine
Ulibarri, credits the secret religious society of Los Penitentes
with strongly upholding the traditions in the hills around
Tierra Amarilla: "If we forget or ignore the Penitentes the
historical picture of New Mexico crumbles. Without them no
history."(6) Ulibarri goes on to laud their preservation of
religion and language: "Through the religious exercises they
kept the language alive and relatively pure. Perhaps we owe
in large measure that mysticism so characteristic of our people
to the Penitentes. So who knows how many New Mexicans
have gone to Heaven and have introduced themselves to Saint
Peter in perfect Castilian, thanks to the Penitentes(7)...
Without them you and I might be worth somewhat less."(8)

Language is in itself an indicator of an influence on many
cultural aspects of human life; the person who expresses
himself first in Spanish actually thinks differently from the
native English speaker. In interpersonal relationships, for
example, the fact that Spanish has a formal and an informal
second person allows the Spanish speaker to feel close in
speaking to someone called "tu" and objectively removed from
an "Usted," while the English speaker is linguistically equally
removed from every "you." Another example is the Spanish
use of the subjunctive and/or reflexive verb form to indicate
emotional connotations surrounding a statement, which in
English is rather cold without many added words. Because
Spanish allows expressions of warmth and love and encourages
them more than does English, it helps to separate the native
Spanish speaker from the dominant culture. This could be a

strong argument in favor of Anglo children learning Spanish to open up a bit of intercultural harmony.

More recent immigrants to the English-speaking U.S. from Mexico came at various times for various reasons, often economic. In 1902, the Reclamation Act and increased irrigation in the Southwest enticed 100,000 workers across the border. In 1910, the Mexican Revolution pushed 800,000 across. Between 1920-30, boom times in the U.S. are estimated to have brought one and a half million pairs of hands for work. However, the Depression made English-speaking Americans jealous about employment, leading to the deportation of half a million Mexicans. At that time, speaking Spanish became a real liability, and the 1930s gave rise to the generation that associates bilingualism with shame. A fear of writing one's Spanish surname on any official document was also established. The new-generation Chicano is working to wash this fear from his parents in his new realization that there is power in the political process.

Immigration from Mexico continues to bring first generation Spanish speakers, who do not always identify themselves as Chicanos, to areas where there are jobs and where some Spanish is spoken. Children fom several Latin American countries are enrolled regularly in the Colorado Springs public schools, and the limited but very good bilingual program benefits such children greatly. U.S. pressure on Latin American economies in such forms as controlling investments has been blamed by some for the poor living standard south of the border; jobs and a better material life continue to lure Latinos north.

The term Chicano, it should be emphasized, is not defined only on a linguistic basis, but in relationship to national and racial origin, physical characteristics, cultural practices, length of stay in the United States, and personal feeling of being Chicano. There is a joke which separates the speakers of Spanish in the U.S. and also points out cultural differences among immigrating groups; the Cuban immigrant is typically ahead of others educationally, quite free of feelings of inferiority, able to integrate while giving up neither language nor culture, and very ambitious to establish himself through political and economic power. The joke is as follows: "the Chicano already has one strike against him in the United States before he can even begin to get ahead, and the Puerto Rican has two strikes against him. But after the Cuban struck out, the catcher dropped the ball, and the Cuban is safe at first base."

During the Second World War, Mexican-American service men formed the largest minority or ethnic group to serve in the armed forces and became the most decorated, a fact little known in the mainstream culture, but beneficial for improving the deprived Chicano self image. The Civil Rights Movement of the 1950s and 1960s and the large Chicano vote for Kennedy

in 1960, indicating a sense of hope, gave impetus to a Chicano
Renaissance. It could even be called a naissance because it
was not a rebirth of anything that existed previously. This
surge is characterized by the search for identity and its
spokesmen ask, " Quienes somos? De donde somos? Adonde
vamos?" "Who are we? Where do we come from? Where are
we going?" However, before the Chicano's self-concept was
raised, he suffered some cultural shocks. The process of
increased involvement with the dominant U.S. culture between
the 1930s and the 1970s, with industrialization, urbanization,
and war, gave the Latino a feeling of being lost; he was in
desperate need for an identity. To the Hispano whose family
had been in the U.S. for many generations, the shift was from
a rural, strongly family-oriented culture to an urban situation
where the family was a decreasing force. In addition, the
culture of western and northern Europe, on which the mainstream of the U.S. is based, is a culture of paper, of
documents, of contracts, of "get it in writing," and "put your
John Hancock there." In contrast, the Hispanic culture, "de
palabra," is one of trust in the spoken agreement and faith in
a man's word. Understandably, the Hispano had many difficulties to overcome.

Since complete integration was precluded by linguistic and
physical characteristics, the Chicano movement emerged in the
1960s, but it has by no means been monolithic, and the language label is divided in several ways. In addition, there are
economic, cultural, and physical differences among people
grouped as Chicanos. Some see three types of Chicanos:
there are professionals and others who are economically well
off; there are those who barely make it in the competition with
Anglos, who are frequently better prepared; and there are
those who don't make it at all and compete with other minorities for menial jobs. For the latter, barrio - literally
neighborhood, but here understood to mean a low income
Chicano neighborhood - living is often a unifying force, and
this group may identify most strongly as Chicanos. Certainly
their frustration in the dominant society is the most acute of
that of any of the groups. Often the young product of the
barrio scrapes together enough earnings and assistance for a
college education, and becomes an effective and vocal Chicano,
pressing for a better life for his people.

Physical characteristics are more important in categorizing
Chicanos. Those who have white skin contrast sharply with
those whose dark hair and skin keep them from the benefits
of the dominant society, which constantly opens the scars of
discrimination and prejudice.

In cultural terms, including interpersonal relationships,
food, art, and music, along with language, Chicanos are
catalogued by some Hispano educators as follows: The traditional is one whose home is monolingual in Spanish, and who

retains Mexican cultural practices in the home. The semi-traditional, is either bilingual or understands Spanish without speaking it, and follows many aspects of Mexican culture. The non-traditional is completely assimilated - except for the surname - and identifies with the Anglo culture.

These three categories are sometimes used in determining the need for bilingual-bicultural education. The child of any of the three types of Chicano homes can experience problems in facing the public school system, in adjusting to conflicting philosophies in and outside the home, and in striking out on his own at adulthood. Bilingual-bicultural education is a vast and complex area, often an emotionally-loaded subject, differing from state to state in philosophy and implementation. To the child of a traditional family and to the Anglo teacher trying to reach that child, use of Spanish helps make the school a comfortable place, a place where one is not an alien and where learning can begin. The teacher's understanding of the Spanish culture keeps both the child and teacher from being baffled into hostility by the other's "strange" behavior. The traditional Chicano child is taught to speak only when spoken to, to pull back from adults, and to help his siblings and neighbors. The white teacher expects children to volunteer and "knows" that the child who fails to raise his hand is "slow"; the white teacher "knows" that the bright children sit at the front of the room, and expects each child to do his/her own work, and not "cheat" by helping or getting help from a neighbor. These are cultural differences between a competitive, aggressive, individualistic dominant culture, and a warm, gentle, loving mutually-supportive society that values harmony. Without bilingual, or at least bicultural education, the Chicano child is faced with a situation in which he is punished for the very things his home has consistently praised, encouraged, even insisted upon. It is little wonder this child has long been the victim of the self-fulfilling prophesy of being a "slow learner," and has become frustrated trying to survive such a subtle form of oppression.

There are, in addition, minor categories of Chicanismo seen differently by every individual. A Chicano teacher remarked that her husband's reluctance to attend social functions was a typical Chicano characteristic, one which she wished could be overcome. She cited two types of machismo: one is typified by conviviality and enjoyment of dancing and music, a willingness to work for better conditions, education, travel, and possibly service in the armed forces; the other is typified by a strong wish to stay at home where the man is the lord, wariness of new things, mistrust of females in action, and a strong mistrust of Anglos and of anything which might upset the Anglo and make him more of a threat than he is. She saw the latter as a cultural pull backward.

This woman herself represents la Chicana, the person who

may suffer as much prejudice and injustice for being a woman as for being a Chicano, not only at the hands of the mainstream of society, but sometimes more harshly from males in her family. The Chicano man frequently feels as deeply threatened by his women as by outsiders, and he feels he can and must exert power over la Chicana. This holdover from the Spanish code of honor and patriarchy is seen by la Chicana and by the liberal Chicano as a negative maintenance of the cultural heritage.

The educated young Chicano often identifies more strongly than his older relatives with La Raza, the raciallymixed "race" with Mexican and North American elements, as has been noted. Esteban Villa, a Mexican-American artist expressed it this way:

> Primero, I want to say that I paint and draw as a Chicano. Not too long ago I was asked by a group of college students, 'Is there such a thing as Chicano Art?' I say there is. All my observations on life are definitely seen and felt as a Chicano. I still believe in 'el dia de los santos,' 'el bautismo,' 'la boda,' and 'la llorona.' I still believe in playing the guitar, and, most of all, I still believe in all the ceremony and folklore that is part of being Chicano.(9)

Another artist, Melesio Casas of San Antonio, made the following statement:

> To me, being an outsider is the next thing to being an artist. I think we are lucky to be born outsiders. The other thing, however, is this. You think that, because you eat tortillas and you think in Spanish or in the Mexican tradition, you can identify yourself. I don't think it's quite true. First of all, because we use liquitex [acrylic paint], and we use canvas, and we use stretcher boards. "No usamos bastidores o manta.' [We don't use the Spanish equivalent.] So we are a mixture. So there is no sense in trying to say that we have that kind of purity. We are entirely different. We are neither Mexican nor Anglos. We are in between.(10)

Jacinto Quirarte, in his book Mexican American Artists, spoke of his heritage in this way:

> English and Spanish [form] a bilingualism that makes us very special. We have a rich heritage; we have our roots in pre-Columbian times; we are

related to a century and a half of American rule.
So that we are all of these and none of them. It
isn't just a duality. It is far more than that. And
of course it is our role to define exactly what that
is.(11)

Thus the role of the emerging Chicano in defining his
own identity can be seen as one compelling, unifying force in
the Chicano movement. It is an effective technique for
handling the frustration of a complex minority in a complex
society.
In the context of the uniqueness of the Chicano minority,
it is ironic that the Anglo establishment treatment leads to
militant rhetoric in such publications as La Cucaracha from
Pueblo, Colorado, a Chicano newspaper that is reminiscent of
The Black Panther and the Native American publication,
Akwesasne Notes. The individual Chicano asks, "Who in
particular uniqueness am I?" And the establishment society
answers, "You are just like any other minority, inferior." It
is no wonder that the rage of the Chicano resembles that of
the black or Native American.
Chicanos have felt justified rage, and have been isolated
from both Mexico and white America. However, a strong
current of thought has been growing, given credence by
people such as Rosa Guerrero, an educator from El Paso, who
emphasized the unique beauty of the minority contribution to
the U.S. Seeing America no longer as a "melting pot where
everything becomes uniform," Mrs. Guerrero, in her beautiful
film, Tapestry, talks about the universal quality of art, music,
rhythm, and dance, and also the singular quality of the
threads of many colors from many sources woven together into
the tapestry of American culture. Her philosophy radiates a
strength and pride that can overcome feelings of frustration.
In discussing Chicano identity, one has to admit that each
person who identifies as Chicano is an individual who defines
the term in his or her own way, and accepts or rejects parts
of the Chicano culture according to his or her individual
preferences. A Spanish-surnamed gentleman in his early
thirties, who has a Masters Degree in bilingual education and
who works for Hispanic causes, says, "I don't really like
Chicano music; give me Soul. I grew up with black people. I
am a human being first, then a man, and then a Chicano."(12)
Although the point has been made that there is great
diversity and individualism in the Chicano culture, it can also
be argued that there is a growing cohesiveness in the Chicano
movement. Abelardo Delgado comments on that movement:

The Chicano community in the United States has
been in a constant state of rebellion against the
economic and foreign mode of life that has been

imposed on us ever since the very first day that a
white man and a brown man crossed paths. This
refusal to acculturate, to be absorbed or assimilated
into the dominant and larger society, is the heart
of the Chicano movement, and it has been ticking
away,   quite   healthily,   without   the   need   of   a
transplant.(13)

This Chicano movement has undergone some important
changes in the twentieth century.   Delgado cites the young
activist's indebtedness to his antepasados (forefathers) for
maintaining the dignity of brown people in the U.S.   However,
he also reminds the reader of the Pachucos, or young activist
Hispanos, of the 1940s and 1950s whose energy and frustration
often took a self-destructive form, with Chicanos attacking
other Chicanos.   Their bold acts of identification with their
Mexican origins and kin took the form of bizarre dress and
speech, daring the scorn of the dominant society.   Delgado
goes on to mention the swing, on the part of some World War
II veterans who had observed the gringo way under duress, to
thinking that the better life could be attained only by going
the gringo way.
        There is a vast accumulation of historical events that
have contributed to the Chicano movement, and there is a
wealth of writing on the history of the movement itself.(14)
Recently three Chicano educators were discussing their increased awareness of their own heritage and history, and the
background of atrocities and injustice their people had endured
in the southwestern states, when they were joined by an
Anglo.   It is indicative of the current strength of Chicano
pride and self-concept that, rather than shift to lighter
subjects, they continued to compare Nazi atrocities to the
treatment of the Chicano in the Southwest: "It goes right back
to what Acuna says.(15)   You can destroy a man physically or
you can destroy him spiritually.   Atrocities can be committed
with no blood being spilled."
        Suffice it to proceed here to current signs of the
movement, which have been identified by Delgado.   Activism
by youth who are not culturally-divorced from their parents
provides a spirit of companionship and a means to protest the
blatant neglect suffered in employment, education and political
recognition.   The name Chicano itself, coined in the barrio to
impose itself on the lingo of the dominant culture, is gathering
respectability as it climbs into the very sacredness of church
and school because there is no shame to the name.(16)   There
is vibrant movement in the arts, particularly in murals, an
interest that is shared with the Afro-American culture.   There
is a growing willingness and eagerness to be seen, heard, and
acknowledged, a pride that is sometimes misinterpreted as
cockiness, but that enables the Chicano to feel equal to others

in society. This feeling of self-esteem is celebrated in the Chicano's festive recognition of El Cinco de Mayo, the Mexican holiday commemorating the overcoming of European dominance. Cezar Chavez, the farm workers union leader, Corky Gonzales, originator of the Plan de Aztlan in Colorado and advocate of meaningful education for Chicano youth, Reies Lopez Tijerina, advocate of justice in land titles, and Jose Angel Gutierrez, advocate of political self-determination through La Raza Unida, have emerged as national leaders. The people have rallied around La Causa "a more adequate place in our communities, in our own country."(17) All these factors have brought about a drive to prove oneself to oneself, not to the gringo; a Chicano Nationalism which is neither un-American nor racist is alive and well.

The mural movement in Chicano neighborhoods is an expression of separatist feelings, as well as an agent in their growth. The style of painting varies with geographic location and individual artists, but it is consistently different from the art of the dominant culture. If it is similar to anything North American, it is strongly akin to Afro-American murals and the art in The Black Panther. Chicano art has visible roots in pre-Columbian, Spanish, and Mexican revolutionary art, both stylistically and thematically, and is an outpouring of feelings about common origins.

As a consciousness-raising agent, outdoor barrio art makes a strong bid for attention. The recurring themes of kinship and unity of la familia and la raza, resistance to economic and political oppression, and the very positive statements regarding the use of primordial Aztec strength to overcome frustration are clearly intended to foster Chicano solidarity and awareness, and to encourage strength for bettering the conditions of Chicano life.

There is an apparent proliferation of groups within the movement working for the same Causa; Mayos, Brown Berets, UMA, MECHA, G.I. Forum, and underground Chicano news-papers numbering in the hundreds exhibit a neighborly feeling of mutual help and support. The well-documented boycotts and strikes against big agricultural interests have been ef-fective because the workers in certain areas are predominantly of Mexican origin, a factor not applicable to other minorities. Many groups work for education, a recognized need among Chicanos. In Colorado, for example, the Latin American Education Foundation, formed 29 years ago, has helped hundreds of college students to reverse the downward spiral of low income, low educational attainment, and low job op-portunity. This organization started out by loaning money, and is now solvent enough to grant scholarships, thereby helping to overcome the unavailability of financial aid to capable Chicano students whose educational background is often inferior to that of mainstream students. Other organizations, such as Hispano Educators extend the term "education" to include political expertise and understanding in the hope that an understanding of the political process will better the Chicano's lot.

In recent actions and statements of these groups one sees an evolution from a militant flailing out against the establishment and the frustrations brought on by an immovable society toward a more positive and self-directed point of view. There is still anger; the news still reports clashes such as the May 7, 1978 riot in Houston that was triggered by injustice in the treatment of Chicanos by police. One cannot pretend that the movement has comfortably subsided into a beatific or academic doldrum. However, the spokesmen of the 1970s are often more articulate and educated than their earlier counterparts, or they are the same people matured by several years' experience. There is a prevailing mood of unity in the face of frustration that extends across Aztlan from coast to coast and from the Rio Grande to Michigan; it is expressed eloquently in the one-year-old magazine NUESTRO, a publication with strength in its convictions. The following is a quote from its publisher, Daniel M. Lopez:

> Our future role, as I see it, depends upon the quality of each individual's devotion to the task of Latino unity. For unity is the single most important factor affecting Latino success. It gives us social force and political power - the things we need to add to our present strengths in order to become a part of the voice that shapes America. It means that we - you and I - are the place we must start to bring about change.(18)

This is a long way from cries against someone else, and incendiary statements of hate for the oppressor.

This statement by Lopez may be indicative of a trend in Chicano thinking which maintains a working relationship with the dominant society but accepts separatism as a viable tool for dealing with frustration in contemporary America. Delgado avers that the most visible sign in the movement is the pride that allows the Chicano to cease whispering when he talks to the Anglo, and to stare directly into the eyes of a man his equal. This pride, "is the characteristic, which, if respected, can end all racism."(19)

NOTES

(1) Amador S. Bustos, "Immigration - The Human Journey and The Human Hunt," La Luz, Hispanic Magazine, Vol. 7, No. 2, February, 1978, p. 11.

(2) William H. Prescott, The World Of The Aztecs, (New York: Tudor, 1970), p. 13.
(3) Nephtali De Leon, Chicanos, Our Background and Our Pride, (Lubbock, Texas: Trucha Publications, 1972), p. 17.
(4) Jacinto Quirarte, Mexican-American Artists, (Austin, Texas: University of Texas Press, 1973), p. XXII.
(5) L'Abbe Brasseur de Bourbourg, Grammaire de la Langue Quichee (Paris: Arthus Bertrand, 1862).
(6) Sabine Ulibarri, Mi Abuela Fumaba Puros, (Berkeley, Cal.: Quinto Sol, 1977), p. 159.
(7) Ibid., p. 161.
(8) Ibid., p. 167.
(9) Quirarte, Mexican-American Artists, p. XXII.
(10) Ibid., p. XXII.
(11) Ibid., p. XXIII.
(12) Ramon Nieto, in an interview with the author in Colorado Springs, 1978.
(13) Abelardo Delgado, The Chicano Movement, Some Not Too Objective Observations, (Denver, Col.: Totinem Publications, 1971), p. 1.
(14) See such books as Rodolfo Acuna's Occupied America: The Chicano's Struggle Toward Liberation, (San Francisco: Canfield Press, Harper and Row, 1972) or Tony Castro, Chicano Power, The Emergence of Mexican America, (New York: E.P. Dutton, 1974).
(15) Rodolfo Acuna, Occupied America.
(16) Delgado, The Chicano Movement, p. 3.
(17) Ibid., p. 4.
(18) Daniel M. Lopez, "Letter from the Publisher," in Nuestro, The Magazine for Latinos, Vol. 2, No. 4, April 1978, p. 5.
(19) Delgado, The Chicano Movement, p. 3.

BIBLIOGRAPHY

Acuna, Rodolfo, Occupied America: The Chicano's Struggle Toward Liberation. San Francisco: Canfield Press, Harper and Row, 1972.

Anaya, Rodolfo, A. Bless Me, Ultima. Berkeley, Cal.: Tonatiuh International, 1972.

Aranda, Charles. Dichos, Proverbs and Sayings from the Spanish. Santa Fe, N.M.: The Sunstone Press, 1975.

Bustos, Amador S. "Immigration - The Human Journey and the Human Hunt," La Luz, Hispanic Magazine, Vol. 7, No. 2, February 1978.

Castro,   Tony.   Chicano Power, The Emergence of Mexican America. New York: E.P. Dutton, 1974.

Cockcroft, Eva, John Weber, and James Cockcroft: Towards A People's Art, The Contemporary Mural Movement. New York: Dutton, 1977.

Cuesta, Benedicto. El Paisano. Santa Fe, N.M.: The Sunstone Press, 1976.

De Leon, Nephtali. Chicanos, Our Background and Our Pride. Lubbock, Texas: Trucha Publications, 1972.

Delgado, Abelardo B. The Chicano Movement, Some Not Too Objective Observations. Denver: Totinem Publications, 1971.

Grigsby, J. Eugene, Jr. Art and Ethnics. Dubuque, Iowa: Wm. C. Brown Co., 1977.

Guzman, Diego Arenas. La Revolution Mexicana. Mexico: Fondo del Cultura Economica, 1969.

Kelman, Pal. Art of the Americas, Ancient and Hispanic. New York: Thomas Y. Crowell Co., 1969.

La Cucaracha, newspaper. Pueblo, Col.: Producciones Estrella Roja, 1977-78.

Ortego, Philip D. We Are Chicanos. New York: Washington Square Press, 1973.

Prescott, William H. The World Of The Aztecs. New York: Tudor Publishing Co., 1970.

Quirarte, Jacinto. Mexican-American Artists. Austin, Texas: University of Texas Press, 1973.

Rendon, Armando B. Chicano Manifesto. New York: Macmillan Co., 1971.

Rivera, Charles R., editor-in-chief. Nuestro, The Magazine for Latinos. New York: Nuestro Publications, 1977-78.

Romero, Orlando. Nambe: Year One. Berkeley, Cal.: Tonatiuh International, Inc. 1976.

Smith, Bradley. Mexico, A History In Art. New York: Doubleday and Co., 1968.

Ulibarri, Sabine R. Mi Abuela Fumaba Puros: My Grandmother Smoked Cigars. Berkeley, Cal., Quinto Sol, 1977.

Ulibarri, Sabine P. Tierra Amarilla. Albuquerque, N.M.: University of New Mexico Press, 1971.

Valdes, Daniel T., editor-in-chief. La Luz, Hispanic Magazine, Denver, Col.: La Luz Publications, Inc., 1975 - 78.

Wagner, Nathaniel N. and Marsha J. Haug. Chicanos, Social and Psychological Perspectives. St. Louis: C.V. Mosby Co., 1971.

West, Robert C. and John P. Angelli. Middle America: Its Lands and Peoples. 2nd ed. Englewood Cliffs, N.J.: Prentice-Hall, 1976.

7 Separatism in Quebec*

George F. Theriault

Will Quebec, which occupies an area as large as Mexico and has six million people - 80 percent of whom are Francophones - remain a part of Canada, or will it become the independent sovereign State of Kebec, fulfilling at long last the aspirations of the Francophone majority to be <u>Maitres chez nous</u>?

The catalytic event that precipitated this latest, and in the eyes of many observers, most serious, confrontation was the November 1976 rise to power of the <u>Parti Quebecois</u>, the first important political party in Canadian history committed openly, frankly, and fully to the cause of separation and independence.

The "<u>pequistes</u>", with a solid majority of 69 of the 110 members of <u>l'Assemblee Nationale</u>, have chosen the issue of language as the decisive battleground for confrontation. Bill 101, enacted into law in August 1977, requires nearly all children in Quebec, irrespective of ethnic background or parental desires, to attend French language schools. The option hitherto enjoyed of attending either French or British schools is now denied to 20 percent of the people of Quebec, and nearly 40 percent of the population of its metropolis, Montreal. Bill 101 also embodies strong measures to make French the language of work at both the management and shop levels, of the courts, and of all other key sectors of Quebec life.

This is powerful medicine. It has met vigorous resistance and resentment from the English-speaking minority of some 900,000, and from other ethnic minorities, notably Jewish and Italian, with a population of almost half a million. The Franco-

---

*Published by permission of George F. Theriault.

phones of Quebec, for their part, are resentful and feel threatened by the fact that most immigrants, who have come in large numbers in the post World War II years, have chosen to send their children to English language schools. This choice, for Francophones, rubs salt in the old wound that speaking French bears the symbolic stigma of second-class citizenship.

A referendum on separation from Canada, which will implement its overriding goal to become a separate sovereign State, has been promised by the Parti Quebecois for 1979.

The question of the dismemberment, if not the dissolution, of Canada is thus clearly posed. The issue is joined. Quebec versus Canada. Separatists versus federalists. The Parti Quebecois versus the Liberal Party, the latter both in its Quebec version and as the national Liberal Party in power in Ottawa. Rene Levesque versus Pierre Elliott Trudeau. The coming year will be a fateful one.

Several scenarios are dimly discernible as we ponder the strains of unfolding developments that may be acted out in the months and years ahead. We venture the enticing, if foolhardy, attempt to assay their prospects. First, however, we take a retrospective look through several centuries of French Canadian and Quebec separatism and their vicissitudes. Depicting in broad brush strokes only the most essential features of developments, much of the color and vivid detail of the French Canadian story must, unfortunately be sacrificed.

In examining Quebec separatism in retrospect and prospect our main goal is to understand the circumstances, influences, turns of events, and their consequences that have nourished and maintained the identity of the French people. After nearly four centuries, they have the vigor, determination and courage to run up the flag over their Quebec stronghold, man the political ramparts, and fling down the gauntlet to the Anglo-Saxon hosts, some 220 million strong, besetting them on all sides.

A RETROSPECTIVE OVERVIEW

Jacques Cartier began the French exploration of North America in 1534. Champlain established the first settlement at Quebec in 1608. Under the governance of fur trading monopolies at the outset, La Nouvelle France became a royal colony in 1663. The siege of Quebec, culminating in the decisive battle of the Plains of Abraham in 1759, ended French rule over the approximately 70,000 inhabitants of French origin or descent. New France became a British colony like those along the Atlantic coast to the south, except that the population of the latter was 1,500,000 at that time.

This striking twenty-fold numerical advantage of English

over French inhabitants in the Northern Hemisphere is significant; because the two countries' enterprises in North America had spanned roughly the same period of time, it reflects important differences in their interests and in what they were engaged in doing. The French enterprises were exploration, the search for treasure soon supplanted by the fur trade, and zealous missionary work to convert the Indians to Catholicism. These aspirations and commitments all tended to draw the French deeper and deeper into the interior of the Continent to the Great Lakes and southward down the Mississippi. Their settlements were a few - Quebec, Trois-Rivieres, Montreal - farming and fishing villages along the St. Lawrence, and small forts and outposts protecting the voyageurs and the fur traders. In sharp contrast, the English did not penetrate far into the interior, but early permanent settlements, substantial capital investment, agriculture and trade brought about cities, harbors, shipping, and compact development in their Protestant colonies along the coast. Contrasting religious motives strengthened these divergent goals. Although Protestant dissenters from the Church of England and French Huguenots from the Catholic Church came to America to settle permanently in the hope of enjoying religious freedom, the French missionaries, clergy, royal officials, soldiers, traders, and settlers in New France all shared the same Roman Catholic faith, and sought to propagate it.

An earnest test of future English-French relations in Canada followed quickly upon the heels of the conquest. The military occupation from 1759 to 1763 was peaceful; the miltary regime, respectful; the French clergy, cooperative; and the habitants, left to themselves, were withdrawn and quietly submissive. The Treaty of Paris in 1763 was followed by a royal Proclamation that established the Province of Quebec; it also brought in English law and English courts, granted land to Protestant clergy and schoolmasters, planned for large scale immigration of English subjects, and denied public office to Catholics. A decade of passive resistance followed, with the numerically predominant French continuing to speak French, practicing their Catholic faith, and following their own customs. After the loss of the fur trade to English merchants, the French retreated to the countryside. There, they lived in isolation, subsisting upon their own resources, interacting only with one another, and ignoring les maudits anglais. This recourse appeared to be vindicated when, in 1774, the Quebec Act restored the French civil law, the Catholic Church, and the right to hold public office. The French clergy were accorded the right to their tithes, the seigneurs to their dues. That the Quebec Act, ofttimes referred to as the Magna Carta of French Canada, came at a time when the American colonies to the south were in revolt, and that its

intent was to defuse disaffection and the potential spread of
revolutionary fervor to the French was a fortunate, if not
providential, coincidence.

The French clergy, mistrustful of the Protestant American
colonists' attitudes towards Rome, remained loyal to the Crown
during the Revolution, as did the seigneurs; and the habitants
were generally indifferent to American pleas for independence
and freedom from economic exploitation.

The 15 years after the conquest, in short, offered a
miniscule preview of the shape of things to come. It set the
stage that characterized the Canadian scene for the better part
of the next two centuries: English Protestants were dominant,
with military and political power, and economic hegemony over
the richest resources and trade; French Catholics were subordinate, engaging in rural farming, fishing, and hunting, and
passively submitting to the authority of both their own clergy
and seigneurs and of English rule. This brief period also
witnessed some abrupt fluctuations between acceptance, restless unease, and angry resentment.

Because of their numerical inferiority uneasiness, fear,
and resentment could also be attributed to the English. Even
after the American Revolution, with a Loyalist immigration of
some 1,000 into the Montreal region and some 6,000 into the
Upper St. Lawrence region that was to become Ontario, the
few English merchants and officials were "badly scared men"
(Wade, 1955, p. 60) trying to control a steadily-expanding
majority. In 1793, Richardson, the leader of the English
Canadians, explained, "Nothing can be so irksome as the
situation of the English members - without numbers to do any
good - doomed to the necessity of combatting the absurdities
of the majority, without a hope of success" (quoted by P.E.
Trudeau in "Some Obstacles to Democracy in Quebec," Wade,
1960, p. 253).

In 1791, the dissatisfaction of both ethnic groups led the
British government to separate Upper Canada - with a population of some 10,000 English-speaking Loyalists - from Lower
Canada - with approximately 150,000 predominantly-Catholic
Francophones. Even then, the latter did not enjoy popular
representative government. Resentment under English rule
continued and intensified as the years went by. In 1834,
although it numbered some 600,000 in both Canadas as compared to only 75,000 English colonists, the French-speaking
element held only a quarter of the official posts in Lower
Canada, and felt it was being exploited by the dominant
majority. Papineau led a rebellion in 1837, but it was quickly
put down by professional soldiers. Finally, the separate
legislative assembly for Lower Canada was done away with in
the Union Act of 1840. Resentment, conflict, and misunderstanding continued, and an enhanced sense of separate and
distinct identities and ways of life followed.

Mid-century, 1850, may be taken as an arbitrary bench-
mark when these separate and distinctive identities were firmly
set in the pursuit of sharply-contrasting, even antithetical
goals.   English Canada was launched upon the course of expansion, the encouragement of large scale immigration from
England, Scotland and Ireland, and the formation of new
provinces.   Canada was to participate in the technological,
commercial and industrial development then gathering headway
in the western world to the extent that its geographic features
permitted.

Few checkreins were in evidence upon the enterprises of
their Yankee cousins to the south.   In the 1820s Francis C.
Lowell introduced mass production techniques in the American
textile industry.   By 1850, Lowell, Massachusetts was the home
of nine major companies, and Charles Dickens had drawn
international attention to "a strange Yankee phenomenon" - the
company town.   "... the little Merrimac," as James Truslow
Adams wrote, "otherwise insignificant as an American River,"
was becoming by mid-century, "the most noted water-power
stream in the world" (Adams, J.T., 1930, p. 7).   A string of
mill towns lined its banks from Manchester, where the
Amoskeag Manufacturing Company had the largest cotton mill in
the world, south to Nashua, Lowell, Lawrence, Haverhill and
Amesbury on its way to the sea.   New England's burgeoning
growth had many facets: canals, railroads, clipper ships, and
commerce challenged Britain's seapower; and there was large
scale Irish immigration into the cities, as farmers emigrated
from their rocky farms in northern New England to the fertile
plains of the Middle West.

By mid-century, French Canada was well launched on a
very different course.   Nearly 100 years had passed since the
defeat on the Plains of Abraham and the loss of control over
the Canadian West, the Great Lakes, and the huge territories
of the Mississippi and its tributaries.   French resentment
against their conquerors had flared into open rebellion only
once, and had been quelled.   For nearly a century, they had
huddled together in their parishes and rangs strung out along
the broad St. Lawrence, small communities of equals, living a
self-sufficient way of life, they farmed, fished, hunted, and
trapped at a tempo and in the cadence set by the four
seasons.

Thus, effectively isolated in all essential respects, the
habitants on the shores and in the proximate hinterlands of
the St. Lawrence looked only to themselves, their immediate
natural resources, and the institutions and ancient traditions
of their forefathers for the course to pursue.   Once found, it
became the one to which they would cling tenaciously for the
next century.   Not the least intriguing feature of their experiment in survival is that it gathered momentum from 1850 to
1950, even as the basic conditions for its continuance were

being eroded.

The hegemony of the Roman Catholic hierarchy over French Canada, securely established by 1850, provided the unchallenged institutional matrix that shaped and colored all aspects of French-Canadian life. The tourists' image of the rural Quebec village - a cluster of modest homes surrounding an angust, granite, slate-roofed, high-steepled church with its nearby school, couvent (convent), and large and imposing presbytere (parsonage) - accurately suggests the contours of French-Canadian culture, and the beliefs and values the habitant continued to live by through the nineteenth and well into the twentieth century.

Salvation, not success, was the central concern. Spiritual worth and humane goodness in preparation for life after death, not material achievement in competition with one's fellow-man, demonstrated one's strength and competence in this life and was the primary test of personhood. Every stage in the life cycle of the individual was deeply-colored by the sentiments, attitudes, and behavior appropriate to a profound Catholicism.

The impress of the Church upon other institutions was great. In a subsistence agricultural economy in which the family was the basic unit of production, children were an asset. Under the spur of divine ordination, large families were idealized; in 1905, a pronvincial government publication published photographs of families with sixteen or more children (Robert, 1975, p. 93). By 1865, the fecundity ratio of Quebec families had reached 7.1 children per family. Through numerous generations, from the late eighteenth century on, French-Canadians actually attained the Malthusian limit by doubling their population every 25 years.

The influence of the Church in education was even greater. The Church was in control of education at all levels, and instruction was carried out by religious orders of priests, sisters, and brothers. Teaching was oriented primarily to religious ends. The main focus of the primary grades was to prepare children for their First Communion; in the secondary years they were prepared for religious vocations, or for the traditional liberal professions of law and medicine. While reading, writing, and arithmetic were taught, schooling was largely irrelevant to the pursuits of every day life, whose requirements were met by word of mouth. In his 1898 Histoire de la Seigneury de Lauzon, J.E. Roy commented that, with the isolation, penury, and demands of continuous manual labor, "barely ten percent of the habitants had learned to read, to write and add sums, and these laboriously, in childhood, and bid adieu to books and paper and pencil once out of school" (Rioux, 1974, p. 51). With their oral traditions, it is little wonder that education and schooling had virtually no meaning for many of them.

The main thrusts of education were thus to inculcate religion in the great majority of French Canadians who were engaged in heavy manual labor in the fields and forests, and to produce a small elite of priests, religious lawyers, and doctors. For a long time, women tended to obtain a somewhat better education than men; they were attracted to the orderliness and discipline of the religious institutions. Those who had obtained more than a rudimentary education, but who did not qualify for the more intellectually demanding vocations, were employed as teachers in one-room rural schools, or as clerical workers, saleswomen, or bookkeepers in the villages.

The rural parish provided the setting that unified and integrated forces in French Canada. The rang, whose farms were close to one another and invariably followed the uniquely Quebecois pattern of long narrow strips of land fronting upon the rang and extending back from it, provided the main locus of social interaction and mutual aid among people sharing basically-equal social status. In these settings, life, as Horace Miner described it in St. Denis, was "a flow of traditional behavior" (Miner, 1939, p. 91).

A conservative traditional outlook accompanied the traditional behavior. Louis Hemon expresses this eloquently in his novel Maria Chapdelaine. His heroine, Maria, describes how all rural French Canadians, feel about the past, present, and future:

> We came here three hundred years ago....Those who brought us here could return among us without bitterness and without regret, because, if it is so that we have learned nothing, it is as certain that we have forgotten nothing. We brought from overseas our prayers and our songs; they remain the same. We brought in our breasts the hearts of the men of our homeland, valiant and lively, as quick to cry as to laugh, the human of human hearts; it has not changed....here all that we brought with us, our culture, our language, our virtues and even our weaknesses have become sacred, and should last right to the end. .....
>
> Nothing has changed, because we are an attestation, an affirmation (of the vitality of a race and the indestructibility of a way of life). Of ourselves and of our destinies, we have clearly understood this duty: to persist...maintain ourselves... And we have done so, perhaps that several centuries hence the world will turn to us and say: These people are of a race that does not know how to die....

Marcel Rioux, the well-known French Canadian sociologist, wrote of his forebears: "If one were to summarize in a word the life of those generations, one could say that their sole concern was to attach themselves to the soil and to survive" (M. Rioux, 1971, p. 7). One of French Canada's foremost political scientists, Leon Dion, agrees: "La survivance became their principal goal," the lynchpin of their first traditional ideology. Professor Dion calls it their "conservative nationalism" (Leon Dion, 1976, p. 115).

It is this sentiment that animates the official motto of Quebec, Je me souviens (I remember).

THE EMERGING SCENE

The French-Canadian experiment in survival we have described, claimed by the geographer Marcel Belanger to have been a most completely successful colonial venture, (Robert, 1975, p. 272) continued under vigorous ultra-montane control until the middle of the twentieth century. Yet, from 1850 to 1950 the conditions for its continued existence were being undermined at a steadily increasing rate of speed.

When the Union Government was established in 1840 and a single government for Upper Canada and Lower Canada came into being in 1841, Canada East (Quebec) and Canada West (Ontario) were allocated an equal number of seats in the assembly. Despite the fact that there were 650,000 inhabitants in Quebec and 450,000 in Ontario, the possibility of another Papineau rebellion was effectively foreclosed, and the future minority status of the French-speaking population in Canada was assured. After mid-century the population balance actually shifted. In 1861, the four provinces in Canada as a whole, New Brunswick and Nova Scotia as well as Canada East and Canada West, had two and a half million people as a result of English, Irish, and Scotch immigration, while the prolific French-speaking population had grown to only 883,569.

The British North America Act in 1867 united Ontario, Quebec, and the two maritime provinces under a central government. This Act, still in force today, permitted the provinces to retain many highly-important powers, including control over education. In contrast to the States in the U.S., the Canadian provinces, later increased to ten, enjoyed a much larger measure of independence and autonomy. The Federal government was, and remains, weaker than its American counterpart. A swelling tide of immigration in the closing years of the nineteenth century, and especially in the decade just prior to World War I, not only played an important part in the development of the Prairie Provinces, but sealed the fate of the French Canadians as a demographic minority - a Quebec island in a predominantly Anglo-Saxon sea.

If its demographic prospects were bleak in comparison with its neighbors, events quickly demonstrated that it had very serious problems accommodating the swelling population within its own boundaries. The expansion of Quebec's ideal society - tradition-oriented, agricultural, French-speaking, deeply Catholic - encountered insurmountable obstacles. Although Quebec is as large as Mexico and three times larger than France, its fertile land area is limited mainly to the lowlands bordering the St. Lawrence and its tributaries, the townships south and east of Montreal, the Ottawa Valley, and the area surrounding Lac Saint-Jean. Together, these areas comprise but a small portion of its territory. These geo-graphic limitations, in conjunction with rapid economic devel-opment in the United States as compared to the Canadian economy, led large numbers of French Canadians to emigrate to the United States in the closing decades of the nineteenth century.

An Appalachia-like existence in a province gripped by endless depression drove many younger sons and young fam-ilies to seek their fortunes elsewhere. While some went west, most emigrants sought the Promised Land in the textile fac-tories and mill towns of New England. A trickle southward began in the 1840s, was slowed by depression in the mid-1850s, and dried up during the Civil War when the mills ground to a halt for lack of cotton. The first great wave of migration came in the post-war boom years, especially 1870-73. A Canadian survey of the exodus in 1873 estimated that 400,000 French Canadians emigrated to the United States (Hansen and Brebner, 1940, pp. 167-168), and that from one-fourth to one-third of the land usually tilted in the Province of Quebec was idle, houses boarded up, their owners at work in New England.

For the remainder of the century the alternating periods of boom and bust in the business cycle of the United States tended to dictate the ebbs and flows of migration to and from Canada. However, the return migration to Canada in de-pressed periods never equalled the flood tides southward in good years. The depression of the middle and late 1870s was followed by another huge influx in the early 1880s, and a third big wave occurred in the 1890s. Subsequent emigration was on a smaller scale as the result of an impetus in the Canadian economy which drew workers to Canadian cities rather than to New England. Meanwhile, a solid base had been established for La Franco-Americanie in New England. In 1891, it was estimated that there were 400,000 French Canadians in New England and New York State (Hamon, 1891, pp. 11 and 456). In that same year, the French-Canadian population in Canada was 1,488,535 (Langlois, 1934, p. 184).

Before modern technology, industrial growth, transportation facilities, commerce and finance began to transform Quebec into a modern urbanized economy, one French Canadian out of four had been drawn into the labor force in New England. Their wave-like migration into the textile centers gave rise to clustered neighborhoods of cold-water flats adjoining the factories. There they built parishes and schools modeled upon those of Quebec, and, for a generation or two, extended the tradition of large families. While immigration from Canada slackened, their numbers continued to increase. In the twentieth century, Franco-American stock constituted one-sixth of New England's population. Their experience of assimilation in different social contexts is instructive when weighing the prospects of the Quebecois for maintaining their ethnic identity.

The closing decades of the nineteenth century brought economic developments in Quebec that had fateful consequences for the traditional French-Canadian rural society. Agriculture changed from wheat to dairy and cash crop farming. Railroads bound regional ties, opened markets in cities and towns, and provided export possibilities for farm products, wood, and other raw materials. Protective tariffs encouraged light industrial production of consumer goods, which drew workers to towns and cities.

With the advent of hydro-electric power after the turn of the century, heavy industry flourished in the form of paper, pulp and mineral-processing plants. By 1920, manufacturing accounted for 38 percent of Quebec's economy (McRoberts and Posgate, 1976, p. 27).

Montreal tripled in size between 1901 and 1921. Smaller urban centers, Sherbrooke, Trois-Rivieres and Hull, doubled in size (McRoberts and Posgate, 1976, p. 27). The flow of French Canadians from the farms to the cities, providing abundant low cost labor, accelerated in the closing decades of the nineteenth century and continued at a high rate until 1920, slackened between the two World Wars, and accelerated again in the post-World War II years.

By mid-century, Quebec was structurally a modern society; its population became predominantly urban after World War I, and by 1951, its urban population was 66.8 percent of the total (Robert, 1975, p. 66). However, these economic and demographic developments were not accompanied by corresponding changes in attitudes on the part of the French-Canadian leadership. Farming, large families, and rural life continued to be idealized. Father Labelle, a priest who led rural colonization efforts in Quebec, viewed the textile centers of New England as le tombeau de la race (the graveyard of the race). In 1915, a government spokesman vigorously opposed migration to the cities and urged pioneer development of new parishes and farms in Quebec:

Canadian French! Do not leave your farms to go to
live in the cities in the dust of the factories and
the ear-splitting noise of machinery. If the pater-
nal homestead cannot provide places for all the
brothers, if for whatever reason you leave your
birthplace, come to Temiscaming, come to Abitibi.
You will expand and enrich the Pronvince, enlarge
its population, you will live among your kindly
fellow-citizens, you will speak our beautiful French
language, your children will learn their religion in
schools formed by Catholic traditions (Robert, 1975,
p. 66).

As late as 1956, colonists in new rural areas continued to be
subsidized by the government. In comparison with the massive
migration movements to the cities and the mineral and mining
processing centers of the province, rural colonization efforts
were insignificant. By 1961, the rural farm population of
French origin in Quebec had fallen to 13 percent of the total,
and was to drop to 6% percent by 1971. (McRoberts and
Postgate, 1976, p. 48).

The French migrants to the cities of Quebec, with their
backgrounds of farm labor and low levels of education, entered
the labor force at the bottom of the economic ladder as factory
.workers and day laborers, just as they had in the New
England mill towns of the nineteenth century. In the 1930s,
Everett Hughes studied an industrial town in the Eastern
town-ships, and described the status of the French-speaking
element in these terms:

... it is in the upper ranks of industry that one
finds the English outsiders. People of local origin
and French culture are in the lower ranks. The
latter are, furthermore, from the lower ranks of the
local society. The people of the higher ranks of
French-Canadian society find little place in the
industrial society (McRoberts and Postgate, 1976,
pp. 38-39).

The "higher ranks" were the products of the classical
education designed to train the fortunate few for the priesthood and the traditional liberal professions.

The emerging scene not only brought French Canadians
from the country to the city. It changed the values they
lived by. The best general measure of these changing values
is the birth rate. Demographers, Jacques Henripin and Ives
Peron wrote that religious and nationalistic factors had long
kept the birth rate high: "Perhaps nowhere else in the world
has the Catholic ideal of large families been more effectively
achieved ... This ideal was reinforced by a vigorous nation-

alistic propaganda and one cannnot question its success"
(Robert, 1975, pp. 72-73). The revanche de berceaux
(revenge of the cradle) "produced some of the highest birth
rates that have ever been recorded, 64.5 per thousand in
1761-1770. ... They remained exceptionally high until well into
the twentieth century" (McRoberts and Posgate, 1976, p. 57).

As late as the 1930s, thoughtful observers speculated on
the possible consequences: "Like some prolific plant that hugs
the earth, they spread at the expense of surrounding
populations" (Hughes, 1943, p. iv). Arnold Toynbee commented upon their invasion of New England: "... and now in
the fullness of time the French Canadian is making a counter-
offensive into the heart of his old rival's homeland. He is
conquering New England in the peasant's way - by slower but
surer methods than those which governments have at their
command" (1934, pp. 72-73).

Even as these observations were made, however, a
dramatic reversal was under way. In 1920, the birth rate in
Quebec was still impressively high. It then dropped
precipitously.

> Historically the province with the highest birth rate
> in Canada, Quebec now has the lowest." It was
> 37.6 per thousand in 1921 (compared to 29.3 for
> Canada), 30 in the late forties, began declining in
> the late 1950s and, with the ready availability of
> "the pill," fell to 16 in 1969 and 13.8 in 1972 (when
> the rate for Canada was 15.9)" (McRoberts and
> Posgate, 1976, p. 57).

Marcel Rioux expressed it in other terms: "In 1951 the
fecundity of the French-Canadians was 23% higher than that of
other Canadians, but in 1965 it was 5% below" (1971, p. 188).

No better indicator of secularization of a traditionally-
deeply-religious people who idealized the large family can be
found than these measures of changing behavior. Other
measures of changing attitudes are also illuminating. An
excellent study by Tremblay and Fortin of economic behavior
in relation to attitudes and values was based upon a 1959
survey of 1465 families of wage earners in rural and urban
settings. They found that French-Canadian society was becoming more and more homogeneous, with an emergent set of
values and norms increasingly common to the whole society.
The authors summarized their findings in these words:

> ... our society is in process of becoming, if it is
> not in fact already, a society in which mass culture
> is preponderant. The traditional French-Canadian
> culture seems no longer to influence the population,
> at least insofar as economic behavior is concerned.

> From the outset of our studies of the rural milieu we hypothesized that the new desire for a high standard of living was in the process of completely transforming the values and social organization of rural society. The present study confirms this hypothesis and suggests that the transformation has already taken place to a large extent (1964, p. 110).

THE QUIET REVOLUTION

Rattrapage (catching up) is the one word used by the Quebecois to wrap up the years of The Quiet Revolution under the leadership of Prime Minister Jean LeSage and the Liberal Party. If the more familiar description is to serve as the key to understanding the critical events of that period from 1960-66, it should be used in the plural. It was an internal revolution that swept most of the traditional culture out of its path, toppled the power elite, transformed the institutions of the family, education, religion and government, unbridled the arts, and began laying the foundations· of a new society. Writing of the early 1960s, the Milners said, "Quebec built up an infrastructure of a modern capitalistic society" (1973, p. 167). Those eventful years also found massive popular support for an external revolution against Anglo-American hegemony. That this revolution was anything but ephemeral was to be demonstrated when the conservative Union nationale came to power in 1966 and, under Daniel Johnson, continued to bring pressure upon Ottawa for greater autonomy. In the 1970s, the return to power of Bourassa and the Liberals, and the Parti Quebecois, with Rene Levesque as the standard bearer for independence, brought increasing pressure for change in Quebec-Canadian and Quebec-American relations. All shades of Quebec political opinion, from the extreme right to the extreme left, press for greater autonomy. "The new ideal of French-Canadian nationalists became a highly efficient technological society led by French Canadians and animated by a French spirit" (McRoberts and Posgate, 1976, p. 98).

While these revolutions appear to have struck with a thunder-clap, the deeper groundwork had been long in the making, as we have seen in the foregoing pages. They were also prefaced by significant events and developments in the 1940s and 1950s. The asbestos strike of 1949 shook, divided, and weakened the old order and served as a clarion call to numerous Quebec academicians, intellectuals, and university students. Pierre Eliott Trudeau and other young intellectuals in the avant-garde Cite Libre attacked the traditional authority structure and espoused liberal belief in government as an agent of popular will. Social scientists at Laval, historians at l'universite de Montreale, liberal priests, and such Catholic voluntary associations as l'Action Catholique, the Confederation des travailleurs catholiques du Canada and the Jeunesse etudiante catholique, among others, prepared the way in the 1950s.

The transfer of political power to the Liberals in 1960, after the long bastion-like regime of the autocrat Duplessis, opened the flood-gates and rattrapage proceeded at a dizzying rate. For a few years, all seemed possible. Union activity was recognized as legitimate. Censorship disappeared when the heavy hand of Church disapproval was removed. A consciously-Quebec art and music appeared. La Presse, under Gerard Pelletier, became a vibrant and open voice of the new Quebec. With the Lesage slogan Maitres Chez Nous (Masters in our own house), an exaggerated self-confidence replaced the passive acceptance of second class status expressed in the saying Ne pour un petit pain (Born for a small loaf of bread). The Quebec Liberal Party became independent of the national Liberal Party. When Manicouagan, the largest hydro-electric power project of its kind in the world, was constructed in Northern Quebec under exclusively Francophone management with French as the language of work, strong sentiments of pride swept through all factions in Quebec.

Cite Libre had done its work. "The State (ed: The Quebec government) assumed a new importance as the primary agent, le moteur principal, of this ... catching up process" (McRoberts and Posgate, 1976, p. 99). A new elite came to power, a middle-class bureaucracy with a monopoly within French-Canadian society on the specialized technical knowledge and management skills required for a technocratic society.

Strong nationalistic sentiments were held by the new technocrats. McRoberts and Posgate suggest several conceivable sources of this sentiment. The new middle class at first tended to be drawn from laymen whose skills had been employed within Church-controlled activities; resentment at the attempt by the Church to retain control may have given rise to nationalist sentiments and diverted loyalty to the Quebec government. The possibility of attaining top management positions appeared to the new middle class as viable only in a French-Canadian society, as in the socialized Hydro-Quebec. Because the new middle class had been recruited largely from the lower class, rejecting Francophone society to become Anglophones and Canadians did not appear to be a viable alternative. The comparatively-small Francophone manufacturing and commercial enterprises felt hard pressed by the competition of American corporations, and Anglo-Canadian firms, and tended to join the new technocrats in seeking help from the Quebec government. Needless to say, Francophones in middle management positions in English-Canadian and American firms shared the same sentiments. Nationalistic sentiments thus drew strength from several well-springs of the new Francophone middle class.

The most drastic and far-reaching measures taken by the Lesage regime in the early 1960s were in education, health, and welfare, and in the socialization of electric power. Under the vigorous leadership of Paul Gerin-Lajoie, the Department of Education was established in 1964, and the government assumed full authority over education at all levels. Education was secularized. The Church retained control only over the confessional aspects in Catholic schools. The new extensive system of two-year colleges, the CEGEPs, was wholly non-confessional.

In 1961, hospital insurance was introduced, completely under government regulation and administration. In 1964, a compulsory contributory pension plan was inaugurated, and former federal welfare programs were taken over by the provincial government.

Rene Levesque was the moving spirit in the nationalization of hydro-electric facilities. Hydro-Quebec came into being in 1962, providing access to top management positions for French bureaucrats. It was completely French-speaking. Even its new projects, such as the gigantic Manicouagan Dam in northern Quebec that was financed by $300,000,000 of American capital, were undertaken with French as the sole working language and carried out by an exclusively Francophone management.

The Lesage years also brought in numerous other economic ventures, none of which were initially as successful as Hydro-Quebec. The Societe Generale de financement, designed to support marginal Francophone business enterprises, was unimpressive, possibly because of limited resources and unclear objectives. SIDBEC was established to build an integrated steel complex that would give Quebec greater autonomy and control over its economy. However, the project proved to be excessively costly and controversial, and, in spite of energetic efforts, its construction was repeatedly postponed.

The structure of the provincial government itself was expanded greatly during this period. Administrative units grew from 39 to 64, the civil service expanded, and employees in public enterprises more than doubled. Although, with the exception of Hydro-Quebec, no radical changes took place and American and Anglo-Canadian corporations continued much as before, the internal revolution had in a few short years taken many essential steps toward attaining modern, highly-developed governing structures and institutions congruent with the requirements and needs of a highly-developed economy and society.

While rattrapage was proceeding on many fronts in the

internal revolution, the Lesage Liberal regime brought into play new rules in the game of relations with Ottawa that have been in effect ever since. This aspect of the external revolution replaced the rhetorical affirmations of autonomy and "going it alone" of the Duplessis years with tough-minded bargaining for real stakes; namely, the provincial government was to get a larger share of tax revenues and to assume responsibility for, and control over, the management of specific programs. For example, one of the first provincial victories was over the funding of universities, with the federal government reducing its share of the corporate income tax yield by one percent, and Quebec increasing its share by one percent. The federal government yielded to several of these demands in the early 1960s, and similar shifts were effected in education, health and welfare. In addition to these shifts involving the provincial government taking over programs formerly administered by the federal government, there was a struggle for control over new programs; perhaps the most bitterly contested was the contributory pension plan, which was eventually taken over by the provincial government.

Other issues also figured in Ottawa-Quebec relations: The right to negotiate unilateral treaties with foreign nations was one. And consultation with the provincial government preceding the introduction of new Federal programs was another. Thus was the contest waged to carve out a new and enlarged role for the provincial government. In numerous respects, a de facto special status for Quebec came into being in successive concessions won by hard bargaining around the conference table, and these victories brought ever-higher aspirations for more provincial rsponsibility and power.

THE CONSERVATIVE REACTION AND DEEPENING UNEASE

The developments we have outlined in the preceding two sections of this chapter may be likened to an ocean rising to full tide in The Quiet Revolution. The next decade, 1966-76, to continue the metaphor, was an ebbing tide, when viewed overall. Waves, large and small, pounded the shore. Street demonstrations, strikes in public services, dynamitings, kidnappings, terrorists' clandestine military training, student unrest, and occupation and burning of university buildings alerted observers and interested parties alike that portentous happenings were churning below the surface.

Conservatives were returned to power in Quebec in 1966, reflecting the continued presence of important traditional attitudes, especially in rural areas, and a more general sentiment that the Lesage regime had moved too far too fast; a breathing spell was needed. That the Union nationale victory, with only 40 percent of the popular vote, was not a rejection of The Quiet Revolution was quickly made manifest in the implementation of many of its key policy decisions by Prime Minister Daniel Johnson and his successor, Jean-Jacques Bertrand.   The reforms of the education system were carried out.   The first CEGEP college was established in 1967, and twenty-nine more were built by 1970.   Even SIDBEC was implemented by the purchase of the Dominion Steel Corporation, subsidized to the tune of $60,000,000 for the next five years.

On the other hand, the Union nationale years curbed many Liberal programs and dropped some of them, slowed the rate of government expenditures and bureaucratic expansion, and reduced demands for the transfer of responsibilities from the federal to the provincial government.   The one area in which the Union nationale pressed the Federal government for greater autonomy was that of international relations, demanding the right to negotiate with foreign powers in matters over which Quebec had constitutional jurisdiction.   Johnson also pressed Ottawa vigorously for broad changes in the Canadian Constitution as the alternative to independence for Quebec. These demands met stiffened resistance on the part of the Federal Government after Trudeau succeeded Pearson as Canadian Prime Minister.

On the key issue of limiting parental choice of English- or French-language schools, the Union nationale at first temporized, then encountered stiff Francophone antagonism to its policy of permitting linguistic choice.   Union demands by teachers in the schools and workers in public transportation were firmly opposed by the provincial government.   Alienation and erosion of popular support for the Union nationale resulted.

The Liberal Party that returned to power in 1970 was a far cry from the Liberal Party of The Quiet Revolution.   Its leader, Robert Bourassa, was a moderate with confidence in the free operation of economic forces without government intervention.   Rene Levesque had led the militant nationalistic interventionists out of the Liberal Party in 1967, and had formed the Mouvement souverainete-association to establish the base of popular support that later found expression in the Parti Quebecois.   Bourassa's Liberal Party was primarily concerned with attracting American capital to a free enterprise system.   Particularly symbolic of this political stance was the delegation of responsibility for the James Bay hydro-electric development to a private corporation rather than to Hydro-Quebec.

In certain minor respects, however, the Bourassa regime followed an interventionist policy in support of Francophone enterprises.   The Societe generale de financement was more successful in the early 1970s than it had been in the 1960s. Continuity with the policies set in The Quiet Revolution was maintained in regard to education, health, and welfare. In health insurance, conditions set for the medical profession were stricter than those in other provinces.

Although the two major parties that controlled the Quebec government from 1966-76 followed moderate conservative courses, certain critical events heralded rougher seas ahead, much as the asbestos strike of 1949 had signalled a train of events that culminated in The Quiet Revolution. Three cut to the quick of different facets of Quebec's thrust for basic institutional change: the language of instruction in the schools, the status of the working class and the role of unions in the emerging society, and the means to be used in the attainment of power.

In 1967, officials of a school district in Montreal transformed the issue of the language of instruction from rhetoric to social action by attempting to force immigrant children to attend French-language schools. The provincial Minister of Education refused to take a stand and formulate a general policy for local school boards to follow. In 1968 and 1969, the provincial legislature considered the issue, against a background of ever-more-insistent pressure for government intervention favorable to a policy forcing instruction in French, and finally passed Bill 63 which guaranteed parental choice of the language of instruction. It is notable that Bill 63 was passed with the support of the Liberal opposition in spite of a demonstration against it by 50,000 people in front of the Legislature. Compromises and concessions built into the measure only served to testify to the steadily-growing insistence by the French majority that its identity and survival required concerted action and government intervention.

After its return to power in 1970, the Liberal Party encountered similar difficulties with Bill 22, which attempted to meet the language issue on the job front as well as in the schools. Departing from the traditional position of both languages being coequal, Bill 22 declared French to be the "official language" of Quebec. Francophone nationalists, however, found it ambiguous and weak both as to education and work in its specific provisions. It shifted the issue in the schools from the politically-tender one of parental choice by requiring children of immigrants to show they knew English "well enough" to be taught in that language, and it granted broad discretionary power to the Department of Education to allocate resources for facilities for instruction in English. The provisions of Bill 22 in regard to the language of work were also diluted in many respects; linguistic practices in different types of business varied widely and effecting changes in language practices would be extremely difficult.

Be that as it may, proponents of French as the language of work took strong exception to Bill 22's moderate, general and, in their view, weak and inadequate provisions. They also objected to the latitude of responsibility accorded to the Office de la langue francaise charged with its administration. Their misgivings seemed to be confirmed by the failure of the Bourassa regime to fill the top positions in the Office de la langue francaise in the year following the passage of Bill 22.

The underlying swell of discontent, frustration, and pressure over the language issue seemed to reflect an ever-deepening fear that the identity of French Canadian society and culture in the new setting of a modern, highly-developed urban society might not survive. That new immigrants to Quebec, especially the Italians who hitherto had been the ethnic stock most disposed to learn French, should intermarry, become assimilated, and send their children to English-language schools was seen as an especially serious threat. This action communicated a clear message: the next generation will be better off if it adapts to Anglo-American society. Unless the French majority that controlled the government and supported education financially took effective counter-measures, it was in effect working for its own demise and, in the long run, for the assimilation of its children and grandchildren into the Anglo-American mass. That a minority of 20 percent should call the tune while the majority of 80 percent paid the piper was intolerable.

A second area of critical interest as background for current and future developments in Quebec is that of the labor movement. It was noted earlier that the asbestos strike of 1949 shook the foundations of the old traditional society and set in motion a train of events leading to The Quiet Revolution. During the Lesage regime the labor movement was further encouraged, with public employees gaining the right to strike. Unions picked up membership and momentum steadily through the 1960s and 1970s.

In 1972, a Common Front of the three major labor con-federations called out 210,000 public and para-public employees in a general strike for job security, a minimum wage of $100 per week, and fair salary increases. After two weeks, the Bourassa regime passed special legislation suspending the right of public employees to strike and forced a return to work. The union leaders who advised the membership to disobey the law, before holding a referendum and reluctantly recommending a return to work were successfully prosecuted by the govern-ment and sentenced to jail for one-year terms. These con-victions prompted a still broader general strike which con-tinued for another week. Of particular note through those critical weeks was the radical tone of the pamphlets and flyers used by the CNTU (Confederation of National Trade Unions). One read, "Il faut casser le systeme" (The system must be destroyed).

This strike was the culmination of a spirited decade of expansion and strife. The earlier, relatively passive, largely

church-controlled labor associations of the Duplessis years had
been replaced by a dynamic, aggressive labor movement on a
scale far beyond that familiar to Americans. In Quebec,
doctors and engineers are unionized, as well as teachers, and
they exercise the prerogative to strike in a manner much more
suggestive of France than of the U.S. For months in 1967,
for example, radiologists were on strike and x-ray examina-
tions were not available anywhere in the province. Nurses,
hospital employees, police, postal employees and teachers have
also gone out on strike. A very interesting feature of the
labor movement in Quebec is that, following the initial impetus
of The Quiet Revolution, the fastest-growing unions, grouped
in the CNTU, and the most dynamic and aggressive were also
the most radical and nationalistic.

Prior to 1960, anti-capitalistic thought and sentiment in
Quebec tended to be limited to intellectuals and academicians.
Although The Quiet Revolution promised a liberation economique
to all, in practice it primarily benefited the white-collar middle
class, except in the matter of health and welfare benefits
which all classes shared.

Political organization of radical elements began on a small
scale in the early 1960s. The RIN (Rassemblement pour l'independence nationale), founded in 1960, was very active in
street demonstrations and received 5.5% of the vote in the
elections of 1966. As early as 1960, the CNTU supported the
NPD (Nouveau Parti Democratique), a nascent political party
with socialist goals. In 1963, Parti Pris, a Marxist nationalist
review, had a readership of only 3500, principally students
and professors. A more solid base of leftist socialist organization emerged in the unions, notably in the CNTU, under the
vigorous leadership of Jean Marchand in 1961 and Marcel Pepin
in 1965. Composed of decentralized unions with a horizontal
distribution of power, the CNTU was set up along industrial
lines, such as hospital services and construction. Working in
close cooperation with the Lesage regime in the early 1960s, its
membership grew from 80,000 to 230,000 by 1970. As it grew,
its demands intensified: more strikes were called, and its dues
were much higher than those of rival unions.

An interesting and important feature of the labor scene in
Quebec since The Quiet Revolution is the extent to which the
Quebec government became the employer of organized labor in
the province. By 1970, the public sector contained 40 percent
of the unionized workers of Quebec, including 37,000 civil
servants and 16,366 employed in public enterprises; the
Government's assumption of responsibility over education and
health and welfare services also expanded its role as employer.
The CNTU, more open than its rival QFL (Quebec Federation
of Labor) in advocating Quebecois nationalism, recruited a
large share of public employees. By 1970, some 50 percent of
its members were in the public sector, as compared to 15

percent in the QFL.   A third important union, the CEQ (Corporation des enseignants du Quebec), was wholly in the public
sector, with 71,360 teacher-members in 1968-69.

The position of the government is complex.   It is the
employer of a very large segment of the union membership,
which, for the most part, is controlled by aggressive radical
leaders who are anti-capitalistic, thrusting for socialist takeovers of business enterprises, urging francization of work,
and pressing for ever greater gains of labor.   Ever since
1960, Liberal administrations have recognized these rights and
promised that they would be realized.   At the same time, the
government has access to, and control over, many measures
not available to private employers.   The general strike demonstrated that the courts and jail terms could be resorted to
quickly and efficaciously; yet such actions necessarily feed the
fires of labor alienation and build pressures for governments
more responsive to labor's needs and demands.

No party in power in Quebec can avoid such confrontations.   L'Universite Laval, the Harvard of Quebec, was
strike-bound in the fall of 1976.   It was only through the
concession of most union demands during arbitration forced by
the Parti Quebecois - just come to power and on a honeymoon
with the unions - that Laval opened its doors in January.

The kidnapping and eventual murder of Pierre Laporte,
the Quebec Minister of Labor, in October 1970 was also the
culmination of terrorist acts and the violence of extremists.
The turbulent 1960s brought the beginning of basic institutional shifts in political power, a process as yet far from
resolution.

The 1960 overthrow of the power structure that had been
perceived as unassailable for over a century created a vacuum,
one that leaders and interest groups across the political
spectrum from the extreme right to the extreme left attempted
to fill.   A baker's dozen of political parties and movements
formed, dissolved, split, merged, and regrouped in this power
struggle.   Confrontations eventuating in irreconcilable conflict
over ends and means inevitably spawned anger and hatred,
and resorted to violence to achieve their goals.   Loosely-
organized in cells, the FLQ (front de liberation du Quebec)
first directed its attacks at British or federal institutions and
symbols by planting small bombs in mail boxes, Mounted Police
headquarters, and before a monument to Queen Victoria.   The
program escalated over the years: more powerful bombs were
used; telephone warnings were fewer; injuries and deaths were
inflicted; and more damage was done against a broader range
of targets, including French-owned and -operated establish-
ments.

Then tactics changed: attempts were made to recruit and
train a revolutionary army; military depots, banks, and a firearms store were robbed to obtain funds, radio equipment, and

arms; in the later stages, strong attacks were launched on government buildings, headquarters of political parties, city halls, and even the headquarters of a moderate labor organization. The nature of the attacks just prior to the kidnappings of Cross and Laporte suggest that the FLQ believed Quebec ready for revolution.

Until the murder of Laporte, widely-publicized FLQ manifestoes received surprisingly favorable popular support, even among some priests, for the goals and objectives they sought. The murder of Minister Laporte, however, was immediately and strongly denounced. Rene Levesque and other moderate separatists called upon the kidnappers to surrender. Both the federal and provincial governments took strong repressive measures. Very few radicals proved to be ready to pursue the road of violence any further. Although the severity and scope of the government's repressive measures were criticized as excessive and unjustified, the course for independantistes was, in effect, set; their goals would be achieved peacefully through the democratic process.

The Rise of the Parti Quebecois

In opposition after its defeat by the Union nationale in 1966 the Liberal Party was no longer able to maintain the precarious unity between conservatives and progressives, a responsibility that its leaders had accepted when it was the party in power. During The Quiet Revolution, party congresses had witnessed many confrontations, the most notable that in which Rene Levesque and his nationalist associates successfully overcame the resistance of the conservatives, including Prime Minister Lesage, and obtained party approval for the government takeover of the electric utilities and the establishment of Hydro-Quebec.

When the October 1967 Liberal Party Congress rejected Rene Levesque's concept of sourverainete-association, he resigned, formed the MSA (Mouvement souverainete-association), and was joined by some of his separatist associates - Jacques Parizeau, who had been a consultant on economic affairs for both Lesage and Johnson, Claude Morin, a specialist in intergovernmental relations, and Jacques-Yvan Morin, who had extensive organizational experience as the leader of Les Etats Generaux in 1966. The latter was an ambitious undertaking that had sounded out interests and attitudes throughout French Canada by organizing discussion groups and assemblies at the local, regional, and national level.

The Parti Quebecois was founded in October of 1968 and immediately launched vigorous campaigns, recruitment drives, and fund-raising efforts in its drive toward power. As the

result of the the single member plurality electoral system, it
won only seven seats in the legislature in the election of 1970
and only six seats in 1973, despite winning nearly 24 percent
of the vote in 1970 and 30 percent of the vote in 1973. In the
fall of 1976, however, the system worked to its advantage;
with only 41 percent of the votes, it came into power with 69
seats of the total 110.

That the appeal of the Parti Quebecois was heavily based
upon the sentiment of separatism is shown in surveys: in 1970,
70 percent of its voters were for souverainete-association, and
an even higher percentage, 77 percent, in 1973. By 1974,
however, surveys found this percentage had dropped to 61
percent. In the 1976 campaign separatist sentiment had declined to a point where the Party waged its successful campaign on the issues of ineptness and alleged dishonesty of the
Bourassa regime. It defused anti-separatist fears by promising that it would not, once in power, move toward independence without first submitting the issue to the voters in the
form of a referendum.

The Parti Quebecois In Power

After ten years of struggle, the coming to power of
Quebec's first avowedly separatist political party marked the
opening of a new scene in the drama of North American political and economic development. In the days of assessment immediately following the election there was a sense that decisive
events had taken place, and that henceforth the political stage
would present new plays. Rene Levesque and the P.Q.leaders
turned to the challenges of implementing the Party's promises
now that power was in their hands. Their followers, the
pequistes, and their Francophone opponents who were
sympathisants generally adopted a wait-and-see attitude. The
comment of a small neighborhood grocery store owner in
Quebec city reflected a prevalant sentiment, "Nos gars sont la.
On ouaira." (Our guys are in. We'll see.)

The winter months of 1976-77 brought a growing sense
that the P.Q. meant business, that the public's disenchantment
with the high rhetoric, empty promises, and half measures of
the preceding decade, whether of Daniel Johnson and the
Union Nationale or of Bourassa and the Liberal Party, was not
to be deepened further by the Parti Quebecois.

The regime's White Paper in April 1977 declared Quebec to
be "a French society," and told the English-speaking minority
it "could no longer dominate economic life." "The Quebec we
wish to build," it said, "will be essentially French. ...The use
of French will accompany, symbolize and favor a reconquest by
the French-speaking majority of the control that belongs to it
over the levers of the economy." Camille Laurin, Minister for

Cultural Development, spoke of the White Paper as "the herald of the springtime of Quebec's collective life." He predicted that the months ahead would see a prolonged discussion in the legislature that would reconcile differences and bring forth a "reasonable document" to effect these basic goals as fairly as possible.

A comprehensive measure was introduced shortly thereafter to make French the official and primary language in government, the courts, and public and para-public administrative agencies. French was also to be the language of work, of business and commerce, and of education. The measure also set forth procedures and methods to attain these ends, and penalties for their infraction.

The serious consequences of the impending changes immediately precipitated vigorous arguments, bitter debate, threats and counterthreats, fears, unrest, and disaffection. Increasing uncertainty, unhappiness, and recrimination marked the ongoing consideration of the measure through the spring and summer. Minor modifications were made and Bill 101 was enacted, over bitter opposition, by a vote of 54 to 31 on August 26, 1977.

This is being written nine months later after a fall, winter and spring of profound discontent and apprehension in the Anglophone minority. This response has many facets. Old English residents fear the extinction of the English community in Quebec and believe their demotion in status forecloses their future in the province. Many are leaving. On April 9, 1978, The New York Times reported that there were 97,000 emigrants from Quebec in 1977; at the same time, 27,000 migrated to Quebec from other provinces, and 20,000 foreign immigrants entered, indicating a net loss of 50,000 - a large proportion of them believed to have been Anglophones. Because the new law requires the great majority of children of English-speaking families to attend French-language schools, English-language schools are declining in enrollment. Eight of the 95 English-language schools in Greater Montreal will be closed at the end of the current term.

Bill 101 strikes home immediately by requiring that the children of most business managers, executives, and professionals attend French-language schools. Its provisions for the broad extension of French as the language of work at the management level, hitherto conducted in English by both English- and American-owned businesses, are also deeply painful and present business with many problems.

Although it is difficult to arrive at precise estimates, the exodus of business firms from Quebec is substantial. Montreal has long been the financial and business heart of Canada. In addition to the assertion of French primacy, Montreal's role has been diminished by a depressed economy and a westward shift of many enterprises. According to The New York Times of April 23, 1978, federal officials estimate that 140 corporate offices have left Montreal in the past two years. Sun Life, a five billion-dollar mutual insurance company, represented the greatest single loss. Smaller enterprises such as Dominion Bridge, a steel fabricator and holding company, Douglas, Ltd., a container manufacturer, and Redpath Industries, a sugar refiner, have relocated in the U.S. Pharmaceutical companies are leaving. Some large firms, such as banks, seem to be quietly shifting some of their operations to other provinces. Some remain - the Aluminum Company of Canada, for example - because they are not transportable. The general climate appears to be a discouraging one, tending to confirm the predictions of federalists that effective steps toward independence would prove to be prohibitively costly. Writing in the January 1978 issue of Atlantic Monthly, Mordecai Richler, expressed the view that "the economy of (an independent) Quebec would be ruined for a generation, maybe more."

The climate of hostility and conflict in the first year of the Parti Quebecois regime is reflected in a sharp drop in support for separatism in Quebec; a recent Gallup poll showed 19 percent for, 70 percent opposed, and 10 percent undecided. Anglophones are fearful that the promised referendum, which will probably be held in 1979, will be rigged by the regime in such a way that a clear, unambiguous vote may not be possible. Federalists, including the Federal government, threaten to conduct their own poll.

Recently, the Liberal Party of Quebec has chosen Claude Ryan as its leader. Ryan, a highly-respected and widely-known journalist who was for many years the editor of Le Devoir, will be the opponent of Rene Levesque in the provincial elections to be held in 1980. Rene Levesque wasted no time in launching the political infighting. He pictured this "Pope" in the solitude and quiet of his editorial office pondering over pontifical and beautifully-written essays that put readers to sleep, while experienced politicians worked night and day to improve the welfare of the Quebecois. While Ryan sat, experienced politicians were wrenching rights and money from Ottawa, and curbing the English and American exploiters of the blue- and white-collar French workers.

REFLECTIONS UPON THE PROSPECTS FOR QUEBEC

"The cultural mutations experienced by Quebec since 1940 are nothing short of astounding" (Dion, p. 201). If that is so, the prospects for the remaining decades of the twentieth century are very likely to be no less so.

Quebec has gone from a church-controlled society where lives were lived in anticipation of the ultimate encounter with

Saint Peter to one with faith in a government that promises all
the "goodies" of this world - from television sets and roulottes
(camping trailers) to welfare and insurance against hardship
and deprivations. Duplessis autocratic, arch-conservative, and
corrupt Union nationale political regime was replaced by the
charm and Gallic wit of the pied piper, Rene Levesque, who
nationalized the electric utilities of Quebec in The Quiet
Revolution, transformed the Liberal Party into the conservative
heir of the Union nationale in the next decade, and developed
astounding skill in the 1970s as a juggler who maintained the
high hopes of all the radical and moderate performers in the
"independentist" Parti Quebecois.

Is anything predictably foreclosed in Quebec's future? A
province with one of the world's highest birth rates now has
not only one of the lowest, but the lowest of any Canadian
province; a highly-moralistic, puritanical "atmosphere" has
been converted to one that publicizes the disgressions of its
Prime Minister; a society that did not encourage the wives of
statesmen to appear in public, and then only as the house-
wifely figures associated with Russian diplomats' wives, now
presents to the world - to again quote Richler - the "stunning
young wife of the Prime Minister of Canada, a mother of three
and a self-declared flower child, abandoning Ottawa to Do Her
Own Thing in New York." That the public could respond to
these events with sympathetic understanding would have been
unthinkable a generation ago.

Another facet of Quebec's astounding mutations is the
economic and ecological transition from an underdeveloped rural
society to a highly-centralized urban society. Half of its
population is now concentrated in metropolitan Montreal, and
only 5.6 percent on farms. Quebec's industrial economy is
predominantly built around the extractive industries, pulp and
paper, smelting and refining. In some respects, Quebec's
economy appears to be moving into a post-industrial phase
faster than many more fully-industrialized societies. Employment in the secondary sector of manufacturing - textiles,
clothing, and tobacco products, for example - has slipped
since World War II from 36 percent to 31.9 percent of the labor
force, and the value of the products has declined from 41.2
percent to 38.8 percent of the provincial total. (McRoberts
and Posgate, p. 34) The service sector, both private and
public, is expanding rapidly in characteristic post-industrial
fashion.

Whatever surprises lie in store for Quebec and interested
observers, this review of developments raises fundamental
questions that will have to be answered in the years ahead.
While we are fully aware of being hostages to fortune in doing
so, we have formed opinions that are offered to the reader for
reflection.

Will Quebec Become an Independent Nation?

In our judgment, probably not.

Canada is a loose confederation of more or less autonomous provinces. Although the constant preoccupation of Canadians collectively, and each of the provinces individually, with the question of identity strikes the outside observer at times as paranoid and at others as futile, it probably reflects the fact that the confederation is more or less continuously renegotiating issues that are in its fine print. It is more likely that this process will continue in the future than that Canada will dissolve into independent states.

What Are French Canada's Prospects for Linguistic and Cultural Survival?

At first blush, this may seem a curious question to pose. French Canadians perceive themselves as one of the two cofounding peoples of Canada, and are proposing, after three and a half centuries, to dissolve the partnership and establish themselves as a sovereign and independent nation-state. Yet these same people have passed a law to enforce instruction in French in the schools on the ground that not to do so is a serious threat to their survival as an ethnic entity.

Sensitivity to the issue of the language used in the transactions of everyday life has long marked the French-Canadian outlook. "Qui perd sa langue perd sa foi" (He who loses his mother tongue loses his religious faith) was the master slogan used in the propaganda campaigns of the traditional society. Today, many thoughtful French Canadians are mulling over the question, "Will he who has lost his religious faith also lose his mother tongue?" And if the twins are thrown out with the bath water what will be left? Will the French become just another minority in the process of assimilation into the American and Anglo-Saxon mass?

The language spoken in everyday life is not only eloquent testimony of a living culture differentiated from other cultures, it is also a formidable barrier between peoples. John Porter, a Canadian sociologist, made the following observation:

> ... there is the barrier of language which can operate as effectively as color differences to reduce friendly interaction between groups. If people from two groups cannot communicate, as is the case in Canada where the French and English have been effectively out of communication with each other, then the language division is as real as that of color (Glazer and Moynihan, p. 268).

The existence and persistence of language as a barrier is in part a function of mass. Concentrations of people speaking a particular language and in intimate interaction with one another afford a convenient index both to the social strength of the language and to its prospects for survival. Where are the French-speaking Canadians? What is their distribution? Where are concentrations of them found?

The largest concentrations outside of Quebec are in the provinces of Ontario and New Brunswick. Of the 1,300,000 French Canadians outside Quebec, about 650,000 live in Ontario and 250,000 in New Brunswick (Levesque, p. 115). The 1971 Census reported that French was spoken by only 6 percent of the Ontarians of French-Canadian stock, and by 34 percent of those in New Brunswick. The latter figures have to be interpreted with care, however. In some parts of northern Ontario, almost half the population is French-speaking: and in some counties of the St. Lawrence-Ottawa river triangle, over 80 percent of the people are French-speaking (Glazer and Moynihan, p. 273). The retention of French as the language of everyday life in these instances appears to be a function of the density of French-speaking population and the relative absence of English-speaking stock.

Actually assimilation, defined as a changeover from another mother tongue to English, has been very marked in Canada:

> While those of English-speaking ethnic origin con-stituted only 45% of the population, English as the language most spoken in the home was 65%. While the non-English, non-French ethnicities made up 28% of the population, only about 12% had the same mother tongue as their ethnic origin, and only about 6% spoke their ethnic origin language most often in the home. (These figures are overall figures, including Quebec, for Canada.) The French ethnic origin showed a minor language loss, with 28% of the population reporting French ethnic origin and 25% as speaking French in the home (Glazer and Moynihan, p. 281).

By contrast to these overall figures for Canada as a whole, the degree to which French is spoken within the Province of Quebec has its bastion-like qualities. Table 7.1 (Rioux, Appendix) reveals the percentage by regions within Quebec that are French speaking.

Table 7.1.   Percentage of the Population that
is Francophone

By Regions

Regions	1961	1971
Bas-Saint-Laurent	93.3%	93.0%
Saguenay-Lac-Saint-Jean	97.2%	97.4%
Quebec	97.0%	97.0%
Trois-Rivieres	96.8%	97.2%
Cantons de l'est	89.4%	91.1%
Outaouais	81.2%	84.3%
Saguenay-Cote-Nord	79.0%	82.7%
Nord-Ouest Quebecois	88.4%	87.2%
Ile de Montreal et ile Jesus	63.9%	64.2%
Banlieue de Montreal	80.3%	74.8%
Grand-Montreal	66.4%	66.4%
Couronne Montrealaise nord	88.6%	90.0%
Couronne Montrealaise sud	86.5%	89.7%

Source: Encyclopedie du Quebec

The portent of the foregoing statistics was not lost upon
the Parti Quebecois. Option Quebec, the political tract in
which Rene Levesque and his colleagues presented their goals
and policies after their resignations from the Liberal Party,
commented on the 1961 Census figures: "Il faut voir d'abord
dans quel etat avance de   decomposition culturelles se trouvent
nos minorites" (One can see that our minorities are in an
advanced state of cultural decomposition). Referring to the
figures in Table 2 as "galloping assimilation," they noted that
some 34 percent of those of Francophone origins now spoke
only English (Levesque, pp. 115 - 116).
        The Parti Quebecois also took note of how the interests of
the French-Canadians of the other provinces, even those
retaining the mother tongue, diverged from those of Quebec.
The former stressed their collective rights, especially as to
language and education, while the latter were concerned with
exercising sovereignty and the powers of governing, objectives
viewed as unrealistic and of little interest by the former.
These considerations led the Parti Quebecois to concentrate
their efforts upon Quebec, and to leave the Francophone
minorities of the other provinces to their own devices.

Table 7.2.   Galloping Assimilation

Province	Of French Origin	French still the mother tongue	Assimilated	Percentage Assimilated
New Brunswick	232,127	210,530	21,597	9.3%
Manitoba	83,936	60,899,	23,087	27.4%
Ontario	647,941	425,302	222,639	34.3%
Saskatchewan	59,824	36,163	23,661	39.5%
Yukon Territories			966	40 %
Alberta	83,319	42,276	41,043	49.2%
P.E.I.	17,418	7,958	9,460	54.3%
Nova Scotia	87,883	39,568	48,315	54.9%
British Columbia	66,970	26,179	40,791	60.8%
Newfoundland	17,171	3,150	14,021	81.6%

Source: Census, 1961

Parenthetically, the experience of the French Canadian emigrants to the U.S. is illuminating. The Cajuns of the bayous of Louisiana survive as a curiosity, not unlike the Amish or Pennsylvania Dutch in Pennsylvania. The estimated one million New Englanders of Quebec and Acadian stock' have lost their cultural and institutional identity almost completely. Even their genealogical societies conduct their reunions and conferences in English.

The homeland, the Francophone bastion of Quebec, is, of course, the big stage upon which the fate of the French language as the language of daily use will be decided. Contemplation of possible scenarios in different ecological settings suggest great variety as to content, process, and timing. Distance and isolation are important factors in this huge province. Towns and fishing villages strung out for hundreds of miles on the Saint Lawrence, and in remote farming parishes in the interior may be French-speaking perhaps indefinitely. However, they continue to lose their young to urban centers and the luring calls of the mass media. Distance and isolation are no longer impermeable barriers to outside influences.

One fact of cardinal importance to the future of French is the centralization of the Quebec economy in metropolitan Montreal; and upwards of two million of Quebec's five million Francophones are concentrated there. They tend to live in ethnically-distinct sections and neighborhoods, and the majority of blue-collar workers in industry, commerce, and public and private service occupations conduct their work, as well as their family and social lives, in French. However, they are constantly exposed to the massive influences of the over-shadowing Anglophone ambiance, which controls status in

the marketplace, television, and sports, and which is supported by the public relations maneuvers of the mandarins of
high finance and the interlocking directorates of the multi-
national corporations.   That the modern society they have
joined carries on its larger and more important affairs in
business and the professions in English, and that the rewards
of income, power, and prestige accompanying the conduct of
these larger responsibilities are enjoyed by those who are fully
at home in English are facts of life.

The displacement of this "alien" ruling class, many of
whose members are imported from the U.S. and England to run
Quebec's branch economy, is a key objective of the Parti
Quebecois.   Those Francophones who are preparing themselves
in the CEGEP, universities, and professional and technical
schools for these higher positions are increasingly finding
bilingualism necessary and advantageous.   The language of
science, technology, engineering, and management is predominantly English.   Students speaking French and attending
lectures in French at colleges and universities in Quebec must
read and study texts and source materials in English as well
as French.

When Rene Levesque makes a pilgrimage to Wall Street he
presents his case to American financiers, and to the American
public, in English.   When Pierre Eliott Trudeau, Prime Minister
of Canada, doubles his opponent in spades, he addresses
Congress, and the American public, in English.

In short, although French will survive and make its
presence heavily and effectively felt for an indefinite period at
all levels of economic, political, and public life in Quebec,
bilingualism will gain more ground as the years go by.   In the
proximate future, French Canadians will have a greater
motivation to acquire and master a second language than
English Canadians and Americans.   In an interdependent world
that has seen the proliferation of more than a hundred new
nations since World War II, each of which has economic, political, military, and social relations with English-speaking
people, provincial unilingualism will prove increasingly
counterproductive, especially as the hitherto underdeveloped
countries share more and more of the resources of the hitherto
developed countries.

The Future Distribution of Wealth

What can be expected regarding the future allocation and
distribution of wealth, benefits, and rights among occupations
and social classes in Quebec?

From its conquest in 1759 until well into the twentieth
century, the traditional rural, theocratic society gave neither
the leaders nor the habitants reason to concern themselves

with business, trade, or the problems of the cities and development. Such matters were for the maudits anglais. However, surplus population, poverty, poor soil, and depression drove many to the cities, where they became the main-d'oeuvre, the cheap labor supply of the new factories. As the pace of industrial growth and modern technological enterprises quickened after World War I, technical, management, and enterpreneurial requirements were met by trained and highly-skilled English and imported personnel. Only the traditional professions - the clergy, the law and politics - provided opportunities of a higher order for the products of the classical Church-run educational system.

Many of the secular intellectuals who began to make their presence felt after the asbestos strike of 1949 were socialists. They were in revolt not only against the corruption and autocracy of the Duplessis era and the shortcomings of the domination of education by the Church, but against a capitalistic system controlled by outsiders. The combination of nationalism and socialist theory, and the growing sense that collectively the French and the resources of the province were being used to benefit outsiders whipped up strong reformist sentiments.

The Quiet Revolution ushered in mass support for political and economic reform, and high expectations for governmental action. Although the gains of The Quiet Revolution were, with the exception of health and welfare reforms, primarily middle class gains, the labor movement was encouraged and given hope for the future. Labor has since established mass support, and has developed aggressive leadership. However, it has yet to win as large a share of the pie as the middle class, quite large segments of which have won their benefits through collective union action.

In 1978, the labor movement is in an uneasy coalition with a moderate, liberal Parti Quebecois. Labor leaders tend to justify this alliance by saying they are pequistes for lack of something better. Currently, the breadbasket aspects of future developments have two faces. Canada's economy is depressed, with unemployment over 11 percent in Quebec; and the Canadian dollar has fallen to below 90 cents of the slipping American dollar. A flight of business from Montreal, because of Bill 101 and the uncertainties created by strong separatist sentiments, is under way. While American capital appears to be holding back on new investments in Quebec, Ontario and metropolitan Toronto appear to be making gains, both because of long-term economic shifts towards mid-continent and because they represent greater security. No political party can long maintain a favorable public image under these conditions.

The more immediate threat is to the ruling Liberal Party of Prime Minister Trudeau. Its fate will be decided by federal elections, probably within a year. The Liberal Party holds

only two trump cards, but they are face cards: one is the
weakness and inept leadership of the Conservative Party; the
second is Prime Minister Trudeau, a man of stature, who is
seen as perhaps the only leader capable of keeping Quebec in
Canada and forcing the separatists to the conference table.

An election will not be held in Quebec before 1980.
There will be at least one referendum in 1979, and perhaps
more, on separatist sentiment in the province. The outcome of
a contest between the Liberal Party and the Parti Quebecois is
unpredictable at this time. The clash between Claude Ryan
and Rene Levesque promises to be a championship fight of
heroic proportions between two gifted and widely-respected
leaders.

Reflecting upon possible future developments, we are
inclined to favor the view that the outcome of the election may
not be as crucial as many are inclined to believe. Daniel
Johnson, after leading the Union nationale back into power in
1966, carried out the Liberal Party's reforms in education and
welfare, and carried the fight over provincial prerogatives to
Ottawa with greater vigor and skill than his predecessor,
Lesage. Claude Ryan and the Liberal Party could be expected
to continue the thrust for French language schools and for
French as the language of work. Negotiations would be
carried on with the unions. The main thrust in relations with
Ottawa would be to seek changes in the Federal constitution
that would give greater rights to Quebec.

The Parti Quebecois would continue to press for sovereignty and autonomy for Quebec. It could be expected to
continue to work toward establishing itself as the Quebec
government built upon the strong nationalist sentiments of
conservatives, liberals, and radicals alike. It could be expected to nationalize sectors of the economy and continue to
refurbish the public image of old nationalistic heroes of the
past; it recently retrieved a statue of Duplessis from a ware-
house and set it up before l'Assemblee Nationale. Relationships between the government and labor unions would be
uneasy and difficult, and confrontations would be the norm.

Led by a vigorous, leftist leadership, labor union pressure for a larger slice of the pie can be expected to continue. Should economic conditions deteriorate further, or
remain poor into the 1980s, the fate that befell the Union
nationale when it dropped to the status of a small minority
party could become that of the Liberal Party as well. Disenchantment with government and politicians is not a feeling to
which Quebec and Quebecers are immune. Should that become
general, all bets and predictions are off. Short of that, we
do not exclude a continued movement similar to that of the
past decade, but further to the left. The Parti Quebecois
could become the party of the middle class. A new labor
party representing blue-collar workers and white-collar service

employees might emerge.

Leon Dion, Quebec's distinguished political scientist and perceptive commentator on the Quebec scene has expressed our inclination well.   In this new order, "listening to society's humblest and most under-privileged ranks" is crucial:

> The pioneer farmers of the lower Saint-Lawrence and the Gaspe Peninsula, clinging to their woodlots and their rocky soil, the people of the forgotten slums of Montreal, Quebec, and other cities ... just as in Ancient Greece the culture of the slaves and not that of the masters carried the day in giving rise to the Stoic values upon which Roman civilization and subsequently western civilizations were largely built, so today we must look towards the poor for pointers to the values that may guide us in choosing sound commitments (Dion, p. 207).

NOTE

The English translations of passages from French sources are the author's unless otherwise indicated.

BIBLIOGRAPHY

Adams, J.T.   The Founding of New England.   Boston: Little, Brown, 1930.

Dion, Leon.   Quebec, The Unfinished Revolution.   Montreal: McGill-Queen's University Press, 1976.

Glazer, Nathan and Daniel P. Moynihan. Ethnicity: Theory and Experience.   Cambridge: Harvard University Press, 1975.

Hamon, E.   Les Canadiens-francais de la Nouvelle Angleterre. Quebec: N.S. Hardy, 1891.

Hansen, M. and J.B. Brebner.   The Mingling of the Canadian and American People.   New Haven: Yale University Press, 1940.

Hemon Louis.   Maria Chapdelaine.   Paris: Artheme Fayard et Cie, 1930.

Hughes, Everett, C.   French Canada In Transition.   Chicago: University of Chicago Press, 1943.

Langlois, O. Histoire de la population Canadian-Francaise. Montreal: Levesque, 1934.

Levesque, Rene.   Option Quebec.   Montreal: Les editions de
l'homme, 1968.

McRoberts K. and D. Posgate.   Quebec, Social Change and
Political Crisis.   Toronto: McClelland and Stewart, 1976.

Milner, H. and S.H. Milner.   The Decolonization of Quebec.
Toronto: McClelland and Stewart, 1973.

Miner, Horace.   St. Denis, A French-Canadian Parish.   Chicago: The University of Chicago, 1939.

Rioux, Marcel.   La Question du Quebec.   Paris: Seghers,
1971.

_____.   Les Quebecois.   Paris: Seuil, 1974.

Robert, Jean-Claude.   Du Canada francais au Quebec Libre.
Paris: Flammarion, 1975.

Toynbee, Arnold J.   A Study of History.   London: Oxford
University Press, 1934.

Tremblay, Marc-Adelard and Gerald Fortin.   Les comportements
economiques de la famille salariee du Quebec.   Quebec: Presses
de l'Universite Laval, 1964.

Wade, Mason.   The French Canadians, 1760 - 1945.   Toronto:
Macmillan, 1955.

_____.   Canadian Dualism.   Toronto: University of Toronto
Press, 1960.

III

Autonomy and Ethnicity in Europe

Introduction

States have the legal authority to establish and regulate their internal social arrangements. Frequently this authority is used to control diverse ethnic groups through the designation of majority-minority groups, which is sure to be followed by a pattern of dominant-subordinant relations. In Europe, this pattern stems from the fact that in the not-too-distant past ethnic groups occupied specific territory as nationality groups; only under the (nation) state did they become national minorities. Hence, adjustments in group status can be attributed directly to changes initiated by the state to expedite its rule. Not surprisingly, some ethnic groups react against state-imposed social and political arrangements that threaten traditional order. The best evidence of ethnic perception of state-imposed arrangements as inimical to ethnic traditional social arrangements is found in movements for autonomy.

In Europe today, as in most developed parts of the world, state control over ethnic relations is modified by transnational military, political, and economic organizations aimed at larger and newer forms of international cooperation. The importance of transnational organizations centers around their potential impact on the internal socio-political dynamics of industrial states. Examples of these supranational organizations include the North Atlantic Treaty Organization (NATO), the organization for the Economic Development and Cooperation (OECD), the European Economic Community (EEC), and the European Free Trade Association (EFTA). In addition to these military and economic transnational organizations, there are multinational corporations (MNCs), a special kind of transnational economic organization.

Transnational organizations and cooperation among European states are the result of modernization and devel-

opment. Although these organizations have the potential for
altering internal political arrangements in individual states, it
is believed that the overall benefits of cooperation in transnational organizations far outweigh the cost of potential minor
alternations in internal policy.

It should follow that increased cooperation among developed European states occurs because of a high degree of
internal cohesion and a low level of ethnic conflict among
diverse groups. However, although the intensity of ethnic
conflict varies from place to place, movements for ethnic
autonomy abound. The persistence of these movements centers
around historical and geographic factors in dynamic interaction
with cultural, linguistic, religious, and economic variables.
Each author in this section combines the different variables in
various ways, placing emphasis on those considered most important in the particular analysis of ethnic autonomy under
discussion.

The first two chapters in this section treat two forms of
conflict in the United Kingdom. The United Kingdom is comprised of Northern Ireland and Britain; Britain itself includes
England, Scotland, and Wales; the Act of Union in 1536 combined Wales and England and the Treaty of Union of 1707
merged Scotland and England. Although the United Kingdom
operates as a unitary political system, it is also characterized
by a form of decentralization that allows local control of
socio-cultural and other effective group values. The Scots,
Welsh, and English are different ethnic groups, with the
English dominant. Britain has a relatively long history as a
unitary state, but that does not mean that it has operated
without regard to ethnic differences.

It is no mere accident that, certain aspects of devolution
notwithstanding, economic control is retained in London. Consequently, except for Northern Ireland where religious differences, with an undercurrent of ethnic animosity, are the
prime causes of conflict, Welsh and Scottish autonomy-oriented
action is a reaction to the economic domination of the English.
However, it should be clear that these self-determination
efforts are not based solely on ethnic differences. This
section begins with Curran's chapter on Northern Ireland.

Separatism in Northern Ireland is the outgrowth of a
long-lived, entho-religious conflict. That conflict began almost
four centuries ago, when the Protestant colonists from Britain
first clashed with the Catholic natives of Ireland's northern
province of Ulster. Fearing and despising Irish Catholics,
most Protestants stubbornly opposed their nationalist efforts to
win freedom from British rule. When Irish separatists finally
achieved that goal after World War I, Ulster Protestants demanded exclusion from the Irish Free State, which has since
evolved into the Irish Republic. The six counties of northeast
Ulster, whose population remains almost 70 percent Protestant,

became the British substate of Northern Ireland with a Parliament to manage local affairs. Using Home Rule to maintain their ascendancy and to perpetuate a caste-bound society, Protestants systematically discriminated against Northern Ireland's large nationalist minority.

In the late 1960s, however, Catholics launched a campaign demanding equal rights. The Protestants' violent reaction was predicated on the belief that the Catholics wanted to subvert Northern Ireland and merge it with the Irish Republic. Communal riots forced the British government to send in troops to restore order in 1969, and further violence led it to suspend Home Rule in 1972. Since then, British efforts to establish an executive in which power is shared by Protestants and Catholics have been frustrated by both camps, and direct rule from London continues.

Although religion is the root of Ulster's problem, the conflict is not simply one of rival theologies. It is religion as a badge of ethnic identity that divides the two communities so deeply. To an extent unknown elsewhere in the Western World, religious allegiance determines one's values, attitudes, and actions in Northern Ireland. Historically, Catholicism is an integral part of Irish nationalism; however, Protestantism plays an ever larger role in the heritage of those whose ancestors colonized Ulster. The separatist ideal of an all-Ireland Republic has a strong appeal for Northern Catholics. And the demands of Protestant ultras for an independent Northern Ireland, in which their caste would enjoy a permanent monopoly of power, spring from a heritage which equates ethnocentrism with religion. With politics and society polarized, attempts at compromise have proved abortive. Curran believes that not only is it impossible to create a just and democratic society within Northern Ireland's present framework, but neither is Catholic nor Protestant separatism possible. If Catholic and Protestant separatism is ruled out, and attempts at structural reform level have failed, what possible solution remains? The only answer appears to be repartition and population transfers. This proposal goes to the heart of the problem by separating two communities whose irreconcilable traditions have bedeviled the history of Ulster, Ireland, and Britain for centuries. The idea deserves serious consideration by all parties concerned.

The selection by Furniss pays particular attention to the political component of Scottish nationality. From the very beginning of its union with England, Scotland has had most of the requisites of a separate state; only its political institutions were merged. It retained its own legal system, educational structure, national church, culinary traditions, national sports, and general popular culture. In short, Furniss observes that "when we combine geographical separation with a past independent political existence, unique and guaranteed institutions of religion, law, and education, a pervasive popular culture, and regionally-oriented media, it is not surprising that Scots perceive themselves as different from other peoples living in the British Isles."

Why, in light of the virtual independence of the Scottish "periphery" from the English "center," should Scottish nationalism emerge now? Furniss argues that the political manifestations of Scottish nationalism stem from the "center's" reactions to external pressure in the EEC for exports. The center in turn pressures its periphery to produce those goods that are politically and economically beneficial to the state, and the periphery demands a bolstering of its own economic position.

What these pressures and counter pressures mean essentially is that Scotland, although it fares relatively well economically in the United Kingdom, is, nevertheless, controlled economically by England. With around 40 percent of its work force in large companies headquartered elsewhere, and with the development of North Sea oil, Scotland is clearly dependent on external economic developments to maintain its economic viability. Hence, the political component of Scottish nationalism is aimed - and Furniss emphasizes this point - not at separatism per se, but at more economic autonomy within the structure of the unitary British state.

On the European continent, Heiberg examines the Basque movement for autonomy in Spain. Basque nationalism is one of the most emotionally-energetic and historically-persistent examples of an ethnic nationalist movement in Western Europe. On one level the Basque problem is but a special case of the perennial Spanish problem of regionalism, but it is a very peculiar case.   When Basque nationalism first emerged in industrialized Bilbao in the 1890s, the Basques were, as they still are, an economically-advantaged group. Moreover, the Basque political and financial elite were an integral part of the wider Spanish elite, and most of the nationalist leaders - if education and language are used as indicators - were culturally more akin to other Spaniards than to their rural Basque counterparts.

Since the 1890s the social base of the nationalist movement, given specific variations, has remained essentially the same. This base consists of those sectors of the Basque middle and petty bourgeoisie who have been marginal to the main thrust of industrialization. Thus they have been economically and politically threatened by, and trapped between, their two main protagonists, the immigrant proletariat and the Basque financial oligarchy.

Heiberg argues that Basque nationalism is based on two fundamental ideological assumptions: first, historically and culturally the Basques and, therefore, the Basque country constitute a "nation"; second, this Basque nation is sovereign

and must be governed by Basques. Basque nationalism divides
the inhabitants of the Basque country into Basque and anti-
Basques;   the   former   are   viewed   as   the   defenders   and
legitimate inheritors of the Basque nation, and the latter as its
enemies.   For   political   purposes,   descent   has   never   been
regarded by the Basques as a sufficient criterion for ethnic
inclusion, or exclusion.   Instead, "Basqueness" is measured in
terms of adherence to certain morally-loaded political and social
prescriptions.   A Basque is anyone of either Basque or immigrant origin who is a Basque nationalist; an anti-Basque is
anyone who is not.   Basque nationalism, in sum, is an attempt
by specific sectors of Basque society to impose via the logic of
nationalism an economic, political, and cultural hegemony over
all of Basque society.   Finally, Heiberg believes that "at the
root of Basque nationalist symbols - lies a profound cultural
crisis and conflict."

The selection by Beer addresses the problem of the re-
appearance of ethnic activism in modern France. He uses both
historical and theoretical approaches to explain this resurgence
of ethnicity.   Historically, the essential dialectic from the 1789
Revolution to the present was that ethnic regions were politically opposed to whatever centralized Jacobian-Francophone
government was in power in Paris.   Thus, in the nineteenth
century, when Paris was Republican, ethnic regionalism was
Royalist; in the interwar period, when Paris was Socialist,
ethnic activism moved toward Fascism. Now that the present
government in Paris is center-right, the ethnic activists have
taken a leftist stance.   Beer discusses the factors that precipitated the most recent ethnic rebirth: the loss of Indochina
and Algeria led to the idea that part of France could be detached, government attempts at decentralization and Socialist-
Communist promises of regional autonomy inspired regional
awareness, the Common Market was accompanied by a decline
in the importance of national boundaries, and the demonstration of other ethnic activist movements in the modern world
had an effect on the French.

Beer's theoretical explanation stems from the theories of
internal colonialism and rising expectations.   The former
argues that there will be a negative association between levels
of socioeconomic development and ethnic political militancy; the
latter suggests a positive association between rates of improvement of socioeconomic indicators and the levels of ethnic
political militancy. Beer argues that both theories should be
modified: "Although there is partial confirmation of both
hypotheses, in neither case is the evidence strong enough to
warrant   the   conclusion   that   these   theoretical   formulations
answer all the questions about the rebirth of ethnic activism in
France and other industrial societies."

Lindgren's chapter deals with racial and ethnic autonomy
in the Soviet Union.   The Soviet Union is comprised of ap-

proximately 100 nationalities, with the Great Russians accounting for about 52 percent of the population. In recent years, national minorities have become an increasing cause for concern to Soviet leaders; not only do they make up 48 percent of the population, but they have substantially higher birth rates than the Great Russians. Moreover, they have become openly critical of Soviet nationality policies, a fact that has caused the Soviet leadership much embarrassment in light of the recent Helsinki Agreements on Human Rights. Of particular concern to the Soviets have been the Central Asians. The Central Asians are Turkic peoples of the Muslim religion who inhabit an area of strategic importance along the Chinese border. When first brought into the Russian Empire in the latter half of the 19th century, the Central Asians were treated as colonial dependencies and their societies were left virtually intact.

After the Revolution of 1917, however, Stalin instituted a program of Russification that had the forcible assimilation of the Central Asians into Soviet society as its primary goal. Ironically, one outcome of Russification was to foster a sense of national consciousness among Central Asians where none had formerly existed. Today, fearful that such consciousness could be encouraged by countries across the border, the Soviets have encouraged Russian immigration into the area. Hence, Lindgren concludes that "the Central Asians face the dilemma of whether to assimilate and enjoy the material benefits of Soviet society, or to retain their cultural identity at the risk of remaining isolated from the Soviet mainstream."

8 Separatism in Northern Ireland

Joseph Curran

Like everything else in Northern Ireland, separatism is either Catholic or Protestant as the result of a history that differs sharply from the rest of Ireland. The divergence began almost four centuries ago when Ulster resisted England's conquest of Ireland and was crushed. That defeat heralded the birth of modern Ulster. Confiscating the lands of rebel chieftains, the Crown colonized them with Scots and English settlers, thereby establishing the only large-scale plantation on the island. All the colonists were Protestants, and most were hard-bitten Scottish Presbyterians. The clash of Calvinism and Catholicism rocked Europe to its foundations in the Reformation era, but nowhere were the consequences of this confrontation so tragically enduring as in Ireland's northern province. From the start of the plantation, religion was the main dividing line between settlers and natives, and it remains so today.

Competition for land heightened sectarian antagonism, and it was not until the end of the seventeenth century that the Ulster plantation and the conquest of Ireland were finally made secure. The victory of the Protestant champion, William of Orange, over his Catholic rival, James II, left the Catholics leaderless, almost landless, and saddled with a savage penal code that reduced them to abject servitude for more than a century. In the eighteenth century, a sense of common grievances brought hope for a Catholic-Protestant alliance against English misrule. This hope was fostered by the growth of secular attitudes during the Enlightenment, and by the American and French Revolutions with their democratic and egalitarian ideals; but it was blighted by a heritage of sectarian strife. When rebellion finally did erupt in 1798, it was primarily the Catholics who revolted, and the excesses committed by both government forces and insurgents confirmed religious animosity.

In an effort to ensure English security and allay Irish
discontent, the British government secured a parliamentary
union between the two countries in 1800. The creation of a
United Kingdom not only did not accomplish these objectives,
but it widened the gulf between Ulster and the rest of Ireland. Rapid industrialization during the nineteenth century
increased Ulster's prosperity and tightened its economic ties to
Britain. In the same period, the striking success of the
Evangelical revival intensified Protestant opposition to Roman
Catholicism, helping to cement an alliance of Episcopalians and
Presbyterians against Popery in politics as well as religion.
When Irish leaders mounted a popular nationalist movement that
was supported by the Catholic clergy, Protestant Ulster would
have no part of it. Even the limited measure of constitutional
autonomy sought by most nationalists was an anathema to
Ulster loyalists, who equated Home Rule with "Rome Rule" and
the economic ruin of their province. Their stubborn opposition to Home Rule in the years just before World War I
convulsed the United Kingdom, weakened the cause of moderate
nationalism in Ireland, and helped revive separatism.

In 1916, a separatist insurrection in Dublin started a
five-year struggle for national independence. Although the
rebels were not able to win recognition for an Irish Republic,
they did gain independence within the British Commonwealth,
and this Dominion status opened the way for a peaceful advance to the Republic. The price of freedom was partition;
under the terms of the 1921 Anglo-Irish Treaty, six counties
of Northeast Ulster were excluded from the Irish Free State
and remained part of the United Kingdom.(1)

At the time of its creation, Northern Ireland was given a
local Parliament to administer internal affairs. For almost half
a century, the Unionist governments used this Parliament to
perpetuate both partition and the subordination of a large
nationalist minority. The irreconcilable differences between
the two communities were aptly summarized in a recent British
White Paper:

> A fundamental problem since the earliest years
> of Northern Ireland's existence has been the dis-
> agreement not just about how Northern Ireland
> should be governed, but as to whether it should
> continue to exist at all. Those in Northern Ireland
> who have supported its continued membership of the
> United Kingdom have seen themselves as faced by
> an unremitting campaign to discredit and dismantle
> the constitutional system. Their opponents, on the
> other hand, have claimed that valid political op-
> position has been treated as subversion, and used
> as a pretext to exclude them from any share of real
> power or influence in Northern Ireland's affairs.(2)

Denied equal rights, Catholics were unable to prevent discrimination in voting, housing, and jobs. Their unemployment and emigration rates remained consistently higher than those of Protestants. They were also denied any emotional gratification by the regime. While Protestants enthusiastically commemorated past triumphs and celebrated their version of history, Catholic attempts to honor the nationalist tradition were suppressed by the government and its supporters. Sullenly, the minority complied with the laws, by withheld allegiance from the regime. Eager to avoid any further involvement in Irish affairs, British governments refused to investigate complaints of injustice in Northern Ireland. The government in Dublin was no better. Although its leaders regularly denounced the inequity of partition, they did little to aid their co-religionists north of the border.

Events in the 1960s produced a confrontation that tore Northern Ireland apart. American civil rights protests, witnessed on television around the world, sparked similar action in Ulster. Although the origins of the Irish civil rights movement were neither sectarian nor separatist, ultra-loyalists such as the Reverend Ian Paisley saw it as the thin end of the Roman-Republican wedge. The regime's cautious efforts to appease the protesters only made them more militant, and roused Protestant extremists to violent action. In August 1969, sectarian riots in Londonderry and Belfast forced the British to intervene militarily to protect Catholics and restore order. To resolve the problem, the British government pressed for a policy of reform that would end discrimination. However, Protestant opposition and continued disorder frustrated this effort, and rough treatment by the military alienated the Catholic community. Although purporting to defend Catholics against Protestant violence, the illegal Irish Republican Army soon moved to attack British troops in order to force their withdrawal and open the way to unification with the Republic.

Internment of suspected Catholic subversives in August, 1971 triggered a rapid escalation of violence. Belatedly realizing that a political solution was impossible under the existing regime, the British suspended Home Rule in March 1972 and resumed direct control of Northern Ireland's affairs. A British initiative in 1973 was supported by Protestant and Catholic moderates, and led to the creation of a power-sharing executive with representatives from both communities. Nevertheless, Protestants grew increasingly fearful of the implications of this experiment; within a year, it was wrecked by a general strike fomented by ultra-loyalists. Since 1974, extremists in both camps have blocked efforts to end the constitutional stalemate; meanwhile, the death toll has risen to over 1800 persons. Throughout the crisis, the Republic has sought to avoid direct involvement. Having no wish for a

united Ireland if it means civil war, the Dublin government's
main preoccupation has been to prevent violence from crossing
the border.

While religion is the real source of conflict in Northern
Ireland, the clash is not one of rival theologies. Despite
controversy over the Papacy, the two communities share
generally conservative views on doctrine, and both deplore
social permissiveness. The real division stems from religion as
a cultural force and a badge of ethnic identity. To an extent
unknown elsewhere in the Western world, religion determines
one's way of life in Northern Ireland. Its influence in such
matters as marriage, social relationships, residence, education,
employment, recreation, and, of course, politics if far greater
than that of any other factor. A man may renounce his faith,
but he cannot easily escape a heritage which has decisively
shaped his values and attitudes. For a Catholic, religion is an
integral part of Irish nationalism, something inextricably joined
with the history of a persecuted and oppressed people
struggling for liberation. For a Protestant, religion is even
more important because of a confusion over national identity
that leaves him unsure whether he is British, Irish, or
Ulsterman.(3)   His religious heritage resolves this ambiguity;
it makes him the heir of those whose swords and Bibles overcame the forces of barbarism and superstition to civilize
Ulster. In the "black North" of Ireland, as in the Middle
East, religion is what distinguishes "us" from "them,"
especially for Protestants.

Yet even though religion is the principal symbol of
national identity in Ireland, neither Catholics nor Protestants
have been willing to entrust political leadership to churchmen,
fearing that they would betray their communal heritage out of
misguided notions about peace and brotherhood. Thus, it is
not surprising that separatism has been a recurring theme in
Irish history, despite the Catholic hierarchy's outspoken
opposition to its violent methods. Although the tradition of
armed resistance to English rule reaches deep into Ireland's
past, Republicanism did not surface until the close of the
eighteenth century, when the Society of United Irishmen
sought to forge an alliance of Irishmen of all creeds to expel
the English. The rebels of 1798 failed to win independence,
but the dream of an Irish Republic persisted, and was given
new life in 1858 by the Irish Republican Brotherhood. Although its initial attempts at revolution proved dismal failures,
the IRB survived, and its leaders planned the 1916 uprising
that began the all-out struggle for national freedom. Five
years later, the revolution culminated in a settlement that
conferred virtual independence on most of Ireland. Most
nationalists welcomed the Treaty of 1921, but many separatists,
notably those in the Irish Republican Army, denounced it as a
betrayal of the Republic. This dispute resulted in a civil war

between nationalists, from which the pro-Treaty forces emerged victorious. Yet, even in defeat, the separatist ideal retained a powerful appeal, which brought it to realization in the next generation. By declaring the Irish state a Republic in 1949, the Dublin government hoped to "take the gun out of politics" by pacifying extreme separatists. However, this was impossible as long as partition remained.

Although internal dissension and loss of popular support had left the IRA moribund by the 1960s, its fortunes were speedily revived by the troubles in the North. With the aid of money and guns from sympathizers at home and abroad, the IRA's militant Provisional Wing waged a guerrilla war against the British. It helped to topple the Unionist regime in 1972, and obstructed efforts to work out a compromise settlement. Nevertheless, the British refused to withdraw their troops, and indiscriminate terrorism eventually cost the Provos Catholic support. Despite the IRA's claim that British evacuation would lead Protestants to accept the inevitability of a united Ireland, the incidence of sectarian murders in the North lends weight to the argument that British withdrawal would set off full-scale civil war.

A more socially-conscious brand of Republicanism is represented by the Official IRA. Disillusioned by their failure to "liberate" the North through the guerrilla campaign of 1956-62, some IRA leaders changed their approach to the problem. They called for intensive efforts to educate workers in both parts of Ireland to militant class-consciousness, asserting that, once this was done, both Orange and Green capitalism could be overthrown and an all-Ireland Socialist Republic established. The Marxist ideology of this program, and its supporters' cautious attitude toward the use of terrorism in the Northern crisis precipitated a split in the IRA in January 1970. Since then, the Provisional faction has gained ascendancy by its ruthless tactics, and the Officials have exerted little influence on events. Like other Republican-Labor groups formed during the last half-century, the official IRA recognizes the limitations of political terrorism, but has failed to grasp that economic issues in Northern Ireland are secondary to nationalism and religion. Protestant workers are unwilling to surrender their privileged political position for economic advantage, while their Catholic counterparts refuse to barter their nationalist allegiance for economic benefits alone. The struggle remains one of castes rather than classes.

Since Ireland was partitioned, moderate nationalists in Northern Ireland have tried to find a via media between Unionism and physical-force Republicanism. To this end, they supported non-violent separatism or unification by consent, but this idea made little headway with Protestants. The Social Democratic and Labor Party, founded in 1970, has sought to unite all opposition to the Unionist regime on a non-sectarian basis.   The party's ultimate aim is an all-Ireland Republic; but, until this idea wins majority consent in both parts of the country, the SDLP is committed to power-sharing and social justice within Northern Ireland.   Despite its pledge of allegiance to the substate, the party has been unable to attract a significant number of Protestants, nor does it exert any control over the IRA; both factions have their own political organizations.   Since the collapse of the coalition executive in 1974, the SDLP has played a minor role.

Protestant separatism is of more recent vintage than that of the Catholics.   It first appeared on the eve of World War I during the heated controversy over Home Rule.   Loyalists saw nothing wrong in defying the government and threatening armed revolt to maintain the Anglo-Irish Union.   Their minimum demand was exclusion from the proposed Dublin Parliament, coupled with hints of secession if it were not met. Exactly how this threat was to be made good was never spelled out, but it served its purpose; and, once the loyalists' position was safeguarded by partition, nothing more was heard of separatism.   The idea was revived when Britain suspended Home Rule in 1972, and made clear that its restoration was conditional upon some sort of power-sharing with Catholics. Ultra-loyalists have never really trusted the British, whom they fear would gladly sell them out to obtain an Irish settlement.   No doubt, some ultras wish they could follow the example set by Rhodesia in 1965 and "go it alone," but such a move would pose insuperable problems: without continuing massive subsidies from Britain, which now amount to almost a billion dollars a year, Ulster's sagging economy would collapse completely; also, a Protestant regime could not maintain order without the British army, and declaring independence would almost certainly lead to confrontation with the British, as well as with the IRA, the Catholic minority, and the armed forces of the Republic.   No Protestant junta could survive such a clash.   The perils of independence are so obvious that threats on this score cannot be taken seriously by any but the most fanatic ultras.

If both Catholic and Protestant separatism are ruled out, and attempts at structural reform have failed, what possible solution to the Ulster problem remains?   The only answer appears to be repartition and population transfers.   Redrawing the border to make it follow religious-political divisions as closely as possible would detach predominantly Catholic areas west of the Bann River.   Those Protestants who chose not to live in the Republic could be resettled east of the Benn.   At the same time, Catholics in Belfast would be moved from their vulnerable ghettos to new homes in the Republic, Britain, or overseas.   Such a plan would involve the resettlement of no more than 300,000 people out of 1.5 million.   It would leave Northern Ireland a smaller, but much more homogeneous entity, with a Catholic minority of 10 percent instead of 35 percent.   In addition to making the substate more viable in every respect, it would reduce its political and economic liability as a part of the United Kingdom, and would give the Republic control of land and people it has justly claimed for generations.   This proposal goes to the heart of the problem by separating two communities whose irreconcilable traditions have bedeviled the history of Ulster, Ireland, and Britain for centuries.   As the one kind of separatism that might work, the idea   deserves   serious   consideration   by   all   parties concerned.(4)

NOTES

1. Originally, loyalists laid claim to all nine counties of Ulster, but Protestants had a majority of only 200,000 in the province as a whole.   Unionist leaders, therefore, withdrew   their   claim   to   the   counties   of   Donegal, Monaghan,   and   Cavan,   all   of   which   contained   overwhelming nationalist majorities.   This left the Protestants with a two-to-one majority in the six counties that make up Northern Ireland.   Despite a higher Catholic birth rate in the last half-century, the Protestants have maintained that majority because more Catholics have emigrated.   At present, Catholics number slightly more than one-third of Northern Ireland's 1.5 million people.   In this article, I have followed common practice in using "Ulster" as a synonym for Northern Ireland, although, strictly speaking, this is inaccurate because three of the province's nine counties belong to the Republic.
2. United Kingdom, Northern Ireland Constitutional Proposals (White Paper).   Cmnd 5259, March, 1973, pp. 24-25.
3. Richard   Rose,   Governing without Consensus, An Irish Perspective (Boston, 1971), pp. 205-209, 485.   Rose's work is a very valuable study of attitudes in Northern Ireland on the eve of the civil rights upheaval, and is essential reading for anyone interested in the subject.
4. For a fuller discussion of this idea, see Joseph M. Curran, "Ulster Repartition: A Possible Answer?" America (New York), January 31, 1976, pp. 66-68.

9 The Political Component of Scottish Nationality

Norman Furniss

Scotland has long had most of the common attributes of a separate nation. Unlike many of the participants in the current nationalist revival in Europe, including Wales, Scotland has had a distinct and recognized identity as an independent state. All Scottish children are taught that this independence has been maintained primarily through foreign alliances and wars against England. Moreover, the Union of 1707 between Scotland and England was not the result of conquest, but a formal treaty ratified by each parliament. Under the provisions of the Treaty, only political institutions were merged; Scotland retained, and still retains, her separate and divergent legal system, educational structure, and national church. With one minor exception, Scottish laws are independent of the law courts in the rest of Britain, a status that "gives the Scottish legal system more independence than the legal systems of federal states," including the United States (Kellas, 1975). Scotland had a public educational system two centuries before such a thing was even seriously contemplated in England; from the outset, education in Scotland was regarded as a tool for social and economic advancement, in sharp contrast to the ascriptive values prevalent in England until well into the twentieth century. The Church of Scotland, with around 40 percent of the adult population as communicants, was established on very different theological bases from the Church of England. Scotland also has about twice the percentage of Catholics as England.

Besides these institutional bases of nationality, Scotland has a strong popular culture, with her own organizations and enthusiasms in sports, her own tradition of food and drink, her own poets and writers, and her own popular symbols - the tartan, the bagpipe, the cross of St. Andrew. Mass communications show a similar, albeit less compartmentalized,

152

pattern: the Scottish BBC has its own administrative structure and program schedule; and most of the popular newspapers are published in Scotland, where the "elite" often read the (Edinburgh) Scotsman and the Glasgow Herald instead of the Times and Guardian. Finally, it should be noted that the geographical distance between the major population centers of England and Scotland - again unlike Wales - has helped reduce the population flow from south to north and has furthered the retention of a Scottish, as opposed to an English, identity.(1) A recent survey reported that 82 percent of the respondents had lived in Scotland all their lives. This was the highest "regional" response in Britain, and compared with 62 percent for the state as a whole. Those who had lived in Scotland ten years or more comprised 97 percent of respondents, also the highest in Britain (Commission on the Constitution, Table 31).

When geographical separation is combined with a past independent political existence, unique and guaranteed institutions of religion, law, and education, a pervasive popular culture, and regionally-oriented media, it is not surprising that the Scots perceive themselves as different from other peoples living in the British Isles. In France, the fact that many Bretons do not consider themselves "French" above all else is proclaimed with astonishment and alarm;(2) in Britain, the fact that over two-thirds of Scottish respondents think of themselves as "Scots" rather than "British" or "English" is a mere routine confirmation that Britain is indeed a "multi-national state" (Rose, p. 57). In 1966, a more politically-significant survey asked whether the respondents had more in common with Englishmen of their own class or with Scots of the opposite class. The former has chosen by 19 percent of the sample; the latter, by 56 percent (Miller, 1977, p. 84). In sum, Scotland has a strong sense of nationality, with at least latent political implications.

NATIONALITY AT BAY

Despite the strong sense of nationality, there has been a progressive atrophy of much of the Scottish national inheritance. The decline is seen clearly in the institutional legacy of the union and in culture. The "angilicization" and loss of vitality of the Scottish legal system have been vividly detailed by Smith (1965, pp. 39-57). Any differences in law most often concern parochialisms that Westminister has not the time to correct, or "Victorian" social sentiments on drink or homosexuality that have been revised in England but are deemed better left undisturbed and unenforced north of the border. The social authority of the Church of Scotland was challenged on more "traditional" principles by the establishment

of the United Secession Church in 1820 and the Free Church
of Scotland in 1843. Reunification 80 years later occurred in a
more secular age. However, even before 1800, the Church of
Scotland was moving away from puritanism toward a theological
position "very similar" to that of the English Church (Smout,
1969, p. 230). And educational initiative has declined to such
an extent that England is now seen as a font of innovative
reforms (Furniss, 1976, pp. 461-462).

The cultural decline has been even more extensive. In
the eighteenth century, Scotland was a major center of Enlightenment. However, the legacy of Ferguson, Hume, and
Smith was not renewed, and the nineteenth century saw a
progressive slide to the mawkishness of the "Kailyard" school
with its celebration of the small town sage.(3) Popular culture
has become firmly identified with kilt and bagpipe, and this
cultural climate has not been greatly improved or exposed by
Scottish media, which have tended to be more cautious and
more decorous than their English counterparts.   "Television
reporters in particular, on crossing the Border, found that
the Scottish BBC expected them to conform to a more respectful, less radical, form of behavior" (Hood, 1970, p. 202).
Small wonder that for many observers the real question "is not
whether an independent Scotland would be viable but whether
it would be bearable" (Marwick, p. 31).

Nor should the distinctiveness of social and economic
conditions in Scotland be exaggerated. Although Scots eat
more starch and drink more whiskey than Englishmen and are
twice as likely to live in council (public) housing, and although their gross domestic product per head is slightly below
the United Kingdom average, these differences are far less
pronounced than regional variations found in France, Italy, or
the United States. In socio-economic terms, the Scots are
more "like" the English than any other nation. "Modernization," in the sense of increasing social and economic development and identity, has had the further, and not necessarily
inevitable, consequence of markedly reducing Scotland's
control of her own economy.

The Political Manifestation of Separate
National Identity

The political component of Scottish nationality seems out
of phase with the pattern outlined above. After the Union, at
a time when national institutions were strong and philosophy
was flowering in Scotland, the nation was integrated within a
unitary state with no separate political forum for the expression of Scottish sentiment. Most Scots were unmoved;
and the few who did urge a renewal of national political
identity spent a large amount of energy quarreling among

themselves. For over 250 years, they failed to project a reasonable public image, or to rally a significant following. A nationalist, writing in the 1920's, described the situation:

> The general movement in favor of a national rebirth has attracted some of the most generous spirits in Scotland - and many of the greatest cranks in Christendon....

> We have people who want all Scotland to speak the Gaelic .... Some hark back to the hope of a sixteenth-century Scotland regained, others suggest a national approchement with France, still others a Jacobite restoration.... All is hubbub, outcry, chaos. There is no chart, no plan, nothing approaching a serious, practical Scotsman-like policy in either art or politics (Hanham, pp. 154-55).

Only in the last ten years has there been growth of a serious political movement based on Scotland and Scottish concerns. Most striking has been the rise of the Scottish National Party, whose policy statement, "The Democratic Road," outlines the party's aspirations (Scots Independent, March 1977):

> a) Self-Government for Scotland--that is, the restoration of Scottish national sovereignty by the establishment of a democratic Scottish Parliament within the Commonwealth, freely elected by the Scottish electors, whose authority will be limited only by such agreements as may be freely entered into by it with other nations or states or international organizations for the purpose of furthering international co-operation and world peace.

> b) The furtherance of all Scottish interests.

As can be seen in the table 9.1, the SNP has risen from obscurity to a position where it is a major contender for Scottish votes. In the October 1974 general election, the SNP finished second to labor, which received 36.3 percent of the votes, and well ahead of the Conservative and Liberal Parties, which received 24.7 percent and 8.3 percent, respectively. Under Britain's "first past the post" electoral system, the SNP won the eleven constituencies in which its candidates finished first. In the most recent election, SNP vote declined, and the number of parliamentary seats was reduced dramatically. This electoral system is a volatile one when there are more than two viable parties; a rise in SNP support above 30 percent could

Table 9.1.   SNP Votes and MPs

Year	Total Vote	Vote as % of Scottish Electorate	MPs
1945	30,595	1.2	-
1950	9,708	0.4	-
1951	7,299	0.3	-
1955	12,112	0.5	-
1959	21,738	0.8	-
1964	64,044	2.4	-
1966	129,112	5.1	-
1970	306,796	11.4	1
1974 (Feb.)	632,032	21.9	7
1974 (Oct.)	839,628	30.4	11
1979	504,259	17.3	2

give the party a majority of Scotland's 71 seats.   In the October 1974 election, for example, the Labour Party was able to
transform a 36 percent share of the popular vote into 41 of the
71 seats.   The SNP would interpret a similar victory as a
"mandate for independence."
        Equally important has been the coincident reorientation of
interest groups, such as the Scottish Trades Union Congress,
around Scottish concerns and their sometimes strident re-
counting of injustices from London.   Renewed attention has
also been given to the Scottish Council, whose aim is to
modernize Scotland's aging economic plant.   Recently, the
Scotsman, which formerly expressed only mild interest in
nationalism, and the Glasgow Herald, which stridently opposed
it, have given it their overt support.   Coverage of the
seemingly-endless "devolution" debate in Westminister has been
exhaustive, and the Labour Government's as-yet-unrealized
efforts to establish some form of a Scottish parliament was
denounced in advance as insufficient.   While many in England
wondered whether the government had gone too far in relaxing
central controls in its 1975 White Paper on Devolution, the
Scottish press termed the Paper little short of treasonous.   "A
black betrayal of the people of Scotland," was the judgment of
the Scottish Daily Express.   (Kellas and Owen, p. 25).
        The first reaction of the central government to the new
political manifestation of Scottish nationality, was to appoint a
Royal Commission and hope the problem would fade away.
When it did not, and when the Labour Party, historically
dependent on a large plurality in the "periphery" to balance
Conservative strength in the English "Home Counties," took
office, there arose a conviction that some political move had to

be made.   Separate Devolution Bills were issued for Scotland
and Wales which would establish a cross between a federal and
consultative assembly.   This assembly would have had power
over some domestic affairs, and would have had the ability to
spend a negotiated block grant, but not to tax; the center
would have the reserved authority to avoid any measure.   The
Scotland Bill was narrowly approved in a Scottish referendum.
It failed however to pass the hurdle, added by amendment late
in the legislative process, of support by over 40% of the
potential electorates.   This ambiguous outcome precipitated the
vote of no confidence in the House of Commons for the Labour
Government.   The new Conservative Government is committed
to repealing the bill.   More consultations and political controversy will ensue.   What can be predicted with some safety
is that the issue of Scottish Devolution will occupy the political
system for some time to come.

The Significance of Scottish Nationalism

Although Scottish political nationalism appears to have
been mistimed, it was quite successful in diverting the attention of the center to Scottish problems and impelling Westminster to broach various reforms.   However, given the strong
sense of Scottish national identity, a political movement urging
more autonomy, such as Sudtiroler Volkspartei in Italy, might
have been expected at least from the time of the appearance of
the Irish Party in the 1870s.   On the other hand, given the
current weaknesses of the national tradition, it could be assumed that any nationalist political gains would be fleeting
(Mansbach).   Because neither assumption was valid, we are
left with the need to explain why the political component of
Scottish nationality should emerge at a time when most of its
traditional features are in decline.   In brief, the question is,
why this political upsurge now?   A tenable response must
include an understanding of why there was not a serious
political movement earlier.

A SEARCH FOR AN APPROPRIATE PERSPECTIVE

The framing of the question - why this political upsurge
now? - makes some explanations of the "Scottish question" less
suitable than others.   England tends to look for the answer by
concentrating on the immediate problems besetting the United
Kingdom.   Britain's institutions and party structure need
renovation, its political leadership has been uninspiring, its
economic progress in general has lagged behind its industrial
competitors; and the Scottish economy in particular has not

even attained Britain's level.   Since 1960, Scotland's per capita
gross domestic product has ranged from 87 percent to 93
percent of the United Kingdom average.(4)   These explanations
are inadequate because of their exaggerated implication of
novelty.   Britain's institutional structure has been in difficulty
for some time; it is also debatable whether it is less responsive
than the institutions of many of its neighbors, France, for
example.   Leadership has been weak before, and the world
contains few political "giants."   The economy has been in
trouble since the 1880s; more particularly, Scotland's current
economic situation, both absolutely and relative to Britain's
performance, is in far better condition than it was in the
1930s, when a separate political movement remained moribund.
In short, even "relative deprivation" (Hah and Martin) must be
part of another answer.

Similar problems confront various "cleavage" approaches.
It is undoubtedly useful to add the split between center and
periphery to the other divisions in discussing key issues in
national   development   (Rokkan).   This   approach,   however,
defines the problem; but it does not lead to a solution.   Specifically, it is too static to account for why some cleavages
exist in some states and not in others, or why some of these
cleavages persist over time while others do not.   Finally, we
should   look   briefly   at   currently   popular   ideas   in   political
science that might link the political movement to either the
advent of "post-industrial" values or - what is probably the
same thing viewed from a different normative position - the
crisis of "ungovernability."   These rather self-defining ideas
address specifically the question of what has caused the
flowering of the political component of Scottish nationality now.
Their immediate difficulty lies in their lack of empirical support.   In a careful study of data from the British Election
Survey, Jack Brand found no link between the espousal of
post-industrial (noneconomic) values and the tendency to vote
for the SNP.   "Ungovernability" is not easy to measure; in so
far as an approach can be made through a study of perceived
alienation, the connection with SNP voting is very weak.   Not
surprisingly, SNP voters tend to express dissatisfaction with
parties and politicians, but then so do voters for the other
parties, including those who supported the victorious Labour
Party.   By itself, the explanation that alienation leads to
anti-system voting is not very satisfactory.

The perspective that can best combine the insights of the
previously-discussed approaches with needed historical and
power dimensions can be called "developmental."   This term is
not used in the "diffusion" sense advanced by writers on what
is often called "nation-building."   A good critique of this
literature is provided by Hechter (pp. 22-30); here, it is
sufficient to note that by most of the indices Scotland is fully
"integrated" - what needs to be explained cannot even be

acknowledged. Rather, in the tradition of Hechter (1975) and Nairn (1977) the term is used to designate the interaction between two main variables over time: uneven economic development and political power. Economic development is not uniform; there are <u>areas</u> as well as groups that lag behind in the battle for development. In this battle a key resource is political <u>power</u> which is almost always predominant at the center. However, the power relationship center-region is not uniform over time or among states.

Political manifestations of Scottish nationality reflect the workings of certain forms of power relationships among the state center, the regional center, and the regional periphery. Political manifestations of nationality arise in one of three ways: the regional periphery is burdened by what it considers to be intolerable pressure by the state center to force assimilation or give up a distinctive way of life; the regional center of the elite calculates that demands from the state center plus the economic costs of union exceed the benefits and opportunities to be derived; the regional center, sometimes in coordination with the regional periphery, determines that the benefits of union would be increased were national sentiments given political expression. In Scotland, with one telling exception, the first has never occurred; and the second could be a possibility; but it is the third that has thus far been the primary political component of Scottish nationalism.

PATTERNS OF CENTER-NATIONAL DEVELOPMENT

The power relationship center-region (nation) takes place within the context of internal uneven economic development.(5) This context changes over time. To give structure to these changes, the forms of uneven development can be divided into the three categories: pre-industrial (mercantilist/commercial), industrial, and advanced industrial. Because the discussion is framed in general terms, it can be applied to other western states. In a larger comparative endeavor, Scotland could be a useful case study because its relationship with England spans all three periods.

Pre-Industrial Context

The main actors are the state center, the regional center, and the regional periphery, here seen as threatening by both the state and regional center. The demands from the state center are the same for both the regional center and periphery - political loyalty to the state center and religious loyalty to the state religion. For most of Scotland, the latter posed no problem because, according to the reasoning advanced by Locke in Letters Concerning Toleration, Protestants were not seen as posing a problem of security. Parliament, on the other hand, would have to go because its function was far less to represent interests than to symbolize sovereignty.

The immediate costs of union for the regional center, those making the decisions, were not large. To be sure, parliament had to be jettisoned, and in its subsequent "governance" Scotland came to symbolize the essence of the "rotten borough" electoral system. Still, as Nairn comments, even this management "was so much better than what Scotland had known that they [the indigenous ruling class] could hardly believe their luck" (1977, p. 136). Moreover, parliament was the only institution Scotland had to give up; all the institutions essential to the economic interest and job security of the aspiring middle class - the church, the legal profession, the privileges of the Royal burghs, schools and universities - were guaranteed. The absence of a parliament was even viewed as a positive advantage; in the words of the Caledonian Mercury (1783), the attention of Scots was better focused on "trade, industry and improvement of the soil," not on "the nonsense and distraction on turmoil of politics" (Campbell, p. 468).

The immediate benefits of the union were direct. Financially, the Company of Scotland, bankrupt - with an assist from England - after its failure to establish a profitable colony at Darien, was abolished by the Treaty of Union, and England agreed to give Scotland nearly 400,000 pounds to liquidate its debts. England also removed the strictures of the Navigation Acts, a central feature of mercantile economic policy, and granted all subjects of the United Kingdom "full freedom and intercourse of trade and navigation to and from any port or place within the said United Kingdom and the dominions and plantations thereunto belonging."(6) Even more important, the Union afforded the regional center the means to maintain order in the lowlands, and then gradually to extend the habit of civil obedience into the highlands.

The opportunities opened by the Union were foreseen at the time: Scotland would share in England's commercial expansion. It took a generation for the fruits to be realized, but afterward the gains were extraordinary (Smout, 1969, pp. 240-247; 1976, pp. 8-11). The opening of the English market to Scottish cattle, the rise of Glasgow in the tobacco trade, the growth of the linen industry, from which it is estimated that four households in five drew some income and which exported two-thirds of its product to England or America - all would have been unthinkable in the mercantile, pre-industrial world in which a state could prosper only at the direct expense of its neighbors.

In summary, the political expression of nationality was

absolutely essential to the negotiations establishing the Treaty of Union. Why should England pay Scotland's debts, guarantee her institutions, and allow her inside the English Mercantile economy if a potential independent Scotland did not pose a real security threat to the English state? Thereafter, any separate political expression would have been harmful to the interests of the regional center. There was no cause to tempt the revival of discriminatory English legislation. Even more, there was no cause to risk being linked to the periodic uprisings in the highlands, to which almost all lowland Scots were unalterably opposed, and the last of which, in 1745, brought the Jacobite armies as far south as Derby.(7) These profitless adventures were precisely what the regional center had embraced the Union to avoid.

Industrial Context

With the advent of industrialization, uneven economic development <u>within</u> <u>nations</u> is intensified. Growth areas developed around energy resources and natural communication facilities. The freeing of labor in other areas swells the population of the center city, where there is a need for economic and political coordination. This phenomenon, when nurtured by preponderant central political power, can divert "natural" uneven economic development toward the center. The classic example is France. France is unique among the nations of the Western world in having a primary city whose population exceeds that of the next eight metropolitan areas combined. Paris also has a disproportionate percentage of key tertiary sector activities: one-third of the nation's doctors, one-half of the engineers, and between one-half and two-thirds of the research and development personnel live in the capital (Statistiques et Indicateurs des Regions Francaises, 1976).

In considering demands from the state center, it thus becomes necessary first to determine whether the region contains "natural" growth points, and whether central demands include a qualitative change in the natural pattern of uneven development. Second, it must be discovered whether the required mobilization of the peripheral mass for industrial labor endangers distinctive national cultural traditions. In the case of Scotland, neither arose. Scotland was endowed with coal, and was located astride the North American trade routes. Industrialization did not take place in an atmosphere of "siege mentality" in which the state center declared it essential or opportune to arrogate all resources to itself at the expense of the regional elite. The consequence, as Nairn relates (1977, p. 177), was that Scotland was able to modernize without the mobilization of separate national power. The institutional guarantees and the middle-class jobs they represented forestalled the decline of Edinburgh, a fate otherwise probable given her lack of heavy industry and a separate political administration. Although Edinburgh grew much more slowly after 1830 and relinquished her position as Scotland's first city to Glasgow, the demand for Scottish lawyers, doctors, church officials, and providers of capital remained strong, and the New Town and the villas to the south retained their place as centers of middle-class life.

Mobilization of individuals in outlying areas for industrial labor introduces a class component to the center-periphery relationship. In the case of Scotland, this mobilization so reduced the population of the highlands that unrest became no longer politically dangerous and - as with the crofter agitations in the late nineteenth century - could be addressed through normal parliamentary procedures. The mobilization of the industrial labor force also occurred in a manner that did not arouse national resentment. The two major ways in which the early industrial states intruded directly upon the lives of in-dividuals were conscription and education. The former was not an issue in Britain; the military traditions of the highlands could even be nurtured and harnassed for the profit of the state. Education remained a Scottish concern. And the ab-sence of language differences further dampened potential reaction. Here, for example, the national development of Britain diverged from that of Belgium. As described by Claes, in Flanders, as in Scotland, the open nature of the industrialization process did not give rise to a political ex-pression of nationality by the regional elite: "Dans la second moitie du XIXe siecle, la situation dans le pays flamand se caracterisait par l'absence d'une elite autochtone" (p. 220). For the masses, however, the reaction was quite different. The imposition of state education in French led to the "spontaneous" creation of "le mouvement flamand [which] realisa son unanimite en adoptant, comme objectif premier, la neerlandisation de l'enseignement" (p. 221).

The isolation of the Clyde region - where most of Scot-land's economic growth took place - from the major population centers in England helped prevent a major immigration of Englishmen. Foremen, technicians, and other middle-range workers in Scotland's industrial society were Scottish; unlike Wales, Scotland emerged from industrialization ethnically distinct. This is not to say that the costs of industrialization were minute, but they were not seen as the outcome of the political subordination of Scotland to England. Quite the contrary, to be effective a public philosophy aimed at con-trolling negative externalities, establishing minimum levels of economic security, and promoting a redistribution of income had to emphasize the unity between Scots and English and the imperative of centralized reforms.(8)

This conclusion was dogma both to the activities of the

Labour Party and to Scottish interest groups, where they existed at all. The formation and early position of the Scottish Trades Union Congress (STUC) is representative. The STUC was established in 1897, very late in the industrialization process, and after the flurry of interest in Gladstone's "Home Rule" proposals had subsided. That it was founded at all was the result of a shift within the British Trade Union Congress. In a generally successful effort to reduce the number of militants at Congress meetings, the British Congress passed motions excluding trades councils from active participation, and requiring delegates to be active workers or full-time union officials. These actions had a particularly devastating impact on the Scottish trade unions. Trades councils played a greater role in trade union actions in Scotland because, being generally smaller than their English counterparts, unions had more need to combine into trades councils to defray expenses, and because the unions tended to be more politically conscious. In addition, Scottish unions were more committed to socialism; in 1898, eight of the ten members of the STUC Council belonged to the Independent Labour Party, and the new swing toward conservatism in the British Trades Union Congress was ideologically grating. Feelings of separatism were not offered when the STUC was founded. The President of the Scottish Trades Union Congress reiterated in 1898, when it was clear that the 1895 BTUC ban on trades councils would not be repealed, that it was "decided to establish a STUC for consideration of national labour questions.... This Congress is in no sense antagonistic to the BTUC but rather intended to assist in lightening its labours, and in proving a helpful ally." The alliance, needless to say, was against capital, and remarks such as "Workers are not free.... They are the slaves of the factory system and the machine" were endemic before World War I. That the "machines" were probably owned by Scots did not raise the speaker's spirits.

While the costs of union were not deemed significant, the benefits and opportunities appeared boundless. Foremost was the ability to share in, and contribute to, Britain's economic growth. Union fostered the free borrowing and exploitation of technology (Smout, 1969, pp. 253-357); and it enabled Scotland to mobilize vast amounts of capital. By the 1880s two-thirds of the British merchant marine - by far the largest in the world - was built on the Clyde. It also encouraged social mobility to the highest levels of enterprise - most firms in Scotland were controlled by Scots. For others, opportunities were opened by the prospect of occupations outside Scotland. Throughout this period, Scotland was able to absorb less than 50 percent of her male university graduates. Even this figure exaggerates the retention of those with industrial skills. Over 80 percent of divinity graduates remained in Scotland; in engineering and medicine, the percentages were 35 and 25, respectively. Most graduates found jobs in England - 35 percent - and the Empire - 25 percent. Because education was an important means of upward mobility, a university population far in excess of what Scotland herself could employ helped channel the benefits of union downward (Furniss, 1976, pp. 451-459).

To summarize, within the industrial context developed in the British center-regional-periphery relationship, the political expression of Scottish nationality was basically irrelevant. The resulting political tranquility afforded the occasion for Victorian political leaders and analysts to indulge their passion for "good government," and there was much talk and even some action toward "devolving" functions from what was thought to be the overburdened center to the region. The Scottish offices of these new institutions could then be operated rationally, unaffected by the ideological turmoil of politics. On the other hand, there was nothing in the state-region relationship that required the abandonment of national feeling in order to share in economic growth and spoils of Empire. As with "tartanry," and the tradition of thrift, some aspects of the relationship could even be mobilized for the promotion of central state power. There was no reason why, succored by her institutions, the national cleavage between Scotland and England could not remain latent.

Advanced Industrial Context

In the advanced industrial context the problem of uneven economic development assumes three principal forms. First, areas of marginal productivity that were never industrialized - the Highlands, parts of Norway, the Ardennes, parts of western France, and most of the Mezzogiorno - experience a collapse of agricultural employment and an out-migration of youth, leaving the center with substantial difficulties in maintaining services and income. Second, states are faced with areas in which formerly vital heavy industries are no longer viable - the Clyde, Tyne and Belfast regions in Britain, northern France, and much of the Great Lakes area in the United States. These areas have a declining or stagnant industrial structure, a below average occupational pattern, and an outflow of skilled labor. Their generally outdated infrastructure and lack of amenities preclude attracting new manufacturing and service industries. When national aggregate demand slows, these regions are often the first to feel the effects, and high unemployment is a constant worry.

The third form of uneven development is found in densely-populated urban areas of the state center - Copenhagen, London, and Paris - where the social costs of congestion are rising rapidly, and where the strain on resources

is acute. The extra cost of housing, office space, and transportation contributes to inflationary tendencies, and thus
exacerbates the problems of other areas where more stimulation
of demand may be in order. Furthermore, the same factors
that underlie the decline of agricultural employment and the
stagnation of heavy industries - the growth of service industries, the increased demand for knowledge skills, and the
expansion of government employment and coordination - are
likely to promote further congestion unless checked by
conscious public policy.

So far, only factors internal to the nation-state have been
considered. Increasing international economic interdependence
and competition, the prominence of multi-national corporations,
and the ensuing battle of exchange rates mandate a further
concentration on export industries or services. This requirement implies greater development in regions that can
produce exports, or import substitutes. Again, this is usually
to the detriment of the marginal agricultural or monolithic
heavy industrial areas. Concern over balance of payments also
limits effective regional policy. Finally, since uneven development occurs among as well as within states, a state that
fares badly in the growth race is usually deprived of resources to deal with unbalanced internal growth. Britain, of
course, is a prime example, and the judgment of a recent
OECD study seems justified:

> Insofar as the required improvements [in depressed
> regions] necessitate investment in infrastructure,
> the rate at which progress can be made is limited
> by the resources which the country can afford to
> devote to this purpose. This being so, the interest
> of the United Kingdom in the attraction of external
> resources from the EEC as a contribution to its
> regional policies is understandable (OECD, 1976, p.
> 43).

The state center itself becomes a supplicant.

What is new about this uneven economic development in
the advanced industrial context is the inherent politicization of
the process. The intrusion and dominance of politics comes
from two directions. The better-informed citizens demand the
maintenance of income and security, and are more than willing
to punish governments at the polls for any failure to deliver.
Interest groups are similarly reoriented. This is why underdeveloped, non-industrial regions cannot be allowed to lan-
guish. Second, as growth industries are liberated geographically from dependence on predetermined transportation networks and mineral deposits, their location becomes a prime
concern of government policy. This concern is particularly
acute because of the costs central congestion imposes on economic growth as a whole. The consequence is an elaborate

system of taxes and incentives, the contours of which, despite
the rhetoric of economic "logic," are shaped primarily by
political pressure.
     In this politicized atmosphere, the demands of the state
center increase.   The regional center of elites must coordinate
its economic activities with those of the center and remain open
to industrial combination.   For Scotland, the cost of these
demands has been high.   The psychological effects of the loss
of autonomous decision-making may be hard to measure, but
other disadvantages are not.   Forty percent of the work force
in enterprises with over 1000 employees is employed in branch
plants of companies headquartered elsewhere, an indication of
the dependence of the Scottish economy on external economic
developments (Firn, 1975, p. 159).   There are growing fears
that this dependence could lead to a further inbalance of the
occupational structure, thereby reducing the demand for local
managerial talent and weakening the Scottish economy's potential for self-generating growth.   These fears are in a recent
study by Hood and Young on American Investment in Scotland:

> A majority of U.S. firms in Scotland either under-
> take no Marketing or R & D in Scotland, or the
> functions delegated are not particularly meaning-
> ful...[Unless more autonomy is allowed] the cost of
> loss of control has to be built into any equation of
> the gains and losses from increasing U.S. direct
> investment in Scotland (pp. 292-93).

Nor is there much indication that indigenous entrepreneurs
could compensate for the lack of autonomous control of branch
plants.(9)   Only 40 percent of all manufacturing plants are
owned by Scots; 40 percent are English, and 15 percent are
American.   The figure for Scottish ownership, however, exaggerates the extent of indigenous control.   When the economy is
divided by sector, the generalization emerges that the more
advanced the sector, and the more rapid its growth, the less
Scottish ownership.   Scottish firms, for example, dominate the
leather and fur industry, but employ only seven percent of
the work force in electrical engineering.   Of the five most
rapidly growing sectors between 1963-73, only 13.5 percent of
the total employment was by Scottish firms (Firn, 1975, pp.
161, 162).
     As a whole, the Scottish economy since World War II has
followed the pattern of a depressed region overly-dependent on
stagnating heavy industries.   Unemployment has been well
above the British average, and wages have usually been
below.   Net migration totaled over 500,000 from 1958-75, by
far the highest both relatively and absolutely of the 11 regions
in Britain.   And growth, because it has tended to lag behind
the British pace, has been particularly discontinuous.   Under
the "stop and go" policies that have constituted Britain's

economic management since the World War II, Scottish heavy industry began to respond to the creation of new demand at the point that inflationary or balance of payments problems at the center forced the imposition of fiscal and monetary constraint.

This is not to say that benefits from the union are non-existent. Beginning in 1960 with the Local Employment Act, the central government has enacted at least 12 major pieces of legislation aimed at "development areas" in general, or at Scotland in particular. Financial resources have been directly diverted; employers have been paid to hire labor; special tax and development concessions have been offered; and industrial parks have been created. Nonrecoverable Exchequer assistance to industry in Scotland rose from an annual average of .5 of a million pounds at the beginning of the 1960s to 40 million pounds at the close (Rhodes and Moore, p. 234). These measures have had a positive impact. The relative economic decline that McCrone (1965) and others noted in the 1950s has been halted and, in many indices, reversed. Emigration, although still high, has been reduced. The unemployment rate is closer to the British average; how much the convergence is the consequence of Britain's usually high rate remains to be seen. Rhodes and Moore have estimated that regional policy generated from 70,000 to 80,000 new jobs between 1965-71. Since 1962, per capita gross domestic product has risen at a faster rate than the British; and average wage rates are now estimated to be above the British regional mean. Another indicator of the impact of regional policy is given by Forsyth: Of the 105 American firms that were asked to rank-order 17 factors in their decision to locate in Scotland, the most important factor by far was "government financial inducements"; This was named first by 32 of the 96 companies that responded, and second by 16 others; all told, 52 firms gave some aspect of central government regional policy as their main reason for coming to Scotland (p. 222).

These benefits have not, however, had the effect of opening new opportunities for the Scottish elite. Hood and Young have described the lack of autonomy in branch plants, and Rhodes and Moore estimate that three-fourths of all new employment came from the establishment of new factories by firms operating outside Scotland. Nothing has arrested the root causes of Scottish industrial decline - "the poor performance of those enterprises in manufacturing that are owned and controlled locally" (Firn, 1977, p. 72). This decline, which probably should be linked to the peculiar pattern of employment of university graduates "is very much the result of a failure of the indigenous industries within Scotland to move into new markers, technologies, and forms of organization"(p. 68). When combined with the loss of jobs and income in the Empire and the slow growth of the central economy, one can

comprehend the dissatisfaction of many Scots with the opportunities provided by the union and the positioning of the
generally acknowledged narrow indigenous talent base to its
operations.

How much of this dissatisfaction is the result of the many
failures of British economic management is hard to say, but it
should be emphasized that there are limits beyond which no
modern non-federal state can go to meet particular regional
demands. Financial inducements, for example, have helped to
attract American firms to Scotland, but it is not unfair to say
that no British government could systematically tout Scotland's
advantages over those of, say, Northumberland. A similar
comment could be made in regard to the tourist industry, in
which efforts on behalf of Scotland are compared unfavorably
to those of the Irish Republic.

Giving immediacy to the dissatisfaction with the inherent
constraints imposed by union and with the particular disabilities ascribed to governmental policy is the presence of
North Sea oil. Although the slogan of the SNP - "It's Scotland's wealth" (Scots Independent, October 1977) - is not
generally supported, and the associated claim -"Scotland has
oil and gas now reckoned to be worth some 150,000 pounds for
every Scottish household" - has thus far failed to arouse an
uncontrollable urge for independent use, Scottish and English
opinion diverge markedly on where the oil revenues should be
spent. The 1974 British Election Survey (the most recent
analysis of electoral data available) asked both Scottish and
English respondents whether the oil revenues should be
"shared equally by Britain as a whole," or whether Scotland
should receive "a somewhat larger" share, "the largest" or
"all." In England, eight percent felt the oil should be shared
equally, while 70 percent of the Scots chose one of the three
alternatives (Miller, 1977, p. 98). Although only 10 percent
of the Scottish respondents wanted "all the oil," this percentage rose appreciably when the issue was presented more
subtly. Recent polls commissioned by the Scotsman, for
example, have shown that opinion in Scotland is sharply
divided, with slightly more than half of all respondents agree-
ing with the statement that "oil in the North Sea belongs to
Scotland, and tax revenues from it should be used for the
benefit of the Scottish people."

The consequence of this mix of costs, benefits, and what
are perceived as unrealized or threatened opportunities has
been a politicization of Scottish national feeling. To promote
the political component of nationality is now seen to be in the
interest of individuals and groups; this feeling is particularly
strong in Scotland as a result of the absence of representative
institutions. (Drucker). Although activity toward this end
generally assumes the form of an articulation of grievances
against the center, there is a concomitant attempt to mobilize

popular support and a strong interest in drawing up a "balance sheet" on independence (MacKay). There is clearly little sentiment for emulating Third World leaders who declared it preferable to go hungry in freedom than to live well in bondage. Rather, there is an effort to determine whether Scotland might not be "better off" alone. If such were found to be the case, one can only assume that it would be desirable to proceed to independence as rapidly as possible.

TOWARD THE UNDERSTANDING OF THE POLITICAL MANIFESTATIONS OF SCOTTISH NATIONALITY

The perspective presented in the previous section enables us to approach an answer to the question - why this political upsurge now? The pattern of uneven economic development in the advanced industrial context fostered the type of center-region power relationship that made a political expression of nationality a rational strategy for Scotland to pursue. That the Scots still have this card to play probably arises from two historical factors: First, the strength of the Scottish political nation in 1707 allowed the negotiated retention of most of the institutional supports of a viable nationality. Second, the manner of industrialization in Britain did not pose for Scots the dilemma of whether to abandon a separate national identity in order to share in economic growth. Indeed, national traditions were mildly encouraged by the state center.

A particular type of political nationalism is advancing in Scotland. It has been determined that the benefits of union would be increased were national sentiment given political expression. An exploration of some of the features of political strategy shows that this calculation has not been wrong.

First, it is most important to look at the behavior of the media and various groups and organizations. Unlike Drucker, I think it more appropriate to see their relationship to the political upsurge not as one of momentary weakness that allowed the politicians in the door, but as one of a fundamental reorientation of concern around the championing of Scottish interests. As far as the press is concerned, only the Dundee-based Thompson group has remained committed to the political status quo (Kellas and Owen, p. 25). The changing attitude of organizations is also strikingly evident in the deliberations of the Scottish Trades Union Congress. During the entire inter-war period, Scotland suffered severe economic hardship. In 1932, 27.7 percent of insured workers were unemployed, and at no time before re-armament did this figure fall below 15 percent. These percentages do not reveal the full extent of the misery. Male unemployment figures were substantially higher, and certain industries and towns were disproportion-

ately affected; in some districts, unemployment rates of 40 to
60 percent were common. On the other hand, as early as
1934, the economic situation in London and Southern England
had greatly improved. By 1937, the unemployment rate was
approximately three times higher in Scotland than in London
and the South East; the unemployment rate in Wales was four
times higher.

This uneven economic hardship, one might think would be
a ready-made issue for the rallying of national or regional
feeling. Yet nowhere in the annual meetings of the Congress
can I find anyone suggesting that independence, autonomy,
decentralization, or even special aids to depressed regions
would be useful. Rather, struggle against the "bosses" was
the great historic issue. Militantly-allied to the Labour Party's
centralizing strategy of redistribution, Scotland's problems
became derivative. Of the 732 motions placed before the STUC
Annual Meetings from 1921-40, at most 22, or three percent,
dealt with Scotland in any way at all. From 1936-40, there
were more motions on the Spanish Civil War than on all aspects
of Scottish affairs.

In the advanced industrial context of unequal economic
development, this orientation has been transformed. Beginning
with the Labour Party victory in 1964 and before the first SNP
by-election triumphs, consideration of Scottish concerns
emerged as an intrinsic component of the STUC activities.
Since 1965, each Annual Report has led off with an increasingly long section of gloomy economic forecasts, summaries
of representations for a better deal for Scotland, and charges
of betrayal of government promises. Motions from the floor
dealing with Scottish problems have similarly multiplied.
Accounting for five to eight percent of all motions in the mid
1950s, Scottish motions rose to 16 percent in 1964, 21 percent
in 1968, 38 percent in 1972, and 42 percent in 1976. The
STUC has also become politically active, pushing the Scottish
council of the Labour Party to sponsor devolution schemes,
advocating taxing powers and other functions for the proposed
Assembly, and encouraging the formation of multi-group alliances to put even more pressure on Whitehall for financial
assistance.

As well as illuminating changes in the behavior of groups,
the perspective also increases our understanding of public
opinion and voting preferences. One of the remarkable aspects of the political upsurge in Scotland has been that it has
occurred independent of any change in expressed attitudes
toward self-rule. Somewhat under 25 percent of Scottish-
survey respondents profess general contentment with the
present system; somewhat under 20 percent opt for independence; the remainder support some form of Scottish
Assembly. This pattern has remained fairly constant during
the whole period of SNP ascendance. Clearly, what the SNP

represents is not a sudden renewal of national spirit, but the effect of a multitude of individual decisions that nationality has become politically relevant. A necessary precondition for these decisions could have been the "marked" dealignment of major-party support" (Crewe, p. 182). This was evident in the February 1974 General Election, although it must be remembered that by then SNP support was already high. What has translated this dealignment into purposeful alternative electoral behavior has been the latent "devolution cleavage" (Miller, 1977, p. 96).

The perspective provides an insight into how this cleavage persisted, why it might be politically relevant now, and why its political expression was not preceded or accompanied by a more wide-spread feeling of nationality. National traditions have not shown a resurgence; what has changed has been the pattern of center-region power relationships. Two connected and intriguing findings can also be incorporated: first, SNP support tends to be above the level of aspiration for independence; second, 76 percent of Scottish respondents in the British Election Survey - including 70 percent of those voting Labour and 69 percent of those voting Conservative - stated that SNP victories were "good for Scotland" (Miller, 1977, p. 100). These data suggest that the SNP is being used as a vehicle for the transmission of Scottish grievances, a strategy felt commendable even by a majority of those who have continued to vote for other parties.

The new political pressure has positive feedback. The strategy works. Central policy is now vitally concerned with "development areas." And, of all the regions, Scotland does the best on an array of measures. Scotland receives the highest proportion of public expenditure per capita (Drucker, p. 184); she benefits from the activities of special agencies such as the Scottish Development Agency and the Highlands and Island Development Board; and she garners a disproportionate share of external support - 45 percent of the value of loans from the European Investment Bank went to firms in Scotland in 1974-75. The Scottish economy has responded favorably, both absolutely and relative to the average British performance. The lesson to be learned, of course, is not that Whitehall knows best, but that militancy pays. The emerging dialogue over oil revenues raises a new issue altogether. No longer can it be assumed that it is sufficient for the center to redistribute resources to bring Scotland in line with the United Kingdom mean. There is now the implicit demand for the channeling of enough oil revenues to put, and keep, Scotland ahead of the mean. It is this functional utility that leads me to expect a revival of SNP support before the end of the Conservative Government.

Renewed movement toward the establishment of a federated institution in Scotland can also be anticipated. This

institution would facilitate the routinized transfer of greater
resources from the center, and would provide a forum for
groups to put pressure on the center at times other than
before general elections. Its precise responsibilities are difficult to foresee. We can speak with more assurance on directions the federated institution would not take. There is no
indication that any major group or interest would promote a
revitalization of national institutions - law, education, church -
or of national culture. Still less can it be anticipated that the
institution would have as its goals more "responsiveness,"
bringing government "closer to the people," or any of the
values professed by advocates of decentralization. An indicator is the interest of the recently-instituted Scottish local
government reform in the implications for the proposed assembly. Beginning in 1975, the diverse collection of 430
elected councils in Scotland was replaced by a "rationalized"
two tier structure of nine regional councils and 53 district
councils; there were also three "most purpose" Island
Councils. The regional councils were responsible for planning,
education, social services, police, fire, and transportation; the
districts were charged with zoning, housing, and a variety of
other matters. How effectively these bodies will operate cannot, of course, be determined definitely (Eyestone, 1977). It
would, however, seem prudent not to establish yet another tier
until the vaguely-defined functions between councils and
districts had been put in some order. Moreover, whatever
else the 1975 local government reform accomplishes, it did
involve a major centralization of power from the locality to a
more remote level. To establish an Assembly overseeing all of
Scotland would create an imbalance in what might already be
seen as a top-heavy administrative structure.

That none of the parties in the center-regional dialogue
has evidenced the slightest concern for these matters points to
the fundamental nature of the debate. The real issue is
power. In the constant power struggles that are imposed by
uneven development, the balance has shifted somewhat, although not preponderantly, toward Scotland. An Assembly
represents an accommodation by the center, a wise accommodation to forestall a more inconvenient situation. The constraints imposed by Scottish opinion and the orientation of
groups suggests that a deal can be struck.

CONCLUSIONS

The framework that has been developed and applied
provides, I believe, the most satisfactory answer to the
question - why this political upsurge now? The politicization
of the pattern of internal uneven economic development has

made the articulation of a unique Scottish position a rational strategy for producer groups to pursue. This reorientation of groups and media has had the further consequence of giving credibility to political parties espousing Scottish autonomy or independence.(10) It is this factor that, in my opinion, has enabled the SNP to take advantage of the political dealignment in Britain and mobilize voters concerned with the devolution issue. That the party should continue to be an important, albeit not a dominant, electoral force is indicated by the feeling of voters in other parties that its presence helps promote the interests of Scotland.

At the same time, particularly in a volume of this sort, the limits beyond which the political expression of Scottish nationality is unlikely to go should be emphasized. There are three major interrelated factors involved. First, although groups may find it useful to impart a national tone to their demands, they strenuously oppose any serious movement toward political separation. The Scottish Trades Union Congress may want more devolution, but there are no longer any purely Scottish unions; the majority of manufacturing enterprises in Scotland are not controlled by Scots. For labor and business groups the idea of an "independent" Scotland - whatever that would mean economically - makes little sense to labor and business groups. And the national institutions are not strong enough to lead a sustained campaign for independence.

Second, Scotland is a heterogeneous nation. Its diverse industrial profile, the uncertain future of the highlands, the aging industrial plant in the Strathclyde region, the large residue of poverty, the lamentable housing stock, the high percentage of recent Irish immigrants, the oil boom in Aberdeen - all attest to the immense legacy of uneven development within the nation. Although all states, both actual and potential, are diverse, a strong argument can be made that Scotland is far less homogeneous than the Scandinavian countries, which nationalist writers are fond of evoking. Tensions can be expected to arise within any Scottish Assembly; given Scotland's vast economic and social discrepancies, an Assembly endowed with any real powers would have to address the issue of redistribution within the nation, and this would likely be contentious. The alliance against what are considered English depredations might soon dissolve. Moreover, because the Assembly would almost certainly lack a strong public philosophy to legitimize redistribution, it is probable that any serious effort to equalize the impact of uneven development would fail. Any failure would channel appeals back to Westminster, putting an additional check on the amount of independent power the assembly could acquire.

Finally, the absence of ethnic or cultural revival to paralleling the political aspect deprives any movement of the

popular fervor necessary to overcome the "rational" behavior
of groups or the economic heterogeneity of the population. An
upsurge of national culture can, however, be extremely
divisive: In Wales, the language issue has narrowed the appeal
of the nationalist party; similar problems exist in Brittany,
where the questions are whether an autonomous Brittany should
make Breton a required second language or the primary one,
and whether residents of French ancestry should be considered full fledged citizens. The political movement for more
Scottish control or benefits has avoided these troubles by
carefully eschewing any systematic appeal to national culture.
The price has been to give the movement in general, and the
SNP in particular, a weaker "grass roots" base. Despite its
rhetoric, the party has a role more analogous to that of a
pressure group than to a Scottish counterpart of the Parti
Quebecois. A credible threat of separatism remains the
missing component in the political expression of Scottish
nationality.

NOTES

1. The extensive Irish migration to the west of Scotland is a
   factor that will be mentioned all too briefly, later in the
   paper.
2. See Jacques Ozouf (1975). In the commissioned poll, 22
   percent of the respondents considered themselves
   "Breton," 26 percent felt equally Breton and French. On
   the other hand, over 80 percent were satisfied with the
   current status of Brittany in the French political system;
   they felt Brittany should be treated like all other French
   regions. Only 12 percent favored a "status d'auto-
   nomie." For an impassioned statement of what "being
   Breton" means in a unitary state see, Xavier Grall
   (1977).
3. This "provincialism," in the worst sense of the term,
   appears to be a pervasive, cross-national phenomenon.
4. The "state of England" literature is too massive (and
   usually too ephemeral) to recount. I might draw the
   reader's attention to a particularly trenchant criticism of
   Britain's political institutions by The Economist ("Blowing
   up a Tyranny," November 5, 1977, pp. 11-16). The
   tension in the devolution debate between the government's
   political purpose of "dishing the Nats" and its ostensible
   aim of providing "good government" is described by Smith
   (1977).
5. Often referred to as "capitalist development," a term
   which is surely wrong. Uneven development was a
   feature of English-Scottish relations prior to the advent

of capitalism. And one of the most striking instances of uneven development today occurs in the Soviet Union, where the phenomenon is generally called the "national-ities problem."

6. The Navigation Acts of 1660 and 1663 declared that no goods could be transported from any of the King's pos-sessions except in English, Irish, or Welsh ships, or in ships with an English captain and crew. Nor could any foreign goods enter England except in English ships, or ships of the country or origin. By these measures, Scottish commerce was effectively excluded. These mer-cantilist acts and the uneven economic development they fostered impelled weaker states to subordinate themselves to, or to amalgamate with, their stronger neighbors.

7. The fate of the highlands, the regional periphery par excellence, helps sharpen appreciation of the pattern of state center-regional and center-regional-periphery power relations. The highland clans were unable to meet the state center's demand for loyalty, precisely as earlier they were unable to meet Edinburgh's. The strength of Catholicism was one major barrier; Gaelic was another. Even more significant, the clan system was designed for war rather than for participation in economic development. And the highland clans were so economically backward that as late as the visitation of Dr. Johnson in 1773 there had yet to be a wheel north of Inverness. To give loyalty to the state would be to undermine the traditional way of life. When geographic remoteness and a fear and hatred of their lowland neighbors were added to these factors, endemic revolt was a predictable consequence.

That these revolts did not result in the development of nationalism on the order of our type I - the reaction of the regional periphery to what is seen as intolerable pressure from the center - is in large part the result of the successful efforts to extirpate all vestiges of highland society after 1745. The leaders of the rebellion were executed and their land seized by the state. Highland dress was forbidden and heritable jurisdictions were abolished. The clans were effectively disarmed. The Society for the Promoting of Christian Knowledge was sent north to teach their children proper behavior - in English. Economically, there was the forced introduction of lowland (modern) economic relationships to overcome what one contemporary writer termed the "constitutional sloth" of the highlander. (This account is drawn from the indispensable work of A.J. Youngson (1973).

The success of the measures is attested to by con-temporary observers. In 1746, Duncan Forbes gave the following description (Youngson, 1973, p. 23): "The inhabitants of the mountains, unacquainted with industry and the fruit of it, and united in some degree by the similarity of dress and language, stick close to their ancient idle way of life; retain their barbarous customs and maxims; depend generally on their Chiefs, as their sovereign Lords and masters; and being accustomed to the use of arms, and inured to hard living, are dangerous to the public peace..." Within 30 years, Dr. Johnson could report (Smout, 1969, p. 342) that "there was perhaps never any change of national manners so quick, so great, and so general, as that which has operated in the Highlands by the last conquest and the subsequent laws. We came hither too late to see what we expected - a people of peculiar appearance, and a system of antiquated life. The clans retain little now of their original character: their ferocity of temper is softened, their military ardour is extinguished, their dignity of independence is depressed, their contempt of government subdued, and their reverence for their Chiefs abated. Of what they had before the late conquest of their country there remains only their language and their poverty."

This transformation was probably not within the power of the Scottish center alone to effect. If this surmise is correct, the Union of 1707 may have forestalled the development of separate highland nationalism. From the perspective of the Scottish center, no greater benefit from the Union could have been possible.

8. To approach this important issue from another direction, I think it is justified to propose that the more decentralized the arenas of power, the less attention will be paid to environment or resource control and to matters of redistribution (For further discussion using primarily European examples, see Furniss, 1974, pp. 979-82). In careful review of the concept of "fiscal federalism," S.H. Beer (1976, p. 28) arrives at a similar conclusion: "In modern society like the U.S the function of redistribution of income or wealth can be effectively performed only by the Federal government."

9. This change from entrepreneurial dynamics and autonomy occurred roughly from 1890 to 1940. This is the same period, probably not coincidentally, in which the decline of the Scottish higher education system took place. What precisely produced these changes, to what extent the immediate causes can be related to the latent disabilities of political integration once industrialization has developed - these are issues that require extensive further research.

10. On the political left, the problem of taking the SNP seriously has been particularly difficult. The efforts of "socialism" to come to terms with "nationalism" are detailed

in Brown (1975). The passage from treating the SNP with amused scorn to grudging respect is shown in Nairn (1970, 1977). For an excellent general discussion, I refer the reader to Heiberg's paper in this volume.

BIBLIOGRAPHY

Beer, Samuel H. "A Political Scientists's View of Fiscal Federalism." Paper prepared for the ISPE Conference on Fiscal Federalism. Berlin, 1976.

Brand, Jack. "Development of National Feeling in Scotland: 1945 to 1977." Paper prepared for delivery at the Annual Meeting of the American Political Science Association. Washington, D.C., 1977.

Brown, Gordon. The Red Paper on Scotland. Edinburgh: Edinburgh University Student Publications Bureau, 1975.

Campbell, R.H. "Anglo-Scottish Union of 1707: The Economic Consequences," Economic History Review 16, 3, 1964. Pp. 486-477.

Claes, Lode. "The Mouvement Flammand entre le politique, l'economique et le curturel," Res Publica 15, 2, 1973. Pp. 219-236.

Commission of the Constitution. "Devolution and Other Aspects of Government: An Attitudes Survey." London: H.M.S.O., 1973.

Crewe, Ivor et al. "Partisan Dealignment in Britain," British Journal of Political Science 7, 2, 1977. Pp. 129-190.

Drucker, H.M. "Devolution and Corporatism." Government and Opposition 8, 3, 1977. Pp. 178-193.

The Economist.

Eyestone, Robert. "Planning in Scotland's New Regions." Paper prepared for presentation at the meetings of the Midwest Political Science Association, Chicago, 1977.

Firn, John. "External Control and Regional Policy," in: Gordon Brown, The Red Paper on Scotland 1975. Pp. 153-167.

_____. "Industrial Policy," in: Donald MacKay, Scotland 1980. Edinburgh: Q Press, 1977. Pp. 62-83.

Forsyth, David. U.S. Investment in Scotland. New York: Praeger 1972.

Furniss, Norman (1974). "The Practical Significance of Decentralization," Journal of Politics 36, 4, 1974. Pp. 958-982.

_____. "Northern Ireland as a Case Study of De-
centralization in Unitary States," World Politics 27, 3, 1974.
Pp. 385-404.

_____. "Internal Colonialism," Development and Change 7,
1976. Pp. 445-467.

Grall, Xavier. Le Cheval Couche. Paris: Hachette, 1977.

Hah, Chong-do and Jeffrey Martin. "Toward a Synthesis of
Conflict and Integration Theories of Nationalism," World Politics
27, 3, 1975. Pp. 361-386.

Hanham, H.J. Scottish Nationalism. London: Faber and
Faber, 1969.

Hechter, Michael. Internal Colonialism: The Celtic Fringe in
British National Development 1536-1966. Berkeley: University
of California Press, 1975.

Hood, N. and S. Young. "U.S. Investment in Scotland -
Aspects of the Branch Factory Syndrome," Scottish Journal of
Political Economy 23, 3, 1976. Pp. 279-293.

Hood, Stuart (1970). "The Backwardness of Scottish Television," in: Karl Miller, Memoirs of a Modern Scotland 1970.
Pp.

Kellas, James. The Scottish Political System. London: Cambridge University Press, 1975.

Kellas, James and Raymond Owen. "Devolution and the Polit-
ical Context in Scotland." Paper prepared for delivery at the
Annual Meeting of the American Political Science Association,
Washington, D.C., 1977.

McCrone, Gavin. Scotland's Economic Progress 1951-1960.
London: G. Allen & Unwin, 1965.

MacKay. Donald (ed.). Scotland 1980: The Economics of Self-
Government. Edinburgh: Q Press, 1977.

Mansbach, Richard. "The Scottish National Party," Comparative Politics 5, 2, 1973. Pp. 185-210.

Marwick, Arthur. "Scottish Nationalism since 1918," in: Karl
Miller, Memoirs of a Modern Scotland, 1970. Pp. 13-33.

Miller, Karl. Memoirs of a Modern Scotland. London: Faber
and Faber, 1970.

Miller, William. "The Connection between SNP Voting and the
Demand for Self-Government," European Journal of Political
Research 5, 1, 1977. Pp. 83-102.

Nairn, Tom. "The Three Dreams of Scottish Nationalism," in: Karl Miller, Memoirs of a Modern Scotland, 1970.

_____. The Break-up of Britain. London: New Left Books, 1977.

Organization for Economic Co-Operation and Development (1976). Regional Problems and Policies in OECD Countries. Paris.

Ozouf, Jacques. "Que Veulent les Bretons," Le Nouvel Observateur 576, 1975 44ff.

Rhodes, Barry and John Moore. "Regional Policy and the Scottish Economy," Scottish Journal of Political Economy 21, 3, 1974. Pp. 215-235.

Rokkan, Stein. "Dimensions of State Formation and Nation-Building: A Possible Paradigm for Research and Variations within Europe," in Charles Tilly, The Formation of Nation States in Western Europe. Princeton: University Press, 1975.

Rose, Richard. Governing Without Consensus. Boston: Beacon Press, 1971.

Scots Independent.

The Scotsman.

Scottish Economic Bulletin.

Scottish Trades Union Congress. Annual Reports.

Smith Brian. "Confusions in Regionalism," Political Quarterly 48, 1, 1977. Pp. 14-29.

Smith T.B. "Legal Imperialism and Legal Parochialism," Juridical Review 34, 1965. Pp. 39-57.

Smout, T.C. A History of the Scottish People, 1560-1830. London: Collins, 1969.

_____. "The Historical Separateness of the Scots," New Society 37, 717, 1976. Pp. 8-11.

Statistiques et Indicateurs des Regions Francaises (I.N.S.E.E.: Series R).

Youngson, A.J. (1973). After the Forty-Five: The Economic Impact on the Scottish Highlands. Edinburgh: University Press, 1973.

10 External and Internal Nationalism: The Case of the Spanish Basques*
Marianne Heiberg

BACKGROUND

For approximately the last 100 years, the Basque country has
been subject to two cogent, powerful, and related centralizing
forces. State centralization enforced political conformity from
Madrid, and industrialization economically integrated the
Basque country from within. Basque nationalism was the
political response to both these forces. Basque nationalism
initially emerged as an ultra-conservative, deeply-Catholic, and
racially-exclusive doctrine in Bilbao, the capital of Vizcaya, in
the early 1890s. Although the nationalist platform stressed
rural Basque culture, traditions, and language as the symbols
of Basque uniqueness and unity, Basque nationalism was an
urban product designed to deal with urban problems. An
analysis of the initial rise of Basque nationalism must be placed
into a wider context. The last quarter of the nineteenth
century in the Spanish Basque country, and especially in
Vizcaya, was a period of severe social crisis. The old, traditional Basque society, governed by foral institutions(1) and
dedicated to commercial and agricultural enterprise, was
superseded by a society founded on a unified Spanish constitution and heavy, rapidly-expanding industrialization.
    On one level, the Basque case could be regarded as a
special case of the perennial Spanish problem of regionalism.
In Spain, a sense of an overarching Spanish "nation" has al-

*This article is based on research originally supported by the
Social Science Research Council, London, and supervised by
Professor Julian Pitt-Rivers. I should also like to thank
Professor Ernest Gellner for his many valuable comments.

ways been weak. Villages or regions provided the principal foci for intense personal loyalties and patriotism. At one time or another, regionalist or secessionist movements have affected almost every part of Spain - Galicia, Catalonia, Murcia, Andalucia, and the Basque country, to mention some examples.

In part, this has been due to the nature and slow development of the Spanish state. Probably only under the authoritarian Franco regime did the state finally gain full integrative powers. Although Ferdinand and Isabella brought Spain together under the personal rule of a single monarchy in the late fifteenth century, each of the regions of Spain continued to enjoy distinct legal codes (fueros), which permitted ample regional autonomies. Only with the secession of the Bourbon Dynasty and, more specifically, in the aftermath of Napolean's defeat in the early nineteenth century were serious attempts made to weld Spain into a unified country with a uniform constitution. The nineteenth century saw the rise of liberalism as a centralizing ideology, the construction of a state-wide education and communication system, the instigation of limited social welfare policies, and the growth of industrialization in Catalonia and the Basque region. However, this period also witnessed severe political instability. The country was shattered by revolts, two prolonged civil wars, the Carlist Wars, and dozens of pronunciamientos by disaffected generals who felt they could run Spain better than the unscrupulous politicians.

From the standpoint of Madrid, the four Basque provinces - Guizpuzcoa, Vizcaya, Navarra, and Alava - that lie in northwest Spain have historically been regarded as constituting a separate political entity. The Basque country maintained its distinct political and legal codes longer than any other region in Spain.(2) Nevertheless, with the exception of the Kingdom of Navarra, which briefly joined the entire Basque country under one monarch in the eleventh century, the Basques, unlike the Catalans, have never formed a political or legal entity. Each of the four Basque provinces were regulated by a distinct set of fueros, which showed important variations from province to province.

Moreover, by the year 1200, the various Basque provinces and districts were all connected in one way or another to the Kingdom of Castilla, although complete annexation occurred at a later date. Alfonso VIII, King of Castilla, peacefully annexed Guipuzcoa in 1200; Alava was invaded in 1181, and integrated into Castilla in 1331; Vizcaya and, finally, Navarra were brought within the domain of the Castillian monarchy in 1379 and 1515, respectively. Although incorporated into the Castillian monarchy, the legal institutions established by the fueros enabled the Basques to have their own courts, parliaments, coinage, militia, and customs boundaries; they were also free from outside taxation.

Not only were the Basque provinces largely autonomous both vis-a-vis Madrid and each other, but the unity of the Basque country was further fragmented by the deep cultural, economic, and political opposition between the urban centers (villas) and the surrounding rural hinterland. From the time the process of urbanization was initiated in the thirteenth century, the urban centers were frequently populated by people of quite different origins from those in the countryside (Caro Baroja, pp. 31-51). Moreover, whereas the latter, residing on dispersed, isolated farmsteads, were peasant agriculturists and spoke the Basque language (Euskera) exclusively the former were dedicated to commerce and administration and tended to use Spanish or French as their daily language. Until the advent of industrialization, these hispanized towns were to a great extent economically independent of, although often in conflict with, the surrounding Basque countryside. Agrarian protests and uprisings against urban expansion have been a constant theme in Basque history.

The Rural Defeat and Urban Ascendancy: The Carlist Wars and its Effects

Throughout the major part of the nineteenth century, the centralizing tendencies of the various Madrid governments and the aspirations of the nascent Basque urban bourgeousie combined to attack the traditional Basque political order based on the fueros. The motivations of the Basque urbanites were clear enough. The foral institutions protected a rural mode of life, and the advantaged position of the rural notables. Merchants, lawyers, and budding industrialists were reduced to second class citizenship (Carr, p. 5), and industrial growth was drastically constricted. In the main, this was due to four features of the foral regime: 1) The Provincial Assemblies, the semi-autonomous organizations governing each of the Basque provinces, were structured on municipal representation. Each of the municipalities in a province, regardless of its population, enjoyed equal representation. Because most of the municipalities were strictly rural, the Provincial Assemblies were disproportionately weighted toward rural interests. 2) In order to hold public office, an individual had to own land. Hence, many urbanites were barred from public positions. 3) The Basque provinces constituted a duty-free zone, with customs lines drawn along the Ebro rather than along the coast. Therefore, Basque industry was cut off from Spanish markets by tariff barriers, while being subjected to an influx of competing industrial goods from abroad. 4) The main resources of the Basque country, timber and iron ore, were municipal rather than private property, and exportation of the extensive supply of iron ore was prohibited.

During the nineteenth century, the tension and conflict between urban and rural interests twice erupted into war. To a significant extent these Carlist Wars were Basque civil wars.(3)   The liberal, anti-fuero urban centers were pitted against the Carlist, rural areas that had been mobilized in defense of the fueros. With the final Carlist defeat in 1876, the foral regime was abolished by decree of the Madrid government. Customs lines were moved to the national frontiers, where they shortly became part of the highest protective tariff barrier in Europe. The supremely-rich iron mines surrounding Bilbao fell into private ownership, and the export of iron was legalized. The effects of these changes on the growth of Basque industry were staggering and immediate.

In the urban areas, the use of the Basque language had been declining for centuries. Basque urban politics and business were conducted in Spanish. Euskera was stigmatized as the language of the stables, the language of unsophisticated rural population. The Basque language was primarily an oral one with almost no literary production, and it lacked the terminology to cover the contingencies of urban life. Euskera was spoken by the coastal fishermen and the Basque farmers (basirratara) in parts of Vizcaya, Guipuzcoa, and the Pyrenean valleys of Navarra. (Douglass, p. 150). There are currently two and a half million inhabitants in the Basque country, and only about 600,000, or 24 percent speak Euskera. Of those who are Basque by descent, slightly under 50 percent have a working knowledge of the language. Although the Basques' separatist argument is based on the claim that they have a distinct culture, Basque culture is a product of rural areas, and is primarily confined there today.(4)

Basque Industrialization, 1876-1900

After the abolition of the Vizcayan fueros prohibiting the export of iron ore, the exploitation of Bilbao's iron mines commenced in ernest. Capital from Basque and foreign, mainly British, investors combined with Basque management to increase the extraction of iron by 10 fold within a period of 25 years. By 1900, well over four million tons of ore, representing approximately 80 percent of production, were exported annually. The capital accumulated by the metallurgical industry spurred the growth of the shipbuilding, locomotive manufacturing, paper, and cement industries. Bilbao became not only the center of Spain's iron and steel industry, but also developed into an important international port, and became a major center for ship building as a result of the readily available resources of Basque lumber. By the beginning of the twentieth century, 45 percent of the Spanish merchant marine, nearly all of Spain's annual production of iron and

steel, and 30 percent of Spanish capital were in Basque hands.
Raymond Carr has stated that Basque bankers were at this
time the single most important financial interest group in
Spain.

In Bilbao, this bustling economic activity generated a vast
number of small, subsidiary enterprises dependent either
directly or indirectly on the rapidly-expanding heavy industry. Most of these enterprises, few of which employed
over 10 workers, were family-owned endeavors. Thus, a type
of industrial and commercial minifundia proliferated in the wake
of the powerful iron and steel interests. This sector of small,
dependent industrial producers has formed one of the main
pillars of Basque nationalist support.

The reigning political atmosphere surrounding this economic take-off was especially favorable. In 1878, the Madrid
government negotiated with the provincial governments of
Vizcaya and Guipuzcoa and conceded a special economic and
administrative regime to them, the conciertos economicos.
Basically, the conciertos economicos permitted these two
Basque provinces to assess their own taxes and pay a fixed
sum into the Madrid treasury. The sums agreed upon could
be raised in whatever manner the provincial government, the
Diputacion, deemed advisable. In Vizcaya, this meant that the
total amount of taxes paid to Madrid in any one year was considerably lower proportionally than in the rest of Spain.
(Payne, p. 158). Furthermore, because political control of the
Diputacion Provincial de Vizcaya was firmly held within the
domain of the big Basque industrialists, these taxes were
raised indirectly. In addition, because of combined Basque
and Catalan pressure fired by the economic crisis of the 1880s,
by 1900 Basque industrial development was further protected
by high tariff walls. The Basque economy also benefited from
generous government subsidies, especially for shipping.

Basque industrialization brought about equally dramatic
social changes. As Basque industry gained momentum, a new,
small, but extremely powerful, social class emerged. Focused
on the banking family, Avellano, and the Ybarra family, owners of Altos Hormos, the Basque economic elite consisted of
about five families, tied by intermarriage, who exercized an
increasingly monopolistic control over much of the Basque
economy. Dominating over 50 percent of the iron and steel
industry and most of the banking activity, this elite retained
tight control over the provincial government through electoral
corruption and clientalism. This uppermost echelon of Basque
society, the Basque oligarchy, never questioned the economic
and political unity of Spain. In fact, the Basque elite became
an integral part of the wider Spanish elite and had a potent
voice in shaping Spain's economic and political policies. Spain
was not ruled by "Spaniards," but by a conglomeration that
included Catalans, Andalucian landowners, and Basque in-

dustrialists.

The lower ranks of Basque society were also radically altered. In response to Basque industry's incessant need for vast pools of unskilled labor, Vizcaya - and especially Bilbao - experienced an immense influx of immigrants, most of whom came from the more-impoverished rural areas of Spain. From 1876 to 1900, the population of Bilbao almost tripled, and Vizcaya became the most densely-populated province in Spain. By the turn of the century, fully 47 percent of Bilbao's inhabitants were non-Basque by origin, and less than 20 percent had actually been born in the city. The Basque and non-Basque workers tended to be separated both by place of residence - the Basques living in the older sections of the town and the non-Basques on the outskirts - and by employment. While the Basques frequently worked in the more desirable, smaller, and personalized factories, the non-Basques were concentrated in the iron foundries and the mines; of the 13,000 workers employed in the mines in 1910, only 3000 were of Basque origin.

An autonomous middle class culture never developed in the Basque country as it did in Catalonia. There was no Basque university, theater, or experimentation in architecture and the arts. Although European cultural influences were enthusiastically received and absorbed in Barcelona, Bilbao remained proletarian in attitude and semi-rural in appearance. Its population of shopkeepers, traders, artisans, clerks and manual workers was enriched only by the financial aristocracy housed in opulent palaces on the right bank of the Narvion.

The whole nature of social life among the middle sectors of Bilbao society deteriorated rapidly under the demographic crush. Many native Basques felt themselves to be a social minority; overcrowding, inflation, and the lack of adquate social services became acute; and the economic policies of the Basque oligarchy only worsened the situation. In 1897, the price of iron was doubled, and many small concerns dependent on iron products went bankrupt. While social and economic grievances were accumulating among the Basques, resentment and rancor were spreading among the immigrant workers who were subject to brutal living and working conditions. The miners were usually housed in substandard, unhygienic barracks located alongside the mine pits. With sanitation and medical facilities non-existent, disease, especially respiratory ailments, was rampant. And salaries for 12 to 16-hour work days were barely above subsistence level.

The first branch of the Partido Obrero Socialista Espanol (PSOE) and the first workers' organizations, which later became incorporated into the Union General de Trabajadores (UGT), were founded among the Bilbao miners in 1890. From 1890 onwards, the mines and heavy industry sector of Bilbao became the scene of violent, bitterly-fought strikes that at

times threatened to explode into generalized armed confrontation.(5)   The strikes, directed against the Basque managers
and proprietors of the mining industry were led by Spanish
socialist organizers with enthusiastic and militant non-Basque
supporters.   In other words, the opposing interests in these
strikes corresponded to the ethnic divisions existing at that
time in Bilbao.   Because few Basques supported the miners'
cause, many immigrants viewed the Basques in general as an
exploiting, privileged class, and the bitterness of these immigrants was reflected in the socialist literature of the period.
In 1893, "La lucha de Clases" ("The Class Struggle"), the
socialists' newspaper and "Sizkaitarra" ("The Vizcayan"), the
magazine of an embryonic group of Vizcayan nationalists,
appeared on the streets of Bilbao almost simultaneously.

To understand Basque nationalism, it is crucial to note
that it evolved out of Vizcayan nationalism.   The first nationalists referred to themselves as bizkainos, Vizcayans, not
Basques.   The initial stage of Basque nationalism was concerned with the problems of industrial Bilbao, and not the
Basque country as a whole.   Only when industrialization
spread to other Basque areas at a later date did nationalist
sentiment become a wider popular phenomenon.

The Rise of Basque Nationalism (1890 - 1936) and the New Traditionalism

When Basque nationalism first made its appearance in
Bilbao, a city which 25 years previously had defended centralizing liberalism against the Carlist uprising, Basque
traditional culture and language were almost extinct in the
city.   Moreover, the urban initiators of the nationalist creed
were only vaguely familiar with Basque culture and history,
although several of them later went to great extents to learn
about both.

Sabino de Arana, the acknowledged founder of Basque
nationalism and its chief ideologue, was born in Bilbao and was
a lawyer by profession.(6)   His father, a constructor of river
barges, had been an ardent Carlist supporter.   Javier
Courcuera, the Basque historian, has described Arana: "The
first cry of Sabino is the cry of Basque traditional society
destroyed by industrialization and centralism.   It is the
mythification of an archaic, democratic and happy past destroyed by Spain and factories." (Corcuera, p. 108).   This
cry was taken up and converted into a political instrument by
those in Bilbao society - middle-level industrialists, shopkeepers, professionals, artisans, the lower Basque clergy -
who were socially, economically, and politically threatened by
the two main protagonists of the Basque industrialization, the
Basque financial oligarchy and the Spanish immigrant
proletariat.

Intellectually inspired by early nineteenth century German nationalism, Catalanism, and a strict Jesuit education, Sabino de Arana's ideology contained an eclectic mixture of romantic foralism, populism, Catholicism, and Carlism(7) - and a profound aversion to capitalistic industrialization. The heart of Arana's ideology was encapsulated in two assumptions(8) that continue to constitute the core of Basque nationalist ideology· Basques, who have a history of struggling to maintain their independence, are bound by racial, cultural, and linguistic ties and, therefore, the Basque country, forms a sovereign nation; by natural right, this Basque nation must be governed solely by Basques. Accordingly, the nationalists concluded - and this conclusion is fundamental to an understanding of the social and political nature and logic of Basque nationalism - a Basque is one who, loving his nation, fights for its liberation. In other words, a true Basque can only be a Basque nationalist.

Because the Basques possessed a natural and moral right to political hegemony in the Basque country, a basic task for Arana - as it is for contemporary Basque nationalists - was to define "Basque" and "Basqueness" as a differentiated, exclusive category. He used two principal means to achieve this. First, he articulated symbols of Basque cohesion and exclusivity, symbols which he regarded as representing the Basque mode as opposed to the non-Basque mode. (Heiberg and Escudero, pp. 87-102). Although nationalistic support was primarily confined to urban areas, these symbols were derived from rural society; they consisted of the Basque language, rural culture such as folkdancing and oral poetry, the fueros, and Catholicism. This last symbol was emblazoned in the nationalist slogan, "The Basques for Euzkadi and Euzkadi for God!" Reigning above these symbols was the supreme symbol of Basque distinctiveness and superiority - the Basque race defined genetically and spiritually rather than linguistically. Arana conceived of the Basque language, the rural culture, the fervent Catholicism, and the purity of the Basque race as walls capable of protecting true Basques from being absorbed by other sectors of society inside the Basque country. These elements were destined to struggle for economic and political power in order to achieve an internal nationalism. The fueros and Basque independence were the means by which the Basque country as a whole could be safeguarded from Madrid centralization, or external nationalism.

Second, explicit factors of exclusion were expounded: the Basque obligarchy was rejected for its key role in corrupting and perverting the Basques' awareness of their own identity; and anti-espanolismo, anti- maketismo(9), and anti-socialismo were espoused. Anti-clerical socialism was seen as the total negation of all the basic values of the Basque spirit. Therefore, no one could be truly Basque if he was part of the oligarchy, or if he expressed favor for Spain or things Spanish, sympathy for the immigrants, or socialist tendencies; these were in essence anti-Basque and morally reproachful. Hence, those who fell on the anti-Basque side of the boundary that nationalist exclusivity helped to create were also perceived of as morally contemptible. In nationalist ideology, both the major factions in Basque industrialization were excluded not only from 'Basque' status, but were also ejected from the moral universe.(10)

All the social problems and evils created by industrialization and Spanish infiltration, Arana concluded, would be resolved almost by definition if the four Basque provinces established a free nation, uncontaminated by foreign influences and governed by inherent Basque egalitarianism, Catholic ardor, and the legal harmony of the Basque fueros.

In 1894, Sabino de Arana and his followers, the large majority from the Basque petty-bourgeousie and several who were born in the rural areas, inaugurated the Basque Society (Euskeldun Batzokija) as a political club. Its statutes, which prohibited membership to anyone who could not prove at least two generations of pure Basque descent, and doctrinal position were faithful to Arana's primitive nationalism. In 1895, the Euskeldun Batzokija was transformed into the Partido Nacionalists Vasco (PNV). If the PNV had rigidly followed the political line of its main theorist and initial membership, Basque nationalism would probably have been condemned to remain the cause of a small group of entrenched Basque romantics.

Because of the tremendous impact of Arana's ideas and the lack of a more politically-sophisticated middle class similar to that in Catalonia, a more moderate formulation of nationalist ideology was most likely precluded. However, in the Basque country, partly in response to the chronic Spanish political crisis and partly because of their own economic vulnerability, large sectors of the non-oligarchical industrial and commercial bourgeousie had for some time been agitating for more economic and administrative autonomy. In a sense these Foral Liberals (Liberales Fueristas) - the political party to which many of them adhered - were being forced into a nationalist position. This sector of the urban Basque bourgeousie was pushed into a nationalist stance not because it necessarily felt a wider Basque unity, but because nationalist arguments had immense utility in helping to achieve its goals. In 1898, an event occurred that was of crucial importance for the future of Basque nationalism as a political creed: Unable to establish an independent political presence of significance, a large group of these liberals, headed by an important Bilbao industrialist, Ramon de la Sota, joined the PNV en masse. Arana's exclusive, moral ideology was the political tool the Basque middle bourgeousie needed. On one level, this event opened the

possibility of changing the PNV into a modern, viable political
option; on another, it introduced a fundamental contradiction
into the heart of the party. The fusion of primitive nationalism and modern economic thinking gave the PNV a hybrid,
and in many respects contradictory, ideology; it also gave
strength.

The contradiction erupted repeatedly into tension and
conflict within the nationalist movement, especially after
Arana's premature death in 1903 at the age of 35. On one
side, the intransigent nationalists, mainly from the petty
bourgeousie and many only recently-urbanized, defended a
political line that absolutely excluded any alliances with
Spanish political parties; their goal was the establishment of an
independent, purified Basque state. On the other, the
moderate, liberal nationalists, economically dependent on
Spanish markets and protectionism, aimed at wresting an
autonomy statute for the Basque country; to achieve their
aspiration, the moderates were willing to ally with Spanish
parties at propitious moments. Regardless of their differences
concerning the desired relation with Madrid, however, both
streams within the PNV were united in their aims for the
Basque country. Utilizing the emotive and moral power of
nationalist symbols and ideology, Basque nationalism was an
attempt to impose political hegemony first in Vizcaya and later
in all four Basque provinces.

The internal history of the PNV from 1898 to 1936 re-
volved around the tensions, separations, and reunifications
between the intransigents and moderates. Except for a brief
period, however, the moderate bloc maintained operational
control of the party structure as a result of their understanding of the requisites of pragmatic political action. In
1921, increasing conflict finally split the PNV into two separate
parties; but with the fall of the Primo de Rivera dictatorship
in 1930, it was reunited under the leadership of another
youthful Bilbao lawyer, Jose Antonio Aquirre. With the
moderates clearly in charge, the PNV was firmly dedicated to
negotiating a statute of autonomy with Madrid and augmenting
its political influence at home.(11)

The cultural and political achievements of the Basque
nationalists were considerable. On the cultural front, partly
because there was a need to instill a sense of nationhood into
the Basque people, a renaissance of impressive dimensions took
place. The Basque language was purged of foreign impurities
and attempts were made to create a unified written language.
Folklore and rural culture were studied seriously for the first
time, and often mythified in the process. Scholarly journals
and popular magazines were published in Euskera. Basque
language schools (ikastolas) were established, and massive
folkloric performances that carried heavy political messages,
became frequent popular events. This cultural revival helped

remove the stigma attached to traditional culture. Euskera, which had been regarded as the language of an uncultured peasantry, became the language, at least symbolically, of an urban political vanguard.

The cultural renaissance served other functions as well. It reenforced notions of Basque cultural distinctiveness, and thus promoted the argument for Basque political autonomy. Moreover, it strengthened the barrier between Basques and anti-Basques. Basque culture became irreversibly equated with nationalist politics, which, in turn, gained a monopoly right to use Basque culture and the symbols it offered as political weapons. In addition, the popular base of the nationalist movement was vastly expanded. This was of special importance during the years of the Primo de Rivera dictatorship 1923-1930, when political nationalism and political parties were prohibited, but cultural nationalism allowed; Basque songs and dances appealed to both urban and rural youth. These frequent mass events, and the organizational activities surrounding them helped to transform nationalist supporters into a growing community bound by shared political, moral, and social codes. This characteristic of the Basque nationalist movement is of crucial importance. Basque nationalism was not only a political movement, but a social one as well. In many families, nationalist sentiment became a tradition imbibed "with the mother's milk." The nationalists came to perceive themselves as a separate social group regardless of their class and other differences. This social cohesiveness provided opportunities for a far-reaching personalized organization and unity that the other main political forces - the socialists and conservatives - lacked.

On the political front, the nationalists were pressed between two equally distasteful poles. On one side, they were violently attacked by the progressively-militant socialists who were rapidly gaining converts throughout the industrial areas of the Basque country, and who were appalled by nationalist conservatism and archreligiosity. On the other, the conservatives and revitalized Carlists hated the idea of Basque separatism, and vehemently denied the nationalists' claim that they alone were the exclusive inheritors of Basque identity and destiny. Despite these two "anti-Basque" enemies at their flank, the nationalists' first election victory came in 1898; Sabino de Arana, with heavy support from Ramon de la Sota and the liberals, was elected deputy to the Bilbao city council (ayuntamiento). The political entrepreneurial skills of the nationalist moderates helped the PNV to grow quickly. As industrialization spilled over into Guipuzcoa, the PNV influence spread with it. The nationalists found especially strong support in those rural areas on the margins of the industrialized zones. With priests, teachers, doctors and lawyers carrying the nationalist message into these rural areas, the nationalists

replaced the Carlists as the chief political power in the rural
parts of Guipuzcoa and Vizcaya.(12)
      By 1918, the PNV had wrested control of the Diputacion
of Vizcaya from the conservatives and liberals, and had managed to send seven of its members as deputies to the Madrid
Parliament (Cortes). However, the nationalists' major electoral
triumph came in 1933 during the Second Republic; the PNV
managed to capitalize on the widespread Basque fear of many
of the policies, particularly those concerning the Church and
land reform, enacted or proposed by the Republican government. The PNV won 36 percent of the vote in Guipuzcoa, 9
percent in Navarra, 44 percent in Vizcaya, and 29 percent in
Alava.(13) In the critical elections of 1936, support for the
nationalists dwindled slightly, but nevertheless, they managed
to capture over 33 percent of the electoral vote. The remaining 66 percent was evenly divided between the nationalists' two traditional adversaries, the socialists and the
republicans. The socialists' main base of support was the
immigrant workers, although many of the leaders were
Basque by descent; and the republicans represented the
Basque economic elite.
      The political successes of the Basque nationalists cul-
minated in October 1936 shortly after the onset of the Spanish
Civil War(14); the autonomous government of Euzkadi was
formed, and Jose Antonio Aquirre was named President. Nine
months later, Euzkadi was overthrown by General Franco's
military crusade.

           The Post War Period, The Emergence of ETA
                and The Reemergence of Nationalism

      Following the Civil War, Basque nationalism was paralyzed
into dormancy by a campaign of harsh political and cultural
repression.(15) Thousands of Basque nationalists were im-
prisoned, or sought the relative safety of exile. Many were
executed. In its initial years, the Franco regime seemed
intent on destroying all vestiges of Basque culture. It was
argued that because Basque nationalism had employed cultural
elements as political instruments, banning Basque culture
would remove signs of separatism. Franco wanted to achieve
that which had eluded all previous heads of Spain - the
definitive unification of Spain. Spain was to become "una,
libre y grande." Public use of the Basque language was
prohibited; all Basque names were erased from public
buildings; displays of Basque folklore were declared illegal;
and severe fines and prison sentences were meted out to those
caught teaching the Basque language.(16)
      With the collapse of the fascist regimes in Italy and Ger-
many at the end of World War II, the Basques were euphoric.

They believed that an invasion of Spain by the Allies, alongside of whom many Basque exiles had fought, was imminent.
In part because of Churchill's fears of another socialist country flanking Europe, the invasion never occurred. The PNV's
dwindling hopes for the overthrow of Franco were finally
crushed in 1953 when, in the atmosphere of the Cold War, the
U.S. signed an agreement to provide economic and military aid
to Spain. Although the Spanish regime liberalized its repressive measures slightly, the PNV had already entered into a
period of inactivity and organizational decline.

Many Basque youths, especially those from the Bilbao
middle classes who had grown up in the family tradition of
nationalism, felt repulsion and impatience with the political
apathy of the PNV. Moreover, it was recognized that, although the PNV was politically oppressed by Franco, many
PNV members benefited from Franco's economic policies. In
1952, a group of Bilbao students started a magazine named
"Ekin," meaning "to do." The magazine published articles
about eighteenth century Basque egalitarianism, the existence
of a unified Basque state in the ninth century, and other
idealized versions of Basque history. Initially, the originators
of "Ekin," who were later to form the leadership of Euskadi
and Liberty (Euskadi 'Ta Askatasuna ETA), had an ideology
similiar to that of the PNV. However, there was one important
exception; because of the Church's avid support of the Franco
regime, this group felt a deep sense of betrayal by
Catholicism, and "Ekin" was staunchly non-religious. During
1955-56, many of the disenchanted PNV youths fused with the
"Ekin" group. In 1959, all ties with the PNV were broken and
the ETA was founded.

Although initially it blended Arana's primitive nationalism
with a deep sense of Christian commitment, four factors
pushed ETA firmly into the camp of leftist militancy: 1) the
model provided by the European student movements in the
1960s, 2) the example offered by the Franco regime on the
political efficiency of violence, 3) the desire to destroy the
image promulgated by the PNV of the inherent passiveness of
the Basque people, and, perhaps most important, 4) the 1962
publication of the book, Vasconia, by the ETA militant,
Frederico Krutwig (Ortzi, pp. 295-313).

Strongly influenced by the Algerian experience, Krutwig
argued that, before its subjugation and transformation into a
colony by Spain and France, Euskadi had been a nation free
from class war. The national and social repression of the
Basques went hand in hand, and, therefore, the fight for
national liberation and socialism must also go together.
Krutwig attacked Catholicism as an instrument of the Spanish
state and as "anti-Basque" because the Basques were, by
nature, pagans. In using Algeria as his model, Krutwig
mapped out the principles of the "revolutionary war for liber-

ation." Basque nationalism was to be part of the revolutionary
nationalism of the Third World. The three major elements in
the Third World model, independence, armed struggle, and
socialism, were all adopted by ETA. In Krutwig, ETA found
both ideological justification and military strategy.

ETA gradually began an armed attack on the symbols of
Spanish domination - railroads, television and radio trans-
mitters, and Spanish war memorials. Finally, in 1968, ETA's
attack stretched to the hated Spanish police. The Franco
regime responded with random, massive repression. The
Basque country became involved in an ever-accelerating spiral
of violence and counter-violence. States of emergency were
frequently imposed, road controls were constant, and Basque
political prisoners swelled the Spanish jails. Stirred by the
militancy of ETA, the draconian measures of the police, the
work of Basque priests in the countryside, and a new influx
of Spanish immigrants, popular support for Basque nationalism
was rekindled. Although few supported ETA's Marxist
ideology, ETA enjoyed the empathy of Basques of all political
persuasions. For many, ETA militants became the new heros,
sounding the bell for nationalism. For the majority, they were
the vanguard of the struggle against the despised Franco
regime.

However, the "colonialist model" did not fit easily into the
economic reality of the Basque provinces. The period of
1950-65 saw the second great wave of Basque industrialization.
Again, capital was mainly in Basque hands and unskilled labor
was supplied by an enormous inflow of immigrant workers, who
brought the total non-Basque population close to 50 percent.
With the industrial prosperity generated, the Basque country
enjoyed a standard of living some 60 percent higher than the
Spanish norm. Moreover, the relations between the Basque
and Spanish communities were marked by mutual distrust and
resentment. The two groups led separate social lives and met
only in their places of employment. On the "grass-roots"
level, and especially in the recently-industrialized areas, the
Spanish workers were viewed as perfidious economic and
cultural competitors.

The combination of socialism and nationalism presented
these young, left-wing Basque nationalists with an un-
resolvable contradiction. The conflict between the ideological
and tactical prerogatives of nationalism and socialism slowly
began to rip ETA apart. From 1967 to date, ETA and the
nationalist movement in general has split repeatedly into
various factions, with the myriad of new political groups each
possessing its own special mixture of nationalism and Marxist
and non-Marxist socialism.

The cultural and political repression of the Basques under
Franco, the general resentment against excessive centralization, the increasing visibility of "minority" nationalism in Eu-

rope, and ETA's militancy combined to give Basque nationalism
a far-reaching legitimacy that it had not enjoyed previously.
Large sectors of both the Basque and immigrant population
were allied in support of many nationalist demands. During
the last year of the Franco regime and the present two years
of the "democratic transition," demands for autonomy and
bilingualism have been increasingly incorporated into the
platforms of even the centralized political parties, such as the
PSOE and the Communist Party. In the tense political atmosphere of the Basque country, the idea that the Basques
constitute a sovereign nation that should be governed by
Basques has gained profound moral recognition. As the
originator and prime defender of this idea, Basque nationalism
has cemented its claim to be the final arbitrator and protector
of Basque identity. It has acquired the moral hegemony it
sought.

Although a broad agreement exists between the Basque
opposition parties - nationalist and non-nationalist - on what
terms should govern the relationship between the Basque
country and Madrid, and although the Basque country has
been granted a restricted Home Rule, tension and antagonisms
within the region are severe. The situation is complex and
subtle, and it functions on several levels. First, although the
nationalists view themselves as part of the same ideological
family, the nationalist ranks are sharply - at times virulently -
divided into two main camps, which unite only in opposition to
the non-nationalist parties. Essentially this split reflects the
continued divergence of the political lines adopted by the
Basque middle and petty bourgeousie. The middle bourgeousie
and important sectors of Basque farmers are incorporated into
the PNV, which reemerged with vigor in 1973 when party
politics again became feasible. By far the most important
nationalist party, the PNV joins nationalist populism with
parliamentary politics. Opposing the PNV are an array of
bitterly-fragmented, radical nationalist groups formed around,
ot descended from, ETA. These groups combine revolutionary
nationalism, utopian socialism, and extra-parliamentary political
action. The social base of this latter stream of nationalists
comprises urban youth, Basques in recently-industrialized
areas, Basque farmers who have mixed agricultural and industrial incomes, and considerable sections of the Basque petty
bourgeousie in general.

Second, in addition to tensions within the nationalist
movement, party politics in the Basque country are unusually
sectarian. In recent years, the Basque region was the only
significant area of Spain that could not unite in political opposition to the Franco regime; the polarization between nationalists and non-nationalists proved unbridgeable. Now,
as previously, the nationalists see themselves wedged in
between their two traditional opponents. This view was amply

verified by the parliamentary election results of June 1977, when the 3 main blocks in Basque politics - the non-nationalist right, the nationalists, and the non-nationalist left - sent almost equal numbers of deputies to the new Madrid Cortes.(17)   Moreover, the PSOE emerged as the largest single party in the Basque country, with the PNV a close second, and the Union Centro Democratico (UCD) running third. Because electoral power is so evenly distributed among the three groups, tactical alliances are a necessity, especially on the critical issue of autonomy.   Although the PSOE and PNV unite to obstruct UCD initiatives, relations between the two are strained.   Nationalist claims to moral hegemony have been successfully translated into claims to political hegemony.   In spite of the PSOE's stronger electoral performance, the PNV has won the struggle for political precedence.   The situation has been made more acute by the radical nationalists' attempts to maintain the heated pre-election atmosphere by continued mass mobilizations and ETA "milis"(18), and renewed armed attacks against the police, Basque industrialists, and state bureaucrats.

However, the key to the Basque political situation lies in the political and social effects and the logic of nationalist ideology itself.   In the multi-ethnic environment of the Basque country, the differentiation, consolidation, and mobilization of one group of people defined as "Basque" in opposition to another group defined as "anti-Basque" remains an inevitable consequence of Basque nationalist ideology.   The core of this ideology continues to be embedded in premises concerning "nationality," and in highly-emotive symbols of separateness. Neither the premises nor the symbols are open to debate; they are popularly regarded and defended as self-evident, a part of a natural order.   The new symbols are similar to the old: Euskera, the Basque language, symbolizes the existence of a separate culture and nationality; Basque culture reaffirms this existence; Basque history underlines the assumption that the Basques always have been independent and, therefore, re-enforces claims for independence now; and finally, the superiority of the Basque social and moral order, symbolized in the pre-war period by Basque advocacy of Catholicism, has been represented in the post-war period by socialism.   Even the PNV has publicly announced itself as socialist.

For political purposes a Basque - or, rather, a true Basque - is one who actively and politically defends these symbols of Basque cohesion and differentiation.   The immoral are those who threaten or go against their moral prescriptions. Ethnic assignation - who is or is not considered Basque - is not determined by criteria of descent.   One of the Basques' most revered martyrs, Juan Paredes Manot, was an immigrant who spoke no Euskera; "Long live free Euskadi!" he cried as he was executed by Franco's police.   A person is "Basque"

when he is seen to adhere to the symbols of Basqueness; and
the symbols of Basqueness are exclusively nationalist property,
a point with which many would violently disagree.

During the late 1960s and early 1970s another cultural
renaissance was launched by ETA with support from all the
opposition groups. Basque literature was published; Basque
language schools (ikastolas) blossomed throughout the region;
and many folk groups singing in Euskera were started. The
defense and revitalization of Basque culture - or what was
sometimes referred to as the "renationalization of Euskadi" -
was regarded as a moral duty of all Basques. Although most
of the people connected to the ikastolas were of nationalist
sympathies, many of the Basque-speaking (euskaldun) teachers
were affiliated with communist parties. Moreover, one of the
most famous of the Basque folk groups was comprised primarily
of communists.

Throughout the early 1970s, the ikastolas were the scenes
of bitter dispute as the nationalists attempted, usually successfully, to oust the non-nationalist Basque teachers. In one
year alone, more than 50 such teachers were dismissed.
Similarly, the folk group was consistently boycotted, and its
performances disrupted, by nationalist supporters; during one
performance, an ETA militant, to the delight of many of his
sympathizers, mounted the stage and bashed the lead singer
on the nose. For the nationalists, Euskera, is more than a
cultural element; it is a political symbol of national legitimacy.
It is a powerful, political resource to which only "Basques"
ought to have access.

In politics, ideology shapes political demands and party
platforms. In the Basque case, these symbols that function to
exclude and differentiate are directly translated into concrete
political proposals that debar and discriminate. For example,
frequent nationalist resolutions have proposed that all public
office holders - elected and non-elected - should be fluent in
Euskera as well as Spanish, thus effectively barring 76 percent of the population from public office. Nationalists have
also proposed that one qualification for a job should be a
knowledge of the Basque language, and that eventually all
public life in the Basque country should be carried on solely
in Euskera. Their argument is that, unless knowledge of
Euskera becomes a political and economic necessity, the
language will disappear entirely within a short time.

Nationalism has created two antagonistic political
communities in the Basque country. Cutting across class and
urban or rural boundaries, a deep polarization divides the
political arena and all areas of public activity. Political
parties, artistic production, amnesty organizations, historical
research, economic enterprises, schools, newspapers, public
work projects, popular festivals - all are categorized
into abertzale (patriotic) or espanolista, nationalist or non-

nationalist, Basque or anti-Basque. Increasingly, this social boundary is being used to achieve differential access to political power and economic and social resources. In the worsening economic crisis now facing the Basque country, scarce commodities are Basque by "national" right.(19)

SOME CONCLUSIONS

Within the limits of this article many crucial aspects of the Basque situation have not been discussed. Basque nationalism has been treated as the struggle for political vis-a-vis Madrid - external nationalism - and the struggle for precedence within the Basque country - internal nationalism Moreover, it has centered on elite political strategies and aims, and not on "grass-roots" nationalist support and sentiment. This is, of course, only part of the situation. The function and meaning of Basque nationalism in the euskaldun rural areas and on the local level present many features absent in the urban politicized context. Nationalist arguments concerning culture cannot be reduced to mere decorations for what are regarded as inherently economic and political relationships. As I have argued elsewhere (Heiberg, 1975) at the root of Basque nationalist sentiment - often obscured by nationalist manipulation of cultural symbols - lies a profound cultural crisis and conflict.

NOTES

1. "Foral" comes from the Spanish word fuero, or fors in French. During the Middle Ages, the kings of Castilla granted the various Basque districts and provinces special charters and privileges called fueros. The legal institutions established by these fueros - general assemblies, local councils, etc. - provided the framework for the traditional Basque legal and political system.
2. The foral regime existed in Navarra until 1842 and in Alava, Vizcaya, and Guipuzcoa until 1876.
3. The Carlist Wars were complicated. Nominally, they concerned a conflict over succession to the Spanish throne, with the champions of Don Carlos, brother of the deceased king, Ferdinand VII, arrayed against the defenders of the late king's infant daughter. However, Carlism was actually a revolt against the economic, political, and religious policies of the liberal regime in Madrid.
4. Basque nationalists frequently argue that Euskera has

declined as a spoken language because Madrid repressed
the Basque culture. This argument, although certainly
valid for the 40 years of the Franco dictatorship, is very
misleading. Arturo Campion, Basque nationalist writing
in the nineteenth century, placed the blame for the disappearance of the Basque language squarely on Basque
families who refused to teach Euskera to their children
because it was deemed an inferior language to Spanish.
Sabino de Arana, writing in the 1890s, estimated that
only a half of Bilbao's Basque population were familiar
with Euskera.

5. The best description and analysis of these strikes and the
labor movement in the Basque country in general can be
found in J.P. Fusi, Politica Obrera en el Pais Vasco
(Madrid, 1975).

6. Whereas prior to the nineteenth century lawyers were
almost a despised class in the Basque country, in the
nineteenth century they came into their own as political
figures. Today in the Basque country almost every
important political leader is a lawyer.

7. These assumptions are most explicitly formulated by Arana
in his book, Bizkaya por su independencia, published in
1892.

8. Arana synthesized his ideas and those of his party in the
slogan, Jaun-Goikua eta Lagi-Zarra, which means, God
and the Old Laws. The early nationalists called themselves JELs, and were often referred to by others as the
JEL, after this principal slogan of the nationalist party.

9. Maketo was a derogatory term used to refer to Spanish
immigrants in the Basque country.

10. I emphasize the moral and symbolic elements in the
nationalist ideology because, in my opinion, it is the
strong influence of these elements in Basque nationalism
that give it a markedly-different character from Catalanism, which was more based on arguments of specific
regional interests and achievements.

11. The constant failures of the Basques in negotiating a
statute of autonomy contrasted markedly with the success
of the Catalans. To protest the PNV's inability to force
through a statute, the most extreme wing of the PNV,
known as Jagi-Jagi after the magazine they published,
left the party and started an intense campaign to achieve
Basque independence. Composed mainly of radicalized
youth from the petty bougeousie, the Jagi-Jagi to a
significant degree was similar to the radical nationalists of
today who function within the orbit of ETA.

12. Nationalist penetration into the rural areas had been slow
partly because the nationalist image of the free, con-
tented Basque farmer, proud and noble in his Basqueness - an image used to mobilize the urban masses - had

little in common with actual rural conditions. Most Basque farmers were tenant farmers, under the political control of the larger landowners, who were Carlist in political affiliation. In the late 1910s, the PNV began to establish farmers' organizations throughout the rural areas. These helped the Basque farmers to buy their own land. Moreover, these organizations provided legal aid and special insurance schemes for the peasantry. It was in this period that the PNV became more aware of the rural situation and began to agitate for bilingualism in the public sphere.

13. The rest of the election results for the 1933 elections were as follows (small parties have been omitted):
     Alava - Carlists - 52%, left-wing coalition - 12%
     Guipuzcoa - Union of the Right - 19%, Socialist - 36%
     Navarra - Carlists - 71%, Socialists - 14%
     Vizcaya - Right-wing coalition - 15%,
              Socialist/Republicans - 37%

14. Because the nationalists had viewed both the right and the Republicans with almost equal distrust, the first weeks of the Civil War presented the PNV with a considerable dilemma. Some nationalists argued that it was a war between Spaniards, and, as such, did not concern the Basques. Several days went by before the PNV could decide which side to join. The promise of a statute of autonomy from the Republican government was important in the nationalists' decision. After the fall of Bilbao, several attempts were made to negotiate a separate peace for the Basque country with the Italians.

15. Although the punishment meted out to the Basque country during the months following the fall of Bilbao was harsh, it did not compare with the level of brutality witnessed in Andalucia. Needing Basque industry, and especially the armament industry centered in Eibar, Franco attempted to avoid unnecessarily alienating Basque industrialists.

16. Particularly hard hit by these measures were the rural Basques, many of whom spoke no Spanish. By government decree also, all church services had to be conducted solely in Spanish. Many of the deeply Catholic Basque farmers felt that the Franco regime had deprived them not only of their culture, but also of their church. Rural allegiance to the nationalist cause today can, in part, be explained by the very direct, hard manner in which the rural Basques experienced the oppressive cultural policies of the Franco regime.

17. The results of the 1977 elections to the Madrid Cortes were as follows (listed in terms of deputies elected)·
     Alava - PNV - 1, PSOE - 1, UCD - 2
     Guipuzcoa - EE (Euskadiko Ezkerra, an electoral alliance
         of radical nationalists) - 1, PNV - 3, PSOE - 3

Navarra - PSOE - 2, UCD - 3
Vizcaya - AP (Alianza Popular, neo-Francoists) - 1,
   PNV - 5, PSOE - 3, UCD - ˉ

18. ETA has undergone many new splits in the last four years. The ETA "milis," or militares, formerly the military wing of ETA, is now an independent organization that aims, primarily by military means, to establish an independent, socialist Basque state.

19. Between December 1977 and February 1978, there were some signs that the campaign against unemployment had to some extent united the nationalists and non-nationalists in the big cities such as Bilbao and San Sebastian.

BIBLIOGRAPHY

Caro Baroja, J. Introduction a la Historia Social y Economica del Pueblo Vasco. San Sebastian: Txertoa, 1974.

Carr, R. Spain 1808 - 1939. London: Clarendon Press, 1966.

Corcuera, J. "Tradicionalismo y burguesia en la formacion del nacionalismo vasco" in Materiales Nr. 5, Barcelona, 1977.

Douglass, W. "Basque nationalism," The Limits of Integration: Ethnicity and Nationalism in Modern Europe. Research Reports Nr. 9, University of Massachusetts, 1971.

Gellner, E. Thought and Change. London, 1964.

_____. i.d. 'Scale and Nation' paper prepared in advance for participants in Burg Wartenstein Symposium Nr. 55, 1972.

Heiberg, M. "Insiders/Outsiders: Basque nationalism," European Journal of Sociology, XVI, Paris: Musee de l'Homme, 1975.

Heiberg, M. and M. Escudero. "Sabino de Arana: la logica del nacionalismo vasco" in Materiales Nr. 5, Barcelona, 1977.

Hobsbawn, E. "Some reflections on the 'Break-up of Britain,'" New Left Review Nr. 105, London, 1977.

Kendourie, E. Nationalism. London, 1966.

Minogue, K.R. Nationalism. London: Methuen, 1967.

Ortzi. Historia de Euskadi: el nacionalismo vasco y ETA. Ruedo Iberico, 1975.

Payne, S. El Nacionalismo Vasco. Barcelona: Dopesa, 1974.

11 Internal Colonialism and Rising Expectations: Ethnic Activism in Contemporary France*

William R. Beer

> Without centralization there can be no France.
> Germany and Italy can exist without it, because
> there is a single German civilization and one Italian
> civilization. But in France there are several
> civilizations. And they have not disappeared....
>
> —Alexandre Sanguinetti

The resurgence of ethnicity as a political and social force
in the developed societies of the world is well recognized, even
though it is still not well understood. The expectation that
modernization would eclipse such primordial sentiments has not
been borne out. Ethnic consciousness and conflict are growing
in Austria, Belgium, Britain, Canada, Spain, Switzerland, and
Yugoslavia.(1) Since 1960, and accelerating after 1968, France
has also experienced an ethnic renaissance in Alsace,
Flanders, Brittany, the French Basque country, French
Catalonia, Corsica, and the portion of southern France known
as Occitania. The activists that have appeared in these
regions consider themselves to be part of an ethnic movement
(Heraud), and focus on language as a distinctive aspect of
their social identity.(2) The level of political mobilization in
each of France's ethnic regions is very uneven, varying from
terrorism through electoral politics to cultural societies, but
there is evidence that its degree is related to levels of
economic prosperity and rates of social change.

---

*The author would like to express his thanks to Professor
Frank Hull of the Brooklyn College Department of Sociology for
his advice, and to Mme. Tuma of the Service de Presse of the
French Consulate in New York for her assistance.

Ethnic activism(3) in modern society defies expectations. Social theories of the late nineteenth and early twentieth centuries assumed that, as capitalism (Marx and Engels, p. 12), rationality (Weber, p. 389), or the division of labor (Durkheim, p. 187) spread and developed, modern social formations would supersede previous social forms, including ethnicity. Modern social theories, such as structural functionalism (Parsons, pp. 172-176), insofar as they have dealt with ethnicity, similarly consider that it is a sentiment antithetical to modernity. And political theorists of "nation-building" (Deutsch, p. 162; Pye, pp. 33-45; Almond and Powell, pp. 299-332; Kautsky, p. 25-34) have also led us to expect that, as social formations are modernized in the framework of nation-states, ethnic differences are supplanted by homogeneous national consciousness.

ʹn this sense, the appearance of ethnic activism in modern societies is an anomaly, an empirical reality that cannot be accommodated by the prevailing pattern of thought in social science (Kuhn, pp. 52-65). Glazer and Moynihan, Fishman Novak, Berger, Connor, Enloe, Heisler, and DaSilva are among those who have tried to come to grips with this anomaly; and Hechter has given us a systematic framework in which to understand it. What follows below is both an attempt to explain the resurgence of ethnic activism in France, and an attempt to resolve one of the principle anomalies in contemporary social science. Two theoretical constructs can be used to explain this apparent paradox: one is the theory of internal colonialism, and the other is a version of the theory of relative deprivation, that of rising expectations. Although France is the context examined in this paper, these theories have relevance to similar phenomena in other developed societies. Although the central problem is a theoretical one, there are explanations which are unique to France. Before examining the generally-applicable theoretical frameworks, a historical background of ethnic activism in France must be sketched.

HISTORICAL BACKGROUND

The ethnic regions of France were added to the nation before, or at the beginning of, the nineteenth century by conquest and annexation, and some have since been lost and regained. Alsace was annexed to the realm by Louis XIV in 1648, following the Thirty Years War. It remained part of France until the Franco-Prussian War. From 1871 until 1918, the region was under German domination. It was again French from 1918 until 1940, when it became part of the Third Reich until its Liberation.

Although French incursions into Flanders began under

Louis XIV, a segment of the Flemish-speaking population did not officially come under French rule until the boundaries between France and Belgium were established in their present form after the Congress of Vienna.

Brittany was formally annexed in 1532, although it had been under French influence ever since the defeat of the Plantagenets.

The areas in France where Basque is spoken were ceded to the kingdom in 1589, when Henri of Navarre became Henri IV of France; and those where Catalan is spoken joined France under the provisions of the Treaty of Pyrenees in 1657.

Corsica was briefly under French control from 1552 to 1559. After that time, it was under Genoese rule until Pascal Paoli founded an independent Corsican state in 1755. In 1768, it was annexed to France, fell under English control in 1790, and was regained by France in 1796.

Occitania, more a linguistic than a geographic entity, refers to the areas where the "oc" dialects of French are spoken. It includes most of southern France, which was joined to the Crown by the Hundred Years' War and the Albigensian Crusades.

Each of the populations in these once autonomous regions is either linguistically distinct from the French-speaking population of the rest of the country, or has vestiges of this linguistic difference in accents, place names, and family names. A German dialect is spoken in Alsace, Flemish in Flanders, Breton in Brittany, Basque in the French Basque country, Catalan in French Catalonia, an Italian dialect in Corsica, and several "oc" dialects in Occitania. That they were conquered, are ethnically-distinct, and, in some cases, have existed as independent states gives weight to the contention that they are colonies within the French nation.

France's ethnic regions long antedated the establishment of departments during the Revolution, but each corresponds to a department, or a number of departments, closely enough so that these modern geographical entities can be used to define the ethnic regions. The equivalencies of departments and regions used in this study are as follows: Alsace(4) includes Haut-Rhin and Bas-Rhin; Flanders, Nord and Pas-de-Calais; Brittany, Ille-et-Vilaine, Cotes-du-Nord, Finistere, and Morbihan; Basque Country, Pyrenees-Atlantiques; French Catalonia, Pyrenees Orientales; Corsica, Corse, which was separated into two departments in 1974; Occitania, Haute-Vienne, Creuse, Correze, Allier, Puy-de-Dome, Cantal, Haute-Loire, Lot, Aveyron, Tarn-et-Garonne, Tarn, Haute-Garonne, Gers, Hautes-Pyrenees, Ariege, Dordogne, Lot-et-Garonne, Lozere, Gard, Herault, Aude, Isere, Drome, Ardeche, Hautes-Alpes, Vaucluse, and Alpes-de-Haute-Provence.(5)

The Revolution can be considered as a starting point in

the history of ethnic activities in France; in erasing the administrative districts of the old regime, it subjected all
provinces to the direct rule of Paris.   Where there had been
differing degrees of autonomy and regional peculiarities, there
was now rigid centralization under the unilingual control of the
capital.   Federalists,   counter-revolutionary   royalists,   and
linguistic minorities were linked together in the Jacobin point
of view, as the following quote from a Revolutionary minister
indicates:

> We have revolutionized the government, customs and
> thought; let us also revolutionize language.   Feder-
> alism and superstition speak Bas-Breton; emigration
> and hatred of the Republic speak German; counter-
> revolution speaks Italian; fanaticism speaks Basque
> (Serant, 1965, pp. 30-31).

The history of ethnic activism in France has been marked
by hostility between Jacobin centralism and regional and ethnic
particularisms.   In considering this history from the Revolution
until the aftermath of World War II, each region is examined in
turn.   This is not meant to be a definitive history of ethnic
activism;   further   references   will   be   cited   for   each   region.
In Alsace, there was no autonomist agitation until the
area was ceded to Prussia.   In 1872, in fact, 5000 Alsatians
and Lorrains emigrated to France to preserve their nationality.
Anti-German, autonomist sentiment rose steadily, and, in 1877,
five autonomist candidates were elected to the Reichstag.   This
drive for autonomy had such an effect that Alsace was granted
its own regional Diet in 1911.
In 1918, Alsace was returned to France without plebiscite,
a violation of the Wilsonian principle of self-determination, that
autonomists were later to point out.   The return of the region
meant the loss of all local autonomy, and a resumption of
Jacobin control.   Nonetheless, the overwhelming majority of
Alsatians welcomed the reunion with France.
During the interwar period, ethnic activist episodes were
confined to the 1920s.   Two autonomist parties had been
founded after World War I, but they received little support.
In the early 1920s, the Premier Edouard Herriot, a radical
socialist, attempted to suppress ethnic languages all over
France, and to separate the Church and state in Alsace - the
Law of Separation of Church and State of 1905 having been
passed when Alsace was still under German control.   These
interventions stirred a heated response from some Alsatians.
In 1926, the Elsass-Lothringer Heimatbund was established,
and it proceeded to publish broadsides against the government's interference.   Twenty-two Alsatian activists were arrested and tried at the Colmar Trial of 1928; a measure of
popular support for the defendants was that one was elected

a deputy while incarcerated. However, from then until the World War II, there was little ethnic activism in Alsace.

Very few Alsatians collaborated with the Third Reich or were Nazis. Over 100,000 men were drafted into the Wehrmacht and sent to Russia, but their military service was hardly voluntary. Although Alsatian troops were present at the reprisal massacre at Curadour in Southern France, they did not participate in the killing. For a further account of ethnic activism in Alsace, see Maugue.

In French Flanders ethnic sentiment was essentially cultural and was not directed against Paris or identified with a foreign power until after World War I. The Comite Flamand de France was set up by de Cousemaker in 1852, but it was primarily a cultural society whose aim was the preservation of local folklore. Although some anti-Parisian clerical elements were attracted to it after the Law of Separation of Church and State, it remained essentially a cultural association.

Abbe Gantois and some other priests founded the Vlaamse Verbond van Frankrijk in 1924; an explicitly autonomist party inspired by the Pan-German theories of Treitschke, it had only about fifteen members until after the German invasion of France. With German support, Gantois remained its head; he also established a youth group, the Zuid-Vlaamse Jeugd, in 1942. However, these were really puppet organizations that had very little appeal to the French Flemings. Although an SS unit was composed of Belgian Flemings, French Flemings never had their own military unit in the Wehrmacht, even though some doubtless participated as individuals. For the history of French Flanders in general, see Trenard (1972); for a discussion of Flemish Nazis, see Dejonghe.

Of all the ethnic minorities in France, the Bretons have the longest and strongest history of ethnic activism - whether cultural, autonomist or separatist. The cultural Association Bretonne was founded in 1829, and the political Union Regionaliste Bretonne in 1898. Catholic activism was wedded to Breton nationalism in the Bleun-Brug in 1905. In 1911, the Parti Nationaliste Breton was established, the first explicitly separatist party in modern France.

The currents of separatist, non-sectarian cultural, and Catholic cultural sentiment resumed in the interwar period: In 1928, the Parti Autonomiste Breton was established to represent the separatists, who came to be known by the name of their publication "Brittany Forever" (Breiz Atao); Ar Falz was a non-sectarian publication whose aim was to promulgate the Breton language by teaching it to children; and Catholic ethnic activism reappeared in Bleun-Brug, which became increasingly nationalistic.

By 1938, the activity of the Breiz Atao group had become serious enough to provoke a law against autonomist activity; groups that threatened the territorial integrity of France were

forbidden. This climaxed a series of incidents that included
the dynamiting of a statue in Rennes commemorating the annexation of Brittany. The group claiming responsibility for
this act called themselves "Black and White" (Gwenn Ha Du),
but there is little doubt that its members came from among
Breiz Atao followers (Reece, p. 127).
       With the growth of fascism in Germany and Italy, the
position of the newly-renamed Parti Nationaliste Breton moved
steadily to the right. When war was declared between France
and Germany, two Breton leaders, Mordrel and Debeauvais,
went to Berlin and were given promises of Nazi support.
They returned to France with the Wehrmacht and made an
unsuccessful attempt to set up military units composed of
Breton soldiers who had been taken prisoner. The Conseil
National Breton was established in 1940, but it remained only a
symbol of Breton self-government throughout the war. In
1943, Breton shock troops (Bezenn Perrot) were formed to
fight against the Resistance; when the Allies advanced the
Bezenn Perrot retreated with the Germans. A measure of the
collaboration in Brittany was that 800 were executed after
Liberation. The bibliography of the Breton movements is vast;
see, for example, Reece and Serant (1971).
       Until the present time, there was practically no
autonomist activity in the French Basque Country and French
Catalonia that was directed against Paris. The cultural
centers of both areas were outside France, and their central
concern was the severity or leniency of Madrid. During the
interwar period, Catalans and Basques were preoccupied with
the ethnic overtones of Franco's war against the Republic;
Guernica is a center of Basque culture, and Basques were
aware that Franco's choice of it for civilian bombing was
related to the Republic's support of limited Basque autonomy.
For further reading on Catalonia, see Bernardo; and, on
Basque nationalism, see Davant.
       Until recently, regional sentiment in Occitania was mainly
apolitical and confined to the literary elite, whose cultural
movement, the Felibrige, was under the leadership of the
Provencal poet, Mistral. From 1854 to 1870, it was a literary
and romantic movement, an attempt to breathe life into the
civilization that had produced the troubadors. After 1870,
until the 1930s, it became increasingly royalist. According to
some, there was a second Felibrige. This so-called "Red"
Felibrige, which supported the vintners' revolt in 1907, was
supposedly a leftist Occitan movement to offset the royalist
Felibrige, but it never amounted to much. For the history of
"occitanism" see, for instance, Espieux (1970) and Lafont.
       Before 1918, Corsican ethnic activism was virtually non-
existent. Chronic banditry was directed not so much against
the French as against any authority, and there was a brief

eruption against the high cost of imports from the mainland in 1910. In 1920, a separatist periodical, A Muvra, was founded by the Rocca brothers, and, in 1922, they set up the Partitu Corsu d'Azzione, later called the Partitu Corsu Autonomistu. Because Corsica was part of Italia irredenta, these groups were subsidized by Mussolini. The PCA held an "Estates General" of Corsica in 1934, but, although some 600 delegates attended, the feeling it reflected did not run deep. After the conquest of France, Corsican prisoners were offered their own military units as part of the Axis forces, as had been tried with Bretons. No Corsican soldier accepted the offer. Desjardins provides a concise history of Corsican regionalism.

After World War II, ethnic activism in France, touched as it was by the stigma of collaboration, was moribund. Brittany was the only region where ethnic activism persisted before the onset of the Algerian War, which was one of the causes of the current resurgence of ethnic activity in France. Algeria had been considered an integral part of France since the turn of the century; however, the fact that it had been separated from the nation by a successful guerrilla movement indicated that France was not "one and indivisible." Following on the heels of the loss of Indochina, the Algerian War encouraged some of France's ethnic regions to think of themselves as colonies that might also successfully wage a war of independence.

The French government itself has also contributed to the growth of regional awareness through its attempts at decentralization. Started during the Fourth Republic and implemented during the Fifth, these established regions - agglomerations of departments - for planning purposes, attempted to build the aerospace industry around Toulouse and the industrial center of Fos near Marseille. Although these attempts may seem feeble in their effects, the government's explicit acknowledgement of the need for regionalization unquestionably had its consequences. A 1969 referendum asked the electorate if they agreed with De Gaulle's plan for regionalization; the real purpose of the referendum may well have been to test the General's legitimacy after the near-revolution of May 1968, but discussion prior to it served to stimulate regional feeling. The opposition has also helped to raise ethnic feelings; during the electoral campaign of 1978, the Socialist Party, within the Union of the Left, expressed sympathy for the ethnic regions. Self-management (autogestion), a part of the non-communist left's program, entailed giving these regions substantially more power over their own affairs.

The Days of May also aided the growth of ethnic activism in France. Breton students fought at the barricades under the Breton flag, symbolism which was widely-broadcast. There had been a modest growth of ethnic activist groups from 1963

to 1968, but after that year scores of groups were established.
Beer (1977) gives a detailed account of these groups. The
success of a small group of revolutionaries in shaking the state
to its foundations indicated that it might be possible for even
marginal groups to have some chance of success. Ethnic
movements outside France have also had a demonstration
effect: many Breton activists admire the Provisional Irish
Republican Army, and claim that Breton youth are being
trained in guerrilla warfare by them; and many of the
"liberation" movements of the Third World are essentially
ethnic nationalist movements.

There are still other factors behind the present resurgence of ethnic activism in France, some of which are
relevant to ethnicity in other advanced industrial societies: the
importance of national boundaries declined with the formation
of the Common Market, and the growth of a worldwide, interdependent economic system; and the political conflict between
NATO and Warsaw Pact countries has reduced the importance
of nation-states.

Until 1945, ethnic activism in France, with the exception
of the Basques and Catalans, had been limited to the royalists
and the fascists. When the central power in Paris had been
Republican, the ethnic regional response was royalist. When
the Republic showed itself to be anticlerical, the regional
royalists were joined by the clergy. During the interwar
period, when the Republic was increasingly dominated by
socialists and, to a lesser extent, by communists, the ethnic
regional response was a drift toward fascism. This dynamic
explains an apparent paradox in the current ethnic revival in
France: with very few exceptions, the groups that declare
themselves to be on the left by using varieties of Marxist
jargon take this position because the government against which
they are pitted is a center-right government. The ethnic
activists of today are simply carrying on a long tradition of
taking the opposite position to whatever government happens
to be in power in Paris.

Now that the background of ethnic activism in France has
been examined, it is possible to turn to the theoretical frameworks of internal colonialism and rising expectations. Because
what is being examined is in the context of France, it should
be acknowledged beforehand that these theories do not explain
everything. Social phenomena have both specific and general
causes; the foregoing has sketched the specific. What follows
is a test of the general and theoretically relevant.

INTERNAL COLONIALISM AND RISING EXPECTATIONS

Although the concept of internal colonialism has been formulated in several versions (Mills, p. 152; Gonzalez-Casanova, p. 33; Horowitz, p. 22), Hechter has provided the most elaborate description of how it has worked to preserve ethnic differences within modern society:

> The spatially uneven wave of modernization over state territory creates relatively advanced and less advanced groups. As a consequence of this initial fortuitous advantage, there is crystalization of the unequal distribution of resources and power between the two groups....This stratification system, which may be termed a cultural division of labor, contributes to the development of a distinctive ethnic identification in the two groups (Hechter, p. 19).

This formulation is systematic enough so that internal colonialism can be treated as a theory.(6)

The theory of internal colonialism holds that ethnic regions are preserved within industrial societies because they are held in a position of economic subordination to the central economy, a relationship analogous to that of colonies of the classical type. They provide foodstuffs, raw materials, and cheap manpower, as well as markets for the finished products. Ethnic stereotypes serve to legitimate the maintenance of these peoples in a politically- and economically-subordinate state. Ethnic activism, whether in the guise of linguistic, cultural, federalist, autonomist, or separatist movements, is a reaction to this subordination. The theory of internal colonialism can be translated into a hypothesis; "Internal colonialism hypothesis": There is a positive association between measures of ethnic political militancy and measures of relative underdevelopment. Conversely, the greater the degree of economic development in an area, the lower will be the degree of ethnic political militancy.

The theory of internal colonialism explains the preservation of ethnically-specific regions in modern states; but it does not explain the resurgence of ethnic militancy in these areas (Hechter, p. 300). Studies of rebellion have made it clear that it is not so much abject oppression that produces militant dissent as it is a disparity between what people have and what they believe they should have. In a phrase, it is not so much absolute deprivation as it is relative deprivation that may be the key to understanding why ethnic militancy has reappeared when it has. There may have been some change in the relative deprivation of France's ethnic minorities to explain the current ethnic revival.

Although relative deprivation was articulated as early as Aristotle (p. 212), it was given its first sociological formulation by Tocqueville (p. 177). In Tocqueville's analysis of the causes of the French Revolution, the promised improvement of circumstances - political, economic, and social - led people to expect more than they previously had. This "revolution of rising expectations" is one kind of revolution that derives from relative deprivation.

Davies has refined this concept, but the most systematic summary of theories of relative deprivation leading to collective and political violence is presented by Gurr. He includes Tocqueville's concept of rising expectations in one of his many hypotheses:

> ...Marginal increases in value capabilities among deprived groups tend to increase the salience of the group's value expectations (p. 118).

In other words, when conditions begin to improve for disadvantaged groups, discontent will increase rather than decrease.

Gurr's hypothesis can by translated into a "rising expectations hypothesis" with regard to the resurgence of ethnic militancy in France: There is a positive association between measures of ethnic political militancy and the rate of increase of measures of economic development. Where economic development is most rapid, ethnic activism will be strongest, and vice-versa. (7)

Thus, we have two hypotheses that can be tested against the data on ethnic political militancy and measures of economic development. These theories and their derivative hypotheses are not contradictory, but complementary. First, the theory of internal colonialism can be incorporated into the general conceptual framework of relative deprivation because the cultural division of labor includes the deprivation of ethnic regions with relation to the core social system. Second, internal colonialism may explain the preservation of ethnic regions in modern states, and rising expectations may explain why the minorities in these regions are becoming restive now.

Testing the Internal Colonialism Hypothesis:
Measures of Ethnic Political Militancy and
Economic Development

A political movement's strength is most easily measured by the number of votes its candidates obtain in elections. However, electoral measures are not enough; some measure of nonelectorally-expressed strength must be used. Direct and indirect data are available about ethnic candidates in presidential and legislative elections in France; there is also evidence of demonstrations, bombings, and terrorist attacks.

In 1974, two federalist candidates ran in the presidential election. The candidacies of M. Guy Heraud from the Parti Federaliste European and M. Claude Sebag from the Mouvement Federaliste European were clearly associated in the public eye with sympathy for ethnic activism. In all regions, the proportion of the vote they received was miniscule, but it can be taken as a measure of the varying levels of ethnic activist feeling in each region. The percentage of the vote for each has been added together to provide a composite measure, which is presented in Appendix Table 11.1.

An indirect measure of electorally-expressed discontent is the percentage of blank ballots that are deposited. Of course, it need not necessarily be an expression of ethnic discontent, but it can be used as a possible indirect measure of the relative level of such feeling in the different ethnic regions of France. Ideally, the blank and null ballots should come from an election where ethnic activist candidates were not running. Because an ethnic candidate ran in the legislative elections of 1973 and 1978, as well as in the presidential election of 1974, blank and null ballots cast in the presidential election of 1974 are used in the figures presented in Appendix Table 11.2.(8)

An important complement to the direct and indirect evidence of electorally-expressed discontent is the presence or absence of bombings, demonstrations, and other signs of nonelectoral protest. In Appendix Table 11.3, the regions are ranked according to the degree of this protest. Brittany is clearly first; there have been waves of bombings in that region since 1968, as well as frequent confrontations between demonstrators and police in Nantes and Rennes.(9) Corsica ranks second; although there was practically no ethnically-motivated violence prior to 1974, the level of bombings, armed attacks, and violent demonstrations since then became very high, a fact that was well-documented by Le Monde throughout 1976, and by Desjardins. The Basques rank third, with large-scale, and occasionally violent, demonstrations in 1965, 1971, and in the summer of 1977. Occitania's large cultural rallies and continuing demonstrations against the French Army's attempted acquisition of land at Larzac are, for the most part, peaceful manifestations (Holohan; Juillien, Kuligowski). Catalonia, Flanders, and Alsace rank equally low on the scale. To date, ethnic militancy in these areas has been primarily restricted to literary, journalistic, and cultural expressions. This ranking involves a certain amount of subjectivity; some might disagree, for instance, that Brittany ranks higher than Corsica, or that Occitania ranks lower than the French Basque country. In any case, the criteria for ranking on this scale have been made explicit.

In summary, three measures of the dependent variable are used: the vote for Heraud and Sebag in the presidential election of 1974, the percentage of blank and null ballots in the same election, and finally, a ranking of the regions nonelectoral protest level.

Now the independent variable, measures of economic development, can be studied. Four measures of the levels of economic development in France's ethnic regions are used.(10) Average annual income is a relative measure of economic development, in that the prosperity of the areas will be reflected in the incomes of the people. These data for 1972 are presented in Appendix Table 11.4. Another measure of economic development is the percentage of the population engaged in agriculture. If an area is economically more developed, there will be fewer people engaged in the agricultural sector relative to the total active population. These data are presented in Appendix Table 11.5. A third measure is the "net regional product per capita." The "net regional product," the chuffre d'affaires des societes et entreprises, regime fiscal du benefice reel, is a measure of the business prosperity in the department. When divided by the population of the department, it provides an indicator of the relative strength of the business sector. These figures for 1972 are shown in Appendix Table 11.6. Finally, the percentage of the population living in urban areas is a measure of the region's urbanization, a characteristic associated with economic development. This figure is used in addition to the percentage of the population living in agricultural regions because people who leave agriculture do not necessarily migrate from country to town. The percentage of the population of each department living in urban areas in 1975 is presented in Appendix Table 11.7.

The degree of association between these variables is measured by correlation, and the correlation coefficients and their significance levels are presented in Table 11.1. When the dependent variable is presented by department, the association is measured by a Pearson product-moment correlation; when the dependent variable is indicated by region, the association is measured by a Spearman rank-order correlation.(11)

Table 11.1.   Correlations of Dependent and
Independent Variables for Internal
Colonialism Hypothesis, with Significance Levels

	Average Annual Income 1972	Percent of Population In Agr. 1968	NRP Per Capita 1972	Percent Urban Population 1975
Vote for Sebag and Heraud 1974	.43 p .02	-.37 p .05	.53 p .01	.41 p .02
Blank and null ballots 1974	-.01 n.s.	-.05 n.s.	.07 n.s.	.03 n.s.
Level of Violence and Demon- strations	-.21 n.s.	.82 p .05	-.49 n.s.	-.65 n.s.

Testing the Rising Expectations Hypothesis:
Measures of Ethnic Political Militancy and
Rates of Economic Development

The same measures of ethnic political militancy are used to test the rising expectations hypothesis, except that blank and null ballots are not used as a measure of nonelectoral protest. The measures of the independent variable are the average annual percentage changes in the independent variable used above, average annual income, percentage of the population actively employed in the agricultural sector, net regional product, and percentage of the population living in urban areas. Appendix Table 11.8 shows the increase rate of the average annual income from 1963-72 in the departments of the ethnic regions. Appendix Table 11.9 shows the departments by rate of decline in the percentage of persons employed in the agricultural sector between 1962-68. Appendix Table 11.10 shows the rate of increase in the net regional product between 1963-72; and Appendix Table 11.11 shows the rate of increase in the urban population between 1962-75 for the component departments of ethnic regions.

These measures are correlated with those of the dependent variable by a Pearson product-moment correlation when the data are presented by department, and by a Spearman rank-order correlation when the dependent variable is ranked by region.   These   correlations   are   presented   in   Table   11.2.

Table 11.2.   Correlations of Dependent and Independent
Variables for Rising Expectations Hypothesis,
with Significance Levels

	Average Yearly Percent Increase in Avg. Salary 1963-72	Average Yearly Percent Decrease in Agr. Population 1962-68	Average Yearly Percent Increase in NRP 1963-72	Average Yearly Percent Increase in Urban Population 1962-75
Vote for Sebag and Heraud 1974	.13 n.s.	-.31 p .05	-.13 n.s.	-.33 p .05
Level of Violence and Demonstrations	.07 n.s.	.32 n.s.	.89 p .01	.50 n.s.

DISCUSSION

Table I tests the internal colonialism hypothesis.   There
appears to be no association between measures of economic
development and the indirect indicator of electorally-expressed
discontent, the percentage of blank and null ballots.   There
is, however, strong and significant association between the
independent variable and direct measures of electorally-
expressed ethnic political militancy.   There is also strong
correlation between the vote for Sebag and Heraud in 1974
and the average annual income in 1972 (.43, p .02), the
percentage of the population in agriculture in 1968 (-.37,
p .05), the net regional product per capita in 1972 (.53,
p .01), and the percentage of the population living in urban
areas in 1975 (.41, p .02).   What is remarkable about these
associations is that the direction of the association is entirely
at odds with the internal colonialism hypothesis.   According to
that hypothesis, the higher the level of economic development
in a region, the lower should be the degree of ethnic political
militancy.   Conversely, there should be more ethnic political
militancy where the percentage of the population engaged in
agriculture is higher.   Therefore, the signs of the first, third

and fourth correlations should be negative, while the sign of the second should be positive.

In contrast, the correlations of extra-electoral protest with the independent variables appear to confirm the internal colonialism hypothesis. Because the number of cases is small, a Spearman rank-order correlation must be very high to be significant. Consequently, the two cases where there are apparently strong associations between violent protest and underdevelopment - new regional product per capita in 1972 (-.49) and percentage of urban population in 1975 (-.68) - could have occurred by chance. Although the correlation of the percentage of population in agriculture in 1968 with measures of extra-electoral ethnic protest is both strong and significant (.82, p .05), it was measured ten years ago, and may be spurious today. Nevertheless, it is clear that at least the signs of the correlations support the internal colonialism hypothesis, with the probability of violence and demonstrations appearing to decrease as relative prosperity increases.

Table 11.2 which shows the associations between rates of economic development and levels of ethnic political militancy, tests the rising expectations hypothesis. Considering electoral measures first, there are two associations with the independent variable that are both strong and significant: the average yearly rate of decline in the percentage of the population engaged in agriculture between 1962-68 (-.31, p .05), and the average yearly rate of increase in the percentage of the population living in urban areas between 1962-75 (-.33, p .05). Because these two measures are related, it is not surprising that their correlations are so similar. The second is more appropriate than the first because it spans a longer period of time and is closer to the election year of 1974. Above all, however, the direction of the associations disconfirms the rising expectations hypothesis. According to that hypothesis, the levels of ethnic political militancy should be positively associated with the rate of increase in measures of economic prosperity; in fact, the direction is negative. The correlations of extra-electoral protest, however, appear to confirm the rising expectations hypothesis. Where the association between protests and the average yearly increase in net regional product from 1963-72 (.89, p .01) is strong and significant, the direction is positive. The faster the rate of business development, the more likely there will be violent and dramatic ethnic protests.

These observations suggest a refinement of both the internal colonialism hypothesis and the rising expectations hypothesis. It seems that the cultural division of labor tends to encourage extra-electoral protest, a feeling of exclusion from the political process evidently going hand in hand with a feeling of exclusion from the fruits of prosperity. On the other hand, to the extent that these benefits are shared by an ethnic region, ethnic feeling will be expressed through the ballot box rather than with bombs. When the social structure is less disrupted by rapid economic development, people's expectations are not as high, and their ethnic political feeling will be likely to express itself in electoral form. Conversely, when the social structure is disrupted by rapid economic development, channels for discontent are not to be found in the regular political process.

In summary, the internal colonialism hypothesis and the rising expectations hypothesis, and by extension the theories upon which they are based, relate to ethnic activism in France. Internal colonialism, the preservation of under-developed ethnic enclaves within advanced industrial societies, serves as a stimulus to violent political dissent, and is in-versely related to electoral ethnic militancy. When a territory is excluded from prosperity, its population is apt to express frustration through demonstrations, bombings, and terrorism. And when a territory does share in the fruits of economic development, its population, to the extent that it expresses ethnic discontent at all, will do so by electoral means.

Even though aspirations as a response to improving economic circumstances must be inferred, it is clear that rapid change is related to the resurgence of ethnic activism in France. When this change is rapid, ethnic discontent appears to be channeled into nonelectoral means of protest. When this change is less rapid, ethnic sentiment is more likely to be expressed through the ballot box. This, too, is consistent with the overall framework of the rising expectations hypo-thesis. When the social structure is transformed too rapidly, a kind of collective anomie sets in; people have no institution-alized means to express their political opposition. Slower social change allows people to accommodate themselves, and remain within the routine boundaries of political expression.

What is the relationship between internal colonialism and rising expectations? There is little question that a cultural-territorial division of labor in France has contributed to the preservation of ethnic regions. It may also help to explain why there has been an ethnic resurgence at the present time. Brittany and Corsica have consistently been excluded from the overall prosperity of France until the present time, while Alsace and Flanders have generally shared in it. In ac-cordance with the rising expectations theory, the frustrations of Bretons and Corsicans appear to be such that, at a time when their prosperity is increasing at a faster rate than the other ethnic regions, their previous exclusion impels them to demonstrate their feeling outside legitimate channels. To put it simply, the areas that were the furthest behind are the areas that are now moving up the most rapidly. Regions that suffered the most from internal colonialism are now undergoing the greatest rate of change. While internal colonialism explains the preservation of ethnic regions, rapid economic development and its attendant rising expectations explains the extra-electoral ethnic protests of the present time.

Although there is partial confirmation of both hypotheses, in neither case is the evidence strong enough to warrant the conclusion that these theoretical formulations answer all the questions about the rebirth of ethnic activism in France and other industrial societies. The historical background sketched above indicates that France has specific antecedents not necessarily common to other advanced industrial societies. However, insofar as the economic factors are concerned, the maintenance of internal colonies and the rapid improvement of conditions in some of these internal colonies partially explain ethnic activism in contemporary France. Comparative studies would show if the same is true for other modern societies where ethnic activism has reappeared.

Appendix Table 11.1. Combined Percentage of Vote for
Claude Sebag and Guy Heraud in Presidential Election, 1974

Alsace	Bas-Rhin	.633
	Haut-Rhin	.552
Flanders	Nord	.208
	Pas-de-Calais	.194
Brittany	Ille-et-Vilaine	.250
	Cotes-du-Nord	.278
	Finistere	.233
	Morbihan	.214
Basque Country	Pyrenees-Atlantiques	.581
French Catalonia	Pyrenees-Orientales	.302
Corsica	Corse*	.148
Occitania	Haute-Vienne	.191
	Creuse	.017
	Correze	.174
	Allier	.157
	Puy-de-Dome	.155
	Cantal	.164
	Haute-Loire	.193
	Lot	.224
	Aveyron	.187
	Tarn-et-Garonne	.267
	Tarn	.196
	Haute-Garonne	.239
	Gers	.239
	Hautes-Pyrenees	.271
	Ariege	.148
	Dordogne	.195
	Lot-et-Garonne	.236
	Lozere	.188
	Gard	.228
	Herault	.197
	Aude	.165
	Isere	.184
	Drome	.216
	Ardeche	.208
	Hautes-Alpes	.221
	Vaucluse	.306
	Alpes-de-Hte-Provence	.257

*In 1974 Corsica was separated into two departments. For
consistency, the island is treated as a single unit.

Source: Le Monde, May 7, 1974.

Appendix Table 11.2. Percent Blank and Null Ballots
in Presidential Election, 1974

Alsace	Bas-Rhin	1.5
	Haut-Rhin	1.7
Flanders	Nord	0.3
	Pas-de-Calais	1.2
Brittany	Ille-et-Vilaine	0.9
	Cotes-du-Nord	0.6
	Finistere	0.5
	Morbihan	0.6
Basque Country	Pyrenees-Atlantiques	0.8
French Catalonia	Pyrenees-Orientales	1.0
Corsica	Corse	0.6
Occitania	Haute-Vienne	1.4
	Creuse	0.9
	Correze	0.8
	Allier	0.9
	Puy-de-Dome	0.6
	Cantal	0.7
	Haute-Loire	1.0
	Lot	0.9
	Aveyron	1.1
	Tarn-et-Garonne	1.2
	Tarn	1.2
	Haute-Garonne	0.8
	Gers	1.1
	Hautes-Pyrenees	0.9
	Ariege	0.9
	Dordogne	1.1
	Lot-et-Garonne	0.9
	Lozere	0.9
	Gard	0.9
	Herault	0.8
	Aude	1.2
	Isere	0.7
	Drome	0.9
	Ardeche	0.9
	Hautes-Alpes	1.1
	Vaucluse	0.1
	Alpes-de-Haute-Provence	1.1

Source: Le Monde, May 7, 1974.

Appendix Table 11.3.   Rank-Order of France's
Ethnic Regions by Level of Public
Violence and Demonstrations

Alsace	6
Flanders	6
Brittany	1
Basque Country	3
French Catalonia	6
Corsica	2
Occitania	4

Appendix Table 11.4.   Average Annual Income in
France's Ethnic Regions, by Department:
1972 (Francs)

Alsace	Bas-Rhin	18,197
	Haut-Rhin	18,379
Flanders	Nord	18,427
	Pas-de-Calais	16,529
Brittany	Ille-et-Vilaine	16,935
	Cotes-du-Nord	15,906
	Finistere	16,806
	Morbihan	16,137
Basque Country	Pyrenees-Atlantiques	17,407
French Catalonia	Pyrenees-Orientales	15,197
Corsica	Corse	13,940
Occitania	Haute-Vienne	16,136
	Creuse	13,686
	Correze	15,446
	Allier	16,989
	Puy-de-Dome	17,841
	Cantal	15,089
	Haute-Loire	15,278
	Lot	15,642
	Aveyron	14,574
	Tarn-et-Garonne	14,861
	Tarn	15,514
	Haute-Garonne	18,536
	Gers	14,373
	Hautes-Pyrenees	15,489
	Ariege	15,351
	Dordogne	14,638
	Lot-et-Garonne	15,159
	Lozere	14,517
	Gard	15,983
	Herault	17,367
	Aude	16,790
	Isere	18,812
	Drome	17,302
	Ardeche	16,338
	Hautes-Alpes	16,007
	Vaucluse	16,885
	Alpes-de-Haute-Provence	18,313

Source: Institut National de la Statistique et d'Etudes Economiques (INSEE), Les Collections de l'INSEE, M 45.   Paris:
Imprimerie Nationale.

Appendix Table 11.5.   Percent of Active Population Employed
in Agriculture in France's Ethnic Regions,
by Department: 1968

Alsace	Bas-Rhin	12.0
	Haut-Rhin	9.5
Flanders	Nord	5.8
	Pas-de-Calais	12.5
Brittany	Ille-et-Vilaine	31.5
	Cotes-du-Nord	41.2
	Finistere	29.8
	Morbihan	34.6
Basque Country	Pyrenees-Atlantiques	23.3
French Catalonia	Pyrenees-Orientales	23.4
Corsica	Corse	24.5
Occitania	Haute-Vienne	23.6
	Creuse	51.2
	Correze	36.4
	Allier	23.6
	Puy-de-Dome	18.7
	Cantal	44.9
	Haute-Loire	37.6
	Lot	41.3
	Aveyron	39.2
	Tarn-et-Garonne	38.2
	Tarn	24.5
	Haute-Garonne	13.5
	Gers	50.9
	Hautes-Pyrenees	24.5
	Ariege	30.7
	Dordogne	37.4
	Lot-et-Garonne	36.8
	Lozere	45.4
	Gard	17.5
	Herault	19.4
	Aude	31.5
	Isere	10.6
	Drome	19.5
	Ardeche	25.6
	Hautes-Alpes	26.1
	Vaucluse	21.0
	Alpes-de-Haute-Provence	22.0

Source: INSEE, Recensement general de la population de 1968,
Resultats du sondage au 1/4, Fascicules departementaux.
Paris: Imprimerie Nationale, 1971.   Vols. I-VI.

Appendix Table 11.6.   Net Regional Product per Capita
in France's Ethnic Regions by Department: 1972 (Francs)

Alsace	Bas-Rhin	29.1
	Haut-Rhin	24.8
Flanders	Nord	28.8
	Pas-de-Calais	14.9
Brittany	Ille-et-Vilaine	10.9
	Cotes-du-Nord	14.7
	Finistere	18.0
	Morbihan	13.4
Basque Country	Pyrenees-Atlantiques	18.2
French Catalonia	Pyrenees-Orientales	14.2
Corsica	Corse	8.9
Occitania	Haute-Vienne	17.2
	Creuse	7.8
	Correze	12.9
	Allier	14.3
	Puy-de-Dome	21.1
	Cantal	9.6
	Haute-Loire	12.9
	Lot	12.1
	Aveyron	13.2
	Tarn-et-Garonne	11.0
	Tarn	22.2
	Haute-Garonne	19.5
	Gers	12.3
	Hautes-Pyrenees	11.9
	Ariege	12.2
	Dordogne	11.1
	Lot-et-Garonne	17.6
	Lozere	9.4
	Gard	13.4
	Herault	15.2
	Aude	12.4
	Isere	21.9
	Drome	19.3
	Ardeche	9.7
	Hautes-Alpes	13.2
	Vaucluse	20.8
	Alpes-de-Haute-Provence	12.2

Source: Ministere des Finances, Statistiques et Etudes Finan-
cieres, no. 325, Jan 1976, 9-12; Annuaire Statistique de la
France (resultats de 1974), INSEE, 1976, pp. 44-46.

Appendix Table 11.7. Percent of Population Living in
Urban Areas in France's Ethnic Regions by Department: 1975

Alsace	Bas-Rhin	71.5
	Haut-Rhin	76.7
Flanders	Nord	89.9
	Pas-de-Calais	80.9
Brittany	Ille-et-Vilaine	56.7
	Cotes-du-Nord	41.2
	Finistere	63.3
	Morbihan	48.9
Basque Country	Pyrenees-Atlantiques	67.3
French Catalonia	Pyrenees-Orientales	71.9
Corsica	Corse	44.7
Occitania	Haute-Vienne	61.1
	Creuse	22.1
	Correze	47.5
	Allier	59.5
	Puy-de-Dome	63.4
	Cantal	33.7
	Haute-Loire	45.6
	Lot	33.4
	Aveyron	42.4
	Tarn-et-Garonne	47.6
	Tarn	64.8
	Haute-Garonne	76.9
	Gers	34.9
	Hautes-Pyrenees	58.5
	Ariege	46.2
	Dordogne	40.0
	Lot-et-Garonne	54.4
	Lozere	32.3
	Gard	71.5
	Herault	77.5
	Aude	53.8
	Isere	77.7
	Drome	66.1
	Ardeche	51.0
	Hautes-Alpes	53.9
	Vaucluse	75.7
	Alpes-de-Haute-Provence	52.4

Source: INSEE, Recensement general de la population de 1975,
Population legale et statistiques communales complementaires.
Paris: Imprimerie Nationale, 1976. Vols. I-VI.

Appendix Table 11.8.   Rate of Increase in Average Annual
Income in France's Ethnic Regions by Department: 1963-72
(Average Percent Per Year, Current Francs

Alsace	Bas-Rhin	24.7
	Haut-Rhin	24.2
Flanders	Nord	23.1
	Pas-de-Calais	23.3
Brittany	Ille-et-Vilaine	24.1
	Cotes-du-Nord	24.2
	Finistere	24.4
	Morbihan	24.9
Basque Country	Pyrenees-Atlantiques	24.2
French Catalonia	Pyrenees-Orientales	23.4
Corsica	Corse	21.2
Occitania	Haute-Vienne	23.9
	Creuse	23.1
	Correze	22.7
	Allier	23.9
	Puy-de-Dome	23.4
	Cantal	26.7
	Haute-Loire	25.0
	Lot	24.9
	Aveyron	23.3
	Tarn-et-Garonne	25.6
	Tarn	24.2
	Haute-Garonne	23.6
	Gers	25.1
	Hautes-Pyrenees	22.8
	Ariege	23.6
	Dordogne	24.2
	Lot-et-Garonne	23.3
	Lozere	22.7
	Gard	22.5
	Herault	23.5
	Aude	25.8
	Isere	23.1
	Drome	23.5
	Ardeche	25.2
	Hautes-Alpes	21.3
	Vaucluse	22.7
	Alpes-de-Haute-Provence	21.6

Appendix Table 11.9.   Rate of Decline in Agricultural
Sector in France's Ethnic Regions by Department: 1962-68
(Average Percent Per Year)

Alsace	Bas-Rhin	0.7
	Haut-Rhin	0.3
Flanders	Nord	0.2
	Pas-de-Calais	0.5
Brittany	Ille-et-Vilaine	1.5
	Cotes-du-Nord	1.4
	Finistere	1.4
	Morbihan	1.7
Basque Country	Pyrenees-Atlantiques	1.3
French Catalonia	Pyrenees-Orientales	1.5
Corsica	Corse	1.2
Occitania	Haute-Vienne	1.4
	Creuse	1.3
	Correze	1.4
	Allier	1.2
	Puy-de-Dome	1.2
	Cantal	1.3
	Haute-Loire	1.3
	Lot	1.6
	Aveyron	1.1
	Tarn-et-Garonne	1.4
	Tarn	1.4
	Haute-Garonne	1.1
	Gers	1.9
	Hautes-Pyrenees	1.3
	Ariege	1.6
	Dordogne	1.6
	Lot-et-Garonne	1.5
	Lozere	1.2
	Gard	0.8
	Herault	1.3
	Aude	1.4
	Isere	0.8
	Drome	1.1
	Ardeche	1.7
	Hautes-Alpes	1.4
	Vaucluse	1.1
	Alpes-de-Haute-Provence	1.4

Appendix Table 11.10.   Rate of Growth of NRP in France's
Ethnic Regions by Department: 1963-72
(Average Percent per Year, Current Francs)

Alsace	Bas-Rhin	34.7
	Haut-Rhin	25.6
Flanders	Nord	25.9
	Pas-de-Calais	33.9
Brittany	Ille-et-Vilaine	28.4
	Cotes-du-Nord	48.4
	Finistere	45.7
	Morbihan	45.0
Basque Country	Pyrenees-Atlantiques	31.0
French Catalonia	Pyrenees-Orientales	28.8
Corsica	Corse	81.0
Occitania	Haute-Vienne	36.1
	Creuse	30.1
	Correze	28.8
	Allier	30.4
	Puy-de-Dome	34.4
	Cantal	36.4
	Haute-Loire	39.1
	Lot	38.1
	Aveyron	38.8
	Tarn-et-Garonne	37.6
	Tarn	34.9
	Haute-Garonne	39.0
	Gers	48.9
	Hautes-Pyrenees	42.2
	Ariege	37.0
	Dordogne	41.8
	Lot-et-Garonne	45.4
	Lozere	44.9
	Gard	29.3
	Herault	14.9
	Aude	26.6
	Isere	30.0
	Drome	36.2
	Ardeche	30.2
	Hautes-Alpes	34.8
	Vaucluse	33.9
	Alpes-de-Haute-Provence	41.9

Appendix Table 11.11. Rate of Urbanization in France's
Ethnic Regions by Department: 1962–75
(Average Percent Per Year)

Alsace	Bas-Rhin	.185
	Haut-Rhin	.085
Flanders	Nord	.086
	Pas-de-Calais	.080
Brittany	Ille-et-Vilaine	.395
	Cotes-du-Nord	.535
	Finistere	.372
	Morbihan	.335
Basque Country	Pyrenees-Atlantiques	.410
French Catalonia	Pyrenees-Orientales	.375
Corsica	Corse	.175
Occitania	Haute-Vienne	.597
	Creuse	.417
	Correze	.668
	Allier	.470
	Puy-de-Dome	.334
	Cantal	.539
	Haute-Loire	.485
	Lot	.405
	Aveyron	.431
	Tarn-et-Garonne	.319
	Tarn	.365
	Haute-Garonne	.284
	Gers	.486
	Hautes-Pyrenees	.332
	Ariege	.487
	Dordogne	.281
	Lot-et-Garonne	.508
	Lozere	.488
	Gard	.128
	Herault	.377
	Aude	.388
	Isere	.357
	Drome	.445
	Ardeche	.605
	Hautes-Alpes	.488
	Vaucluse	.200
	Alpes-de-Haute-Provence	.402

NOTES

1. Ethnicity is also undergoing a rebirth in the United States, but American ethnic groups consist largely of urbanized, and more-or-less assimilated immigrants. The theoretical expectations discussed in this paper does not necessarily hold for the American variety of ethnic groups.

2. On the relation between language and ethnicity in France, see Beer.

3. The word "activism" is used here to be as inclusive as possible, referring to separatist, autonomist, nationalist, federalist, as well as cultural and linguistic groups and organizations.

4. Alsace alone, rather than Alsace and Lorraine, is studied because the Germanic linguistic influence has greatly diminished in Lorraine, and because there is no sign of ethnic activism there.

5. There is considerable vagueness about the exact boundaries of Occitania. In this study, it is considered to include all of southern France with some exceptions: the department of Landes is excluded because it is a littoral plain where the Occitan influence was not as strong as in the interior; Pyrenees-Atlantiques is excluded because it is considered as coextensive with the Basque country; and Pyrenees-Orientales is excluded because it is considered French Catalonia; Bouches-du-Rhone and the Cote d'Azur are excluded because of their great Mediterranean-related prosperity. Lafont (1971, p. 12) has a larger definition of Occitania, while Marti has a much smaller one. The definition used here is similar to that of Lafont.

6. There are some problems with it, however. The first is a semantic difficulty with the use of the term "colonialism." Strictly speaking, a colony is formed by settlers from a mother country. A colony is thus the result of a more-or-less organized set of expeditions to areas that may or may not be inhabited by natives. In this sense, there were attempts to colonize uninhabited areas of France during the Middle Ages (Bloch, pp. 9-11); but there is little correspondence between areas of France colonized in this fashion and those parts of France that could be called internal colonies in the sense meant by Hechter. A better term might be "imperialism" because in this type of system little attempt is made to send settlers to subordinated territories. However, this term is also unacceptable because imperial systems, from Rome to Austria-Hungary, have been so heterogeneous that it would clarify little; and, in addition, "imperialism" has value-

laden implications. The question of whether or not
"internal colonialism" is a slogan or a theory is a second
criticism. Some modern activists in Europe (Lebesque,
176ff; Marti,; Salvi, 1973) and in the U.S. (Carmichael
and Hamilton, pp. 6, 16-23; Moore, p. 194) have used
the term with little concern for theoretical precision.
Despite the imprecision and value-laden implications of the
term, internal colonialism can be stated as a theory. It
has a wide enough currency so that, after its drawbacks
have been pointed out, it can be used in a sociologically-
exact sense.

7.   Although neither Tocqueville nor Gurr connect the revolution of rising expectations to ethnic activities, the
theory can be used in the context of ethnic discontent
because these groups clearly suffer some degree of relative deprivation. Although ethnic militancy is not always
revolutionary, nor is it always violent, the framework of
rising expectations can be used to explain it because it
represents a rejection of the accepted political formations.
Ethnic politics cut across all "normal" lines of cleavage in
modern society, and at times reject the legitimacy of the
state entirely. This is as deep a rejection of the existing
political system as that implied in revolutionary politics –
more, perhaps, because the nation-state is still generally
accepted as a political arena by revolutionaries. As for
violence, guerrilla activity is present and increasing in
Brittany and Corsica. Another difficulty with this and
other types of relative deprivation is that they infer the
states of people's expectations. The rising of expectations is expected to occur as a result of improving circumstances, but there is seldom any direct evidence of
this. A recent study (Miller, et. al., pp. 964-981) has
even shown that, in one empirical context, there is very
little relation between people's expectations and the actual
state of affairs. Because there are no studies which have
systematically measured expectations over time in France's
ethnic regions, rising expectations as a result of improving circumstances will have to be inferred in this
case also.

8.   Besides blank and null ballots, a common way of
measuring electorally-expressed opposition in France is
the percentage of abstentions. However, these figures
are not presented because their correlations with the
independent variable were not substantially different from
those of the percentages of blank and null ballots.

9.   See, for example, Le Monde for April 30, 1968; January 28, 1969; December 28, 1973; and July 28, 1976.
These are only representative accounts of the events.
There are literally hundreds of articles substantiating the
ranks assigned to the regions for this measure. In the

case of this and the other ethnic regions, only representative articles are cited.

10. French census data are notoriously irregular in their
compilation and comparability; in each case, the year used
is as close as possible to the years used for the
dependent variable, 1974 and 1978.

11. For all internal colonialism measures, the figures for each
department ought, in theory, to be divided by the equivalent value for France as a whole to give an index of
relative development. This would have simply meant
dividing them all by the same denominator, and thus was
not done in the Appendix Tables.

BIBLIOGRAPHY

Almond, G. and G. Powell. Comparative Politics: A Developmental Approach. Boston: Little, Brown, 1966.

Aristotle. Aristotle's Politics. New York: Random House,
1943.

Beer, W. "Language and Ethnicity in France," Plural Societies, 7, 2, (1976), 85-94.

_____. "The Social Class of Ethnic Activitists in Contem-
porary France," in M. Esman (ed.), Ethnic Conflict in the
Western World. Ithaca: Cornell University Press, 1977.

Berger, S. "Bretons, Basques, Scots and Other European
Nations." Journal of Interdisciplinary History 3, (1972): 176-
175.

Bernardo, D. "Catalogue-Nord: le traumatisme de la
coupure." Pluriel-debat 7, (1976): 5-28.

Bloch, M. Les caracteres originaux de l'histoire rurale francaise. Paris: Colin, 1964.

Carmicheal, S. and D. Hamilton. Black Power: The Politics
of Liberation in America. New York: Random House, 1967.

Connor, W. "Nation-Building or Nation-Destroying?" World
Politics, 24, 3, (1972): 319-355.

Coornaert, E. La Flandre francaise de langue flamande.
Paris, 1970.

DaSilva, M. "Modernization and Ethnic Conflict: The Case of
the Basques." Comparative Politics (January, 1975).

Davant, J. Histoire du Pays Basque. Bayonne, 1970.

Davis, J. "Toward a Theory of Revolution." American Sociological Review 27 (Feb. 1962): 5-19.

Dejonghe, E. "Un mouvement separatiste dans le Nord et le Pas-de-Calais sous l'occupation (1940-1944): le Vlaamse Verbond van Frankrijk." Revue d'histoire moderne et contemporaine (1970: 1150-1177.

Desjardins, T. La Corse a la derive. Paris: Plon, 1977.

Deutsch, K. Nationalism and Social Communication. Cambridge: MIT Press, 1953.

Durkheim, E. The Division of Labor in Society. New York: Free Press, 1964.

Enloe, C. Ethnic Conflict and Political Development. Boston: Little Brown, 1973.

Espieux, H. Histoire de L'Occitanie. Agen, 1970.

Fishman, J. Language Loyalty in the United States. The Hague: Mouton, 1966.

Galloy, M. "Euzkadi (Pays Basque)" Europa Ethnica 23, 2, (1966): 50-57.

Glazer, N. and D. Moynihan. Beyond the Melting Pot. Cambridge: MIT Press, 1963.

Gonzalez-Casanova, P. "Internal Colonialism and National Development." Studies in Comparative International Development 1, 4, (1965): 27-37.

Gurr, T. Why Men Rebel. Princeton: Princeton University Press, 1970.

Hechter, M. Internal Colonialism: The Celtic Fringe in British National Development, 1536-1966. Berkeley: University of California Press, 1975.

Heisler, M. (ed.). Politics in Europe. New York: McKay, 1974.

Heraud, G. L'Europe des ethnics. Paris: Presses Universitaires de France, 1963.

Holohan, W. "Le conflict du Larzac: chronique et essai d'analyse." Sociologie du travail, 8, 3, (1976): 283-301.

Horowitz, I. Three Worlds of Development: The Theory and Practice of International Stratification. New York: Oxford University Press, 1972.

Juillien C. "Les revoltes du Larzac." Le nouvel observateur (August 1972), pp. 10-16.

Kautsky, J. (ed.). Political Change in Underdeveloped Societies. Huntington: Krieger, 1976.

Kuhn, T. The Structure of Scientific Revolutions. Chicago: University of Chicago Press, 1970.

Kuligowski, E. Le Larzac veut vivre. Paris, 1973.

Lafont, R. La revolution regionaliste. Paris: Flammarion, 1967.

_____. Clefs pour l'Occitanie. Paris: Seghers, 1971.

Lebesque, M. Comment peut-on etre breton? Paris: Seuil, 1970.

Marti, C. Homme d'Oc. Paris: Stock, 1975.

Marx, K. and F. Engels The Communist Manifesto. New York: Appleton-Century-Crofts, 1955.

Maugue, P. Le particularisme alsacien. Paris: Presses d'Europe, 1970.

Miller, A. et al. "The J-Curve Theory and the Black Urban Riots: An Empirical Test of Progressive Relative Deprivation Theory." American Political Science Review 71 (Sept. 1977): 964-981.

Mills, C. "The Problems of Industrial Development." In I. Horowitz, ed. Power, Politics and People. New York: Ballantine, 1962.

Moore, J. "Colonialism: The Case of the Mexican-Americans." In L. Rainwater (ed.). Inequality and Justice: Social Problems and Public Policy. Chicago: Aldine, 1974.

Novak, M. The Rise of the Unmeltable Ethnics. New York: Macmillan, 1971.

Parsons, T. The Social System. New York: Free Press, 1968.

Pye, L. Aspects of Political Development. Boston: Little, Brown, 1966.

Reece, J. The Bretons Against France. Chapel Hill: University of North Carolina Press, 1977.

Salvi, S. Le nazione proibite: guia a dieci colonie interne dell 'Europa occidentale. Florence: Vallecchi, 1973.

Serant, P. La France des minorites. Paris: Robert Laffont, 1965.

_____. La Bretagne et la France. Paris: Fayard, 1971.

Tocqueville, A. The Old Regime and the French Revolution. New York: Doubleday, 1959.

Trenard, L. Histoire de Pays-Bas Francais. 1972.

Weber, M. Economy and Society. G. Roth and K. Wittich, eds. New York: Free Press, 1968.

12 Racial and Ethnic Conflict in Soviet Central Asia
David T. Lindgren

INTRODUCTION

According to a 1979 estimate, the Soviet Union is a
"nation" of 262 million people representing approximately 100
nationalities. Of these nationalities, 15 are sufficiently
numerous and sufficiently developed politically to have been
awarded union republic status, the highest level in the
several-tiered territorial-administrative system. The Great
Russians are the largest group - representing about 52 percent of the total population - and their republic, the Russian
Soviet Federated Socialist Republic (RSFSR), encompasses
nearly two-thirds of the Soviet land area, as well as a substantial number of the lesser nationality groups. The remaining 14 republics, located around the periphery of the
RSFSR, are much smaller, both in terms of population and
area.

In recent years, the national minorities have become an
increasing cause for concern among the Soviet leadership.
One reason has been their rate of growth: The national
minorities represent about 48 percent of the Soviet Union's
population; with their high birth rates, they will soon outnumber the ethnic Russians. Furthermore, a number of the
nationality groups have become quite open in their resistance
to certain Soviet policies, particularly since the signing of the
Helsinki Agreements on human rights. For example, the plight
of Soviet Jews attempting to emigrate to Israel has not only
received worldwide news coverage, much to the embarassment
of Soviet leaders, but it has also delayed passage of a much-
sought-after trade reform bill with the U.S. Similarly, other
nationality groups have been waging their own compaigns
against policies which they find repressive.

Theoretically, the Soviets face a problem common to most modernizing societies - how to integrate a number of diverse peoples into a single political system. Where the Soviets differ is that, as Marxist-Leninists, they view nationalism as a remnant of the capitalist past destined to wither away. However, in the immediate post-Revolutionary years, they found that nationalist forces were not spent and so a number of nationality groups were granted their own territories temporarily. The effect of this was to strengthen the very forces of nationalism that the Soviets had believed would fade. A good example of this can be seen in the case of Central Asia.

Soviet Central Asia is located in the southernmost part of the Soviet Union (Fig. 12.1) and is generally considered to be comprised of the five union republics of Turkmen, Uzbek, Kirghiz, Tadzhik, and Kazakh.(1) The region is bordered to the west by the Caspian Sea, and to the south by a series of rugged mountain ranges that effectively separate it from neighboring Iran, Afghanistan, and China. To the north and east, Central Asia lies virtually open - a vast desert merging only gradually with the Russian steppe. These particular factors of geography have had a significant impact upon the region's history.

The population of the five Central Asian republics is 37.8 million, a figure which represents about 14.7 percent of the total Soviet population, according to a 1976 estimate. Turkic peoples, primarily the Uzbeks, Kazakhs, Kirghiz, and Turkmen, make up about 60 percent of the Central Asian population, while the Tadzhiks, a group ethnically akin to the Iranians, make up another five percent. Much of the remaining 35 percent of the population is Slavic, and primarily Russian. The latter now constitute the largest minority in each of the Central Asian republics with the exception of Kazakhstan, where they actually outnumber the indigenous population.(2)

CENTRAL ASIA UNDER THE TSARS

Russian penetration into Central Asia began during the 1860s. It was motivated by a number of factors: First, there was a need to protect the settlers and traders moving into the more fertile steppe areas to the north - present-day Kazakhstan - from the raids of nomadic tribesmen. Later, the more southern sections of Central Asia were coveted as a potential source of cotton, imports having been cut-off by the American Civil War. And finally, there was a desire on the part of the Tsarist government to head off any possible move into the area by the British, who were already establishing themselves in Persia and Afghanistan.

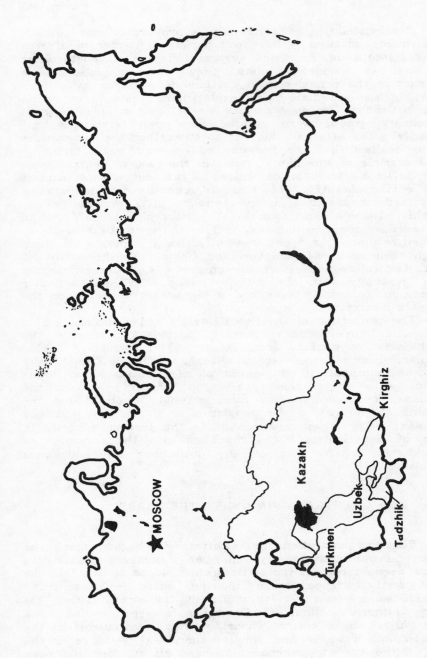

Fig. 12.1. The USSR: Soviet Central Asia

MOSCOW

Kazakh

Kirghiz

Uzbek

Tadzhik

Turkmen

236

Operating from a base at Orenburg (Fig. 12.2), a succession of ambitious military officers systematically, although
often without official authorization, advanced the frontier
southward and eastward. The Russian armies proved too
strong for the poorly-equipped troops of the khans, who on
occasion suffered heavy losses. In 1866, Tashkent and a
portion of the Bukharan khanate were the first to fall. The
following year, these territories were combined to form the
Russian province of Turkestan. Next, in 1868, the Russians
gained control of Samarkand, and forced the Emir of Bukhara
to accept their protection. Khiva became a vassal state of the
Russian empire in 1873; and Kokand was conquered and made a
part of Turkestan in 1876. With the defeat of the Turkmen in
1881 at the battle of Geok Tepe, the Russians were able to organize the whole area, with the exception of the Bukharan and
Khivan khanates, into a series of new administrative units: the
Governate-General of Turkestan, the Governate-General of the
Steppe Region, and the two west Kazakh oblasts of Turgay and
Ural'sk. This system would last until the Revolution of 1917.

The acquisition of Central Asia added nearly a million
square miles and approximately seven million people to the
Russian Empire. The majority of the people were Moslem and
illiterate, and the Tsarist government chose to treat the area
as a colonial dependency. Although military governors administered the various districts and a governor-general was
placed in charge of each province, the traditional way of life
of the Asians was left virtually intact. The Moslem agencies of
authority, which exercised strict control over the local communities, were used by the Russians as intermediaries between
themselves and the Asian population. The only condition
imposed by the Russians was that the Asian community "fulfill
the requirements of the new government" (Rakowska-
Harmstone, p. 14).

From the beginning, the Russian community in Central
Asia conducted itself as a privileged elite. There was little
intermixing or contact with the indigenous population. Most
Russians, in fact, chose to live in the garrison towns which
sprung up alongside the old native cities of Tashkent,
Samarkand, Pishpek (Frunze), and Vernyy (Alma-Ata).

The Russians directed their major efforts towards the
development of irrigation and transportation systems. The
irrigation systems were required for the expansion of cotton
production, and necessitated the expropriation of much of the
Central Asians' best agricultural land. The construction of a
railroad network was of most immediate importance; not
only was it needed for shipping cotton to the textile mills in
Moscow and St. Petersburg, but also for the movement of
military personnel and equipment from European Russia to
Central Asia in times of emergency. The first line built was
the Transcaspian, which ran from Uzun Ada on the Caspian to

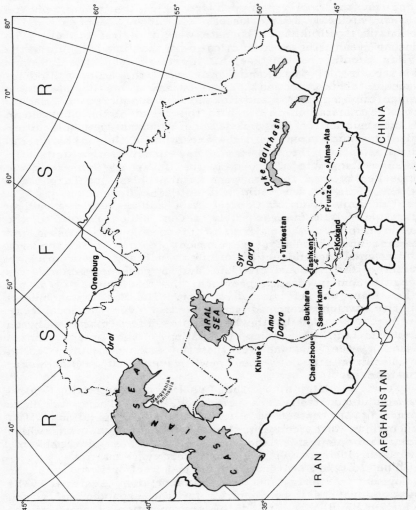

Fig. 12.2. Soviet Central Asia

Kizyl-Arvat and Chardzhou on the Amu Dar'ya. This was
extended to Samarkand in 1888, and to Tashkent in 1898. A
second line was later built from Orenburg to Tashkent,
providing a more direct connection between European Russia
and Turkestan.

For approximately two decades preceding the Revolution,
the Asian community expressed little overt opposition to
Russian activities. In part, this was a result of the absence
of any strong feelings of national consciousness. An individual's loyalty was directed primarily to the joint family and
the clan. Then too, the Asians were lulled into quiescence by
many of the material improvements introduced by the Russians
- the regularization of the land tenure and taxation systems,
the construction of transportation and communication facilities,
and the improvement in medical services. Still, resentments
and frustrations built up and, on occasion, found release.

The convening of the Duma in 1905 presented the Asians
with an excellent opportunity to express their grievances
because, for the first time, they were given representation.
They demanded an immediate halt to further Russian colonization of their lands, and they called for the right to elect
their own deputies. Significantly, there was no request for
independence; Russian control was not even questioned. The
Asians were actually demanding little more than the opportunity for freer cultural and political expression within the
Tsarist administrative system.

A more dramatic expression of Asian resentment towards
the Tsarist government occurred during the summer of 1916.
The "great revolt," as it was called, was ostensibly a protest
against a Tsarist decree calling all citizens, including Central
Asians, to service in the army. Although the decree specified
that the Asians would not be used in front-line positions, they
strongly resented being conscripted to participate in a war
that little concerned them. The revolt that ensued resulted in
"horrible blood-baths and the wholesale slaughter of entire
villages by the natives" (Pahlen, p. 193). It is probable that
the revolt was as much a response to continued Russian
colonization of Asian lands as it was to the decree itself.
Nevertheless, thousands of Central Asians were forced to flee
to Chinese Turkestan to escape Russian retribution.

THE REVOLUTION AND THE STALIN YEARS

The Moslems of Russian Turkestan and the neighboring
khanates of Bukhara and Khiva were quite unprepared to play
any significant role in the revolution of 1917. Even the
Moslem clergy, anxious to retain their authority, remained
neutral. Instead, the revolutionary struggle was waged

primarily by the area's Russian minority.(3) In fact, by the
time the Moslem leadership became aware of the significance of
the Revolution and its implications for Central Asia, power was
securely in Bolshevik hands.

For their part, the Bolsheviks did little to encourage
Moslem participation. They viewed the Central Asians as
cultural inferiors, and expressed nothing but contempt for
the Moslem religion. Moreover, fearing the numerical superiority of the Central Asians, the Bolsheviks interpreted the
revolutionary struggle in this region less as one involving
class differences than as one pitting the Russian minority
against the Moslem majority. Given this situation, it is not
surprising that the Central Asians responded with feelings of
suspicion and hostility towards the new Soviet government.

Still, many of the more liberal Moslem leaders hoped that
some kind of a unified Turkestan could be established within
the evolving Soviet system. To that end, a congress was
convened in Kokand during November 1917. The participants
demanded territorial autonomy for Turkestan and proceeded to
elect a council to serve as a Moslem provisional government.
Again, there was no demand for independence. Nevertheless,
fearful that the newly-elected Kokand provisional government
might begin to attract local support, the Russian-dominated
Tashkent Soviet(4) ordered its armies to attack. Without
popular support and, in fact, with the increasing hostility of
many conservative Moslem leaders, the provisional government
was toppled with ease. It had lasted less than four months.

The destruction of the Kokand provisional government
dashed whatever hopes the liberal Moslem leadership held of
negotiating with the Bolsheviks. Conservative leaders were
now largely unchallenged in their call for a "holy war" against
the infidel Russians. When the Tashkent Soviet ordered its
armies against the Emir of Bukhara in March 1918, the Russians were repulsed by an army raised to almost fanatical
heights by the Moslem clergy. Of even greater significance,
however, was the Basmachi, a guerrilla movement that, by
1920, numbered its supporters in the thousands. The
Basmachi drew much of its strength from the khanates of
Bukhara and Khiva, whose continued existence now appeared
threatened by the growing power of the Bolsheviks.

The early successes of the Basmachi became a source of
increasing concern to the Soviet government. The Soviets
were particularly fearful that the Basmachi would unite the
various forces demanding a single autonomous Islamic state for
Central Asia. Thus, as a means of weakening the movement,
Soviet armies were sent to destroy the Khivan and Bukharan
khanates. Khiva fell in February 1920; Bukhara was taken the
following September. The two were reorganized and admitted
into the Soviet system as People's Conciliar Republics.

By 1920, the Bolsheviks were certain of victory in the
Civil War; more than anything else, they needed a respite in
order to consolidate power. Furthermore, the economy was in
shambles and it too needed time for recovery. Lenin
responded with his New Economic Policy (NEP), a program that
temporarily relaxed many of the rigid controls of the War
Communism period and allowed for the return of a free-market
system to a substantial portion of the economy.(5) Similarly,
attitudes toward the national minorities were relaxed as Lenin
began to realize that their support was necessary to the consolidation process.

In Central Asia, this change in attitude was accompanied
by a number of consiliatory gestures towards the Moslem
religion: the clergy recovered some of their lost powers;
church lands were returned; and Moslem schools were allowed
to reopen. In their political discussions with Moslem leaders,
the Soviets voiced support for the creation of a federal
system. It is apparent, however, that Lenin intended
federalism to be but another temporary measure, one that
would be in effect only until nationalism - including Russian
nationalism - had withered away:

> To Lenin, national distinctions were products
> of the bourgeoisie class environment. He believed
> that by reconstituting the economic foundations of
> society on socialism, national differences would
> disappear, and nations would merge into a world
> community of socialism (U.S. Congress, p. 20).

The relatively-relaxed mood of the early NEP period encouraged a number of nationalist groups to begin pressing for
the creation of a single, unified Moslem state. The most
articulate of these groups was the Young Bukhara movement,
which had been given power by the Soviets after the fall of
Bukhara in September 1920. The Young Bukharans were well
aware that little feeling of national consciousness existed
among the Moslem masses, but they were hopeful one could be
superimposed over the tribal identities. They were particularly desirous of eliminating the racial animosities between
Bukhara's Turkmen and Tadzhiks by integrating them into a
unified Bukharan nation:

> When the Young Bukharans spoke of a
> Bukharan nation and a Bukharan homeland, they
> were consciously manipulating these associations and
> memories to promote their concept of Greater
> Bukhara or Turkestan, embracing all of Soviet
> Central Asia, although for the present they were
> compelled to limit their activities to the people's
> republic (Allworth, 1973: 163).

The concept of a unified Moslem state embracing all of Central Asia was not an entirely unrealistic one. For centuries, the various tribes had intermingled with one another; they shared a common history, common religion, and a common culture. And because nearly all of the Turkic peoples spoke similar dialects of the same language, even the idea of a common language had some basis in fact. Thus, had the Young Bukharans been given sufficient time, perhaps they might have had some chance for success. However, such time was not to be forthcoming.

By late 1922, the Soviets had begun to adopt a harder line toward the Central Asians. One reason for the change was the Red Army's increasing success against the Basmachi. However, a second and more compelling reason was the Soviet fear of Turkish nationalism, which was viewed as a threat to the unity of the Soviet state. Stalin, the Commissar for Nationality Affairs, now launched a vigorous purge of the Communist Party to rid it of all those who had joined to foster Turkish nationalism. He withdrew his support of the Young Bukharans for "trying to develop the national consciousness of the Bukharan populace" (Allworth, p. 165). These events, moreover, were but a prelude of things to come.

The first Soviet Constitution, adopted in 1924, effectively ended Central Asian hopes for a unified state. Instead, five, well-defined nationality units were created along the lines of the major ethnic groupings, and the degree of political autonomy given to each of the new units was dependent upon the level of political development. Two, Turkmenia and Uzbekistan, were given Union Republic (SSR) status, while three others became Autonomous Soviet Socialist Republics (ASSR). Of the ASSRs two, Kazakh and Kirghiz, were subordinated to the RSFSR, while the third, Tadzhik, was subordinated to the Uzbek SSR. Tadzhik attained republic status in 1927; Kazakh and Kirghiz were not granted it until 1936.

The Soviets were now able to claim legitimately that they were granting political autonomy to the various Central Asian groups in line with their policy of national self-determination. In fact, they were effectively undermining any pan-Islamic movement by forcing the local nationalities apart. Members of nationalist movements, such as the Young Bukharans, were faced with a choice of either fleeing, perhaps to the Basmachi, or of cooperating with the Soviets in the administration of the new republics. Some indeed chose exile, but most chose to cooperate. Many of those opting for cooperation were to become victims of Stalin's purges in the 1930s, which eliminated almost all native Party personnel.

The Stalin years, 1924-53, were characterized by unusual harshness towards the national minorities. Whereas Lenin had felt the support of the national minorities was essential to the political consolidation process, Stalin viewed their support

quite differently. Stalin's overriding concern was to in-
dustrialize the country as rapidly as possible, and this would
require the support of the Great Russians. He foresaw clearly
that the Soviet citizenry would be forced to make great
sacrifices and that their patriotism would often have to be
called upon to justify the hardships. His revival of what was
essentially traditional Russian patriotism "strengthened the
uniquely Russian quality of the Soviet state and conversely
weakened the position of the nationalities; but in another and
more fundamental way it enhanced basic nationality doctrine by
moving another step along the way of ultimately merging all
nationalities in the USSR, albeit according to Soviet Russian
norms" (U.S. Congress, p. 23).

Stalin's industrialization program required tightly-
centralized control of the entire political system. Such control
drastically reduced the independence that, at least on paper,
had been given to the national minorities. This apparent
contradiction between the federal concept on one hand and the
need for centralized control of the state on the other was
resolved by Stalin with the phrase "nationalist in form but
socialist in content." This concept provided the basis of his
nationality policy.

As a part of his nationality policy towards Central Asia,
Stalin introduced a vigorous program of Russification. The
educational system was restructured, the Moslem religion was
curbed, and an attempt was made to establish Russian as the
first language. Russian "was now to enjoy the status of being
the only medium of high culture, science and industry, and
urban civilization in the non-Russian republics." It appears
that Stalin "considered linguistic unity a major factor in
determining the chances of large empires to survive"
(Szporluk, pp. 31-32).

Not content, however, with just changing the present,
Stalin also attacked the past. The literature was purged of
references to national heroes, while local histories were re-
written to present Russian activities in a more favorable light.
"The tsars were discovered to have been progressive historical
figures, and the various peoples of Russia, previously described as victims of colonial conquest, were now said to have
been saved by the Russians from their own as well as from
Western oppressors" (Szporluk, p. 32).

The Central Asians were probably affected far more by
Stalin's economic policies than by his program of Russification.
Mass collectivization of land and livestock, for example, destroyed the traditional way-of-life of the region's nomadic
tribes by forcibly settling them on farms. The Kazakhs, in
particular, offered fierce resistance to this program. During
the first five years of collectivization, thousands of Kazakhs
slaughtered their herds and fled across the border to China
rather than submit to a policy which would end their nomadic

existence. The livestock losses were ultimately to reach such proportions that pre-collectivization levels were not attained until the mid-1950s.

Further compounding the difficulties for the Central Asians was Stalin's objective of freeing the Soviet Union from dependence upon the outside world. Such an autarkic policy required regional economic specialization where unique circumstances favored it. With its hot summer days and long frost-free season, Central Asia was unusually well-suited for the growing of cotton. However, as cotton production was expanded, less land was available for food production. The result was to transform Central Asia from a self-sufficient region to one increasingly dependent on outside areas for its food needs.

In 1936, Stalin promulgated a new Constitution affirming the autonomy of the union republics, and even going so far as to grant them the right to maintain national armies and even to secede. However, the effect of this Constitution upon the national minorities was minimal. The purges of the late 1930s and the forced resettlement of several nationality groups during World War II represented further examples of Stalin's mistrust of the national minorities. By the time of his death in 1953, Stalin's Soviet Union "was, in effect, a Russian empire run by Great Russians in which only the indispensable minimum of lipservice was still paid to the rights of the national minorities" (Pipes, 1954, p. 80).

THE PRESENT

In the quarter of a century since Stalin's death, Central Asia has received relatively lenient treatment from the Soviet leadership. First Khrushchev and now Brezhnev have had to devote special attention to the region as strained relations with China and an increased involvement in the Middle East have given it an unusual strategic importance. For this reason, as well as the desire to raise the living standards of all Soviet citizens, there has been a heavy capital investment in the improvement of transportation and communication facilities, the education system, and the distribution of medical services. There has been also an intensive investment in agriculture. The Central Asian cotton producer in particular has received very favorable treatment from the Soviets and as of 1970, the earned income of Central Asian collective farm families was significantly higher than that of their European counterparts. Yet, for all this apparent attention Central Asian leaders are convinced that Soviet control over the republics has tightened and that the leadership in Moscow remains committed to the goal of assimilating and eventually merging the nationality groups into a unified Russian state.

The most recent Constitution, ratified in 1978, once again affirms the principle of federalism, but Central Asian leaders tend to view it largely as window dressing. Although the Central Asian republics have separate party and governmental structures, they exercise little independence. The republic parties, for example, are but provincial branches of the national Communist Party (CPSU); their primary task is to implement directives originating in Moscow. In the Russian-dominated CPSU, the national minorities, and in particular the Central Asians, are numerically underrepresented. Furthermore, the minorities are underrepresented in positions of party leadership although recently the number of Turkic representatives on the Politburo has been increased from one to three.

The Central Asians are afforded some autonomy by the governmental structure, at least in those local matters deemed unimportant by Moscow. However, the role of the governmental structure is largely to approve actions already taken by the Party. It is, in essence, the formal structure through which the power of the party is transmitted to society. Thus, through their domination of the Party, the Russians effectively exercise control over the republic governments. Still, nothing is left to chance, even the key posts in the governmental hierarchy of the republics are held by Russians. The President of a republic vs Council of Ministers is always a national, but the Vice-President is almost always a Russian. And whereas Asians hold those positions giving the appearance of authority, such as the ministries of health, justice, and social security, Russians occupy the ministries of state security and communications. Russians are also conspicuously numerous in the army and police (U.S. Congress, p. 59).

Because they have the right to secede, the union republics have the final word constitutionally if their grievances are not properly redressed. However, this guarantee has been shown to be only a fiction; In 1974, 14 Armenians were sentenced to long prison terms simply for suggesting a referendum on secession (U.S. News, p. 53). The continued existence of this guarantee, if only on paper, is illustrative of the concern the Soviets feel for their image in the outside world.

A significant change in the new Constitution has been the elimination of any reference to the right of republics to maintain their own armies. As recently as the early 1970s, requests that conscripts be assigned to units stationed in their home republics were routinely granted. It appears, however, that the fear indigenous troops might support nationalist challenges to Moscow's authority, has necessitated the stationing of Central Asian troops primarily within the RSFSR. A further fact not lost on the Soviets is that by the late 1980s almost 40 percent of the prime draft-age males will be non-European

(Azrael, p. 374).
      Perhaps most disturbing to Central Asians has been their
continued underdevelopment in comparison with other union
republics. The Central Asian economy, like the governmental
system, is heavily controlled by Moscow through the mechanism
of central planning. The Central Asians are particularly
critical of what they perceive to be the policy of exploiting
their regions' resources for the benefit of Moscow, and at the
expense of their own republics. This criticism is not without
validity. In 1957, Khrushchev attempted to solve the problem
by dividing the country into a number of administrative
regions, each containing a council of national economy
(sovnarkhoz) to manage industry; agriculture was not included
in the plans. The sovnarkhozey replaced the ministerial form
of planning and granted to the republics - each of the four
Central Asian republics had one sovnarkhoz and Kazakhstan
had 9 - greater control over the development of their own
resources. They were too successful, however, and in 1962,
Krushchev abolished the sovnarkhozey in Central Asia and
replaced them with a joint Central Asian Bureau under the
direct control of the CPSU's Central Committee. Much to the
resentment of the Central Asians, the chairman of the Central
Asian Bureau and his two deputies were Russians. In 1965,
the entire system was scrapped by the Brezhnev-Kosygin
administration, and the ministries were restored to their former
positions of significance.
      The Central Asian economy has much in common with that
of a Third World country. It is heavily dependent upon
agriculture for income and employment; in fact, Central Asia is
reliant upon a single agricultural crop - cotton. Over half the
irrigated farmland is planted to cotton and the region now
accounts for 90 percent of the country's production. However, as in Tsarist days, the bulk of the cotton is sent to
European Russia for processing. Ironically, this has caused
Central Asia to become a net importer of cotton textile goods.
      The livestock industry represents the other important
part of Central Asia's agricultural economy. Sheep and goats
provide the main source of livelihood, outnumbering cattle five
to one. Wool is a major export, and karakul wool a particular
speciality. Unfortunately, this heavy dependence upon raw
materials for the textile industry makes the Central Asian
economy dangerously vulnerable to competition from the
country's expanding synthetic fiber industry.
      Central Asia is also underdeveloped industrially, and
remains heavily dependent "upon imports of heavy metals,
mineral fertilizers, oil products, coal and cement" (Conolly, p.
128). Most of the industry that has been developed is an-
cilliary to agriculture - textiles, cotton-ginning, food-
processing, irrigation-machinery, and fertilizer production.
Nevertheless, even these industries are not sufficiently devel-

oped to meet local needs. The cotton textile industry, as one example, was introduced to the region during the period of the First Five-Year Plan; it was expected to soon satisfy local demand, as well as to provide a surplus for export to neighboring countries. At present, it meets less than half the local demand and represents only eight percent of the country's cotton textile industry, which continues to be concentrated in the Moscow and Ivanovo oblasts.

Bukharan natural gas and Mangyshlak oil have also become important sources of income to Central Asia in recent years. However, as in the case of the cotton textile industry, both of these resources are sent primarily outside the region. The Uzbeks, in particular, have been critical of a natural gas policy that sends over half their production to the Urals and Moscow for use as fuel. The Uzbeks would prefer that the natural gas remain in the region to provide the basis for a local chemical industry, or at least for use as fuel, which at present must be imported.

This low level of industrialization has vastly complicated the region's employment situation. At present, the Central Asian population is the fastest growing in the Soviet Union. Its rate of growth is amost five times that of the Russians.(6) However, with few industrial skills and relatively low mobility, the Central Asians tend to remain in the small towns and on the farms. As a consequence, considerable reserves of labor have begun to accumulate in the countryside. Nevertheless, many apparently prosper on the proceeds of family cottage industries and private household plots.

> The problem of underemployed rural masses is, of course, familiar to most developing countries, whether still under colonial rule or newly independent. The anomaly is that it should exist at all in the planned society of the Soviet Union (which so loudly denounces this problem elsewhere). Moreover, the Soviet Union has no plan to cope with rural unemployment and no central organ with direct responsibility for population-migration problems, as such (Conolly, p. 357).

Most of the new industry in Central Asia has been located in the larger cities where construction costs are lower. With so few skilled, indigenous workers available, the Soviet government has encouraged an in-migration of skilled workers from Western Russia. The magnitude of this influx can be seen from the following figures:

> Between 1959 and 1970 the Russian population of Bukhara Oblast (exploitation of natural gas and gold) increased by 60,000 or 124 percent, of Kyzl-

Orda Oblast (the Tiuratam space complex) by 42,000
or 83 percent, and of Guriev Oblast (Mangyshlak
oil) by 77,000 or 128 percent, compared with an
average increase in the Russian population in the
country as a whole of only 13 percent (Sheehy, p.
561).

Ironically, if the Soviets were to rapidly build up the industrial capacity of Central Asia, it would necessitate the
recruitment of even more skilled workers from European
Russia. This would have the effect of not only straining
European Russia's labor force, but more importantly of Rus-
sianizing Central Asia's larger cities, thereby further detering
the indigenous population from migrating there. A similar
effect would result if the Soviets were to recruit foreign
workers, though it is doubtful they would do so.

Finally, even in those areas where the Soviets claim the
most solid progress, health care and education, there is
criticism by the Central Asians. In the case of health care,
complaints are primarily about the quality of the facilities and
staff. In rural areas particularly, hospitals are few and
poorly-equipped. Because there is also a great shortage of
doctors, much of the work is done by "felshers," a combination mid-wife and first-aid attendant. Although the
situation is much better in the cities, it is the Russians rather
than the Central Asians who are the primary beneficiaries.

The complaints against education run much deeper. By a
1966 decree of the Presidium of the Supreme Soviet, the
republics lost their formal authority over the education system
to a new federal Ministry of Education. Moscow now exercises
control over such matters "as school curricula in the non-
Russian school, the hours of Russian language to be taught,
the length of the school term, choice of examination requirements, etc" (Szporluk, p. 37). Even Stalin was reluctant
to be quite so overt in the restrictions placed upon non-
Russian schools.

There has clearly developed, then, a dichotomy in Central
Asian society, represented by the Russians on the one hand
and the indigenous population on the other. The Russians are
characteristically urban and, in the Soviet context, urban "is
a good surrogate for the attributes of an advanced society:
industrialization, higher education institutions, skilled employment and services (Allworth, 1973, p. 39). The Central
Asians are typically rural, an indication that they are not
active participants in the industrial society. To be sure, their
life-style has materially improved, but they are becoming
increasingly aware that the benefits have not been shared
equally.

For both the Soviets and the Central Asians, the situation
is becoming critical. The rural population is increasing dra-

matically and, "with mechanization remaining the order of the
day (however irrational in the circumstances), with more and
more youngsters reaching working age, and with wages bound
to drop even if yields rise, it is doubtful that this situation
can continue much longer" (Sheehy, p. 562). Ultimately, the
Central Asians may be forced to migrate to the cities in substantial numbers. If they do, and are unable to find employment there, either because the Russians have preempted
them or industry has not been sufficiently developed, their
frustration with the system can only grow.

CONCLUSION

In one sense, Soviet nationality policies have demonstrated success: they have transformed an area that was once
ethnically heterogeneous, although linked by a common history
and religion, into one of five union republics defined on the
basis of ethnolinguistic criteria; and the attachments that the
inhabitants have formed towards their respective nationality
areas have helped reduce the threat of a pan-Islamic or pan-
Turkic movement. These same attachments, however, now
present an obstacle to the Soviets' ultimate goal of merging the
nationalities into a single nation built upon the Russian
language and culture. The Soviets are therefore faced with
either having to force Russification upon the reluctant Central
Asians or admit that nationalism is not about to wither away,
and allow Central Asians greater freedom of cultural expression. If, as it appears, the Soviets wish to influence developments in the Muslim states to the south-Afghanistan, Iran,
Turkey - they may almost certainly have to do the latter.
Meanwhile, the political and economic frustrations that the
Central Asians have been experiencing have served to further
strengthen their national identities. Although they have felt
powerless to contest Soviet control of their region, they have
attempted to counter policies of Russification. Societies have
been established for the preservation of cultural landmarks,
and efforts have been made to purify local languages by removing Russian words. Even the use of Russian as the lingua
franca of the region has been discouraged. Census data for
the period 1959-70 show a decline in the percentage of Central
Asians speaking Russian; only about 16 percent of Central
Asians speak Russian with some fluency (Azrael, p. 373).
The struggle to arrest Russification poses a serious
dilemma for the Central Asians. If their young are not to
learn Russian, they will not be able to compete successfully
for entrance into scientific and technical universities. Without
such an education, the opportunities for finding skilled employment and for moving into positions of leadership are seri-

ously reduced. There is evidence to suggest that many Central Asians have been pursuing programs in the social sciences and humanities rather than the sciences because of their inability to speak Russian (Allworth, 1973, p. 93). What, then, are the alternatives facing the Central Asians? Must they allow assimilation to take place in order to reap a larger share of the material benefits? Or should they confront the Soviets with the demand for an authentic federal system that would allow them greater political and cultural autonomy? And if the latter, to what extent are they willing to go to achieve it? Until now, the "divide and rule" principle has effectively kept the Central Asian republics apart, but as their numbers increase they may take more concerted action to protect their cultural identities.

NOTES

1. Only the southern half of Kazakhstan is functionally integrated with Central Asia. The northern half is more industrialized and has become closely tied to the RSFSR.
2. According to the 1970 census, Kazkhs make up only 32 percent of their republic; Russians comprise 42 percent of the population, with Ukrainians accounting for another 7.2 percent, and Belorussians, 1.5 percent.
3. By this time, the number of Russians in Central Asia was between two and three million.
4. Moslems were excluded from the Tashkent Soviet and from all governmental posts in Tashkent.
5. The Government retained control over the key sectors, heavy industry and mining, but allowed agriculture, transportation, and retail trade to operate under an almost free-market system.
6. The RSFSR has a rate of natural increase (births minus deaths) of 5.9/1000, while the average rate for the four Central Asian republics is 27/1000, and for Kazakhstan 25/1000.

BIBLIOGRAPHY

Allworth, Edward (ed.). Central Asia: A Century of Russian Rule. New York: Columbia University Press, 1967.

_____. Soviet Nationality Problems. New York: Columbia University Press, 1971.

_____. The Nationality Question in Soviet Central Asia. New York: Praeger, 1973.

Azrael, Jeremy (ed.). Soviet Nationality Policies and Practices. New York: Praeger, 1978.

Becker, Seymour. Russia's Protectorates in Central Asia: Bukhara and Khiva, 1865 - 1929. Cambridge, Mass.: Harvard University Press, 1968.

Conolly, Violet. Beyond the Urals: Economic Developments in Soviet Asia. London: Oxford University Press, 1967.

Economist. "101 Problems for Mr. Brezhnev." March 19, 1977.

Goldhagen, Erich (ed.). Ethnic Minorities in the Soviet Union. New York: Praeger, 1968.

Kaushik, Devendra. Central Asia in Modern Times. Moscow: Progress Publishers, 1970.

Krader, Lawrence. Peoples of Central Asia. Bloomington, Ind.: Indiana University Publications, 1963.

Nove, Alex and J.A. Newth. The Soviet Middle East: A Communist Model for Development. London: Praeger, 1966.

Pahlen, Count K.K. Mission to Turkestan (1908 - 1909). London: Oxford University Press, 1964.

Pierce, Richard A. Soviet Central Asia: A Bibliography. Berkeley: Delo Press, 1966.

Pipes, Richard. The Formation of the Soviet Union, 1917 - 1923. Cambridge, Mass.: Harvard University Press, 1954.

Rakowska-Harmstone, Teresa. Russia and Nationalism in Central Asia: The Case of Tadzhikistan. Baltimore: John Hopkins Press, 1970.

Rywkin, Michael. Russia in Central Asia. New York: Collier Books, 1963.

Schroeder, Gertrude. "Soviet Wage and Income Policies in Regional Perspectives." ACES Bulletin (Fall 1974): 3-19.

Shapiro, Leonard B. The USSR and the Future: An Analysis of the New Program of the CPSU. New York: Praeger, 1963.

Sheehy, Ann. "Some Aspects of Regional Development in Central Asia." Slavic Review, (Sept. 1972), 555-563.

Sokol, Edward. The Revolt of 1916 in Soviet Central Asia. Baltimore: John Hopkins Press, 1954.

Szporluk, Roman. "Nationalities and the Russian Problem in the USSR: An Historical Outline." Journal of International Affairs (Jan. 1973): 22-40.

Taaffe, Robert. Rail Transportation and the Economic Development of Soviet Central Asia. Chicago: University of Chicago, Department of Geography, Research Paper No. 64, 1960.

U.S. Congress, Senate Committee on Judiciary. The Soviet Empire: A Study in Discrimination and Abuse of Power. Report by the Subcommittee to Investigate the Administration of the Internal Security Act and Other Internal Security Laws. 89th Congress, 1st. Session, 1965.

U.S. News and World Report. "In USSR, Minority Problems Just Won't Wither Away." February 14, 1977.

Wheeler, Geoffrey. The Modern History of Soviet Central Asia. London: Praeger, 1964.

Wilbur, Charles K. The Soviet Model and Underdeveloped Countries. Chapel Hill, N.C.: University of North Carolina, 1969.

IV

Ethnicity and Ethnic Autonomy in the Developing World

Introduction

In general, states of the developing world are comprised of ethnically-heterogeneous populations to a greater extent than those of the developed world. Because ethnic heterogeneity contains potential for conflict, the greater the degree of heterogeneity, the more difficult it is for states to manage it. In the developing world, the absence of ethnic conflict in states with multiple ethnic groups is the exception rather than the rule. And the most severe test of ethnic pluralism will have to be met in those states with democratic orientations.

Ethnic conflict in the developing world stems in part from European colonialism, which tended to enlarge indigenous political and social territorial units and to centralize resources, power, status, and privilege in the administrative state center. In many cases, these arrangements forced or strongly influenced diverse ethnic groups to enter into new social and political relationships that contravened their traditions. Before colonialism, potential or actual ethnic adversaries had attempted to work out generally-satisfactory ecological arrangements; they usually respected each others' physical and psychological boundaries, either because there was little or no choice in the matter, or because no one group had sufficient power to overwhelm the others. It is not surprising, therefore, that the most vehement ethnic conflict occurs in states that have experienced colonial domination. Prior to the European incursion, conflict was usually limited to local, small-scale disputes. These became national when new states emerged on the European model; the demise of colonialism did not result in a return to pre-colonial boundaries and social arrangements. The concept of the state in theory and practice was maintained, along with the boundaries drawn up by the former colonial masters. This resulted in the creation of minorities, and caused ethnic social conflict resembling that found in

Europe.   Consequently, ethnic relations and ethnic conflict in
the developing world exhibit characteristics not unlike those
found generally in the developed world.

A first glance, it appears that ethnic conflict in the
developing world stems in the main from a natural tendency for
groups to coalesce around what Clifford Geertz calls "primordial sentiments."   That is, in societies characterized by
"mechanical solidarity," individuals have no identity outside
the ethnic group; they derive their sense of security and
power from membership in it.   A close look, however, suggests
that the new heterogeneity imposed by the state to achieve its
goals creates an atmosphere wherein groups compete with one
another for scarce material and status resources.   Hence,
ethnic solidarity is the most efficacious means of competing
for state-controlled resources.

Again patterned after the developed world, the developing
world uses various strategies and approaches to deal with the
problem of heterogeneity.   In the developed world, "pluralism"
is the concept used to manage diversity; in the developing
world, it is "political integration."   Hence, the selections in
this section address in various ways the political aspects of
pluralism, and the means by which states in the developing
world attempt to deal with the problem of multiple ethnicity.

The first two selections address problems of ethnic
conflict in two East African States, Uganda, and Ethiopia.
Doornbos focuses attention on the Kumayana and the
Rwenzururu movements in Ankole and Toro respectively, two
"neighboring districts in the Western Region of Uganda. Both
districts are ethnically-divided, but the ethnic division has a
different socio-geographic pattern in each case, as have the
proportions of the subgroups."   Doornbos makes it clear that,
despite many common factors, the two movements were distinct:
they originated independently of each other, only partially
overlapped in time, and never became linked.   Although "the
movements found their roots in basically identical factors of
social inequality, structural factors caused them to develop
along quite different lines."   As in the situation in Northern
Ireland, religion played a key role in how the movements
operated, and especially in the recruitment and mobilization of
members.   In addition, the process of modernization prompted
both movements to pay attention to the manner in which unequal benefits accrued to subgroups, "thus causing ethnic
inequality to be a dominant feature of both societies."
Doornbos concludes that these movements may be interpreted
"as the products of emergent class structures [and that]
ethnic grievances, as much as anything else, can be manipulated to build positions of leadership, a requisite for entry
into the government elite."

The selection by Abate on Ethiopia addresses a number of
points: political integration, multiple ethnicity, religious con-

flict of a schismatic nature, secessionism, irredentism, and nationalism. He believes that the most serious problem facing African states is that of national integration, and that, because of its ethnic, religious, racial, and cultural pluralism, "Ethiopia is faced with the most serious problem of national integration of any African country."

The specific areas of conflict consist of Eritrea, the Afar region of the Rift valley, and the Somali-inhabited area of the Ogaden. The eastern area under discussion is hot and dry and is the home of a predominantly Muslim and nomadic population, as opposed to the core region, which is easily cultivated and inhabited by a predominantly Christian population. A combination of ethnic, religious, historical, economic, and political factors are used to explain the secessionist movement in Eritrea, and irredentism in the Ogaden. Christianity was introduced into Ethiopia in the fourth century, and has been the state religion ever since. The conversion of the eastern region to Islam began in the eighth century, and engendered a contest for dominance between the two religious groups. The present conflict is an extension of this age-long conflict. Colonialism, the policy of "divide and rule" and arbitrary drawing of boundaries, has made national integration a formidable task. Nationalist aspirations for self-determination in Eritrea and Somalia are challenging the territorial integrity and sovereignty of Ethiopia.

Moving from specific examples of ethnic movements in East Africa, Anise undertakes the task of treating synoptically the problems of ethnicity and national integration in the 17 states of West Africa. At the outset he makes two important points: every black African state is confronted with "The primary and existential pervasiveness of ethnic groups and identities," and this "ethnicity continues to be the single most readily-identifiable social-structural characteristic of the new states in Africa." And African political leaders and elites persistently identify ethnicity as the principal devisive factor in national politics." He goes on to restate an important point made in the introduction to this volume: "It is not the existence of ethnic heterogeneity or social pluralism per se that causes social and political instability, but rather the uses to which the structures of heterogeneity are put in society." He then focuses attention on relationships between ethnicity, development, resource allocation and ethnic competition for social equity and distributive justice. He concludes that "only the institutionalization of categoric equality and elite disinclination to exploit ethnic, cultural, religious, linguistic, and regional differences in the process of competition for resource scarcity will redirect nation-building energies toward the integrative mode."

In Africa, except for Zimbabwe-Rhodesia and the Union of

South Africa, interethnic conflict takes place among groups of
the same race. The same is true for Europe, save for the
situation in Soviet Central Asia. In the U.S. the most pervasive movements for autonomy involve racial conflict among
blacks, Chicanos, Native Americans, and whites. Race is the
single most important variable explaining power and privilege
in the U.S. Although Chicanos are classified as Caucasians, it
is unclear whether they are generally accepted by whites as
fellow Caucasians.

Different societies attach widely divergent meanings to
real or perceived dissimilarities between peoples. The significance of phenotype varies from place to place, depending
on the importance a particular society places on cultural or
social differences. In contrast to the U.S., race and color in
Latin America are not automatic determinants of individual or
group status; they are but two of the many status components. Some argue that the class structure in Latin America
does carry ethnic overtones, that higher status positions are,
in fact, dominated by those of European descent, with race
and color being the chief determinants. Others argue, however, that an individual with non-white physical traits may in
fact be socially regarded as white, and vice versa, and that
Latin American class culture is multicolored and multi-ethnic.

Although there is debate on whether race and color
significantly shapes the nature and character of intergroup
relations in Latin America, there is less argument that Indians
are the objects of discrimination. However, most agree that
Indians are discriminated against not because of race, but
because of other differences defined as important by the
majority. Indians are not distinguished because of genetic or
phenotypic inheritance; they are discriminated against because
Indian culture is regarded as uncivilized or even savage, and
anyone of Indian descent - even though the person may no
longer occupy Indian status - is associated with that culture.

Indians in Latin America and blacks in the United States
experience discrimination for different reasons. In Latin
America, the Indian and Hispanic populations are distinguished
by language, customs, beliefs, values, and residence. The
dominant Hispanic population in Peru, for example, regards
Indian culture as inferior and, therefore, prohibits the Indians
from participating equally in the social system. By the same
token, most Indians are not eager to be integrated into the
Hispanic mainstream; they are separatist in the sense that they
would prefer the two ethnic groups to remain separate.

There is yet another difference between black American
and Latin American Indian autonomy efforts: black Americans
rebel because they have been excluded, and their rebellions
tend to take place within the mainstream, in cities; Indians
in Latin America rebel in the countryside to maintain their
distinctive cultures. Both efforts to achieve autonomy stem in

large measure from the nature of the colonialism experienced by the two groups. Indians in Latin America were the original inhabitants, and they have refused to become part and parcel of a post-colonial society. In contrast, blacks in the United States were forcibly removed from their native Africa and brought to the Americas, where they remained systematically subordinated; hence, most of their efforts have centered on attempting to become a part of the American mainstream.

Not all black Americans have sought integration as a solution to black-white conflict in the United States; and not all Indians in Latin America have sought to remain separate from the dominant Hispanic mainstream. Both groups fell victim to the majority in the cultures: Most blacks were resigned to the idea that they could not exist separately from whites; and the structure of Indian society in Latin America collapsed in the face of the Hispanic onslaught. Traditions are maintained by those Indians who fled to the periphery. This total subordination of Latin American Indians is the chief reason Castro-Klaren begins her essay with the observation that ethnic separatism "in Latin America is at first glance tantamount to the contemplation of an absence. For the most part, separatism is absent in Latin America because by the end of the fourteenth century Indians had succumbed to the power of the colonial invaders and the forces of integration they put into play." However, she does make the further point that "the war of the castes of Yucatan in 1848 stands out as the only large-scale historical event that expressed the continuance of a desire for separate ethnic rule."

Although the 1848 war may be regarded as the last large-scale expression of Indian separatism, it should also be seen as an expression of a much older historical desire to expel Spanish influence. Because history is always a factor in ethnic movements for autonomy, Castro-Klaren focuses on an important historical figure whose influence is still felt among segments of the Indian population in Peru - Huaman Poma de Ayala. In the sixteenth century, Poma had a plan that would expel the Spaniards from what is now Peru and bring about an ethnically homogeneous state. This was to be accomplished in two stages: The Spaniards and their black slaves would occupy the cities and towns, while the Indians would return to their villages and pre-Inca agrarian life styles. Once secure in this setting, the blueprint for "good government for the Indian states is modeled on the past ... Most especially the old, for they remember, and they also embody a series of negations [of Spanish culture] basic to the administration of good government." Poma's "good government" was to be modeled after the Incan culture in its heyday, and those most capable of bringing it into reality would be the Indians themselves.

While Castro-Klaren narrates a chapter from Peru's past, Segal describes the complexity of the interconnection among

race, class, and ethnicity in contemporary Peru.   In fact,
Segal's discussion and analysis of the relationship among these
three variables, along with the particular attention he pays to
urbanism, modernization, and outside influence, are detailed
explanations of why Poma's blueprint for Indian autonomy has
not materialized, and probably will not be realized in the
future.   For very different reasons, both Poma and Segal
agree that Peru is fertile ground for autonomy action by
Indians: Poma explained to Phillip II and Phillip III why they
should sanction Indian separation; Segal elaborates on why
separatism has not occurred.

Why has it not occurred in Peru?   Segal argues that
"exclusivist central control institutions linked with processes of
inclusion have kept separatist consciousness from arising and
spreading.   Inclusion has never been more than partial, and it
probably would not have been sufficient to diminish a
separatist thrust if the central controlling institutions had not
been so strong."   Although Indians still constitute a large
segment of the population, most of them are poor and isolated,
and Segal thinks it too simplistic to label Peru a dual society
or two separate nations.   He observes that it is still "a
country marked by harsh class divisions re-enforced by ethnic
stratification.   Despite conditions like these, Peru has not had
a significant separatist movement since 1870.   There have been
other, smaller Indian revolts earlier and later, but all were
put down easily.   Not until the 1960s did a set of largely
autonomous peasant movements accomplish major structural
changes in the highland agrarian sector; but, by then, they
were led and carried out by Indians and peasants who desired
social justice within Peruvian society, not separation from it."

Across the Atlantic in the subcontinent of India, the
forecast of a continuation of unity is only cautiously optimistic.
India is the world's largest democracy and faces the most
severe test of ethnic pluralism.   This stems in part from the
diversity of Indian society and the existence of a variety of
movements for autonomy.   What is significant, and deviant with
respect to this volume, about some of these movements in India
is that they are not ethnically based.   Erdman observes that
"virtually every dimension of India's diversity has at one time
or another been brought into play, as religious, tribal, and
linguistic-cultural groups have been involved in the process.

Although some movements have been explicitly secessionist, more numerous ones have included nonsecessionist
demands for territorial redistribution of powers within the
Union.   So far, the state has been able to manage these
demands without significant internal strife; but that is not to
say that there is universal agreement on the government's
ability to do so ad infinitum.   Nevertheless, Erdman points out
that India's "seasoned political leaders are not likely to embark
on policies which will alienate large segments of the population

simultaneously; and they should, moreover, be able to cope
with autonomy-oriented movements as they continue to manifest
themselves." Indian leaders should be able to cope with
movements for autonomy because they are constantly aware
that they must never become complacent about the success of
unity. Erdman, in the final analysis, believes that while "a
bit of guarded optimism is entirely appropriate, there is a
difference between guarded optimism and wishful thinking."

13 Protest Movements in Western Uganda: Some Parallels and Contrasts

Martin R. Doornbos

INTRODUCTION

Ankole and Toro are neighboring districts in western Uganda. Until 1967, they ranked as kingdoms, with quasi-federal relationships to the national center. Although both districts are ethnically divided, the ethnic division has a different socio-geographic pattern in each case, and the proportions of the sub-groups in each are also different. In Ankole, a cattle-owning Bahima elite - constituting approximately only five percent of the population - ruled the Bairu agricultural population; whereas in Toro the Batoro, approximately 55 percent of the population dominated the Bakonzo and Baamba, who live separately in the western part of the district. Common to the two situations, therefore, was the fact that unequal benefits accrued to the different subgroups, thus causing ethnic inequality to be a dominant feature in both societies.

In recent years, ethnic inequality in Ankole and Toro has been challenged by protest movements that attacked the assumptions of hierarchy and subordination underlying the political structure. In Ankole, it was the Kumanyana movement; and in Toro, the Rwenzururu movement. These movements were rooted in the subordinate populations, who reacted against established orders which appeared too inflexible to accommodate participation by new political groups. Resentment over disproportionate allocations of chieftainships and other government posts, inadequate distribution of educational opportunities, inequalities in tax burdens, and obstacles to upward social mobility were among the immediate factors precipitating the movements. Equally as important as these issues, however, were grievances about the contemptuous

263

treatment to which the subordinate groups in Ankole and Toro
had allegedly been subjected. Significantly, the reaction
against political, economic and psychological inequality was
stimulated by processes which had begun to reduce these very
discrepancies. The spread of education, a relative increase in
incomes following the expansion of cash-crop cultivation, and a
general diffusion of more egalitarian values throughout Uganda
all militated against the continued acceptance of inequalities in
other spheres of life.

Notwithstanding these common factors, the two situations
were quite distinct. Although Ankole and Toro were adjacent
districts, the Kumanyana and Rwenzururu movements
originated independently and never became linked to each
other, or to other expressions of protest in the country, an
indication of the district-centered politics of Uganda. They
only partially overlapped in time; the Kumanyana movement was
over its peak when the Rwenzururu movement was in its
infancy in 1962. As a prelude to conflict, there had been a
series of comparable incidents and organizational activity in the
two district-kingdoms; in Ankole, these inaugurated a
movement which gradually grew and then declined, in contrast
to a belated, sudden, and severe outburst of enmity in Toro.

Most important was the fact that, although the movements
found their roots in basically identical factors of social
inequality, structural factors caused them to develop along
quite different lines, to the extent that they ultimately found
themselves pressing for widely divergent demands. One such
difference was the effect of mechanisms designed to widen
popular participation in decision making. In Ankole, these
accommodated demands to a substantial degree, and were thus
conducive to political integration; in Toro, however, they were
incapable of coping with the challenges they had fostered and
eventually broke down. Because political adjustment was
achieved by slow and progressive means in Ankole, the Bairu
movement against Bahima overlordship is little known outside
that district. In Toro, on the other hand, the Rwenzururu
movement rapidly evolved from an internal Toro affair to a
national concern with international implications. An analysis of
the two situations may throw some light on conditions which
promote accommodation or disintegration in sub-national
political frameworks. A brief overview of each case should,
therefore, be helpful.(1)

ANKOLE

Semantics alone would suggest that the Kumanyana
movement should be integrative. Depending on the extent to
which Bakiga, Baganda, and other immigrants to Ankole are

regarded as having been assimilated, the term Bairu (singular, Mwiru) refers to between 85 and 95 percent of the population of Ankole, which totals about 800,000. The term is not without ambiguity; it denotes an ethnic group, the peasant class and serfs, which historically were seen as coterminous. Because no specialized term for this new group has developed, the word "Bairu" inevitably carries negative connotations and, not surprisingly, is unpopular with many people in Ankole. Only a very few people, primarily some of those who have been in the vanguard of the Kumanyana movement, use the term "Mwiru" with a sense of pride. Most people prefer to speak of themselves as Banyankore, while some may go on to specify that they mean "pure" Banyankore, a difference which stresses political rights for the "original" inhabitants of Ankole. In any case, the identification with Ankole is crucial, even if some people may seem to claim Ankole for the Bairu to the exclusion of others.(2)

Possibly in reaction to this, the Bahima have also increasingly identified themselves as Banyankore. As they have been losing power, their numerical minority position, their distinct ways of life, and their recollections of past Bahima domination have tended to keep them on the alert for possible discriminatory measures. However, social distance is still great between the two groups, as evidenced by the infrequency of intermarriage. If one further notes the view of some Bairu that the "Hamites" - a term uncritically adopted from an earlier generation of anthropologists - are invaders who came to Ankole some 500 years ago and who should go back to where they came from, it becomes understandable that the Bahima, at least outwardly, seek to tone down their ethnic identity. Both the Bahima and the Bairu wish to reach a common denominator, but for different reasons. The contemporary lack of appeal of the terms "Bairu" and "Bahima" across ethnic boundaries thus strengthens the unifying qualities of the word "Banyankore."

Beyond terminology, however, a propensity for integration could also be anticipated due to socio-geographic factors. As the Bahima and Bairu lived dispersed throughout most of Ankole, even if not in equal proportions, it was necessary for the latter to press for equality in status and an exchange of leadership roles. Rather than seeking their own separate kingdom, they were induced by these conditions to apply pressure for integration on the existing political hierarchy. The role of the Kumanyana movement was to aggregate forces and exert influence towards this end.

The strategy followed by the Kumanyana movement should be seen in the light of the Ankole context; a comparison with Rwanda is illustrative in this regard. The question which asserts itself is whether slowly-sustained pressure for integration was the only alternative open in Ankole. A violent

revolution in neighboring Rawnda, another ethnically-stratified
society, although not in every respect identical, abruptly
threw off Batutsi rule. The Kumanyana movement, however,
although at times apparently imbued with revolutionary zeal,
was never involved in any serious clashes, nor did it intend to
be. There were no demonstrations, no fights, no imprison-
ments, and it never actually mobilized the peasant masses. As
a matter of fact, it appears that after 1955, when the Bairu
movement had swollen to its most inclusive size, it became too
unwieldy to be very effective.

In retrospect, one would be inclined to assume that the
Rwanda situation was more serious than that in Ankole, and
hence led to a revolution. However, at some points in time
dissensions in Ankole were probably at least as profound as
they were in Rwanda. As late as 1956, for example, the King
(Omugabe) of Ankole, upon his return from a visit to Rwanda,
felt prompted to hold up ethnic relationships in that country
as an example to the Banyankore:

> In Ruanda, there are three types of people, namely
> Bahutu, Batutsi and the Batwa. They work
> together in cooperation and ... their motto is
> "Omuguha gw' enyabushatu' (a rope with three
> strands) representing these classes of people in
> Ruanda. You will all agree with me that no country
> should expect progress if there is lack of co-
> operation and disunity. Division and hatred en-
> gineered by subversive elements in a country
> exhibit a gloomy picture and their ends are fatal.
> I should like you to be 'Omuguha gw-enyabushatu'.
> That is when we shall achieve Ankole's will as a
> nation. (3)

The Ankole situation may not have led to a similar sudden
avalanche because the issues were handled in a different way,
and because certain conditions made it possible to handle them
differently. Unlike the Rwanda situation, in Ankole there was
no sudden realization of the changes of time, and a subsequent abrupt transfer of political support from one group to
another on the part of administrative and clerical authorities.
Beginning in 1945, various new ordinances were introduced
that regulated the powers and compositions of district administrations in Uganda. Although these were issued in a
somewhat piecemeal fashion, they guaranteed the Bairu progressively increasing participation in Ankole affairs and
satisfied demands to some extent. At the same time, they
continued to whet appetites; hence, there was fairly constant
strife, and, at times, it may have seemed graver than in
Rwanda. However, it never culminated in violence.

There were other conditioning elements in Ankole that

made the situation there different from the one in Rwanda. One of these was demographic: the Batutsi comprised approximately 15 percent of Rwanda's population, while the Bahima accounted for only five percent of Ankole's. The Batutsi also appear to have been distributed somewhat more evenly than the Bahima were, and a far larger proportion of Batutsi stood in a directly hierarchical position vis-a-vis Bahutu subordinates than did Bahima in respect to Bairu. The majority of Bahima in Ankole still lead a semi-nomadic, pastoral life, detached from, and disinterested in, the affairs of government. In fact, during the first half of this century, the key positions in Ankole were held by a small group of Bahima chiefs. Most of the pastoral Bahima left for Buganda during the critical years of transition - the late 1940s until the early 1960s - because of an encroachment by the tsetse flies. It may be doubted, however, whether the presence of these Bahima in Ankole would have made much difference as far as the revolutionary potential was concerned. Although their superior military skills had made them a formidable force to be reckoned with and formed the basis for their hegemony in previous centuries, these qualities had not been a factor, or even a consideration, during the last two decades. It is possible that the Batutsi political elite was stronger and more firmly entrenched in Rwanda than was the Bahima ruling group in Ankole. The Batutsi were powerful enough to put up resistance; the Bahima, too weak.

Most decisive, however, seems to be the fact that, in a closed system such as Rwanda, the incumbent elite has no choice; if it wants to remain an elite, it has to fight to maintain its position. In Ankole, on the other hand, many Bahima and Bairu who could not find positions in the local establishment were able to secure alternative employment in the wider universe of Uganda and East Africa. The fact that Ankole was part of a larger entity took much of the steam from its political situation. Hence, the contrasting cases of Ankole and Rwanda suggest that, other things being equal, ethnically-stratified sub-units within wider frameworks are in a better position to reach internal political adjustment than are similarly-divided "national" societies. When the educated class has potential alternatives in the larger unit, there is likely to be a diminution of tension in the sub-units.

However, some aspects of the social setting in which the Kumanyana movement originated served to prolong ethnic strife and factionalism, and at the same time reduce their impact and effectiveness. The Bairu did not constitute a unified force primarily because religious differences in Ankole cut across the ethnic division: the Bahima were almost exclusively Protestants; the Bairu were divided almost evenly between Catholics and Protestants. This weakened the stand Kumanyana could take and reduced the generality of the

Bairu-Bahima confrontation, while at the same time it tended to prolong conflict.

Although the scope of its concerns was Ankole-wide, the movement attracted its following primarily from the central and more heavily-populated parts of the district because they were the most accessible. The centrally-situated counties of Ankole - Shema, Igara, and parts of Rwanpara and Kashari - are also the areas where coffee and other cash-crops had long been successfully cultivated; thus the Bairu living there had comparatively high incomes and educational opportunities. Shema and Igara, with populations almost wholly composed of Bairu, radiate a greater spirit of militancy than can be found in other parts of Ankole. Most of the militant Bairu leaders who came on the scene after the 1940s were from these areas, and a majority of them attended the same primary school at Kabwohe in Shema. Finally, because of the vagaries of history, these central areas also have more Protestants than Catholics. Catholics predominate in the outlying counties of Ankole, such as Bunyaruguru, Buhweju, and Ibanda.

Thus, the Kumanyana movement was basically Protestant, as its various antecedents had also been. Since the 1930s educated Protestant Bairu had been concerned about their position in Ankole society; and the early student agitation of the 1940s took place exclusively among Protestant students. Only a few Roman Catholics are known to have been involved in the Kumanyana meetings from the beginning. It was not until 1955, when the first Prime Minister (Enganzi) was elected by the Council (Eishengyero), that Catholics and Protestants joined in the movement. Yet Catholics account for slightly more than 50 percent of the Bairu, and they had been discriminated against more clearly in the allocation of jobs. Their differences with the Bahima were much greater than those of the Protestant Bairu, who had been in contact with Bahima in school, church, and government service.

Is it a paradox, then, that it was the Protestant Bairu, and not the Catholics, who reacted against the Bahima rule? The proposition has often been advanced that conflict will be less profound between groups having some common values and identifications than between groups divided on the basis of a greater number of criteria. Why then does this thesis seem not to apply in Ankole?

Max Weber has contended that there is an element in the nature of the two religions that made the Protestants more militant, the Catholics more submissive. Although theirs was not the "King's religion," Catholic Bairu were definitely more respectful of the Omugabe's authority than their Protestant counterparts. The latter at one time titled their leader Ruterengwa (Nothing compares with him in stature), which in royalist circles was taken to suggest superiority to the king; and many of them regarded Bagyendanwa (the royal drums and

traditionally the source of all power) as no more than a piece of wood, and the kingship itself as of little consequence.
     Probably, however, it was the closeness of contact which prompted the Protestant Bairu to challenge the status and privileges of the Bahima. Because of their greater social proximity to the Bahima, the Protestant Bairu were more sensitive to the advantages given to their Bahima schoolmates, fellow congregationists, and co-workers in government service. Catholics, on the other hand, were absorbed in their own affairs and out of touch with what went on at the political center of the district. Perhaps a lack of awareness of alternative perspectives had resigned them to their status as second class citizens.
     Equally important was the fact that Protestant Bairu were more educated than the Catholics. On the whole, they also fared better financially as a result of cash-crop cultivation. Thus, Protestants generally seemed to display more "achievement orientation" than Catholics; they felt that they could further improve their standards of living if they were given a chance, and they believed that failures were largely the result of obstacles put in their way by the Bahima. Obviously, these notions can easily lead to scape-goat theories, a phenomenon not unknown in Ankole. In any case, the pattern of interaction of ethnicity and religion in Ankole points to the need for a more complex thesis than one which merely states that the greatest conflict will occur where there are the greatest differences. Indeed, the greatest conflict may well occur between groups that differ the least from each other. This applies particularly if factors of social mobility lead to competition between the groups that have the most in common.
     Generally, there is no denying that ethnicity or religion may have important effects on the nature and depth of a conflict; and the conflict may well be more severe if there are important socio-cultural differences than if there are overarching social values. Ethnicity, religion, language, and race have too often been known to increase sensitivities and intensify conflict. However, one should not draw the conclusion that group conflict results from the distinguishing properties and symbols that divide rather than from the relative differences in educational achievement, economic prosperity, and social and political advancement generally. Conflict seems most likely to occur and increase when changes take place in the social distance between groups, no matter which group is moving and in what direction. Challenges to the leadership position of an ethnic or religious sub-group may thus come from a group which approximates its socio-economic standing, whether or not, and however much or how little, it is culturally different, rather than from a group, whatever its differences may be, that lacks social mobilization and does not have the motivation and perspective to enter into competition for

additional political and social benefits. This is suggested by
the Ankole experience.

The fact that the Kumanyana movement drew its main
strength from the Protestants was one of its weaknesses.
Catholics were induced to join the Bairu meetings in the mid-
1950s, when the fullest possible pressure seemed needed to get
a Mwiru Enganzi elected. Although they came in somewhat
reluctantly, they expected to share in the rewards once a
Bairu administration came into office. However, they soon
became disenchanted when the Protestants continued to reap
most of the benefits. Protestants, on the other hand, considered that they had done more for Bairu advancement, had
more people available for positions, and were more deserving
of rewards. The Catholic disaffection soon caused them to
defect from the Bairu camp. The successes of the Bairu
movement were thus followed shortly by its decline.

From 1955 onwards, the Bahima saw their position go
down as well. When party politics made its entry in the years
immediately before independence, the Bahima found allies in
the Catholic Bairu. In the late 1950s, a coalition grew
between Protestant Bahima and Catholic Bairu, which finally
found its organizational basis when the Democratic Party
branched out into Ankole. They won the first general
elections held for the Eishengyero, and formed the Ankole
government from 1961-63, when it was replaced by the Uganda
People's Congress.

As of 1960, a large majority of the Protestant Bairu gave
their support to the UPC. The UPC was the result of a
merger between a wing of the Uganda National Congress and
the Uganda People's Union, which was based mainly in western
Uganda. Because Ugandan political parties originated primarily
at the center, it took some sorting out before local complexities
found their expression in party rivalries. Although the UPU
and the UNC had to some extent cut across ethnic divisions,
their membership was probably too small and their leadership
too impermanent to allow any conclusions to be drawn from
this. In the late 1950s, and early 1960s, however, potential
election returns became a major consideration in Ankole
politics. Because the vast majority of voters - the Bairu -
were organized along religious lines in the DP and UPC, it
became imperative for the leaders of both parties to try to tip
the balance. The largely Catholic Bairu DP had Bahima
support, but the Protestant Bairu increasingly felt that they
needed Bahima votes for the UPC. Hence, ethnic rivalries
were played down in the 1960-62 period, while religious conflict assumed major proportions. At the popular level, the
Democratic Party was identified with Catholics and the Uganda
People's Congress with Protestants. Because members of the
two denominations were believed to vote for the corresponding
parties, "political baptizing" was needed to convert the re-

maining "pagans," and conquer the floating vote they represented.

The UPC was not able, however, to attract a substantial number of Bahima votes, although some influential Bahima had entered into its leadership. After all the efforts to mobilize the Bairu during the preceding decade, a significant part of the leadership of both the Ankole DP and UPC in the early 1960s was in the hands of Bahima, and three Bahima were among the six M.Ps. returned by the UPC and DP to the National Assembly in 1962. From that time until the present, Ankole politics has further evolved within the threefold framework of Bahima, Protestant Bairu, and Catholic Bairu.

In view of the longstanding lack of empathy between ethnic groups in Ankole, it is not surprising that some suspicions and friction should have developed in both political parties, although most pronounced and openly so within the UPC. As a matter of fact, there is among the Bairu a widely-held theory that the Bahima deliberately stirred up Catholic-Protestant and DP-UPC rivalries to keep the Bairu divided; and then, distributing themselves between the two parties, they managed to gain control over both. There are also certain issues connected with land tenure and the allocation of development resources that some Bairu feel have been manipulated to give disproportionate privileges to "those who have fallen into things," many of whom are Bahima.

These charges have unmistakably added fuel to further articulation of Bairu aggrievances. As a result, a continuation of the Kumanyana movement can be found in one of the factions that has divided the UPC in recent years; the remaining hard core of the movement acts as a ready-made source of political support for the leaders of this group. The rival UPC group feels that times have changed and that the issue of the day is no longer one of Bahima domination; they believe that co-operation and understanding between Protestants and Catholics, Bairu and Bahima, are necessary and possible, and that accentuating differences will in the long run work to no group's advantage.

This latter faction, the Kahigirizagroup, constituted the Ankole government from 1963-67. They were replaced by the Bananukagroup, the present UPC administration in Ankole. However, it is doubtful whether the difference between the two factions is as great as it may appear. There does not seem to be much difference in the nature of the policies pursued and, quite naturally, each has an interest in gaining control over the affairs of the district in order to be able to place followers in administrative positions. If these are pragmatic matters, perhaps their respective followers may be equally pragmatic. Thus, whereas the Bananuka group could rely on a solid core of Protestant Bairu for support, the Kahigiriza group has needed to look for coalitions. Nonetheless, over the past few years both groups have attracted additional support from former Catholic Bairu DP members, at times in active competition against each other.

It is clear that the nature of the Kumanyana movement has changed considerably over time. As an emancipatory movement, it built solidarity and self-esteem, and contributed positively to the transformation of Ankole society. Although originated and carried forward mainly by Protestants, it could with some justice purport to speak for all Bairu in its earlier stages. At one time it represented Catholic as well as Protestant Bairu; but, when disagreements developed over the distribution of rewards, it lost strength and its base once again consisted of the most militant Protestant Bairu. After its earlier concern over the need for improvement in standards of living, it increasingly found itself pressing for spoils for its followers. With political emancipation now achieved in many respects, the successors of Kumanyana engage in Ankole group politics on basically equal terms.

TORO

Rwenzururu, "mountains of heavy rainfall," is the Lukonzo name for the mountain range along the Congo border, which, since the time of Stanley, has been called Ruwenzori or "mountains of the moon." Its precipitous terrain stands in sharp contrast to the gently hilly areas of Toro that begin east of its slopes. Northwest of the Massif, also on the Congo border, are the plains of Bwamba that stretch into the Ituri forest. The Bakonzo of the mountains and the Baamba of the plains have both maintained links with groups of their peoples who live in adjacent Congo. Together, they account for about 35 percent of the population of Toro, which now totals over 400,000.

Since 1962, Rwenzururu has been the name of a movement which pressed for a separate district for Bakonzo and Baamba. It has also become the name of a secessionist state, the Rwenzururu Kingdom. This does not exhaust the significance of the term, however. It has been a political symbol evoking strong emotional appeals, repeated in songs and legends, and encompassing a wide range of attitudes, of which the common element is opposition to Toro rule. There have been sharp differences of opinion and policy among various sections of Bakonzo and Baamba, yet most of them would subscribe to the label "Rwenzururu" to designate their particular political aspirations. Thus, whereas in Ankole the word "Bairu" tends to avoided, in Toro the term "Rwenzururu" is a password. In addition, terms such as "Ankole" and "Banyankore" have some integrative quality to them, but the opposite is true for "Toro"

and "Batoro." Bakonzo and Baamba have been regarded, and
have for long been led to regard themselves, as different from
Batoro. To call themselves Batoro would be inconceivable to
most Bakonzo and Baamba. Rwenzururians, the members of
the Rwenzururu Kingdom, see Toro only as an area east of the
mountains, and prefer to have as little to do with it as possible. A squabble over some of these names was actually one
of the incidents which brought the Rwenzururu crisis into the
open. Prior to Uganda's independence, consultations took
place in the Constitutional Committee of the Toro Rukurato of
the contents of the future constitution for Toro. Bakonzo and
Baamba leaders, who had only belatedly been admitted to these
discussions, insisted that the new Toro constitution should
explicitly recognize Batoro, Bakonzo, and Baamba as the three
tribes of Toro. However, the Toro government could not see
its way to granting parity in recognized status to Baamba and
Bakonzo. The request was declined, and, in response, the
leaders of the two tribes walked out of the proceedings and
boycotted the Rukarato.

Until early 1962, the Bakonzo and Baamba acknowledged
the legitimacy of the Kingdom of Toro. After their bids for
equal status were denied, the Bakonzo and Baamba underwent
a rapid evolution until, less than a year later, they claimed
not only their own area but all of Toro as the territory of the
Rwenzururu Kingdom. Unfulfilled demands for parity in Toro
thus led to parity in stakes on the whole of Toro. According
to traditional history, the Batoro came in the 1830s as invaders
from Bunyoro into Rwenzururu under the rebel prince,
Kaboya. This version does not have Toro break away from
Bunyoro on the basis of the population living in Toro, which
is a more generally-accepted interpretation. This invasion
would have had the effect of pushing the Bakonzo into the
mountains and separating them from the Baganda, to whom
they consider themselves remotely akin. In language and
customs, the Bakonzo have more in common with the Baganda
than they have with the Batoro, although so far no fully
satisfactory explanation for this connection has been found.
The present position of Rwenzururu is, therefore, that the
Rwenzururians were the original inhabitants of Toro, which the
Batoro must vacate by going back to Bunyoro.

Was there - contrary to Ankole, where structural conditions seemed to dictate pressure for integration - some
inherent "logic" in the Toro situation, in the sense that it
should lead to demands for a separate district, and ultimately
the establishment of a secessionist state? It is difficult to say
that there was no alternative; nonetheless, a variety of conditions made these steps understandable. Especially important
was the pattern of distribution of the population of Toro, and
the conditions of the terrain that provided the habitat of the
Bakonzo and Baamba. Territorially, the Bakonzo and Baamba

had long been living separately from the Batoro. Only in
recent decades, and particularly in the 1950s, had Bakonzo
come down the slopes of the Ruwenzori to cultivate cotton on
the plains of Busongora. At the same time, Batoro had gone
to Bwamba to grow coffee. Thus, day to day contacts between
Bakonzo and Baamba on the one hand and Batoro on the other
had become more frequent. However, Bakonzo and Baamba
had in many ways been treated as different and inferior, and
the limited increase in contacts tended to accentuate these
attitudes. The historical traditions of the Bakonzo and
Baamba, which do not suggest evidence of their submission to
the King of Toro at any time before the arrival of the British,
confirm the previous autonomous position of the minority
groups. Thus history, as well as the distinct location of the
people concerned, could easily suggest the solution of a
separate district when political relationships within Toro
deteriorated. Later, when the Toro government had shown
itself to be inflexible in regard to Bakonzo and Baamba
aspirations, and the central government indicated it could not,
on grounds of national unity, give in to the demands for a
separate district, the special characteristics of the habitat of
the Bakonzo enabled them to declare their independence. The
Ruwenzori mountain areas are almost inaccessible; effective
administration had never become established in the higher
altitudes and, in a sense, anybody could set up an independent government there without facing the consequences
for at least some time. As it turned out, the Rwenzururu
Kingdom has held its own from 1962 until the present, 1970, a
longer record than that of any other African secession.

In a number of regards, the case studies of Ankole and
Toro are quite limited. Nonetheless, they suggest certain
differences in the potential for the adjustment of conflict,
which might be formulated in the following terms: other factors
being equal, in situations of ethnic domination, political integration may more easily be achieved if members of the dominating and the dominated strata live in physical proximity to
each other throughout the territory than if the dominant
stratum has a different territorial basis than the dominated
strata.

The isolated existence of ethnic sub-groups within the
same political framework leaves fewer checks on the development of stereotypes and increases the possibility of organized hostility. The chances for reconciliation in Toro thus
seemed to have been more limited from the beginning than in
Ankole. Yet it is difficult to know whether a radically-differ-
ent approach by the Toro authorities might not have maintained
the minimum of rapport essential to a lasting solution of the
conflict. For instance, if there had been any chance of a
substantial increase in the number of Bakonzo and Baamba in
representative positions, or in the bursaries, or if medical
facilities and other social benefits had been allocated to them

on an equal basis, an escalation of conflict might well have been averted. Equally important would have been an attempt to appreciate the grievances involved and, of course, a preparedness on the part of Batoro to regard Bakonzo and Baamba as fellow-citizens and equals. In all these respects, however, the Toro Kingdom utterly failed. Instead, when the request for a separate district was considered by the Toro government, it was dealt with in a most obtuse and insensitive manner. When the moderate leaders of the Baamba and Bakonzo made approaches to the Toro government, they were met with intimidation and high-handedness.(4)

The deadlock in the constitutional deliberations and a range of additional issues which arose between the Toro government and the Bakonzo and Baamba leadership do not need to be related here. Suffice it to note that, after the Toro government had let its chance for rapprochement slip by, positions on both sides became rigid, giving the Rwenzururu movement a major impetus.

However, other factors surrounding the emergence of the Rwenzururu movement should be considered. In eastern Uganda, the Sebei had for long been in a position in respect to the Bagisu that was remarkably similar to that of the Bakonzo and Baamba in respect to the Batoro. When the Democratic Party formed the government of Uganda from 1960-62, Sebei was granted separate district status. The Bakonzo and Baamba were thus alerted to the possibility to having their own district. After a visit by the DP leader, Mr. Benedicto Kiwanuka, the impression was left, correctly or not, that a DP government would further their case for a separate district if they would support the DP in general elections in 1962. This they did; but the Uganda People's Congress won the election. Moreover, the independence constitution made it infinitely more difficult to change the existing boundaries of districts. It is possible that, if the Bakonzo and Baamba had presented the idea of a separate district half a year or more before, they would have had a fair chance of getting it.

Moreover, during the pre-independence period, the Bakonzo and Baamba had seen Toro political leaders make exaggerated claims for Toro's future status in Uganda. Toro made strong demands for a real federal relationship with the center, partly because it was anxious to keep royalties from the Kilembe copper mines to itself, and partly because it wanted to see its Omukama accorded the same privileges as the Kabaka of Buganda. At one point the demand was that "Toro be recognized as a nation first" before any consideration would be given to the nature of its relationship to the rest of Uganda. The Toro government also campaigned for the recovery of the larger part of the province of Kivu in Congo, which it claimed had been "lost" in the Anglo-Belgian boundary settlement at the beginning of this century. These bids for more territory and increased autonomy directly involved the Baamba and Bakonzo, although they did not have any voice in them. Inevitably, however, an impression was left that demands for a revision of the political framework were an appropriate means for improving one's status.

It is useful to consider the antecedent of the Rwenzururu movement. Much of the groundwork and early agitation for the movement took place in Bwamba County. Apart from the Baamba, a few pygmies, and some groups of mixed ethnic origin, one sub-county in Bwamba, Harugali, is predominantly populated by Bakonzo. Although several Baamba were in the vanguard of the movement, it is mainly from these Bakonzo in Bwamba county that the movement received its first major spur.

In 1954, a small group of Bakonzo, led by the primary teacher, Isaya Mukirane, founded the Bakonzo Life History Research Society in Harugali. The Society was the first formal undertaking by the Bakonzo to look into their own history and culture and revive past traditions. Its existence was almost certainly indicative of wider and deeper reflections concerning the role and status of Bakonzo in Toro society. The function of the Society, limited though it may have been in the numbers of people reached, was able to infuse the Bakonzo with more self-awareness and confidence. Inevitably, its major pre-occupation was with past and present relationships between the Bakonzo and the Batoro. Elder members contributed traditions of lost independence, and recounted memories of injustices inflicted upon Bakonjo in the earlier decades of this century. One result of the Society's activities was an awakening and heightening of Bakonzo grievances against the Batoro. The Bakonzo Life History Research Society, whose chairman, Mukirane, was to become leader, President, and King of Rwenzururu, thus was a direct antecedent of the Rwenzururu movement.

The Baamba had a series of short-lived organizations prior to the Rwenzururu movement. In early 1962, Rwenzururu had its base mainly in Bwamba. The Baamba were induced to joint the Bakonzo in the fight for a separate district; and, in fact, two of three original Rwenzururu leaders, Jeremia Kawamara and Peter Mupalya, were Baamba. Although most Baamba joined the movement because they had been subject to the same ill-treatment as the Bakonzo, some may have followed because they felt they did not have any choice; the Ruwenzori range separated them from Toro proper, and an easily-blocked escarpment road formed their only access to Uganda government support if it were needed.

However, when defections from the movement occurred, many were from among the Baamba. In 1964, after the central government took over the administration of government services in the Baamba and Bakonzo areas from the Toro government as an emergency measure, Bwamba seemed ready to accept the role of the central government's Administrator. Nonetheless, attitudes in Bwamba would long retain a marked degree of ambiguity, and one might say that, in more recent years, Rwenzururu was not absent there, but was invisible. It was clear that the Bakonzo were stronger supporters of Rwenzururu. Most of the symbols, songs and communications of the movement were in Lukonzo, and the secessionist Rwenzururu Kingdom that Mukirane established in the mountains was also essentially a Bakonzo affair.

However, not all Bakonzo were part of the Rwenzururu movement. For a limited period, from 1962-64, this one movement involved the great majority of the Bakonzo; this roughly coincided with the time when there was more general support among the Baamba. Particularly in the early stages, when there was profound indignation over the Batoro's blunt rebuffs and expectations ran high that a separate district would eventually be granted, there was general support for the goals of the movement all along the mountain. During the initial periods of violence, there was also widespread popular involvement. The organization proved itself capable of combining a high level of tactical mobility with centralized leadership, sending down waves of raiding parties from quite unpredictable spots into Batoro areas. Men, women, and children had their roles in what was generally considered a just war. However, the decision of the Mukirane faction, taken when the other principal Rwenzururu leaders were in gaol, to establish a government in mountainous seclusion, and adopt armed resistance as a major means to achieve their goals, caused a crack in the movement. Over the years, this crack proved impossible to heal and, in fact, widened.

This rift led to abandoning the demand for a separate district in favor of one for the creation of a separate and independent state. Many hitherto-loyal Rwenzururu members felt this was not realistic and deplored the weakening of the movement's stand on the original issue. Henceforth, therefore, although Rwenzururu still meant opposition against Batoro rule, it covered the widely different strategies of militant rebellion on the one hand and continued efforts to reach a solution through the Uganda government on the other. Later, when the Uganda government took over responsibility for administering the areas, the issue became even more complex. Many people around the Ruwenzori considered that their removal from Toro rule, and the fact that they had come directly under the protection of the central government was an acceptable solution to their problems; and they anticipated more rapid development as a result of the takeover.

The Rwenzururu Kingdom, however, had reached a point from which it was difficult to return. Its vanguard had first demanded a separate district, and it certainly was not ready to

discuss anything short of that. If this status had been given,
it would have remained within Uganda. However, after the
central government opposed the demand, independence was
declared; subsequent efforts at conciliation have proved
abortive, and, for several years now, virtually all communication has been at a standstill. Meanwhile, Mukirane
organized his state; he has appointed a cabinet, chiefs, and
teachers and is running an administration, a tax system, an
army, schools, and prisons. He himself was crowned King of
Rwenzururu. After the exalted position he and his aides had
assumed, it would have been a gross moral defeat and a blow
to their image to give in for what clearly would be less than
district status. Moreover, if any settlement were reached, it
would not be the core group of the Rwenzururu Kingdom that
would be called upon to fill new posts, but rather the Bakonzo
and Baamba who had been campaigning for compromise. From
the secessionist point of view, therefore, the choice became
one of holding on to the Kingdom no matter how little recognition it might receive from outside Rwenzururu, or falling
into oblivion and possibly facing prison terms.

The Rwenzururu government thus carried on, but its
basis of strength progressively shifted from popular support to
a reliance on coercion and punishment. Shortly after June
1964, when a general flare-up of violence occurred as the
result of massive retaliatory actions by the Batoro, a considerable number of Bakonzo were prepared to assist in the
persecution of Rwenzururu forces, whom they had begun to
regard as the greater danger to their survival. Nor is this
surprising. During its earlier stages, the secessionist regime
had directed its attacks primarily at Batoro living down the
mountain. However, when a substantial Uganda security force
was stationed in the area to act as a buffer, Rwenzururu
violence was increasingly directed at Bakonzo living further
down the slopes. The purpose of these raids upon fellow
Bakonzo was to ensure continued loyalty to the Rwenzururu
regime, to inflict punishment for any form of cooperation with
other authorities, and, perhaps above all, to collect tribute
needed for the upkeep of the government. For years,
Rwenzururu gangs have forcibly taken money, food, and goats
from Bakonzo in the lower mountain regions, whose lot has
worsened since the outbreak of open conflict. Many people
have had one or more relatives killed. For a long time, crops
were neglected, destroyed, or without a market. Medical care,
scarce though it was previously, shrank to a point which gave
free play to epidemics visiting the area. Schools, so much
needed to uplift the Bakonzo and Baamba, were closed down
for prolonged lengths of time and many of them still are.
Attempts by the Rwenzururu government to maintain the barest
minimum of these services have not been particularly successful. The prospects it could hold out were dim and certainly

could not compensate for the years of misery.

In recent years, the Rwenzururu government often seemed to be surviving on minority support. Indications are that it has become increasingly fragmented after the death of its first Omukama Kiganzangha, Mukirane, at the end of August 1966. Yet it has held on tenaciously to the imagery of its independent state, which became adorned with neo-traditional titles, a hereditary monarchy, and its own God of Rwenzururu. It has been able to do so largely because of the protective conditions of its terrain. A military action to terminate it might well have had the effect of solidifying and increasing its support. It has not produced a major security challenge to the country as a whole, and, in fact, few people outside Toro even hear about the movement. Thus, its victimized population carries a heavy burden, and may have to bear the brunt of shaking it off.

In this situation, only the most flexible and innovative approach might have led to any solution. As it was, however, each of the major parties to the conflict rigidly held to its position, defying any possibility for rapprochement. The Toro government maintained the view that the Rwenzururu movement constituted an illegitimate reduction of its authority, and expected to have the area brought back under its administration. The Uganda government occasionally repeated its position that a separate district was out of the question, but basically failed to work out alternative solutions. And little initiative could be expected from the Rwenzururu government that might lay the basis for a lasting compromise.

Unfortunately, a variety of Bakonzo and Baamba groups belonged to none of the formal structures and, in more than one sense, were caught in the middle; some people in this category served prison terms with each of the three governments. Over the years, many suggestions for compromise solutions have been made by these people, some of them quite sensible, but with very little success. The confusion among those in this "middle" zone has meanwhile been considerable. For years they were exposed to three competing hierarchies of chiefs and were in great uncertainty about their future.

Finally, there is still another group, those Bakonzo and Baamba who have aligned themselves with the Toro administration. The underlying view was that this collaboration constituted the most realistic way towards an improvement of conditions, but the individuals concerned enjoy very little support among Bakonzo and Baamba.

Some uncertainties about the future have now been lifted, although this change has not brought the desired peace and reconciliation. In 1967, with the adoption of the new Uganda constitution, the Toro monarchy was abolished, along with the removal of kingship elsewhere in the country. Bakonzo and Baamba reactions to this abolition were generally favorable, because it eliminated the symbol of Batoro domination. Also, the new governmental framework was based on a greater extension of centralization, and thus seemed to reduce the chances of a disproportionate allocation of resources within the district.   An attempt was made to balance the leadership of Toro District through the inclusion of a Mwamba and a Mukonzo among the key officeholders as Assistant Secretary General and Chairman of the District Council, respectively. Finally, some central government officers stationed in Toro have done what they could to promote the welfare of Bakonzo and Baamba.   Through their efforts, schools in the areas were re-opened.

However, only a few Bakonzo and Baamba were ready to accept the opinion that Rwenzururu had merely constituted opposition to monarchical rule in Toro.   To most of them the extent of their involvement in the running of government affairs remained the critical and open question.   Among several aspects of this, two were particularly salient in the public mind.   One was the fact that out of several hundred positions at the Toro district headquarters, only a handful were held by Bakonzo and Baamba.   This had been the situation before 1962, but by 1970 it was essentially the same.   The other point concerned the single line of chiefs who were appointed in the Bakonzo and Baamba areas in 1969 to replace both the former Toro chiefs and the central government agents who had been performing their functions.   With a few notable exceptions, the pattern has been for henchmen of the Toro administration to be appointed, sometimes notwithstanding the fact that better qualified people were available.   Consequently, these measures have not been very conducive to inspiring public trust.

On January 1, 1970, a final uncertainty was eliminated. At a ceremonial meeting of the Toro district council, the "disturbed" counties were handed back to the Toro district administration.   Apart from the council, there was little rejoicing.   The secessionist Rwenzururu government reacted by demanding the retirement of the newly-appointed chiefs and threatening to kill them if their warnings were not heeded. During the early months of 1970, there were several such casualties.   Other Bakonzo and Baamba, not belonging to the Rwenzururu Kingdom, felt that little had changed to distinguish the situation from pre-1962.   These people, however, had no effective means to communicate their views; the regular channels would be through the Toro administration, and any expression of discontent could easily be branded as "Rwenzururu."   They do not necessarily doubt that the Uganda government is sincerely trying to promote equity, but believe policies often turn into difficulties in the hands of the "middle men" who implement them.

CONCLUSION

The Rwenzururu movement as much as the Kumanyana movement was, at one point, generally representative of the people who supported it. The Kumanyana movement, which originated amongst Protestant Bairu, came to include Catholics at the peak of its involvement; but Catholics were the first to drop out, and divisions subsequently grew among Protestant Pairu. The Rwenzururu movement, which originated among the Bakonzo, encompassed Baamba at the height of its involvement; but Baamba defected, and dissensions soon widened among the Bakonzo.(5)

Both movements commanded their greatest strength and popularity when the issues were simplest and most clear-cut. The Kumanyana movement declined once its major aims were in the process of being fulfilled. This happened largely before independence, and the movement dwindled in the course of disputes over the fruits of victory. The Rwenzururu movement, on the other hand, disintegrated before it had achieved its goals. This was after independence, and its fragmentation was largely due to the fact that its targets could not be realized.

Both movements had the support of the peasantry, whose grievances they expressed, and whose emancipation they claimed to advance. In Ankole, however, the rural population was never activated to any significant extent, whereas in Toro its mobilization became a major feature of the movement. Rwenzururu was more clearly a grass-root revolt than the Kumanyana movement was, or than it needed or wanted to be.

The two movements were led in considerable part by teacher-politicians, products of their time and incipient elites of their communities. It is the interests of their class, in respresentation and influence, chieftainships and other sinecures, that commanded a high priority among the pursuits of the movements. In time, this may allow for an interpretation of these movements as the products of emergent class structures. Ethnic grievances, as much as anything else, can be manipulated to build positions of leadership, a requisite for entry into the government elite.

NOTES

1. A more detailed account of the conflict situations in Ankole and Toro is given in Martin R. Doornbos, "Kumanyana and Rwenzururu: Two Responses to Ethnic Inequality," in Robert I. Rotberg and Ali A. Mazrui (eds.), Protest and Power in Black Africa (Oxford: Oxford University Press, 1970).

2. A survey-study of self-identifications was undertaken between 1965-68 in collaboration with Marshall H. Segall. An analysis of these data is in preparation.
3. Speech by the Omugabe of Ankole, January 17, 1956.
4. Report of the Commission on Inquiry into the Recent Disturbances among the Baamba and Bakonjo People of Toro (Entebbe: Government Printer, 1962).
5. It is of interest that most of the leadership of the Rwenzururu movement had a Protestant background, similar to that of the Kumanyana movement; this again suggests a greater Protestant propensity for militant protest, even in situations far removed from the origin of the idea of the Protestant Ethic. However, there is no evidence that Protestant-Catholic confrontation has been a significant variable within the Rwenzururu movement.

14 Secessionism and Irredentism in Ethiopia

Yohannis Abate

INTRODUCTION

Ethnic, religious, racial, and cultural pluralism are creating serious problems in African countries on their way to national integration. In most parts of Africa, interests and loyalties still tend to be defined predominantly in terms of traditional, tribal, religious, and communal reference groups. The problems besetting national integration in such societies revolve around making a cohesive society out of a number of traditional societies, each with its own culture and values, and commanding the loyalty and devotion of the individual to the claims of the state. In short, the problem of integration in such societies is essentially one of getting people to shift loyalty from a structure based on tradition to a new territorial and political entity, the nation-state.

Ethiopia faces more serious problems with national integration than any other African country. The entire eastern part of the country, comprising about one-third of its land area and one-sixth of its population, has been in revolt against the central government for the last 15 years. Like many African countries, Ethiopia is a multi-ethnic and multi-religious state. About 40 percent of the population embraces Islam, and an equal number are Christians. Prior to 1974 Ethiopia had a Christian minority church that integrated its teachings with the ideology of the ruling class, and retained absolute political, economic, and social supremacy over the other religions - especially Islam. This situation created a Church-State power that alienated the majority of non-Christian Ethiopians.(1)

The eastern lowland region of Ethiopia - Eritrea, the Afar region of the Rift Valley, and the Somali-inhabited area of

Ogaden - is the home of a predominantly Muslim population; it came under effective Ethiopian control in the last 25 years because of European colonial occupation (Fig. 14.1). A combination of ethnic, religious, historical, economic, and political developments led the people in this region to mount a revolt against the Ethiopian government that has been raging since 1960.(2)

In 1974, the Ethiopian government, then dominated by a Christian ruling class, was overthrown and replaced by a Marxist military government. This new government has found it even more difficult to contain secessionist and irredentist movements in the eastern part of Ethiopia.

This paper is an examination and analysis of the dynamics of secession and irredentism in Ethiopia. The objective is to identify the historical, colonial, ethnic, religious, social, political, and economic factors that, separately or jointly, explain these political phenomena.

CONCEPTS AND PROPOSITIONS IN NATIONAL INTEGRATION

The concepts of centrifugal and centripetal tendencies in a state are an attempt to examine how the diverse elements of the state can be brought under one government harmoniously.(3) The main approach is to examine the coincidence between the nation and the state, and the political loyalty of the peripheral ethnic minorities to the dominant group in the core area. It is an attempt to identify whether political and territorial integration have been achieved. Weiner defines political integration as "the process of bringing together culturally-and socially-discrete groups into a single territorial unit and the establishment of national identity; territorial integration refers to "the problem of establishing national central authority over subordinate political units or regions which may or may not coincide with distinct cultural or social groups.(4)

When a political community is not well integrated there are many indicators.(5) A segment of the population questions the legitimacy of the state to exercise certain powers because it does not identify with the state and, therefore, the state does not deserve its loyalty; hence, a demand for secession indicates a withdrawal of commitment to the existing system. Or a government's lack of·authority is shown by a high incidence of the breakdown of law and order, and a general prevalence of political violence in parts of the territory.

These nation-building problems are prevalent in the Third World, although countries such as Britain, Canada, and Spain are also afflicted by threats of secession. Observations show that secessionism almost always starts in outlying provinces away from the present or historical core area of the state. A

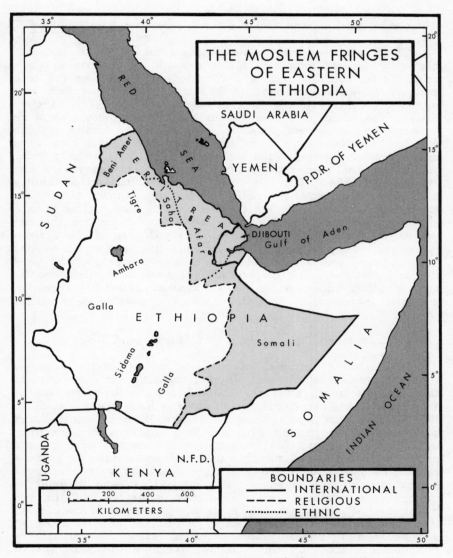

Fig. 14.1.   The Moslem Fringes of Eastern Ethiopia

secessionist attempt was successful in Pakistan, and such
efforts almost succeeded in Nigeria and Zaire. Presently,
there are secessionist forces in the outlying provinces of
Chad, Sudan, Ethiopia, and Kenya.

Historical Background and the Concept of the Raison d'Etre

It is assumed that a state has a raison d'etre, an ico-
nography for its existence,(6) a precept or underlying philosophy that holds it together. The raison d' etre for the core
area of Ethiopia has been Orthodox Christianity, which was
introduced into Ethiopia in the fourth century. For 13 centuries, the history of this region has been replete with wars
between Christians and Muslims. Although the Muslim attacks
on the Christian areas came from many directions, they were
not effective because the Muslims were not united; consequently, the Christian kingdom was able to repulse or absorb the attacks. The Christians attributed this indomitability
to their religion; their belief that God was on their side
strengthened their self-righteousness. Christianity thus became
a symbol of their identity, and the raison d'etre for the existence of the Christian kingdom. The influence of the Church
permeates every aspect of the national life, and often verges
on fanaticism and intolerance of other religious groups, particularly Muslims. For the politically-conscious Muslims, this is
an alienating factor which works against national integration
and the interests of the state and the people as a whole.

Colonialism and the Policy of "Divide and Rule"

The problem national integration faces in Africa is one of
the heritages of colonialism. During the scramble for Africa in
the late nineteenth century, colonial powers drew up boundaries separating members of the same ethnic group, such as
the Tigrean and Somali peoples of the Horn of Africa; and
sometimes ethnic groups with age-long conflicts were brought
under the same flag. The situation was worsened by a colonial
policy of "divide and rule," which fostered ethnic differences
rather than common heritages.(7) When the colonial powers
retreated and independence was achieved, it was difficult to
integrate some ethnic groups into the mainstream of the political life of the state. This lack of integration manifested
itself in the form of civil wars, rebellions and attempts at
secession and irredentism. African states accepted the
boundaries created by the colonial powers in the belief that it
was politically expedient to do so; there was fear that success
of secession and irredentism in one state would encourage
others.

Ethnicity and Socio-Political Organization

African states can be grouped into five categories according to their ethnic and socio-political organization(8): There are countries in which one ethnic group is dominant both numerically and politically, such as the Arabs in the Sudan; There are countries in which one ethnic group is dominant politically but not numerically, such as the Amhara in Ethiopia and, formerly, the Watusi in Rwanda; There are countries in which one or more minorities cut across international boundaries, such as the Somali in the Horn of Africa; There are countries in which no single group is dominant either numerically or politically such as Tanzania; and there are countries where one ethnic and cultural group predominates such as the Somali and Arabs of Egypt. Many African countries in the first three groups have experienced political instability because of their ethnic and political organization, while countries in the last two groups have been spared such experiences. The situation in Ethiopia can be explained by the second and third categories.

Interaction and Communication

Secession arises because of inadequate interaction among the various ethnic groups in a state. An integrated territorial community is maintained by a complex pattern of information exchanges and transaction flows throughout the territory.(9) The adequacy of this integration can be determined by studying the development of mass communication and transportation. Political and territorial integration are functions of the degree of interaction among the various parts of the state, and particularly between the peripheral and the core areas of a state. The higher the degree of positive interaction, the more integrated the state is.

Socioeconomic Development

Secession is generated by a lack of socio-economic development.(10) Ethnic groups that feel excluded from the socio-economic growth of the country as a whole, could embark on a path of separatism to redress their grievances. The corollary of this proposition is that ethnic groups that are developed or endowed with resources, but are a minority politically, may be reluctant to share their resources and/or resent their political impotence, and hence attempt to secede.

Political Development

Secession arises because of a lack of political development. It is a response to dictatorial regimes where there
is no mechanism to express political dissent; hence, alienated
ethnic groups concede that the state does not represent their
interests.(11) The prevalence of multi-party governments in
many African countries immediately after independence was
followed by one-party governments, which gave way to military
governments; this attests to the fact that the rules of the
political game have not been internalized, and hence political
development is in its infancy in Africa. Thus, one could
postulate from the experience of politically-mature states that
secession accompanies the early periods of political development; hence, the existence of secession in African countries,
and Ethiopia in this case, is an inevitable stage in political
development.(12)

HISTORICAL ORIGINS OF THE PROBLEM

The present problem of integration and territorial control
in the eastern region of Ethiopia is a result of Islam-Christian
rivalry and the partition enforced by colonialism.

Islam-Christian Rivalry

The rise of Islam, an event of world importance, was a
turning-point in Ethiopian history. The history of Islam and
Muslim in this region has been dominated by the history of
Christian Abyssinia, as Ethiopia was then called; and "nowhere
has there been any escape from it. In fact, Islam in the
region would have no history without Abyssinia".(13) The
conversion of Ethiopia to Christianity in the fourth century
gave the Kingdom of Aksum a cultural link with the Mediterranean world; it also set the stage for Christian-Islam rivalry
after the emergence of Islam in the seventh century.
The Kingdom of Aksum, the predecessor of the Ethiopian
state, was located in the northern-most plateau region, in what
are now the provinces of Eritrea and Tegre. With the expansion of Islam into the eastern lowland region adjacent to the
Red Sea the Christian Kingdom was confronted by Muslim
aggression and encirclement; it created apprehension that still
persists in the area. The rise of Islam hastened the rapid
decline of Aksum; Arab conquests of the Red Sea Coastal area
and North Africa, severed the Christian Kingdom from its
Byzantine ties. This period started the isolation of the Kingdom. Faced with the rising tide of Islamic expansion, the

Aksum people confined themselves in the impregnable mountains.   Although this virtual imprisonment undeniably had
adverse effects on many aspects of life, it did create solidarity
among the diverse elements.   In the face of a common danger,
they abandoned their centrifugal idiosyncrasies and became
aware of their unity.(14)   The isolation also transformed
Christianity into an indigenous religion.

The weakened and isolated Aksum Kingdom was assaulted
by Beja tribesmen from the north, even as Islam continued to
spread among the population of the eastern coastal region.
The dual pressures of Islam and the Beja forced the Aksum
Kingdom to move southward in the first half of the eighth
century.   During the ninth and tenth centuries it reached the
valleys of the Awash and Omo Rivers.(15)

These people spread their language and the Christian
religion into the southern region and "there began that process of fusion which produced the Abyssinian nation.(16)
This was also the beginning of a shift of political power away
from the Tigre people of the Aksum region to Lasta and Shoa.
A missionary zeal to spread Christianity arose when the political power was in Lasta during the Zagwe Dynasty, which
ruled from 1137 to 1270. After the restoration of the so-called
"Solomonic line of Kings," the political power shifted still
further southward to Shoa, the geographical heart of the
plateau.   At that time, the Kingdom barely reached beyond the
central provinces of Lasta, Tigre, parts of Begemder and
Gojjam, and northern Shoa.   The aim of the king was to consolidate control over this area before undertaking the liquidation of the Muslim principalities that had emerged in the
eastern lowlands.

Between the tenth and twelfth centuries, Islam reached
the Dahlak Archipelago, the Afar and Somali coasts, the Beja
in the north and the Sidama in the south, the Yifat Sultanate
of eastern Shoa, Harar in the east, and Lake Zway in the
west.   These Muslim sultanates spread in a semi-circle along
the northern, eastern, and southern part of the Christian
Kingdom.   However, these sultanates were not united; had
they been, they would have threatened the existence of the
Christian Kingdom.   In the fifteenth century, a Muslim leader,
Ahmed Gragn, welded the Afar and Somali into a formidable
military power that devastated the Christian Kingdom, burning
churches and monasteries, and forcibly converting large
numbers of Christians to Islam.   After a few years, the Muslim
invaders were defeated with the help of Portuguese soldiers
who had come in to support the beleaguered Christian Kingdom
against the Turkish-supported Jihad of Ahmed Gragn.

The Muslim invasion destroyed much of the base of the
Christian Kingdom but "the state itself survived with its basic
traditions and its sense of historical mission and continuity intact.(17)   Christian identity and national defense were themes

that were stamped upon Ethiopian consciousness as early as this period.(18) This incident also led to the further strengthening of the bond between the monarchy and the Church; they emerged as the key integrating elements of the state and the people. Christianity had become the symbol of their national independence, and it was to be defended against Islam, which had isolated them for the last millenium. The centuries of isolation had prompted the development of a stronglyconservative and nationalist spirit, and had created a deep attachment to the doctrines and customs of the Christian National Church. The Church had, in effect, become the raison d'etre of the state and the people. It is this religious conflict, reenforced by ethnicity, that has been one of the exacerbating factors in the political evolution and territorial control of this eastern region of Ethiopia over the last thirteen centuries.

The fortunes of the Ethiopian Church and monarchy have been intertwined. These two forces have rallied the people, particularly when they have been threatened by Islam. The emperor and the Church have worked together and provided the unifying elements which continually countered the centrifugal forces of geography, tribalism, and aristocracy.(19) The Ethiopian polity through the years was not renowned for unity when it came to internal matters, but, when the concern was an external enemy, warring and rival princes laid aside their differences and came together to combat the common foe. During the eighteenth and the first half of the nineteenth century, at the time of the "Era of Princes, the Christian Kingdom disintegrated into many rival principalities whose link became the Christian Church, "the binding force of a very precarious political system."(20) A three-pronged attack by Egypt was beaten back from the eastern coastal region in 1875; "the whole country down to Menelik's Shoan hills reverberated with excitement and the call to deal a final blow to the Muslim foe," although Menelik and the Tigre Emperor Yohannes IV were not on good terms.

Actually, Islam was as great a force in unifying the Christian Kingdom because it was the threat that produced unity. Even as recently as 1935-41, during the Italian invasion of Ethiopia, the Church stood as the most unyielding force in the nation. Failing to break the moral and religious patriotism of the people and clergy, the Italians directed their attention against the Church as a symbol of Ethiopian resistance and nationalism. They publicly killed two bishops, systematically burned churches, plundered religious objects, desecrated shrines, and massacred the clergy and the educated youth. These atrocities only reenforced the iron will of the people to resist the invaders as they had done for centuries.

The power of the Church has enabled it to play a decisive role in the success or failure of an emperor. Many

Ethiopian kings were either made or broken by the influence of the Church. In the two instances when an emperor abandoned the Christian Church, one for Roman Catholicism and another for Islam, the former was forced to abdicate and the latter was deposed.   Hence, in the Ethiopian polity, authority is tempered by the moral and spiritual force of the Church.

The Church and emperor have been mutually dependent. The Church has served the emperor by creating a link between him and the people, by anointing and consecrating him, and by investing a divine role in the kingship.   In return, the Church has received land and other royal favors, and has been given support to establish churches in newly occupied territories.(21)

Although the Church has been an important component of the state and a central social institution, its intolerance of other religions has been divisive, and its conservatism has hampered modernization.   There has been a gradual decrease in the actual political influence wielded by the Church in the operation of the Ethiopian state.   This results in part from a declining governmental emphasis upon the struggle between Christianity and Islam in postwar Ethiopia.   However, the resistance of Muslims in Eritrea, Harar, Sidamo, Arussi, and Bale provinces to the previous government's policy of national integration showed that the religious problem will have to be reckoned with in the future.(22)   Emperor Haile Selassie, a devout Christian, had curbed all powers that did not emanate from him, and he had taken many steps to reduce the effective authority of the church by relegating it to his own supervision.(23)

The Colonial Background - Partition of the Horn

The events that precipitated the conflict in the Horn of Africa have their origin in the colonial partitioning of the area.   Two events that affected political and territorial developments in this part of Africa in the latter half of the nineteenth century were the opening of the Suez Canal in 1869, and the Italian defeat at Adwa by Memelik in 1896. After the opening of the Suez Canal, the European scramble for Africa accelerated.   The Christian Kingdom of Ethiopia had to ward off attempts by Britain, France, and Italy to acquire parts of its territory.   The three European powers were particularly active in the coastal region of the Red Sea and the Gulf of Aden.   This European scramble in the Horn, diverted attention from the centuries-old war between the Christians and the Muslims; both had to fight new enemies in order to survive. In this effort, the Christian region managed to stave off the colonizers, while the divided Islamic areas fell easy prey to them.   Italy acquired Eritrea, which included the

northern tip of the plateau and the Red Sea coastal region;
and the wide expanse of lowland inhabited by the Afars and
Somalis was partitioned by treaty among Ethiopia, Britain,
France, and Italy. King Menelik of Shoa participated in the
partition, and, because he was suspicious of the motives of the
Europeans, garrisons were stationed in areas he effectively
occupied.

The Italians had gained a foothold on the coastal region
of Eritrea during the reign of Yohannes IV in the 1880s, and
they tried to play off Menelik of Shoa, who paid allegiance to
Yohannes, against Yohannes in their effort to gain more territory. However, Yohannes permitted Menelik to acquire as
much territory as he could in the southern and eastern regions
of the country. Italian effort between the 1880s and 1935
focused upon joining Eritrea and Somalia by annexing Ethiopia.
The French were also attentive to Italian overtures to Menelik.
They were interested in building a railway from their port of
Djibuti to the interior plateau region of Ethiopia, thereby
controlling Ethiopia's foreign trade. They succeeded in obtaining a 99 year concession for the line.

There were many motives behind Menelik's efforts to
bring more territory under his effective control. Undoubtedly, the first was to occupy buffer areas, and thus prevent the
colonial powers from further encroachment. Menelik also wanted
to redeem all territories that according to Ethiopian traditions,
were once a part of the Empire. Ethiopian's have the same
view today. The Somali Republic views Menelik as a partici-
pant with the colonial powers in the "scramble for Africa,"
while admiring his skill in conducting his external affairs with
the colonial powers to safeguard his country's territorial integrity.(24) The fact remains that Menelik doubled the area
under his effective occupation between 1872 and 1893, aided by
large quantities of firearms that were imported from France
and Italy.

Menelik's occupation of Harar in 1887 gave him much
easier access and control of the neighboring Afar and Somali-
inhabited lowlands. He then sent his forces to Jijiga, an important watering point 100 kilometers from Harar and a center
for camel caravans from Harar, Berbera, and the Ogaden; this
brought Ethiopians in direct contact with the Somalis. On the
pretext that he had become an ally of Italy, Menelik also sent
his army against the Sultan of Aussa in Afar territory on the
eve of the battle of Adwa in 1896. Thus were added Afar and
Somali areas of the eastern lowlands that had embraced Islam
for centuries. Menelik's army then moved to occupy the Kingdom of Kaffa, and the areas of Sidamo and Borena. These conquests added immense territory in the south, east, and west
to the Christian Kingdom, which traditionally was made up of
the areas of Gojjam, Begemder, Lasta, Tigray and Shoa.(25)

Italy's attempt to make Ethiopia a protectorate and to
extend the colony of Eritrea culminated in a disastrous Italian

defeat at the Battle of Adwa in 1896. This incident had a decisive effect on the history of the Horn. The fact that Menelik did not drive the Italians from Eritrea following their defeat is still resented by many Eritreans and is the origin of the present problem in this region. This was the core area of the Kingdom of Aksum, a predecessor of the Ethiopian state, and many Tigreans of the region felt that they had been abandoned by the Amhara monarch. This period signified a shift in the locus of power, from Tigray to Shoa.

The Italian defeat forced the three European powers to recognize Ethiopia's independence, and to settle their territorial claims with Menelik. The European concept of administrative control within fixed frontiers was foreign to Menelik and his predecessors, who had been claiming territories by name without reference to boundaries. In 1897, Britain, France, and Italy sent representatives to Addis Ababa to settle the boundaries of their respective territories with Ethiopia. The boundary between Ethiopia and Italian Eritrea was concluded in 1896; and the one between French Somaliland and Ethiopia, in June 1897. The British Somaliland agreement recognized the right of the tribesmen on either side of the boundary to cross the line for grazing cattle and obtaining water. The Somali Republic regards the French and British boundary agreements as illegal and unwarranted because both countries had signed treaties of protection with the Somali clans in their respective areas before 1897. In these, they agreed not to cede territory to Ethiopia without the consent and knowledge of Somalis.(26) The boundary between Ethiopia and British Somaliland was demarcated accordingly.

In 1897, the Horn of Africa was divided politically into five parts: Ethiopia controlled the Haud and the Ogaden; the French held the port to Djibuti, and a small hinterland of sand and scrub; the British and Italians had their respective Somalilands; the British controlled the northern frontier district of Kenya; and the Italians were consolidating their hold over Eritrea.

The boundary between Ethiopia and Italian Somaliland, although agreed upon in principle, is still undemarcated and was one of the points that precipitated the Italian attack on Ethiopia in 1935. In 1897, an Italian envoy was sent to conclude a boundary and Menelik agreed upon a line 180 miles parallel to the coast of the Indian Ocean. Menelik affixed his seal to a map showing this line. No treaties or agreements were signed, but Italian acceptance of the proposed line was acknowledged on September 3, 1897.(27) However, confusion soon arose between the official declaration of the envoy in writing and the cartographic agreement that referred to the 180-mile limit parallel to the coast. As a result, no demarcation was made.

Between 1897 and 1908, the Italians urged Menelik for

territorial concession under the guise of the unsettled boundary questions. The Italians agreed to pay three million lires to
compensate for about 50,000 square kilometers of territory.
On this basis, a new boundary agreement was signed in 1908,
an   agreement   considered   a   masterpiece   of   ambiguity.(28)
Because of the ambiguous nature of this agreement, no demarcation could be effected. However, it became certain that
this was intentional, a means by which the Italians could
secure more territory through a series of deliberately inconsistent boundary delimitations. Ethiopian attempts to finalize
the 1908 agreement by demarcating the line failed until 1934,
when   an   EthiopianBritish   boundary   commission   encountered
Italian   troops   100   kilometers   within   Ethiopian   territory   at
Wel-Wel. This Location was shown as Ethiopian even on Italian
maps,   which   were   withdrawn   after   the   confrontation.(29)
Ethiopia brought the case to the Council of the League of
Nations, and this triggered the Italian invasion of Ethiopia in
1935, and an occupation that lasted until 1941.   After the
Italian defeat in World War II, Ethiopia claimed Somaliland and
Eritrea; the former claim was rejected in 1950, and Eritrea was
federated with Ethiopia in 1952 for a 10-year period.
      When the United Nations made Italy the administering
power of former Somaliland under the UN Trusteeship in 1950,
there was hope that the boundary issue could be settled.
Attempts to do so failed, and in July 1960, both the British
and Italian portions of Somaliland gained independence, and
revoked all boundary agreements that had been concluded
between Ethiopia and the former colonial powers. The Constitution of the new Somali Republic also pledged to reunify
the Somali-inhabited areas of Kenya, Ethiopia, and Djibouti.

                        SECESSION OF ERITREA

            Background-British Administration, 1941-52

      The Eritrean population, estimated at about 1,100,000 in
1950, is made up of various religious and ethnic groups:
Tigre-speaking Christians occupy the plateau region; the nomadic Muslim Beni Amer tribes inhabit the western lowlands;
the Belen and the nomadic and semi-nomadic Moslems are in the
north; the Muslim Afar and Saho nomads can be found further
south of the Gulf of Zula; the Baria and Kunama agriculturists
live in the extreme west; and the urbanized groups reside in
Asmara,   Massawa,   and   other   small   towns.   These   various
ethnic and religious groupings re-enforce political differences
and have greatly influenced Eritrean politics since 1941.
      During the early days of the British administration Erit-
rean society was shaped by ethnicity, religion, and occu-

pation.(30) In this system of social hierarchy, the Christian Eritreans were the poorest and weakest, although numerically superior to all the other groups. They were the first to feel the adversities of the war. Before the Italo-Ethiopian War, for which Eritrea was the launching ground, the economic situation of the people had been improved by the opening of small-scale industries. After the capitulation of the Italians and the onset of the British occupation, economic activity virtually stopped. The Christian population suffered. The more prosperous Arabs and Eritrean Muslims became the target of the Christians, who had been made to feel economically inferior to the indigenous and alien Muslims they despised.

When the British assault on Italian troops in Eritrea was launched from the Sudan, Eritrean Christians were promised that they would be reunited with Ethiopia after the war if they would support the war effort against the Italians.(31) The British did not keep their promise; in fact, they retained Italian administrators and police against whose racist policy there was a rising tide of hatred. An unkept promise, the retention of the Italians in their dominant position, and economic adversities led to a growing political awareness among the Christians. They saw the need to establish a political front dedicated to the reunion of Eritrea and Ethiopia.

Ethiopia, which had a national interest in these developments, kept this political movement alive, and, to arouse further interest in the reunion struggle, started appealing to the people through the Christian Church. The Church, which had been the custodian of Ethiopian Christian tradition, had been dispossessed of its land during the Italian administration, and only union with Ethiopia could restore its prestige and property. Ethiopian appeal through this media was so effective that, by 1942, every priest had become a supporter of union with Ethiopia, and every church was a center of Ethiopian nationalism.(32)

As might be expected, the Muslims formed a political party in response to the Christian moves. Many other splinter groups drawn along ethnic and religious lines also emerged; all were united only by an opposition to union with Ethiopia. The separatist parties made up 40.5 percent of the politically-active population, while the Christian Eritreans had 44.8 percent.(33)

In late 1949, the fourth session of the UN General Assembly recommended that a UN Commission be sent to Eritrea to appraise the political situation. The UN Commission found the historical, geographical, and ethnic aspects of the Ethiopian claim to Eritrea justifiable. Economically, the two units complemented each other. Ethiopia depended on the use of Massawa and the transport storage facilities in Asmara, while Eritrea depended on Ethiopian agricultural produce. With union, the economic interdependence would be enhanced, and would help create a national economy that could reenforce the

sense of nationhood and the loyalty of its citizens. Stra-
tegically, Eritrea is vital to Ethiopia; between 1868 and 1935,
Eritrea was the launching ground for six major attacks on
Ethiopia. Ethiopia did not want Eritrea to fall into the hands
of any alien power and risk a repetition.

Although union with Ethiopia seemed a practical solution,
the Muslims who were in opposition formed a significant portion
of the population, and their wishes had to be weighed. Partition of the territory into Christian and Muslim areas, as the
British had suggested, was rejected because it would seriously
disrupt a regional pattern of life that had developed over a
long period of time. The UN Commission recommended federation, with a guarantee against Ethiopian interference in
Eritrean internal affairs. The report of the UN Commission
went to the General Assembly, which passed a resolution rec-
ommending that "Eritrea should constitute an autonomous unit
federated with Ethiopia under the sovereignty of the Ethiopian
crown." The Federal government was to control "defense,
foreign affairs, currency and finance, foreign and interstate
communications including ports." The Eritrean government
was to have "legislative, executive and judical powers in the
field of domestic affairs."(34)

When the elections preliminary to federation were held in
March 1952, the unionists got 32 of the 68 seats; the Muslim
league and affiliated parties polled 19, and other parties combined got the rest.(35) The Federal arrangement was a
victory for the Muslim league, but it was also close to what
the unionist Christians wanted.

Aftermath of Federation, 1952-62

The federation of Eritrea and Ethiopia in 1952 brought
together diverse groups, some of whom were experienced in
nationalist political movements. Included among these were a
large number of Muslims who did not believe that their interests would be safeguarded in a fanatically-Christian state.
The Ethiopian government's first steps should have been to
fully integrate these Muslims into the national life. However,
the federal administration began with the suppression of all
political parties that had opposed reunion with Ethiopia.

The federal arrangement had not been welcomed by
Ethiopian authorities, and the spirit enshrined in the federal
constitution was not respected. Federalism was considered
tantamount to separatism, and, therefore, a potentially dangerous idea which might corrupt other parts of Ethiopia.(36)
The federation was doomed from the start. A further com-
plication was the fact that Eritrea had its own democratic
constitution, which had been drawn up by the UN Commission
for Eritrea, and it was in sharp contrast to that of Ethiopia
with its highly-centralized monarchial tradition.

From the beginning, Eritrea was treated more as a new province than as a federated territory with autonomy for its internal administration. The Emperor's officials in Eritrea took all possible steps to undermine the federal constitution and draw the territory into total amalgamation with Ethiopia.(37) By 1955, three years after the federation came into effect, there was a great deal of dissatisfaction in the Unionist Party about the status of the federation with Ethiopia. There were Eritrean complaints of violations of local autonomy, use of tax funds for imperial rather than local interests, and suppression of the free press. Eritreans were discouraged from using their language in schools and institutions. Eritrean political parties had faded under constant pressure and coercion, and thus the Eritrean parliament provided no effective opposition to Ethiopian policy. The Ethiopian government's attitudes and actions alienated many Muslim and Christian Eritreans. Despite these grievances, the Eritrean Assembly voted to end the 10-year federation in favor of full integration with Ethiopia. In announcing the change on November 16, 1962, Emperor Haile Selassie remarked, "Federation contained inherent dangers of creating misunderstanding among the people and furthermore created a duplication of administrative apparatus".(38) To protest Ethiopia's annexation of Eritrea, separatist Muslims received arms and money from Arab governments and organized the Eritrean Liberation Front (ELF).

Arab Involvement in the Eritrean Conflict

During the 1950's a rising tide of Arab nationalism and Egyptian propaganda was aimed at dissatisfied Muslim Eritreans, who were described by Radio Cairo as victims of black imperialists. After 1965, the strength of the ELF increased as more aid was received from the Arab countries. When arms were smuggled overland from sudan to western Eritrea, the Ethiopian government decided to cut off Eritrean Muslims from contact with the Sudenese. However, the attempt to seal off the desert boundary was never fully successful. The Sudanese government never went so far as to provide sanctuary for the ELF for fear that Ethiopia might retaliate by helping Sudanese dissident groups.

Since the creation of the Organization for African Unity, Egypt has offered no overt encouragement to the ELF by Egypt, although Kuwait, Saudi Arabia, Iraq and Syria have become active supporters, and Syria has provided headquarters for the organization. As soon as the new regime of Colonel Qadaffi came to power in Libya, it granted $7.2 million to the ELF, and declared a holy Muslim war (Jihad) against Ethiopia.(39) However, Arab arms support stopped immediately

after the Arab-Israeli war of 1967. This was followed by a
cleavage within the ranks of the ELF between the majority
Muslim members and the minority Christians. The separation
between the Christians and Muslims was supposedly caused by
the dominant position of the Muslims and their close relations
with the Arabs. If the move for secession was successful, the
ELF wanted to make Eritrea an extension of the Arab world, a
plan so resented by the Christian members that they gave up
their arms and surrendered to the government. Infuriated,
the Muslim members started taking punitive measures against
Christian areas of Eritrea, thus widening the rift between the
two groups.

Another aspect of this Arab involvement concerns
Ethiopia's friendly relations with Israel, both before and after
the Arab Israeli War of 1967. Ethiopia is on the periphery of
the Arab world, and Israel's great interests in that world are
safeguarded through good relations with Ethiopia. The only
ports friendly to Israel on the Red Sea are the Eritrean ports
of Massawa and Assab, which command a strategic position on
the western shore and at the northern approach to the Bab-
el-Mandeb Strait leading out to the Indian Ocean. This is the
line along which Israel transports its crude oil supply from the
Persian Gulf region of Iran. Ethiopia has sought to stay away
from the Arab-Israel issue, but it finds itself inextricably
embroiled in the conflict. Arab support, partly on religious
grounds and partly in retaliation for Ethio-Israeli relations,
has sustained the guerrilla activites of the ELF. In December
1970, a state of emergency was declared in the Muslim regions
of Eritrea, and the western, northern, and entire Red Sea
coastal plain areas were placed under military control. Only
the central plateau region, where the Christian population is
concentrated was excluded. The state of emergency was
declared because increasing activity of the ELF against government forces had culminated in the murder of an Ethiopian
general.

Military Dictatorship and Political Suppression

In early 1974, Government troops in Eritrea and other
parts of the country mutinied. The Ethiopian government was
overthrown on September 12, 1974, and a Provisional Military
Government was installed, with General Aman M. Andom, an
Eritrean, as Head of State and Chairman of the Provisional
Military Council. The Military Council ordered a ceasefire in
Eritrean, and the General initiated talks with Eritrean leaders
in September and October of 1974. He indicated that grievances would be redressed, but that Eritrea should remain a
part of Ethiopia. In the latter part of November 1974, the
General was killed by the Provisional Military Council, while

allegedly resisting arrest. One of the accusations against him
was that he opposed sending 5000 troops to Eritrea to fight
the secessionist forces. He had been of the opinion that,
under his leadership, a negotiated settlement of the Eritrean
situation was possible, and that a military solution was unnecessary and would be counterproductive. In the view of
many observers, the death of the General removed the last
opportunity for a peaceful resolution of the Eritrean conflict.

The government sent more troops to Eritrea and accelerated its campaign against the ELF, and the newer and
more dynamic Eritrean Popular Liberation Front (EPLF), which
had broken away from ELF in 1970. Because it is a predominantly Muslim-inspired organization whose leaders reside in
Arab countries, the ELF was thought to have lost touch with
the "grassroots." The EPLF, a Marxist-oriented group led by
the young and highly-educated has a tremendous appeal for
young Eritreans. When the government stepped up its campaign against the ELF and the EPLF, there were many indiscriminate military operations against alleged sympathizers of
the secessionist forces not only in Eritrea, but also in and
around Addis Ababa, the Capital of Ethiopia, where many
Eritreans live. Such repression, following the death of the
General whom many considered to be their defender, caused
large numbers of Eritreans to join the EPLF, which has become
the stronger of the two secessionist forces. The war has
rendered thousands homeless, many fleeing to Sudan not only
to avoid the war, but to obtain the food and medical supplies
that are in short supply in Eritrea. Neither the government
nor the secessionist leaders are willing to compromise; the
Eritreans will not settle for anything less than independence,
and the government is determined to defend the unity of the
country. In January 1977, Sudan recognized the ELF and
ELPF, a development which enhanced their military operations.
By early 1978, about 90 percent of Eritrea was under the
control of secessionist forces; only the capital city of Asmara
and the ports of Massawa and Assab were outside their sphere.

The military government's effort to increase its military
operation in Eritrea has been thwarted since the summer of
1977, when Somali government forces, supported by guerrillas,
occupied Ogaden and inflicted heavy damage.

IRREDENTISM IN THE OGADEN REGION OF ETHIOPIA

Introduction

Although the Somali occupation of the Ogaden area of
southeastern Ethiopia is a recent phenomenon, Somalis have
been migrating southwards from the small area they occupied

in the northern part of Salia since the fourteenth century.   As
a result of population pressures and the need for a better
grazing area for a growing cattle population, a million Somalis
now inhabit the entire southeastern region of Ethiopia, an area
of about 80,000 square miles, or one-fifth the size of Ethiopia.
Somalis are a minority in the three big towns of the area, Dire
Dawa, Harar, and Jujiga.

The Ogaden, a territory coveted by the Somali Republic,
is a desolate area, and it is this environment that makes water
and grazing land the primary concern of the people.   In
search of these necessities of life, they are against frontiers
that restrict their movements.   Hostility between Ethiopia and
Somalia has affected them and there have been clashes between
Somali and Ethiopian government forces in the Ogaden region
since Somalia became independent in 1960.   While Ethiopian
sources attribute the conflict to Somali government incursions,
the Somali government charges them to an upsurge in pan-
Somalism and a desire for self determination.

The Somali, who occupy the entire horn of Africa are
divided into many tribes and clans.   The two major divisions
of the people are the Samaale and the Sab.   The Samaale, who
are considered the noble tribes, consist of the Digil, Rahan-
wein, and Tunni; they inhabit the valley of Juba River, and
are mainly cultivators.   The dominant Somali's in Ethiopia are
the Ogaden of the Darod tribal-family.   The Somali comprise a
hierarchy of segmented groups, which - according to I. M.
Lewis - could be called nation, tribal family, confederacy,
sub-confederacy, and tribe.(40) Loyalty is to the tribe rather
than to the nation; and within the tribe, clan loyalty is predominant.   The tribe itself is a highly segmented group with
its own name, traditions, and sentiments.(41) Fighting among
tribes over grazing land and water, very important resources
in a meager environment, is common. The satisfaction of these
needs has been throughout the ages, more crucial than the
sentiment of a common language or religion.   The scarcity of
such resources has generated hostility among the various
tribes, making tribal coexistence less than enduring.   This
lack of unity persists in the Somali Republic and is a sore
point for Somali nationalists, who view the tribal nature of the
socio-political tradition as incompatible with the pan-Somali
movement.   The present distribution of Somalis in the Horn of
Africa is the result of a series of tribal wars that culminated
in the occupation of the land by the victor.(42)   Because
these tribal wars have been going on for centuries, Somalis
lacked any national sentiment.   Only after World War II did
Somali nationalism become an issue.

The Colonial Background-Somali Nationalism and "Greater Somalia"

Somali nationalism as a movement dedicated to bring all somalis under "Greater Somalia" has become a force to be reckoned with by Ethiopia and Kenya, the main targets of the pan-Somali movement. It was kindled by the forces of Italian and British colonialism, sometimes deliberately when it served their purpose, and sometimes unwittingly. During the Italian rule of Ethiopia from 1935-41, the ethnic and religious differences of the Ethiopian population were emphasized through administrative organization of the occupied territory.(43) Italian-occupied territories during this period were lumped together as Italian East Africa, which was divided into provinces corresponding to ethnic divisions. A large chunk of Tigre Province of Ethiopia was added to Eritrea, and the new province, Somalia, comprised the former Italian colony and most of the Ethiopian Somali-inhabited region of the Ogaden, a situation which brought all the Somalis under one administration. This was when the seed of "Greater Somalia" was planted. Somali national consciousness in the Horn of Africa received a powerful stimulus during the Italian invasion of Ethiopia. By inciting traditional Somali disdain for Ethiopian Christianity, and by unwittingly encouraging "Greater Somalia," the facist government nourished the growth of Somali nationalism.(44)

In August 1940, British Somaliland was merged with the Italian province of Somalia, thus placing the majority of Somalis under one administration. After several months, however, the Italians were defeated, Ethiopia was liberated, and the British Military Administration took over the administration of the Somali-inhabited region. This included British Somaliland, what was formerly Italian Somaliland, and the Ethiopian region of the Ogaden. The Ethiopian Somali region was administered by the British under a 1942 Ethio-British agreement, which stated that "the conduct of military operations by (British) Imperial forces in parts of Abyssinia will require temporary measures of military guidance and control."(45) This temporary territorial exclusion, which was extended further by a 1944 agreement, alienated the Somalis by playing on their sentiments of Somali nationalism and unity.

Although all Somali-inhabited regions came under British Military Administration, the Somalis of the Ogaden were treated very differently than those of British Somaliland. The latter were allowed to migrate to the Ogaden region for water and pasture, and were permitted to carry arms, while the tribes in the Ogaden were disarmed. Under this arrangement, the better armed Somali tribes from the British Somaliland were overgrazing and exhausting the Ogaden grounds and wells to the detriment of the Ogaden Somalis, who were dependent on them

for their existence all the year round.(46)   What is more, in
the bitter rivalry that ensued for use of water holes and
grazing areas, the British always took the part of the
British-protected tribes.(47)   This treatment by alien governments, first the Italians and then the British, gradually gave
rise to the development of Somali national consciousness.

In June 1946, the British Foreign Secretary, Mr. Bevin,
proposed that a "Greater Somalia" be created under British
Trusteeship: "British Somaliland and the adjacent part of
Ethiopia, if Ethiopia agreed, should be lumped together as a
trust territory, so that the nomads should lead their frugal
existence with the least possible hindrance and there might be
a real chance of a decent economic life as understood in that
territory."(48)   The British offer to add the British Protectorate to the scheme was conditional upon the whole area
being placed under British trusteeship, and was, to a large
extent, designed to safeguard British colonial interests in the
region.   Ethiopia would not agree to part with its territory to
satisfy the British desire for an extended presence in the
region.

The question of the future disposition of the former
Italian Somaliland was under discussion at the UN in the late
1940s.   The British proposed a "Greater Somalia" under their
tutelage, while the Italians lobbied to administer their old
colony under UN trusteeship.   The UN sent a four-power
commission to the region to assess the political situation; it
stimulated new local political organizations and activities.
When support for an Italian return seemed to gain strength,
the Somali Youth League, nurtured on the idea of "Greater
Somalia," asked for immediate independence or temporary UN
trusteeship to prevent the restoration of Italian administration.
The proposed return of the Italians was resented by the
Somalis because of previous fascist policies of repression and
racism, and because it would mean the end of the "Greater
Somalia" plan that had been given a boost by the British.
The Somali Youth League grasped the "Greater Somalia" plan
as a scheme that would prevent the return of Italian rule.(49)

Ethiopia also opposed the Italian return to Somalia because
it was Italian reluctance to demarcate the boundary according
to the 1908 Ethio-Italian agreement that was used as a pretext
for the 1935 invasion.   However, the Four Powers agreed to
the Italian return; Britain handed over the administration of
Somalia to Italy in April 1950, after establishing a new
provisional boundary between Ethiopia and the former Italian
Somaliland.   The boundary was "a unilateral arrangement by
Britain, of an entirely provisional and non-prejudicial
character, to which both Ethiopia and Italy expressed their
strongest reservations."(50)   Throughout the 1950s, the UN
urged the Italian and Ethiopian governments to resolve the
boundary dispute throughout, but all attempts at negotiations

failed, and the boundary remains undelimited. The British finally transferred the administration of the Haud to Ethiopia in 1954. This area is a rich grazing ground in Ethiopian territory adjacent to the protectorate, which was used seasonally by half the population of the protectorate. Most Somalis considered this transfer of territory a betrayal of the protectorate treaties that Britain had signed with traditional leaders between 1884-86.(51)

Territorial manipulation by the Italians and the British governments aroused and strengthened Somali consciousness and national identity, and helped promote Somali nationalism. Previously, the divisive forces of tribalism had been so strong that political nationalism was non-existent. Clan interaction had no wider purposes than fighting one another for water and pasture.(52) Even after Somali independence, national politics were strongly influenced by the loyalty of the individual to his kin and clan. The myth of "Greater Somalia" has, therefore, been used to fight clannism, and Somali political parties before 1969 usually resorted to this myth to invoke tribal loyalty and national unity. The Arab world has also actively encouraged Somali nationalism by providing both moral and financial support. The glories of the Islamic wars that were conducted against the Christian kingdom in past centuries have been revived and their heroes resurrected as symbols of nationalism.

"Greater Somalia" is not based merely on the desire to unite the Somalis under one flag, although this appears to be the main argument behind pan-Somalism. There is a strong economic motivation behind Somali unity. Because Ethiopian territory forms a wedge between northern and southern Somalia, it is difficult to link the two population nuclei of Somalia. Ethiopia and Somalia have not come to an agreement on the use of the two rivers, Wabi Shebeli and Juba, that flow into southern Somalia from Ethiopia. The two rivers pass through arid areas in Ethiopia, and a significant diversion of the water for development in Ethiopia would severely affect Somalia's economy, which depends on bananas grown along the river bank. "Greater Somalia" would enable Somalia to control a substantial portion of these rivers.

Somali Irredentism

After Somalia gained independence in 1960, it launched a policy to unite all the Somalis in Ethiopia, Kenya, and French Somaliland. The fact that the boundary between Ethiopia and the former Italian Somaliland had not been demarcated was only a marginal consideration. Somalia claims one-fifth of Ethiopia, and one-fourth of Kenya.

The year which brought independence to Somalia was also

marked by clashes between Ethiopian troops and Somalis.
Reportedly, these incidents were instigated by Somalia, a point
it denies. As independence for Kenya approached, the Somalis
of the Northern Frontier District of Kenya (NFD) informed a
British Crown Commission that they wanted to secede from
Kenya, but the British refused to comply. Kenya got its
independence in December 1963, and the Somalis created a
National Liberation Front for the secession of NFD. A series
of Somali raids were launched against Kenya security forces in
the region. The confrontations cemented a relationship
between Ethiopia and Kenya, which was formalized by an
agreement of cooperation and mutual defense assistance clearly
aimed at containing pan-Socialism. Strained relations between
Somalia and its neighbors continued until September 1967,
when the Organization of African Unity met in Kinshasa.
There, new agreements were reached between Somalia,
Ethiopia, and Kenya at the suggestion of President Kaunda of
Zambia. New Somali policy was made operative through a
change in the Somali government that brought a new president
and prime minister into office in the summer of 1967. The new
leadership did not renounce the principle of uniting the
Somalis, but it believed that unification should be sought in
ways other than aggression. However, the prime minister
made it clear that this did not mean that any effort would be
spared "to champion the independence of, and self-
determination for, Somali territories under alien rule."(53)
     Somalia had also been isolated from other African states
because of its insistence that colonial boundaries be redrawn,
a move that African countries feel would invite widespread
political instability. African states believe that tribalism
should be stamped out in Africa, and they find the Somali
ambition of pan-Somalism inconsistent with the prevailing mood
of pan-Africanism. In the Organization of African Unity's
summit meeting in May 1963, all member-states pledged themselves to respect the borders inherited with national independence, a resolution which Somalia refused to accept.
The Somali leaders, nevertheless, persist in their belief that
pan-Somalism is a positive contribution to peace and unity in
Africa; they believe that the basis for African unification
should be founded on ethnic and cultural homogeneity, and on
the principle of self-determination on which pan-Somalism is
built. I.M. Lewis explains the problem:(54)

> The conflict highlights the extent to which Somali
> nationalism differs from the nationalism of most
> other African states. The issue turns essentially
> on the distinction between the Somali concept of
> culturally defined national identity, an identity
> which is part of their traditional heritage, and the
> rather different concept of a territorially defined

nationality embracing different tribal and language
groups, current in most of the other ex-colonies of
Africa.

Ethiopia and Kenya consider the Somalis as just one of the
many tribal groupings in their territories. Hence, the Somali
claim to the people and territory of this area is an affront to
the multi-ethnic foundation of Ethiopia, and Somali demand for
self-determination for the people of the region is regarded by
Ethiopia and Kenya as a violation of their sovereignty and
territorial integrity.

There has been some attempt by the Ethiopian government
to integrate the Somalis. Because the British Military Administration delayed the effective occupation of this region by
Ethiopia from the time of liberation in 1941 until 1954, efforts
at integration barely span two decades. Its semi-aridity and
physical isolation, and the sparseness and nomadic character of
its population limit efforts to develop the region. The gradual
development of communications from the plateau and central
region has made more economic and social interaction possible.
Schools and hospitals have been opened in the urban and
administrative centers. Somalis are being gradually appointed
to administrative positions, particularly in Harar Province.
The region has always been accorded special attention, and the
problems associated with its development are on the whole
problems of nation-building and social-mobilization that prevail
in other parts of Ethiopia.

As far as Ethiopia is concerned, therefore, the idea of
"Greater Somalia" is a colonial heritage; the Italians planted
the seed of this irredentism, and the British gave it articulation in the "Bevin Plan." The Ethiopian view is that although all Somalis are culturally homogeneous, there is no
sentiment binding them as a nation. Somalis remain loyal to
their kins and clans, and tribal warfare is part of Somali
history. The present attempt at pan-Somalism is essentially an
attempt to make the Somalis more conscious of the state than of
the tribe. The concept of "Greater Somalia" is, therefore, a
"myth" to consolidate the various family-clans into one Somali
nation. The Ethiopian view is that renunciation by Somalia of
its claim on Ethiopian territory could pave the way toward
solving Somalia's problems regarding the two rivers, its
uneconomic shape, and the question of grazing land.

Developments Between 1970-78(55)

The Somali government was overthrown by the military in
late 1969, and a policy of "scientific socialism" was proclaimed.
It received the largest Soviet military aid in sub-Saharan
Africa. Relations with Ethiopia deteriorated after 1972, when a

U.S. company, Tenneco, discovered gas only 30 miles inside the provisional boundary in Ethiopia. By 1977, Somalia had almost twice the number of combat aircrafts, and about three times the number of tanks and armored personnel carriers as Ethiopia; and Somalia's army of 30,000 was better-trained than Ethiopia's 40,000-man army. When a Somali supported Western Somali Liberation Front intensified its military activity in the Ogaden region of Ethiopia in 1974, relations further worsened. The Somali government forces began their all-out invasion of the region in July 1977; by October, they were in control of Jijiga and a key pass to the highlands, and were consolidating their territorial gains by adding the two major cities of Harar and Dire Dawa to their conquest. The Somali government and Western Somali Liberation Front apparently took advantage of Ethiopia's preoccupation with the secessionist war in Eritrea, where over half its military forces were engaged. The two countries broke off diplomatic relations in September 1977. By the end of November 1977, Ethiopia had been completely cut off from its three major outlets to the Sea - Massawa and Assab Eritrea, and Djibouti - and had to negotiate with Kenya for the use of its port of Mombasa. The Organization of African Unity's attempt to resolve the dispute failed when the Somalis walked out after a special OAU committee refused to recognize the Western Somali Liberation Front. The conflict has the potential to divide the OAU between the Arab countries, which are supporting Islamic Somalia, and the black African countries, which are pledged to accept colonial boundaries.

A potential factor of confrontation between Ethiopia and Somalia was defused when both agreed to respect the independence and territorial integrity of Djibouti, which received its independence in June 1977. Djibouti's population of about 200,000 is equally divided between Somalis who want union with the Somali Republic, and Afars, who do not. It was fear of incorporation into a Somali state by the Afars that delayed independence for the small territory. About 80 percent of the Afar people in the Horn of Africa live in the Rift Valley area of Ethiopia. Ethiopia is also faced with the Afar Liberation Front, a group that is attempting to join all the Afar people under one flag. The Sultan of the Afar had been at odds with the military government in Ethiopia, which attempted to dispossess him of his traditional ownership to land through its land-reform program. The Sultan fled to Saudi Arabia, and his followers have harrassed Ethiopian government troops in the Assab region, and along the railway from Djibouti to the interior. The Afar Liberation Front is also supported by the Somali Government and Arab countries.

There has been a political realignment in the Horn of Africa since early 1977, when the Marxist government in Ethiopia severed its military links with the U.S. The entire

Ethiopian military hardware had been supplied by the U.S. under an agreement signed in 1953, and Ethiopia had been the recipient of the largest amount of U.S. military aid in Africa. It was because of these long standing U.S.-Ethiopian good relations that Somalia turned to the Soviet Union for economic and military aid in the first place. The U.S. severely criticized the Ethiopian government's violation of human rights, and, after the break of military links in April 1977, it stopped virtually all military supplies that had been paid for by the Ethiopian government. The Soviets were willing to provide the military supplies that Ethiopia needed, a development that angered the Somali government. The Soviet government also condemned the Somali invasion of the Ogaden region of Ethiopia, and, in mid-October 1977, the Soviets announced that they were ending military aid to Somalia. In retaliation for Soviet support of Ethiopia, the Somali government renounced its friendship treaty with Moscow, and expelled all Soviet advisers. Soviet use of Somalia's strategic naval facilities in the Indian Ocean and the Gulf of Aden was also suspended. The U.S. applauded Somalia's actions and decided to resume economic aid, which had been discontinued in 1971, but both the U.S. and its Western European allies refrained from supplying Somalia with weapons. However, the U.S. warned Ethiopia not to carry the war across the Somali border once the counter-attack on Somali forces began. Iran, Egypt, and other Arab countries have provided money and small arms to the Somali government.

By February 1978, the Soviet Union had airlifted military hardware into Ethiopia estimated at one billion dollars, and Cuba had sent 10,000 troops. These were deployed on the Ogaden front, and a successful counter-attack was launched in early March. By the end of the month, Ethiopia was again in full control of the Ogaden. Although Somalia decided to withdraw its troops from the Ogaden, Ethiopia refused to end hostilities until Somalia renounces its claim to the Ogaden, Djibouti, and Somali-inhabited areas of Kenya. The Western Somali Liberation Front has vowed to continue fighting the Ethiopians, but it is doubtful whether they can pose any real threat unless they have the support of the Somali government.

It is possible that the Soviet arms and Cuban soldiers might be used to fight Eritrean secessionist forces, who have laid siege to the last Ethiopian stronghold of Asmara, the Capital of Eritrea. However, this may not be as brief as the Ogaden military operation because both the ELF and the EPLF are well-organized politically and militarily, and are well-financed by the Arab countries.

CONCLUSION

There are many factors to explain the secession of Eritrea and Somali irredentism in the Ogaden. The historical rivalry between the followers of Islam and Christianity in the region is of long-standing; Their religions are the raisons d'etre of their existence, the central philosophy that holds them together, a symbol of their nationality and identity. The historical antagonism between the two groups has made the Christians apprehensive about Muslim resurgence on the eastern fringes of the nation. The Christians of the core region of Ethiopia have always feared Muslim encirclement. Whenever Muslim groups in Eritrea, the Afar region, and the Ogaden receive political inspiration from the Islamic world, the Christians feel threatened. However, the failure of the Ethiopian government to handle the question of national integration skillfully, rather than use the "encirclement syndrome," is at the root of the conflict in Eritrea and the Ogaden.

This religious antagonism was exacerbated by the colonial powers; during the scramble for Africa, they drew boundary lines that separated ethnic groups, and found it convenient to play one ethnic group off against another, using the policy of "divide and rule" to maintain their position. Consequently, when independence was achieved and African states decided to accept colonial boundaries, differences that had been played up during the colonial era burst into the open. Italian presence in Eritrea had created enough differences in economic orientation and political outlook to make it an incompatible partner when it was federated with Ethiopia. European colonial powers divided up the Horn of Africa and later nurtured Somali nationalism and "Greater Somalia," which could not be realized.

After colonialism, the Ethiopian government, led by an absolute monarch, considered Eritrea a "returned province." He sought to undermine the federal constitution, suppress Eritrean political parties and their newspapers, and foster the use of the Amharic language. The Eritrean secessionist movement is a cultural rebellion as much as a political one; in the absence of any peaceful mechanism to express their dissatisfaction, the Eritreans found it expedient to resort to military measures. In the early years of the secessionist movement, they would have been satisfied with a guarantee of internal autonomy, but after 1975, when they took the military initiative, they would not settle for anything less than independence. The conflict in Eritrea and the Ogaden is made worse by the intervention of neighboring countries. The support of the Arab world is indispensable to the Eritrean movement, and to the Somali government's quest for the

Ogaden.   Although Arab support for Eritrea was justified on religious grounds and on Ethio-Israeli good relations prior to 1977, recently its purpose has been to offset Soviet influence in Ethiopia, which is geopolitically destabilizing the region. Thus, the conflict in Eritrea can be attributed to political insensitivity on the part of successive Ethiopian governments, and the support of the Arab world.   Whereas that of the Ogaden is triggered by the Somali government, which has pledged to bring all Somali-inhabited areas in the Horn of Africa under one Somali flag, a policy that has been supported by all Somali governments since independence in 1960.

Both Eritrea and the Ogaden are located on the periphery of Ethiopia, far from its core region.   However, Eritrea and Tigre were the core areas of the Aksum Kingdom, the predecessor of the Ethiopian state.   Led by the Amhara, the core of the Ethiopian state shifted southwards from Eritrea and Tigre to Lasta and Shoa, except for a brief period between 1871-89.   The consequent dominance of the Amhara in the political life of Ethiopia, and the relegation of Tigreans to less political eminence has always been resented.   Tigreans have been reluctant to accept Amhara political dominance, and even less willing to accept the imposition of Amhara culture. Hence, a great deal of interaction, both historically and presently, between Eritrea and the rest of Ethiopia has been of a negative nature.   Interaction between the core area and the Ogaden has been hindered by the nomadic character of its population, religious rivalry, and the lack of transportation and communication facilities.   Although the Somalis in Ethiopia have religious freedom, the dominant culture is Amhara and Christian, and this serves to retard national integration.

There are also economic arguments to justify the secession in Eritrea and irredentism in the Ogaden.   A large part of the west and north, and the coastal plain of Eritrea are unsuitable for agriculture.   Although small-scale commercial plantations thrived during the colonial period, these light industries were closed when the Italians were defeated, bringing allegations that the Ethiopian government deliberately closed some of these industries to undermine the Eritrean economy.   There is widespread belief that an independent Eritrea can revive all these industries, and develop Massawa and Assab to bolster its commerce and trade.   Copper extraction, although on a very small scale, had been started by a Japanese firm when it was sabotaged by the EPLF in 1975.   There have also been findings of natural gas on the Red Sea coast of Eritrea, and the possibility of striking oil is high.

The Somali government has accused Ethiopia of not developing the Ogaden, and the Ethiopians have countered that the region is no less developed than other parts of Ethiopia. However, it has been shown that the Ogaden, the southern part with its agricultural potential and the northern part with its good grazing area, would be a tremendous addition to the territory and resources of the Somali government. There is also the possibility of finding oil and natural gas, thereby making the region economically viable. The possibility of jointly developing the region for the benefit of the people in the area has not been considered by the Ethiopian and Somali governments.(56)

Successive Ethiopian governments have been faced with the problem of national integration in the eastern part of Ethiopia. The territorial evolution of the region saw a continuous struggle between the Christian Kingdom and Muslim groups. Colonialism added a political, and even more serious, dimension to the religious and ethnic differences in the region. The population of Ethiopia is a conglomeration of many ethnic groups, and, as long as religion and ethnicity remain factors of self-identification, national integration and territorial control in Eritrea and the Ogaden are going to remain formidable national tasks.

NOTES

1. M. Ayalew, "Problem of Religion in Ethiopia" and H. Gebre Yesus, "Problem of Regionalism in Ethiopia," Challange: Journal of the World-Wide Union of Ethiopian Students 10, no. 1, (Feb. 1970): 31, 36.
2. For an extensive discussion of this point see Y. Abate, The Moslem Fringes of Eastern Ethiopia: Problem of Integration and Territorial Control (Masters thesis, University of North Carolina, Chapel Hill, 1972).
3. This concept is discussed in R. Hartshorne, "The Functional Approach in Political Geography," Annals of the Association of American Geographers 40 (1950): 95-130.
4. M. Weiner, "Political Integration and Political Development," Annals of the American Academy of Political and Social Science 358 (March 1965): 52-64.
5. C. Ake, A Theory of Political Integration (Homewood, 1967), pp. 37-38.
6. See Hartshorne, "The Functional Approach" and Jean Gottman "The Political Partitioning of Our World: An Attempt at Analysis," World Politics 4 (1952): 512-519.
7. Many aspects of pluralism in Africa are discussed in L. Kuper and M.G. Smith (eds.), Pluralism in Africa (Berkeley: University of California Press, 1969); and C. Young, The Politics of Cultural Pluralism (Madison: University of Wisconsin Press, 1976).

8. The first four categories of sociopolitical and ethnic organization are adopted from Clifford Geertz, "The Integrative Revolution: Primordial Sentiments and Civil Politics in the New States", Old Societies and New Nations Clifford Geertz (ed.) (New York: Free Press, 1963).

9. Karl Deutsch has published extensively in this area, see his "Transaction Flows as Indicators of Political Cohesion" and "Communications Theory and Political Integration," in P.E. Jacob and J.V. Toscano (eds.), The Integration of Political Communities (New York: J.P. Lippincott, 1964). Also see his "The Growth of Nations: Some Recurrent Patterns of Political and Social Integration," World Politics 4 (1953): 168-195. An application of transaction flows in Africa is E.W. Soja, "Communications and Territorial Integration in East Africa: An Introduction to Transaction Flow Analysis," The East Lakes Geographer 4 (December 1968): 39-57. A more general study is Lucien Pye (ed.), Communication and Political Development (Princeton: Princeton University Press, 1963).

10. Harry Eckstein, "On the Etiology of Internal Wars," in Why Revolution? Theories and Analyses, C.T. Paynton and R. Blackey (eds.), (Cambridge: Shenkman Publishing, 1971), pp. 124-150.

11. Ibid., pp. 130-31, and also Ake, A Theory of Political Integration, p. 38.

12. Works of interest in Political Development are G. Almond and G.B. Powell, Jr., Comparative Politics: A Developmental Approach (Boston: Little Brown, 1966); and Lucien Pye, Aspects of Political Development (Boston: Little Brown, 1966).

13. John S. Trimingham, Islam in Ethiopia (London: Oxford University Press, 1952), p. 143.

14. Edward Ullendorf, The Ethiopians: An Introduction to Country and People, (2nd ed.; London: Oxford University Press, 1965), p. 59.

15. See Trimingham, Islam in Ethiopia, p. 47 and Ullendorf, The Ethiopians, p. 60.

16. Trimingham, Islam in Ethiopia, p. 49. For a study of this period, see Tamrat Tadesse, Church and State in Ethiopia, 1270-1527 (Oxford: Clarendon Press, 1972).

17. J. Jesman, The Ethiopian Paradox (London: Oxford University Press, 1963), p. 29.

18. See a further elaboration on this topic in Donald N. Levine, "Ethiopia: Identity, Authority and Realism," in Political Culture and Political Development, L. Pye and S. Verba (eds.) (Princeton: Princeton University press, 1965), pp. 245-281.

19. M. Perham, The Government of Ethiopia (2nd ed. London: Gaber, 1969), pp. 103-4.

20. Trimingham, Islam in Ethiopia, p. 144. This period is
    studied in detail in Mordechai Abir, Ethiopia: The Era of
    the Princes (New York: Praeger, 1968).
21. Ullendorf, The Ethiopians, p. 90.
22. Robert L. Hess, Ethiopia: The Modernization of Autocracy
    (Ithaca: Cornell University Press, 1970), p. 112.
23. Christopher S. Clapham, Haile Selassie's Government (New
    York: Praeger, 1969), pp. 82-3.
24. Somali   Government,   The Somali Peninsula: A New Light
    on Imperial Motives (Mogadiscio, 1962), p. xi.
25. Three recent additions to the study of this period are Z.
    Gabre-Sellassie,   Yohannes IV of Ethiopia: A Political
    Biography (Oxford, 1975); Harold G. Marcus, The Life
    and   Times of Menelik II: Ethiopia 1844-1913   (Oxford:
    Clarendon Press, 1975); and S. Rubenson, The Survival
    of Ethiopian Independence (Addis Ababa: Addis Ababa
    University Press, 1976). See also D.N. Levine, Greater
    Ethiopia: The Evolution of a Multi-ethnic Society (Chica-
    go: University of Chicago Press, 1974); Ch. 5, "Patterns
    of Expansion and Unification," is of special interest in
    this context.
26. Somali   Government,   The Somali Peninsula, pp. 59-61.
27. Ibid., p. 50.
28. Mesfin Wolde Mariam, The Background of the Ethio-Somalia
    Boundary Dispute   (Addis   Ababa: Berhanena   Selam
    Printing Press, 1964), p. 40.
29. S. Pankhurst, Ex-Italian Somaliland (New York: Philo-
    sophical Library, 1951), p. 102.
30. G.K.N. Trevaskis, Eritrea: A Colony in Transition 1941-
    52 (London: Oxford University Press, 1960), pp. 46-7.
31. S. Pankhurst, Ethiopia and Eritrea 1941-52, Woodford
    Green: Lalibela House, 1953), pp. 30-1.
32. Trevaskis, Eritrea, p. 60.
33. George A. Lipsky, Ethiopia: Its People, Its Society, Its
    Culture (New Haven: Hraf Press, 1962), p. 202.
34. Final Report of the United Nations Commissioner in
    Eritrea, G. A. O. R., 7th Session, Supplement 15
    (A/2188), 1952, 75-6.
35. Lipsky, Ethiopia, p. 202.
36. M. Perham, The Government of Ethiopia, 2nd ed., p.
    XXXII.
37. Robert L. Hess, "Ethiopia," in National   Unity   and
    Regionalism in Eight African States   G.   Carter   (ed.)
    (Ithaca: Cornell University Press, 1966), p. 503.
38. Africa Report 7, no. 11 (December 1962): 22.
39. The Christian Science Monitor (March 19, 1971), p. 9.
40. I.M. Lewis, Peoples of the Horn of Africa: Saho, Afar,
    Somali (London: International African Institute, 1955), p.
    14.
41. Ibid.

42. Ibid., p. 89.
43. Saadia Touval, Somali Nationalism (Cambridge: Harvard University Press, 1963), p. 76.
44. A.A. Castagno, "Somali Republic," in Political Parties and National Integration in Tropical Africa J.S. Coleman and C. Roseberg (eds.) (Berkeley: University of California Press, 1964), p. 519.
45. House of Commons Debates, Feb. 4, 1941, col. 804.
46. Lord Rennel of Rodd, British Military Administration of Occupied Territories 1941-47 (London: HMSO, 1948), p. 182.
47. S. Pankhurst, Ex-Italian Somaliland (New York: Philosophical Library, 1951), p. 164.
48. House of Commons Debates, June 4, 1946, cols. 1840-1.
49. S. Pankhurst, Ex-Italian Somaliland, p. 179.
50. J. Drysdale, The Somali Dispute, p. 73.
51. A. Castagno, "Somali Republic," in Political Parties p. 542.
52. M. Perham, The Government of Ethiopia, 2nd ed., p. XXXV.
53. C. Hoskynks, Case Studies in African Diplomacy: 2, The Ethiopia-Somali-Kenya Dispute 1960-67 (Dar es Salaam: Oxford University Press, 1970), p. 79.
54. I.M. Lewis, The Modern History of Somaliland (New York: Praeger, 1965), pp. ix-x.
55. For recent developments in the Horn of Africa, see Y. Abate, "Africa's Troubled Horn: Background to Conflict," in Focus (American Geographical Society) 28, no. 3 (January-February 1978), and Tom J. Farer War Clouds in the Horn of Africa (Washington: Carnegie Endowment for International Peace, 1976).
56. See Farer, War Clouds in the Horn of Africa, pp. 136-151, and M. Wolde Mariam, The Background of the Ethio-Somali Boundary Dispute, pp. 65-67.

15 Ethnicity and National Integration in West Africa: Some Theoretical Considerations

Ladun Anise

THE NATURE OF THE PROBLEM:

A basic paradox exists about the role of ethnicity, or tribalism as it is properly known in African politics. First, a simple cursory examination of the social structure and group composition of every black African state shows the primacy and existential pervasiveness of ethnic groups and identities. In this respect, ethnicity continues to be the single most readily-identifiable social-structural characteristic of the new states in Africa. Secondly, African political leaders and elites persistently identify ethnicity as the principal divisive factor in national politics. According to Coleman and Rosberg (p. 690), this orientation of political leaders "helps to explain the firm, indeed frequently ruthless, repressive action taken by ruling elites regarding any tribal or regional manifestation of separatism, as well as the specific outlawing of tribal or regional parties by several governments." Because national political integration is taken by all African governments as a major nation-building objective, it is appropriate to reexamine the assumed relationship between ethnicity and national integration.

National unity and development are the two most often-encountered problems in the rhetoric of African politicians and elites. Both problems are real and complex. Both are generally very difficult to manage effectively. In the long run, the successful management of the problem of national integration depends on the management of the process of economic and social development; especially important in this regard is the allocation of scarce national resources to achieve a moderate level of social equity and distributive justice among contending ethnic groups. The relationships between ethnicity,

development, resource allocation, and ethnic competition for
social equity and distributive justice constitute the point of
departure in this essay.

The analysis is focused primarily on the 17 states of West
Africa, although many of the generalizations and conclusions
drawn from this region may very well apply to the rest of
black Africa. On the whole, the relationship between ethnicity
and national integration is a most complex one.

First, there is a general presumption in the literature
that ethnic heterogeneity tends to threaten the social and
political stability of any society (Rodee et al.; Said and
Simmons; Young; Heisler; McRoberts; Das Gupta; and Enloe).
This may be so, but it is not the existence of ethnic heterogeneity or social pluralism per se that causes social and
political instability, but rather the uses to which the
structures of heterogeneity are put in the society. In West
Africa, it is the sociopolitical and competitive mobilization of
ethnicity within the context of transitional uncertainty, consolidation of power (Markovitz, 1977, pp. 198-229, 284-348),
and material scarcity that engender chronic instability. In a
sense, instability seems inevitable, given the patterns and
characteristics of the political processes as a whole
(O'Connell).

Second, there is a tendency to assume the primacy of the
nation-state, and to assign universal legitimacy to its existence
without ever elaborating the normative justifications for the
validity of the nation-state. This is an inherited problem in
LDCs, where the problems of development are usually analyzed
almost exclusively in national terms. Essentially, it was the
nationalism of the struggle for decolonization that gave the
assumed legitimacy to the new nation-states. The new states
are thus the children of the new nationalisms, except that it
would be more analytically correct to treat the new political
entities as state-nations rather than nation-states. Even the
idea of nation-building, which is assumed to be the central
focus of sociopolitical activities in newly-independent states, is
more closely reflective of a process of transition from state to
nation rather than from nation to state.

The assumptions of the new nationalisms notwithstanding,
it seems more analytically correct to view the structural
evolution of politics in Africa as a process of transition from
ethnic agglomerations to the fusion of nation-states. This
analytic view represents the major contribution of Cohen and
Middleton in their study of the incorporation process in Africa.
This view assigns less structural cohesiveness to a "state"
than to a "nation." Thus "nation" would imply a greater sense
of community or "we feeling" than is to be found in a "state."

Third, the grand theories of political and economic development have contributed to the imposition of the legitimacy of
the nation-state in LDCs. "Grand theories of development

apparently accept this view and thus put a premium on
analyzing the collective attainments of a nation rather than the
relative gains or losses of specific groups in the population
within nations" (Das Gupta, p. 126). This orientation, Das
Gupta further argues, leads to the neglect of the distributive
issues involved in the process of internal political competition
among ethnic groups within states. When such issues are not
directly neglected, the ethnic behavior associated with the
competition and its mode of expression or organization are
treated as negative, or disassociational patterns. They are
thus presented as illegitimate forms of sociopolitical action.
This view of the problem tends to deny the group basis of
politics.

Finally, the assumed legitimacy of the nation-state a
priori tends to neglect the primacy of politics in LDCs in
general, and in Africa in particular. According to the late
Kwame Nkrumah of Ghana, the political kingdom is primary; on
it rests the substantive changes to be expected in the
economy, society, and culture. "Politics is the process by
which a community deals with the issues arising out of its
common problems. The basic functions of politics ... are the
formulation of issues, the deliberation of issues, the resolution
of issues, and the solution of the problems that give rise to
issues in the first of these four phases" (Spiros, 1966, p.
158). One cannot escape the centrality of competition in this
political process. Political competition requires mobilization of
groups and forces in order to achieve desired allocations.
Given what Das Gupta calls the "scarcity of initial political
resources" that characterizes the early states of development
(pp. 128-9), it becomes necessary to examine the means
available in any multi-ethnic society for successful competitive
bargaining for the authoritative allocation of values and scarce
resources.

The scarce political resources over which ethnic groups
compete include power, influence, authority, leadership
positions, representativeness, economic goods and services,
decision-making autonomy, security, cultural autonomy, and
categoric or relative group equality. In almost all cases, the
competition over these scarce resources will adopt various
means deemed appropriate for competitive advantage. The core
of the competition is the disposition to differential claims to
distributive justice among groups in society. Such claims to
justice imply potential conflicts. Thus, political competition
breeds inevitable conflicts; conflict is endemic to politics. It
is a rule worth noting that competing groups in society tend to
use those means at their disposal to mobilize support for group
action that can secure preferential allocation in an environment
of relative scarcity.

In West Africa, the means most readily available for
competitive ethnic mobilization is political ethnicity, or the

politics of ethnic mediation in the political arena.(1) In these
societies, there are political demands for social equity, removal
of regional disparities or imbalances, alleviation of ethnic
disadvantages, prevention of ethnic or regional domination,
and guarantees for ethnic representativeness in the decision-
making structures and processes of the state.

How much social disruption or disintegration results from
this process of competition depends on the means used for
support mobilization, group perception of the fairness or
unfairness of the political process, and the perceived
responsiveness of the political authorities to increasing group
demands for access into the precincts of power, influence, and
status. Because every society has unequal ethnic groups
numerically, unequal levels of ethnic development, and unequal
power and influence groups, the problems created by these
incidences of perceived ethnic, religious, and regional disadvantages must be taken as normal characteristics of the
political process in multi-ethnic societies.

STRUCTURE AND PROCESS IN WEST AFRICAN POLITICS:

Tables 15.1, 15.2, 15.3, 15.4, 15.5, and 15.6 present a
brief analysis of the basic social structures and compositional
characteristics of the West African States. When superimposed
on one another, these Tables provide a basis for some instructive generalizations. First, 8 of the 17 states, or 47
percent, are now under civilian rule. The remaining 9 or 53
percent, are currently under direct military rule, or under
mixed military-civilian regimes. Given the less than constitutional means used in the transformation of civilian into
military regimes, it can be said that most West African States
have not maintained political stability since independence. In
fact, only 35 percent, or six countries - Cameroon, Gambia,
Guinea, Ivory Coast, Liberia and Senegal - have retained
civilian rule throughout their existence as independent states.
This says something about the fact of instability, but not very
much about the causes of such instability.

About 30 percent of the states have experienced two or
more military coups. Only Liberia and Guinea Bissau have not
reported serious attempts or plots to overthrow the governments by force. This adds to the pervasiveness of instability.

Table 15.1.   Major Ethnic and Language Units
in West Africa

Country	Number of Major Ethnic and Language Units	Percentage of Total Population
Benin	3	91.6
Cameroon	6	84.0
Chad	4	91.0
Gambia	5	81.0
Ghana	4	81.5
Guinea	4	97.0
Guinea Bissau	8	88.0
Ivory Coast	7	95.0
Liberia	4	92.0
Mali	6	98.0
Mauritania	2	95.0
Niger	5	93.0
Nigeria	11	96.6
Senegal	5	93.0
Sierra Leone	4	90.0
Togo	6	91.0
Upper Volta	8	100.0

Source: Data adapted from Donald Morrison et al., Black
Africa: A Comparative Handbook (New York: The Free Press,
1972); and Africa Guide, 1977.

Table 15.2.   Relative Numerical Strength of
The Three Largest Ethnic Groups in the
Population by Percentage

Country	G1	G2	G3	Percentage of Total Population
Benin	55.5	22.5	13.6	91.6
Cameroon	27.0	18.0	15.0	60.0
Chad	46.0	28.0	9.5	83.5
Gambia	41.0	13.5	13.0	67.5
Ghana	44.0	16.0	13.0	73.0
Guinea	48.0	28.0	11.0	87.0
Guinea Bissau	31.0	17.5	12.5	62.0
Ivory Coast	25.0	18.0	15.0	58.0
Liberia	44.0	37.0	8.0	89.0
Mali	43.0	20.0	15.0	78.0
Mauritania	82.0	13.0	----	95.0
Niger	46.0	19.0	13.0	78.0
Nigeria	29.0	20.0	17.0	66.0
Senegal	37.0	24.0	16.0	77.0
Sierra Leone	45.0	36.0	8.0	89.0
Togo	44.0	23.0	7.0	74.0
Upper Volta	50.0	16.0	7.0	73.0

Source: Same as for Table 15.1.

Table 15.3. Structure of Religious Distribution
in West Africa By Percentage

Country	Percentage of Muslims	Percentage of Christians	Percentage of Traditional Religions	Total
Benin	15.0	20.0	65.0	100
Cameroon	20.0	35.0	45.0	100
Chad	45.0	10.0	45.0	100
Gambia	80.0	10.0[a]	10.0[a]	100
Ghana	19.0	43.0	38.0	100
Guinea	85.0[a]	10.0[a]	5.0[a]	100
Guinea Bissau	30.0	5.5	65.0	100
Ivory Coast	24.0	14.0	62.0	100
Liberia	20.0[b]	15.0[b]	65.0[b]	100
Mali	65.0	15.0	20.0	100
Mauritania	100.0	----	----	100
Niger	85.0	1.0	14.0	100
Nigeria	47.2	34.5	18.3	100
Senegal	80.0	10.0	10.0	100
Sierra Leone	40.0	7.4	52.6[c]	100
Togo	7.5	25.0	67.5	100
Upper Volta	15.0	5.0	80.0	100

Notes: (a) Estimates: H. Nelson, et al., Area Handbook for
          Guinea (Washington D.C.: U.S. Govt. Printing
          Office, 1975).
          (b) (Officially a Christian State) T. Roberts, et al.,
          Area Handbook for Liberia (Washington D.C.: U.S.
          Govt. Printing Office, 1972).
          (c) I. Kaplan, et al. Area Handbook for Sierra
          Leone (Washington D.C.: U.S. Govt. Printing Of-
          fice, 1976).

Sources: Africa Guide 1977 Country Survey, pp. 79-276;
          United Nations Year Books 1967-75.

Table 15.4. Percent Control of Cabinet Posts by Three
Largest Ethnic Units at Independence

Country	G1	G2	G3	Percentage of Total Population
Benin	70	20	10	100
Cameroon	40	20	0	60
Chad	38	38	0	76
Gambia	43	15	42	100
Ghana	62	23	7.7	92.7
Guinea	60	30	0	90
Guinea Bissau	na	na	na	na
Ivory Coast	25	8.3	8.3	41.6
Liberia*	0	0	0	0 (2% Settler pop. hold 100%)
Mali	43	43	7.1	93.1
Mauritania	100	0	---	100
Niger	9.1	55	18	82.1
Nigeria	39	26	17	72
Senegal	42	17	17	76
Sierra Leone	29	36	0	65
Togo	67	22	0	89
Upper Volta	57	21	0	78

*This is an unusual case; in 1960, the settler descendant
population of 2 percent controlled 100 percent of the cabinet
posts.

Source: Morrison et al., 1972.

Table 15.5. Percentage in Control of Cabinet by Three Largest Ethnic Units at Critical Years, and in 1967

Country	Critical Year			Percentage of Total	1967			Percentage of Total
	G1	G2	G3		G1	G2	G3	
Benin (1965)	92	8	0	100	73	18	9	100
Cameroon	--	--	--	--	40	7	0	47
Chad	--	--	--	--	43	50	0	93
Gambia	--	--	--	--	44	11	33	88
Ghana (Pre Coup 1976)	71	12	12	95	25	13	38	76
Guinea	--	--	--	--	65	27	0	92
Guinea Bissau	--	--	--	--	na	na	na	na
Ivory Coast	--	--	--	--	47	12	24	83
Liberia*	--	--	--	--	0	0	0	0
Mali	--	--	--	--	33	40	0	73
Mauritania	--	--	--	--	83	17	0	100
Niger	--	--	--	--	40	33	6.7	79.7
Nigeria (Pre Coup 1966)	31	34	19	84	--	--	--	--
Senegal	--	--	--	--	44	28	5.6	77.6
Sierra Leone	--	--	--	--	13	62	0	75
Togo (Pre Coup 1963)	70	20	0	90	25	42	8.3	75.3
Upper Volta (Pre Coup Cabinet 1966)	54	15	7.7	76.7	54	31	0	85

Source: Morrison et al., 1972.

WEST AFRICA 323

Table 15.6. Incidences of Elite and Communal Instability,
Present Form of Government and Composite Profile
of Cleavages in West Africa

Country	Instability		Present form of Government	Composite, Cleavage Profile
	Elite	Communal		
Benin	Chronic; 5 coups between 1963-75	Chronic; ethnic violence in 1964	Military (after One Party Rule)	Chronic Regionalism; ideological cleavages; ethnic cleavages; coincident with three region polarization; ethnicized military
Cameroon	Moderate	Ethnic violence in 1962, 1967	Civilian One Party System	Ethnic-Religious splits coincident with North-South cleavages and language divisions
Chad	Chronic; attempted coup, 1971; violent coup, 1976	Civil War 1968-present; Rebellion, 1965-68	Military (after One Party Rule)	North-South regional cleavages coincident with ethnic religious, and ideological cleavages

Table 15.6.   Continued

| Country | Instability | | Present form of Government | Composite Cleavage Profile |
	Elite	Communal		
Gambia	none	none	Civilian Multi-Party System	Stable, little regional, ethnic, or religious cleavages
Ghana	chronic; 3 coups, 1966-78.	controlled communal tensions; Rebellion, 1969	Military (after Military, after Multi-Party, after One Party Rule.	Ewe ir-redentism against Togo; ethnic cleavage coincident with regional cleavage
Guinea	Moderate	Slight ethnic tensions	Civilian One Party System	One Party Rule; Marxist ideological dominance
Guinea Bissau	None; armed struggle; Revolution-ary Leadership	None	Revolution-ary One Party System	One Party Rule; Socialist Revolution-ary Populist

Table 15.6.   Continued

Country	Instability		Present form of Government	Composite Cleavage Profile
	Elite	Communal		
Ivory Coast	Mild	Rebellion in 1959, 1969; feeble secession attempts; near civil war secretly conducted in 1969	Civilian One Party System	North-South Regionalism coincident with mild ethnic cleavage and religious-cultural divisions
Liberia	Mild; minority settler elite complete domination	Slowly increasing tension between settler and indigenous population	Civilian One Party settler descendant dominance	Unusual case of subnational unit supremacy; no dis-integrative movements since 1955; coastal-interior regional cleavage
Mali	Moderate; coup in 1969	High; ethnic rebellion 1963-64	Military-Civilian Coalition Regime after One Party Rule	Regional cleavages coincident with ethnic cleavages
Mauritania	Almost none, until war in Western Sahara brought coup in July 1978	Language riots in 1966; racial tensions	First Military Coup in July 1978	North-South regional cleavage coincident with racial-linguistic cleavage

Table 15.6.   Continued

Country	Instability Elite	Instability Communal	Present form of Government	Composite Cleavage Profile
Niger	Almost chronic	Continual mass agitation since 1960; ethnic violence 1964-65	Military rule after One Party Rule	Chronic north-south cleavage coincident with ethnic violence and ideological polarization
Nigeria	Chronic; three coups; one attempted coup; bloody consequences, ethnicized military	Chronic; ethnic pogrom, 1966 Civil war and secession, 1967-70; always volatile.	Military Rule, 1966-79; succession of three military since 1966, mostly unstable civilian regimes, 1960-66.	Extreme regionalism, statism, ethnic-religious cleavages that tend to violent confrontations; civilian rule expected Oct. 1979
Senegal	Almost none	Almost none	Civilian One Party dominance, but return to ex-perimental three party system in 1978	Ideological and personality cleavages; Some Muslim-Christian cleavages

Table 15.6.   Continued

Country	Instability		Present form of Government	Composite Cleavage Profile
	Elite	Communal		
Sierra Leone	Almost chronic; ethnically based; four coups; ethnicized military	Severe ethnic violence in 1968; continual ethnic tensions	Civilian One Party Rule; ethnic dominance	Regional cleavages coincident with chronic ethnic cleavages; mostly Mende-Temne factionalism
Togo	Chronic; four coups alternating military civilian regimes	Chronic ethnic rivalry; Ewe irredentism between Togo and Ghana	Military dominance	North-South cleavage coincident with ethnic-religious cleavages; periodic shifts in ethnic control of cabinets
Upper Volta	Relatively high; coup in 1966	Ethnic rivalry, but no serious confrontations	Mixed Military-Civilian rule; military dominance	Regional-ethnic-religious cleavages

Second, only Mauritania can be said to be ethnically and linguistically homogeneous. Even so, Mauritania can easily be differentiated regionally. Sixteen states, or 94 percent are characterized by significant ethnic, religious, linguistic, and regional heterogeneity. Most critical, however, is the fact that ethnic, religious, linguistic, and regional cleavages tend to converge in the political structure of West African States. This convergence of multiple cleavages is clearly identifiable in Table 15.6. Thus, given this structure of cleavages, one would have expected a different approach to the politics of value allocation from the one practiced in West Africa, or advocated in the literature of development that assumes a "national" focus without much sensitivity to the structure of cleavages in multi-ethnic societies.

Finally, there is a common sense orientation that is often missed in a discussion on national integration. All the cleavages, especially in their tendency to converge in each state, are easily transformed into political currencies in the process of direct mass-support mobilization or competitive group struggle for comparative advantage in the allocation of scarce political factors and values. Whether or not groups in competition use these political currencies in securing their demands and expected allocations will depend on the nature of the political arena, the political rules of the game, and the presence or absence of alternative currencies with which the same objectives can be achieved. Assuming a limited degree of rationality, or at least some minimal degree of economic-orientation, in the behavior of participants in the political process, there will be a tendency on the part of competitive groups, parties, and leaders to use those currencies that result in immediate, tangible gains over those that promise distant, uncertain rewards. Thus, the readily-available symbols tend to have greater appeal over more costly symbols. In West Africa, the cheap currencies are ethnic, religious, and regional symbols. There are very few crisscrossing cleavage structures, few crosscutting loyalty institutions, and few multiple-membership social formations to limit the excesses of the primordial loyalties of the readily-available symbols of competition. A brief and direct review of some of the events in some of the countries will sharpen the nature of the problem.

Benin continues to be plagued by chronic regionalism; ethnic and religious splits have been translated into political behavior, currencies of mass mobilization, and sources of national disintegration. These cleavages have been introduced into the army, thus institutionalizing regional and generational differences, communal instability, and ethnic violence (Morrison, pp. 227-233; Staniland).

In Cameroon, a north-south split is coincident with ethnic-religious and linguistic cleavages. Fear of northern

Muslim domination of the government tends to breed ethnic violence and mass instability, which, in turn, leads to harsh government measures that are <u>justified</u> in terms of national unity and ethnic and religious cooperation and tolerance (Morrison, pp. 192-98; Johnson, 1970, pp. 671-92).

Civil wars have divided both Niger and Chad since 1960 and 1968 respectively. Foreign military intervention has attempted to stabilize both regimes. The military regimes in both countries have had no more success than the civilian politicians they overthrew. In both countries, a chronic convergence of ethnicity and regionalism continues to produce separatist political movements and intensive ethnic mass violence, fought sometimes under the cover of ideological polarization and elite power competition. Both Niger and Chad tend toward massive national disintegration (Morrison, pp. 204-9, 305-9).

Guinea Bissau enjoys remarkable political stability, dynamic revolutionary leadership, and equitable political allocations and developmental programming. A decade of armed struggle against Portuguese colonialism provided the ideological and the organizational context in which ethnic-religious cleavages were rendered politically insignificant. The prolonged struggle forged the unification of the ethnic and regional groups in the country.(2)

Gambia maintains relative stability and progressive national unity primarily because there is no significant regional split, no translation of religious differences into the currency of elite competition or political mobilization (Morrison, pp. 246-50). The same could be said of Mauritania until its involvement in the western Sahara issue with Morocco, Algeria, and the Polisario brought about a military takeover in July 1978 (Morrison, pp. 300-304). Senegal enjoys a high degree of stability, with a loosely-integrated ideological leadership within a weak structure of Muslim-Christian religious cleavage, and radical-conservative ideological polarization. National integration seems to be making some headway in Gambia and Senegal (Morrison, pp. 324-9). The Ivory Coast has subnational identities, north-south regionalism, and religious-cultural divisions. In spite of its rapid economic development, there is an increasing social polarization as the result of maldistribution of income and the general neglect of 40 percent of the population. These stresses produced feeble, ethnically-motivated secession attempts in 1959 and 1969 that were secretly and brutally suppressed by the government (Amin; Morrison, pp. 264-9).

Liberia is a unique example of political stability. There is an absence of ethnic agitation, despite absolute political and economic domination by the descendants of the settler population in the coastal region. This ruling group, which constitutes only two percent of the total population, is both ethnically and regionally identifiable. Yet there is no major national disintegrative movement in response to obvious subnational unit supremacy, as can be seen in Chad, Niger, or even Nigeria. Much of Liberia's political fortune can be attributed to a lack of political consciousness on the part of indigenous ethnic groups, and to the absence of efficacious indigenous political mass organization. The situation is slowly beginning to change; indigenous ethnic groups have started to demand political and economic equity, thus creating tensions and polarizations between indigenous groups and the minority descendants of the settler population (Morrison, pp. 282-87; Frankel).

National integration was forged in Ghana in the early years of the Nkrumah regime, although strong regional and communal tensions remain. Ghana's chronic elite instability has produced an oscillation between civilian and military regimes, all of which have been unable to cope with the problems of modernization and economic development. Ethnicity continues to be contained within a strong sense of nationalism, challenged periodically by an equally strong sense of regionalism. The latter has not been seriously expressed in terms of convergence of religious and ethnic cleavages. Ewe irredentism against Togo was noticeable in 1957-63, but that has subsided in the wake of severe economic problems (Card; Morrison, pp. 251-58).

Sekou Toure's Guinea enjoys religious and radical Marxist ideological homogeneity, as well as continuity of civilian leadership. However, ethnic tensions exist, and there have been reported challenges to the ruling elites, usually followed by purges and mass arrests of identified counter-elites. On the whole, "the role of ideology and widespread Islamic culture seems to be of special importance in achieving a substantial degree of national integration."[3] The iron hold of one-party, ideological, and authoritarian rule cannot be discounted in assessing the Guinean achievement (Johnson, 1978, pp. 36-65; Dunn, p. 211).

Mali and Upper Volta exhibit similar dynamics. In Mali, elite instability has been dominant, although communal instability occurred in 1963-64, when northern nomadic ethnic groups - the Tuareg group, for example - rebelled against overtaxation and administrative control. Elite competition for power has caused a great deal of tension, leading to a military takeover in 1968. The takeover was explained exclusively in economic terms; according to Moussa Traore, "the state has been living far beyond its means" and the "demagogic and sterile radicalism of the Keita regime has frightened away foreign investors"[4] (Morrison, pp. 294-99). In Upper Volta, much of the instability is elite in nature, regional, and ethnic differences have not been transformed into serious political currencies partly because of the mediation of religious homogeneity (Morrison, pp. 372-76).

Togo,(5) Benin, Sierra Leone, and Nigeria present cases
of dynamic, troublesome, and often disintegrative covergence
of ethnic, regional, and religious cleavages. In these countries, the cleavages have often been translated into political
currencies at the competitive arena. All have had persistent
and chronic elite and communal instability, and multiple military
intrusions into politics. All these military regimes have been
plagued by the ethnicization of both politics and the military
organizational structures and hierarchies. Although Benin,
Togo, and Sierra Leone have managed to avoid outright civil
wars, they cannot be said to be politically-integrated. Like
Chad and Niger, Nigeria has actually pursued the politics of
ethnic, religious, and regional cleavages to the point of
violent, bloody, and disintegrative civil war. In a way,
Nigeria represents the most troubling and most complex
aggregation of all the structural problems in African politics
today. These countries represent varying degrees of the
disintegrative pattern in West Africa. In Sierra Leone, elite
competition for power takes place within perennial ethnic
rivalries, especially between Mende and Temne, either among
civilian leaders or rival factions within the military as it in-
tervenes in politics. In 1968 ethnic violence resulted from
such chronic instability (Morrison, pp. 330-35; Kilson; Allen).
All these countries have witnessed shifts in ethnic control of
cabinet posts at different times in their histories. The ethnic
composition and control of cabinet posts (Tables 15.4 and 15.5)
at different time periods serves as a useful indicator of representativeness, or of a conscious intent to achieve an
equitable structure of power sharing.

Nigeria deserves special attention. Since independence,
Nigeria has witnessed chronic elite and communal instability,
ethnic riots, rebellions, several coups d'etat, ethnic pogroms,
and a three-year, bloody civil war. The country was in the
grip of chronic disintegrative forces from 1962-70. Of all
countries in Africa, Nigeria is unique in its special combination
and convergence of chronic regionalism, ethnic exclusivity and
intolerance, religious polarization, and political, organizational
power drives within a structure of ruthless, even banal,
competition.

The Tiv rebellion between 1960-64 gave a signal of things
to come. Nigeria was overcome by the political power confrontations of regional-ethnic parties from 1959-64, the political
opposition liquidation trials of 1962-64, the three coups of
1966, the ethnic pogrom of May-October 1966, the declaration
of Biafran secession of May 1967, and the outbreak of civil war
in July 1967. The civil war lasted until January 1970. Four
years of reconstruction culminated in the bloodless coup of
July 1975, which was followed by a murderous, attempted coup
in February 1976. Few other countries have been more un-
stable than Nigeria. Naturally Nigeria has received long and

extensive analytical attention because of these problems, the
size of the country, the potential for rapid economic development, the factor endowments, and the many complex contradictions (Coleman 1955, 1958; Varma; Akiwowo; Schwarz;
Dudley; Anise; Melson and Wolpe; Mafeje; Luckham; Dare;
Olorunsola, 1972, 1977; Morrison, pp. 310-18). Undoubtedly
therefore, it can be said with disconcerting justification that
Nigeria's "problem of national integration spans the entire
spectrum of African experience."(6) What is more, the very
structure of regional, religious, and ethnic cleavages found in
civilian politics has found its way into the organizational and
behavioral structure of the Nigerian military establishment
(Dunn; Williams and Turner; Decalo; Dare; Callaway;
Luckman; Welch).

The problem of national political integration in West
African States is serious; the coincidence of multiple cleavages
is at the core of the problem. Ethnicity per se is only a
complicating factor, whose impact must be seen in the light of
the total structure of sociopolitical, historical, and cultural
dynamics. To fully understand these dynamics, analysis
should focus on the nature of political allocations, support
mobilization dynamics, and the cruciality of leadership recruitment and group representativeness in the decision-making
processes. The complicating factors of urbanization, emergent
class conflicts, and social status stratifications must also be
included if such analysis is to be explanatory and relevant.

THE ANALYTICS OF ETHNIC CALCULUS:

The states of West Africa face the same problems encountered by all states that have emerged from the crucible of
colonialism. They all began as arbitrary entities encapsulated
within colonially-determined boundaries. They face what
Edward Shils calls the "vicissitudes of the aspiration toward
the establishment of political society,"(7) the fusion of old
societies to form new, modern, and coherent states and
politics. This modern and coherent society should be more
than a complex of modern institutions. "It is a mode of integration of the whole society,"(8) including the conscious
transcendence of "narrow loyalties, petty jealousies and
ignorant prejudices engaged in mortal conflict."(9)

Like all such states, West African states are "abnormally
susceptible to serious disaffection based on primordial attachments...that stem from the givens...of social existence: immediate contiguity and kin connection mainly, but beyond them
the givenness that stems from being born into a particular
religious community, speaking a particular language...and
following particular social practices."(10)

According to Apter (1963, pp. 57-104), these states have generally adopted a "political religion" to replace the old values and have preferred mobilization systems and structures to reconciliation systems and structures. Reconciliation regimes tend toward democratic pluralism, but mobilization regimes tend toward autocracy and illiberal attitudes.

The choice of mobilization systems in West African States was not derived from the prior analysis of the institutional requirements for building a coherent political community from the socio-structural givenness of ethnic pluralism or of primordial attachments, but rather from the assumptions of the unexamined constitutional legitimacy of the new nation-state. This was a singular failing and a false premise. In effect, political integration was already assumed, and hence the emergence of the coincidence of multiple primordial cleavages was perceived as a treasonable departure from the assumed natural evolution of the nation-state into a homogeneous social and political order. The point of analytic departure here is that, given the primacy of politics in the new states, given the politicization of all aspects of social, cultural, and economic life in the new states, the emergence of the coincidence of multiple cleavages and primordial loyalties and identities, and their massive translation into the political currencies of mass, ethnic, sectional support mobilization, should be treated as a natural logical tendency in such societies. Treating the problem this way would suggest a different calculus of ethnic mediation and regional balancing in the politics of allocation. Not treating the problem in this fashion has created, or at least complicated, the problems of the politics of ethnic, religious, and regional confrontations in West Africa.

Guinea Bissau is the only West African State where the leaders first undertook a critical analysis of the social and structural factors in their society as a foundation for the forms of political and organizational structures of mass mobilization to be introduced. In this experiment, the leaders may have neutralized the saliency of the ethnic, religious, or regional factors in their national politics. In effect the other West African states turned politics upside down. This truncation of expected political engineering largely accounts for the instability of West African regimes and societies. In almost all the countries, the ethnicized politics of confrontation have tended to replace the politics of ethnic mediation. The politics of exclusion have tended to replace the politics of accomodation. Given the fact of "political factor scarcity" at the core of modernization and nation-building, the politics of resource allocation is bound to engender ruthless competition in a winner-take-all political arena. Arthur Lewis (pp. 30-32) has aptly summarized the characteristics of the politics of intolerence, and the zero-sum conception of politics in West Africa:

No politician will admit that he suppresses his political opponents primarily because he wants to stay in power; he will more usually say that their policies or their tactics endanger the country. ...But it would also be mistaken to forget that much of what is going on in some of these countries is fully explained in terms of the normal lust of human beings for power and wealth. The stakes are high. Office carries power, prestige and money. The power is incredible. Most West African Ministers consider themselves to be above the law, and are treated as such by the police. Decision-making is arbitrary...The prestige is also incredible. Men who claim to be democrats in fact behave like emperors. Personifying the state, they dress themselves up in uniforms, build themselves palaces...and generally demand to be treated like Egyptian Pharoahs. And the money is also incredible. Successful politicians receive...salaries two to four times as high as they previously earned...There are also vast opportunities for pickings in bribes, state contracts, diversion of public funds to private uses...To be a Minister is to have a lifetime's chance to make a fortune.

In this kind of political arena, only the most ruthless can succeed. Because total societal resources are scarce, this kind of politics does not favor accommodation. Hence, there is the fear of losing; the fear of domination by the winners over the losers, and the expected recriminations against those who lose create the politics of ethnic anxiety and the reality of the politics of exclusion. It is in this kind of political atmosphere that the routine politics of ethnic mediation is reduced finally into the disintegrative arena of ethnicized politics. There is also a simple rule of logic, even of rational cost minimization, involved in the ensuing political calculus: people, groups, elites, and individuals in competition, aware of the high stakes, will utilize available symbols and sociostructural linkage instruments as economical factors of ready or easy or least-cost support mobilization. This means, in effect, translating ethnic symbols, religious differences and regional differentiation factors into political currencies to purchase mass support, gain access to status roles and positions, and seek vertical mobility in the rigidly pyramidal and hierarchical power systems found all over West Africa.

This structure of politics also suggests that it is erroneous to treat ethnic identifications and the conflicts between ethnic groups in the new states as vestiges of traditionalism and parochialism, something many West African leaders, elites, and even scholars continue to do. Ethnicity is a given structure of multi-ethnic societies. However, political ethnicity and the ethnicization of politics are a modern response phenomenon exacerbated by the ruthless competition for economic power, social status, bureaucratic command, and other allocative advantages in the process of modernization in the new states (Apter, 1971; Melson and Wolpe; Lemarchand; Huntington and Melson; Das Gupta; Heisler pp. 1-57; Horowitz, 1977). Beyond that, recent findings of social science research in more developed, industrial states show that the phenomenon of political ethnicity, as well as the separatist, disintegrative forces it unleashes in modern society, is universal. That this phenomenon is internationally widespread can be seen in Belgium (Heisler, pp. 32-46), Canada (McRoberts), Northern Ireland (Terchek), the Soviet Union (Harmstone), Yugoslavia (Bertsch), China (Dreyer), India (Das Gupta), and the United States (Glazer and Moynihan; Said and Simmons, pp. 9-47).

> It is necessary to reiterate that the ethnic group is not an anachronism of feudal and preindustrial society, but that these antagonisms of modernization dogma continue to demonstrate remarkable persistence even in postindustrial nations (Said and Simmons, p. 33).

The socioeconomic imperatives of political ethnicity, its social psychology, are bound up with the search for a sense of community on one hand, and on the other, with the allocative dynamics of modernization, industrialization, and the principles of collective social equity. It represents the success of political socialization in a way. In the modern states, all groups develop the consciousness of their identity and their right to categoric equality. This represents the process of "domestication of international politics," especially its conflict-inducing competitiveness:

> Conflict is not necessarily irrational but the roots of cultural expression that produce conflict are psychosociological. Cultures and ethnic groups have an inner logic that determines behavior, values and attitudes that confound objective description or absolutism. The complexity of cultures necessitates a multidimensional appreciation of the intertwining institutions and people that synthesize a political cultural and collective consciousness (Said and Simmon, p. 21).

Thus, it matters little whether with new or old industrial states are considered; the politics of choice and the politics of allocation (Apter, 1971) require mobilization of group consciousness and identity in order to achieve any significant allocative advantage in the context of political-resource scarcity. When the ethnicized politics of West Africa is added to this dynamic process, when personalism, the politics of ethnic exclusion, the politics of arbitrary and capricious use of power are added, then instability and continual disintegrative eruptions in the new states are inevitable (O'Connell). Eruptions such as those in Chad, Niger, Benin, Sierra Leone, Zaire, Uganda, Ruwanda, Burundi, and Angola may lead to serious bloodshed, but they are not intended to bring about the dissolution of the new state. They represent group-based contests for power and challenges for allocative advantages in the transitional process of encadrement and consolidation of power (Markovitz, 1977; pp. 198-348). In Huntington and Nelson's terminology, this could be called the process of "developmental embourgeoisment." Among the 17 states of West Africa, only in Nigeria did such extreme contestation result in an actual attempt to dismember the state; that failure may have spared the whole of Africa from opting for state dissolution as an effective answer to ethnic political confrontations. The ongoing war between Ethiopia and Eritrea casts a shadow on how well the lesson of the failure of Biafra has been learned on the continent.

It would seem far more theoretically useful to analyze the problems of political ethnicity, self-determination, and ethnic mediation in terms of a comparative group approach to politics. Interest and pressure groups in industrial societies compete for allocative advantage in the political process. Their competition can be destabilizing. What distinguishes them from ethnic-group competition is two fold. First, they often have crosscutting, multiple memberships that tend to contain conflict potential within manageable boundaries. Ethnic groups tend to be exclusive, single-membership organizations. They also have the primordial attachments that enforce psychosociological linkages that are not easily overcome during politically-competitive situations.

Second, interest- and pressure-group competition in developed industrial states tends to abide by the constitutional rules of the game. That is, they tend to observe a generalized state of legitimacy for the authority of the state, provided all elite groups, leadership styles, and mass mobilization strategies do not severely abuse the rules that guarantee legitimacy. This constitutionally-or legitimacy-constrained behavior is either absent, or, if present, too fragile and superficial in the new West African States. Thus, the zero-sum nature of political competition tends to leave every ethnic, religious, or regional group free to make their own rules as they move along in the competitive game. The nature of the game also tends to encourage extreme behaviors and demands that are presented in non-negotiable, non-compromisable modes. As groups, their behavior reveals either the painful absence, or the fragile and inadequate development of other restraining, routinized institutional mechanisms for conducting political competition.

It is of theoretical, and even practical political interest to observe that, as the developed industrial countries face significant declines in the politics of resource abundance, the possibilities of unlimited growth and economic expansion, the rate of growth of standard of living, expected relative shares of competitive groups, and the expected fairness in governmental as well as decision-making allocative processes, interest and pressure groups have become more organized into narrow and exclusive lobbying groups, that defy the existing legal or constitutional constraints. Labor unions in the U.S., France, Britain, and Italy now engage in seriously-destabilizing industrial actions, often in open defiance of the law. The extremism of ethnic and religious groups in Canada and Northern Ireland suggests that almost all groups could resort to any number of primordial attachments in times of perceived social, political, and economic deprivation and competitive disadvantage. Thus, even in developed industrial societies, the perceived failure of the politics of distributive justice is increasingly producing nationally disintegrative behavior patterns among well organized competitive interest and pressure groups. This behavior pattern is, therefore, not the exclusive property of modernizing new states, although the problems of social, political, and economic equity may be more troubling and more intractable in them. Thus, a conscious adoption of the group theory of politics, and its application to political competition in multi-ethnic societies could help to expose the theoretical prejudices about ethnicity, or tribalism, in analyzing African politics.(11)

The theories of social pluralism (Young; Kuper and Smith; Wallerstein; Lijphart, 1968, 1969; Rodee, pp. 212-218) provide another supplementary point of departure for the analysis of ethnicity and the convergence of multiple cleavages in African societies. These theories suggest the importance and desirability of accommodation, tolerance, and representativeness in political processes and institutions, as well as a categorical institutional and leadership commitment to the principles of equity in the allocative process.

In the early 1960s when civilian and electoral politics were in operation in West Africa, Lewis argued that a system of proportional representation should be put into practice in party politics. The fear of proportional representation was that it would encourage a multi-party system based on ethnic or regional parochialism. As such, the process would tend to be nationally disintegrative. Those states that had a multi-party system - Nigeria, Benin, and Sierra Leone - also had regionally-and ethnically based parties, whose behavior did not encourage national unity. Thus, proportional representation in the absence of commitment to the politics of group equity would naturally tend to produce chronic instability. What Lewis did not foresee was the massive movement toward military dictatorships in West Africa. This development, continuing through the late 1960s and the 1970s, has almost put the notion of political representation beyond the reach of most groups in West Africa. It seems, therefore, that multi-ethnic societies in the process of modernization and encadrement require the rational, systematic, and strategic calculus of ethnic mediation and democratic practice. The politics of ethnic, religious, or regional domination or despotic authoritarianism are more prone to social conflict and disintegration than those that make conscious efforts to engineer an equitable balance. The saliency of a group-conscious propensity for equality is an irresistible force in modern international politics and communication. Only the politics of an engineered group equality can meet that challenge.

In fact, a paradox has developed across West Africa in the process of ethnic political competition. Mobilization of ethnic support for party politics and electoral advantage in Nigeria, Benin, and Sierra Leone, especially during civilian rule, led to greater unification of ethnic groups than before. Thus arises the paradox of a dual process, involving increasing subnational integration on one hand, and increasing national disintegration on the other. This was most pronounced in the cases of Benin and Nigeria (Anise, pp. 479-561). Often, the behavior of elites exacerbates this dual process. Ethnic elites in aspiring for power, status, or advantage may adopt ethnic symbols and rhetoric, either to mobilize support or to dramatize personal individual grievances, in competition with individual elites from other ethnic groups. This phenomenon constitutes a deliberate exploitation of ethnic, religious, or regional difference in order to secure individual - not group - advantages in the competitive arena. As happens frequently in West African politics, the exploited group in whose name or identity the individual claims are made often does not receive any direct benefits from the resulting mediated allocation. At best, individual members of the group may secure indirect benefits through the patron-client linkage structures of the given ethnic, religious, or regional groups. This process, too, must be seen as a modern manifestation of the use of ethnicity or religion or regionalism for competitive advantage in the allocative process.

CONCLUSION

Political integration is the central problem of nation-building and modernization. The given structures of the new

states cannot be assumed to be nations. A nation must be
forged from the dynamic fusion of its multiethnic, particularistic identities under the reality of modern group disposition
to categoric equality. As such, the process of political integration in the new states involves five major processes:
"first, the achievement of some degree of cultural and normative fusion; second, the promotion of economic inter-
penetration among different strata and sectors of society;
third, the process of social integration; fourth, the building of
institutions for effective conflict resolution; and fifth, the
psychological accumulation of a shared national experience"
(Mazriu, p. 277). The problem of ethnic particularism and the
process of ethnicized political competition can be contained only
when conscious ethnic mediation is introduced into the political
and economic calculus of the new states. In the final analysis,
only the institutionalization of categoric equality and elite
disinclination to exploit ethnic, cultural, religious, linguistic,
and regional difference in the process of competition for
political resource scarcity will redirect nation-building energies
toward the integrative mode. The calculus of ethnic mediation
is an inevitable demand for the politics of allocative equity and
fairness among groups and regions, as well as among individual
citizens in the new states. Political parties can play a role in
this process, provided their leaders have the bold foresight
and statesmanship that transcend elemental parochialism and
exclusivity. For those West African states under civilian rule,
party politics are critical (Emerson; Coleman and Rosbergh);
for those states under military rule, a calculus of mediation
must rest with the military's disposition to inclusiveness and
representativeness. Such a calculus may well test the leadership capabilities of both the military leadership and the
leadership of its bureaucratic allies in the administration of
allocative equity and efficiency. In either type of regime, the
challenge of categoric equality and allocative fairness must be
met before the stable, integrative nexus can be guaranteed.
In most cases, the demand for ethnic self-determination in the
new states is not really a demand for separatist political
sovereignty, but an insistence on social equity and allocative
fairness. The calculus of ethnic mediation can, therefore, be
generalized into the calculus of mediated group competition.
This will require the abandonment of the present conception of
political roles and rules in Africa. Up to the present time,
the conception of politics as an exclusionary process has
institutionalized a high degree of structural violence and
chronic instability. This is because "political elites not only
seek to monopolize leadership roles, but (also) the machinery
of the state is used to deny political opportunities to competing
elites, while popular demands are, where not ignored, physically repressed."(12) The result, of course, is the politics of
deprivation, which creates mounting discontent among ethnic,

regional, and religious groups. Only the transformation of these politics into one that institutionally incorporates distributive justice can ensure national integration.

NOTES

1. Jyotirindra Das Gupta, "Nation, Region and Welfare: Ethnicity, Regionalism, and Development Politics in South Asia," The Annals 433, Sept. 1977, p. 130.
2. Africa Guide 1977 (Saffron Walden, Essex: Africa Guide Co., 1977), pp. 148-150.
3. Donald G. Morrison et al., Black Africa: A Comparative Handbook (New York: The Free Press, 1972), p. 263.
4. Ibid., p. 298.
5. Ibid., pp. 361-64.
6. Ibid., p. 315. The new structure of 19 states in the Federation has narrowed these problems, but it has created the new problem of parochial statism.
7. Edward Shils "On the Comparative Study of New States" in Clifford Geertz (ed.), Old Societies and New States (New York: The Free Press, 1963), p. 6.
8. Ibid., p. 21.
9. Clifford Geertz, "The Integrative Revolution," in Old Societies and New States, p. 106. This phrase is quoted from Pandit Nehru in reference to his unsettling discovery of the tenacity of the problems of linguistic identities in India in 1948.
10. Geertz,, "The Integrative Revolution," p. 109.
11. For a brief discussion of theoretical approach, see James A. Bill and Robert L. Hardgrave, Comparative Politics: The Quest for Theory (Columbus: Charles Merrill, 1973).
12. B.J. Dudley, Afriscope, January 1976, p. 6, as quoted in African Freedom Annual 1977, Southern African Freedom Foundation, 1978, p. 24.

BIBLIOGRAPHY

Africa Guide 1977. Saffron Walden, Essex: Africa Guide Co., 1977.

Akiwowo, A.A. "The Sociology of Nigerian Tribalism." Phylon 5, no. 23 (1964): 155-163.

Allen, Christopher. "Sierra Leone." In Dunn, (ed.). West African States: Failure and Promise. pp. 189-210.

Amin, Samir. "Capitalism and Development in the Ivory Coast." In I.L. Markovitz (ed.). African Politics and Society New York: The Free Press, 1970, pp. 277-97.

Anise, Emmanuel. The Impact of Federal Structure and Party System on Political Integration in Nigeria. (Ph.D. dissertation, Syracuse University, 1970).

Annals of the American Academy of Political and Social Science The. vol. 433, Ethnic Conflict in the World Today, Sept. 1977.

Apter, David. "Political Religion in the New States." In Geertz (ed.). Old Societies and New States 1963, pp. 57-104.

_____. Choice and the Politics of Allocation. New Haven: Yale University Press, 1971.

Bates, Robert. "Ethnic Competition and Modernization in Contemporary Africa." Comparative Political Studies 6, no. 4 (1974): 457-484.

Bennett, G. "Tribalism in Politics." In P.H. Gulliver (ed.). Tradition and Transition in East Africa. Berkeley: University of California Press, 1969.

Bertsch, Gary K. "Ethnicity and Politics in Socialist Yugoslavia." The Annals 433 Sept. 1977, pp. 88-99.

Bill, James A. and Robert L. Hardgrave, Jr. Comparative Politics. Columbus: Charles Merrill, 1973.

Callaway, Barbara. "The Political Economy of Nigeria." In R. Harris (ed.). The Political Economy of Africa 1975, pp. 93-136.

Campbell, Bonnie. "Ivory Coast." In Dunn (ed.). West African States 1978, pp. 66-116.

Card, Emily. "The Political Economy of Ghana." In R. Harris, (ed.). The Political Economy of Africa 1975, pp. 49-92.

Clapham, Christopher. "Liberia." In Dunn, (ed.). West African States 1978, pp. 117-131.

Cohen, Ronald and John Middleton. From Tribe to Nation in Africa. Scranton: Chandler Pub., 1970.

Coleman, James S. "The Problem of Political Integration in Emergent Africa." Western Political Quarterly 8 (March 1955): 44-58.

_____. Nigeria: Background to Nationalism. Berkeley: University of California Press, 1958.

Coleman, James S. and Carl Rosberg (ed.). Political Parties and National Integration in Tropical Africa. Berkeley: University of California Press, 1970.

Dare, L.O. "Nigerian Military Governments and the Quest for Legitimacy, January 1966-July 1975." Nigerian Journal of Economic and Social Studies 17 (July 1975): 95-118.

Decalo, Samuel. Coups and Army Rule in Africa. New Haven: Yale University Press, 1976.

Dreyer, June T. "Ethnic Relations in China." The Annals 433, Sept. 1977, pp. 100-111.

Dudley, B.J. "Federalism and the Balance of Political Power in Nigeria." Journal of Commonwealth Political Studies 4, no. 1 (March 1966): 16-29.

Dunn, John (ed.). West African States: Failure and Promise. New York: Cambridge University Press, 1978.

Emerson, Rupert. "Parties and National Integration in Africa," in J. LaPalombara and M. Weiner (eds.). Political Parties and Political Development, Princeton: University Press, 1966, pp. 267-302.

Enloe, Cynthia. Ethnic Conflict and Political Development. Boston: Little, Brown, 1973.

Frankel, M.M. Tribe and Class in Monrovia. London: Oxford University Press, 1964.

Geertz, Clifford (ed.). Old Societies and New States. New York: The Free Press, 1963.

Glazer Nathan and Daniel Moynihan, ed. Ethnicity Theory and Experience. Cambridge, Mass.: Harvard University Press, 1975.

Das Gupta, Jyotirindra. "Nation, Region and Welfare: Ethnicity, Regionalism, and Development Politics in South Asia." The Annals 433, Sept. 1977, pp. 125-136.

Rakowska-Harmstone, Teresa. "Ethnicity in the Soviet Union." The Annals 433, Sept. 1977, pp. 73-87.

Harris, Richard (ed.). The Political Economy of Africa. New York: John Wiley, 1975.

Heeger, Gerald A. The Politics of Underdevelopment. New York: St. Martin's Press, 1974.

Heisler, Martin O. "Ethnic Conflict in the World Today: An Introduction." The Annals 433, Sept. 1977, pp. 1-5.

_____. "Managing Ethnic Conflict in Belgium." The Annals 433, Sept. 1977, pp. 32-46.

Horowitz, Donald. "Three Dimensions of Ethnic Politics," World Politics, 23, no. 2 (Jan. 1971): 244-51.

Horowitz, Donald L. "Cultural Movements and Ethnic Change." The Annals 433, Sept. 1977, pp. 6-18.

Huntington, Samuel P. and Joan M. Nelson. No Easy Choice: Political Participation in Developing Countries. Cambridge: Harvard University Press, 1976.

Johnson, R.W. "Guinea" in Dunn, (ed.). West African States 1978, pp. 36-65.

Johnson, Willard. "The Union des Populations du Cameroun in Rebellion: The Integrative Backlash of Inurgency." In Rotberg and Mazrui, (ed.). Protest and Power in Black Africa New York: Oxford University Press, 1970, pp. 671-92.

Kilson, Martin. Political Change in a West African State. New York: Atheneum, 1969, Part V, Chapters 14-17, pp. 219-296.

Kuper, Leo and M.G. Smith. Pluralism in Africa. Berkeley: University of California Press, 1969.

Lemarchand, Rene. "Political Clientelism and Ethnicity in Tropical Africa." APSR (March 1972).

Lewis, W. Arthur. Politics in West Africa. New York: Oxford University Press, 1965.

Lijphart, Arend. The Politics of Accommodation: Pluralism and Democracy in the Netherlands. Berkeley: University of California Press, 1968.

_____. "Consociational Democracy." World Politics (Jan. 1969).

Luckham, Rubin. The Nigerian Military. London: Cambridge University Press, 1971.

Mafeje, A. "The Ideology of Tribalism." Journal of Modern African Studies 9, no. 2 (1971): 253-261.

Markovitz, Irving L. (ed.). African Politics and Society. New York: The Free Press, 1970.

Markovitz, Irving L. Power and Class in Africa. Englewood, N.J.: Prentice-Hall, 1977.

Mazrui, Ali A. Cultural Engineering and Nation-Building in East Africa. Evanston: Northwestern University Press, 1972, Chapters 6-9, pp. 85-146.

McRoberts, Kenneth. "Quebec and the Canadian Political Crisis." The Annals 433 Sept. 1977; pp. 19-31.

Melson, Robert and Howard Wolpe. Nigeria: Modernization and the Politics of Communalism. East Lansing: Michigan State University Press, 1971.

Morrison, Donald G., R.C. Mitchell, J.N. Paden and N.M. Stevenson. Black Africa: A Comparative Handbook. New York: The Free Press, 1972.

O'Brien, Donald B.C. "Senegal." In Dunn, (ed.) West African States, 1978, pp. 173-188.

O'Connell, James. "The Inevitability of Instability." Journal of Modern African Studies (Sept. 1967).

Olorunsola, Victor A. (ed.). Politics of Cultural Subnationalism. New York: Doubleday, 1972.

_____. Social Reconstruction in Two African States. Washington, D.C.: University Press of America, 1977.

Parenti, Michael. "Ethnic Politics and the Persistence of Ethnic Identification," APSR 62 (1967): 717-726.

Rathbone, Richard. "Ghana." In Dunn (ed.) West African States, 1978. pp. 22-35.

Rodee, Carlton C., T.J. Anderson, C.Q. Christol, and T.H. Greene. Introduction to Political Science (3rd ed.). New York: McGraw-Hill, 1976.

Said, Abdul A. and Luis R. Simmons. Ethnicity in an International Context: The Politics of Disassociation. New Brunswick: Transaction Books, 1976.

Schwarz, F.A.O. Nigeria: The Tribe, the Nation or the Race. Cambridge: M.I.T. Press, 1965.

Spiro, Herbert J. Africa: The Primacy of Politics. New York: Random House, 1966.

Staniland, Martin. "The Three-Party System in Dahomey." Journal of African History 14, nos. 2-3, 1973.

Terchek, Ronald J. "Conflict and Cleavage in Northern Ireland." The Annals 433 Sept. 1977, pp. 47-59.

Varma, S.N. "National Unity and Political Stability in Nigeria." International Studies 4 (1963), pp. 265-80.

Wallerstein, Immanuel. "Ethnicity and National Integration in West Africa." Cahiers d'Etudes Africaines 3 (Oct. 1960), pp. 129-39.

Welch, Claude E. Jr. (ed.). Soldier and State in Africa. Evanston: Northwestern University Press, 1970.

William G. and T. Turner "Nigeria." In Dunn, (ed.). West African States 1978, pp. 132-172.

Young, Crawford. The Politics of Cultural Pluralism. Madison: University of Wisconsin Press, 1976.

16 Huaman Poma and the Space of Purity
Sara Castro-Klaren

To speak of ethnic separatist movements in Latin America is at first glance tantamount to the contemplation of an absence. Historically, one can easily, if perhaps hurriedly, explain this phenomenon by making reference to the swift and almost total collapse of the structures of the two Indian civilizations whose fate was to face European horses, arms, and disease, let alone civil war.(1)

Immediately after the conquest, the only groups that managed to escape the freshly-released forces of integration were those ethnic communities at the periphery of the great empires, such as the Yaquis of Mexico and the American Southwest. The resistance of the Incas in Vilcabamba lasted barely forty years, from 1532-72.(2) In spite of the fact that they managed to improve their army with horses and swords, defeat was written in the wind when Manco Inca met the Spaniards and their Huanca allies in battle. The empire crumbled. The ethnic groups that the Incas had forcibly brought under their rule were on the loose,(3) and the now rebel Incas simply could not secure enough territory to afford the luxury of a separate realm. After Viceroy Toledo's execution of Tupac Amaru I in 1572, the Inca aristocracy gave up and "collaborated very closely with the interest of the metropoli."(4)

The collapse of an Indian leadership capable of expressing the desire for separation from the Spanish colonial world does not, however, tell the full story of the forces of ethnic separatism or its manifestations in Latin American history. Under close scrutiny and with an ear attuned to the underside of history, that is to the history of the majorities, one can detect a large number of social and political phenomena in the history of Latin America whose importance and meaning has been overlooked because ethnicity has been ignored to a large

extent.   One reason for this neglect has been the delicately
complex nature of the ethnic factor in Latin American society.
Even before the conquest, but especially after the widespread
miscegenation that it brought about, ethnic categories constantly shifted, and the composition and destinies of ethnic
groups changed as the result of economic, legal, social, and
political modifications.

Nevertheless, there were a number of rebellions and
millenarian movements in Brazil and Peru, just to give two
examples, in which a desire for ethnic separation, may have
played a much larger role than is customarily assumed.
Antonio Conselheiro, a peasant who preached about the end of
the world and wanted to restore the moral order of the
monarchy, led the famous rebellion of the Canudos in northeastern Brazil in 1896.   This challenge to the central government by the impoverished peasantry of a drought-ravaged area
has several of the characteristics of other ethnic separatist
movements.   Euclines da Cunha, a writer whose coverage of
the rebellion changed the Brazilian elite's image of the country, squarely faced the question of race and ethnicity when he
recognized that a "new Brazilian race made out of the mixed
population of racial hybrids - Indian, black, and European -
would become the bedrock of the country."

Perhaps the clearest example of an ethnic separatist
movement can be found in the Yucatan war of the castes of
1848,(5) a war fought by the descendants of the Maya in order
to overthrow their white and mestizo masters.

Furthermore, it is no longer considered a wild assertion
to say that the diversity of pre-Columbian ethnic nations along
Andean South America should be counted as an important
factor in the splintering of the Spanish Colonial Empire after
the wars for independence.   This does not mean that Chibcha,
Quito, Aymara, and Quechua Indians, had the political or
military wherewithal to fight for nations of their own, or even
for ones which they would be included.   What it means is that
some of the substantial differences that marked the pre-
Columbian nations remained after the devastation of the
conquest.   In time, these differences silently shaped the
colonial societies that were to emerge into independent nations
after Spain left its American dominion.

Perhaps the most striking examples of a history of ethnic
separatism can be found in Peru.   The sixteenth century was
plagued by a series of Indian and mestizo - the offspring of
Spaniards and Indians - rebellions.   For very good reasons,
each of the groups - the mestizos, the Indians, and the
Spaniards - saw itself as the proper heir to the land and the
power.   At every turn, the crown proved to be the master of
the situation.   In 1737, after a long period of peace, Ignacion
Torote, a Pangoa Indian, led a war against the Spanish missionaries, who were destroying the Indian culture while prop-

agating the faith. With the help of the inhospitable, subtropical nature of his area, Torote and his followers managed
to hold off the Spanish missionaries for a long time. Fewer
than ten years later, in 1742, Juan Santos Atahualpa, pro-
claiming himself a direct descendant of the Inca Atahualpa, led
a huge rebellion in the central, subtropical area of Peru, with
the full intention of recapturing the entire territory of the
viceroyalty and reestablishing an Indian kingdom. His
thousands of followers believed that he was divine.

By far the most successful and famous of these rebellions
was led by Jose Gabriel Condorcanqui. A highly-educated and
influential mestizo, Condorcanqui had tried repeatedly, and
unsuccessfully, to gain some justice for the Indians of his
district. In 1780, he changed his name to Tupac Amaru II -
after the pubescent heir to the Incan throne whom the
Spaniards had executed in 1572 - and, with the secret support
of many highly placed individuals, embarked on the most
serious challenge the colonial administration had yet seen. His
armies and thousands of followers believed that he would
restore the Inca kingdom, and that those Indians who killed
Spaniards would be born again. Tupac Amaru II won several
battles, thus dispelling the myth of Spanish invincibility, but
eventually his forces waned. In 1781, he was quartered, after
having been made to witness the execution of his family and
friends. Tupac Amaru II has been used by the Peruvian
leftist military regime as a symbol of social and economic
justice for the peasantry.

In the nineteenth century, Pedro Pablo Atusparia led a
revolt against the central government after it imposed yet
another intolerable tax on the Indians. Atusparia was the
mayor (varayok) of several Indian villages in Huaraz, a
province in the central highlands of Peru. His poorly-armed
followers swept through the area, but were finally defeated by
the armies of the central government. Unlike Tupac Amaru II,
Atusparia was not put to death; the Indigenista movement was
in full swing, and Atusparia was praised in newspaper articles
and orations. Since then, there have been many other Indian
rebellions, usually as the result of population pressures.
However, none have had the character of a separatist movement. This is not surprising in view of the departure of the
Spaniards, the tremendous recovery of the Indian population,
and the enormous forces for national integration which have
been at work. The recent efforts of the central government to
make Quechua the second national language must be read
within the context of nationalism, and the recovery of the
Indian culture as part of that national identity.

Although the question of separation has been rendered
mute by the fact that the Indians constitute the great majority
of the population, ethnic pride,(6) the restoration of the Inca
empire,(7) and a latent hostility to Spanish rule and its repub-

lican variants have far-reaching roots.(8) It is the depth of
this ideology and desire for Indian supremacy, as articulated
by an Indian writer, that I wish to analyze; in one way or
another, it has spoken to people such as Tupac Amaru, and it
continues to address the many problems of ethnicity that per-
meate the social and political processes of contemporary Peru.

As a member of the Inca ruling class on his mother's
side, Huaman Poma de Ayala lived and wrote within the
political issues of the sixteenth century. His plan for an
ethnically-homogeneous state had two stages. The first would
use the newest tool available to his vanquished race - the
written word. The second would establish his "good
government."

Dazzled by the political power of writing, Poma saw
himself bypassing the Colonial administration and addressing
the King of Spain through (folio 960-63) his book, El Primer
Nueva Cronica y Buen go bierno.(9)   His book would accomplish what his physical and legal being had failed to do at
every court and before every corregidor to whom he had taken
his complaints. After reading his long historical reflexion, so
Poma thought, the King could not help but conclude, and order in writing, that the Indians of Peru could and should
rule themselves in order to ensure the survival of the Spanish
Empire. Huaman Poma would use a pen rather than the arms
that could not be turned into victory at Vilcabamba. This
writing project was conceived only a few years after the
execution in 1572 of the last Inca heir, the adolescent Tupac
Amaru I; for which Huaman Poma reproaches Toledo bitterly
(folio 937). Separation by force had proven futile. It was
time to face the invaders within the space they had just inaugurated and within the set of rules that they claimed organized and justified their cosmos, and thus their recent
conquest of the Inca empire - the written word.

With easy hindsight, Huaman Poma's project sounds at
best paradoxical, and, at worst, naive. Yet an examination of
the deft manipulation of the data and arguments contained in
El Primer Nueva Cronica y Buen Gobierno shows that Poma's
intellectual tools, political aims, and challenge to the Christian
ideology that made the conquest possible were chosen with
great care and intelligence. His chronicle is not at all the
garbled product of a primitive mind, refusing that light of the
European Rennaissance as some early commentators wrote.(10)
That the thrust of his project was historically valid was
demonstrated by the chorus of Spanish voices that advocated
separation, but not separate rule, for the Indians. The
establishment of Franciscan millenarian kingdoms and Jesuit
utopian states constituted the partial actualization of his
dream.(11) Silent for over three hundred years, his manuscript sets down the blue-print that would maintain Indian
ethnic integrity, even at the risk of advocating separatism.

Throughout writing, he never tires of repeating "Dios permita que no nos acabemos." (May God grant that we shall not disappear.)

What we know about Poma is what he has chosen to tell the King about himself in El Primer Nueva Cronica y Buen Governo.(12) On his father's side, he was a descendant of the Yarovilcas, lords of the northern part of the Inca Empire. His mother was one of the legitimate daughters of Tupac Inca Yupanqui, (folio 15 and also 1920-22) the penultimate Inca. Born after the death of Atahualpa in 1532, he claims to have spent most of his 87 years resisting Spanish abuses ("mira cristiano a mi todo se me ha hecho," folio 916). Having been expelled by the greedy corregidors from his own province he travelled during the last thirty years of this life collecting materials for his letter to the king; observing and protecting the condition of his fellow Indians in the viceroyalty of Peru.

Huaman Poma spent a great deal of his time reconnoitering the land, quizzing the memory of the elderly and observing the brutal behavior of the Spaniards with the detailed care, and the soundless rage of a Spanish inquisitor. His reflexions - a labor of pain, for he tells us that to write is to cry - eventually became an enormous manuscript, with 500 illustrations and over 1000 pages of text. Almost nothing is known about how, when, or where he became conversant with newly-introduced European categories of thought,(13) as well as the Spanish controversy about the human rights of Indians. Professing not to know Latin or to have the benefit of any degree or schooling ("no soy letrado" [folio 8]), he apologizes for whatever blunders he may make in writing. Coming from the vanquished culture and from a purely oral native tradition, he approaches writing, a totally new category of thought, with trepidation.(14)

The Primer Nueva Cronica, like the Bible, perhaps the closest model Huaman kept in mind, is about many things, and can be put to many uses. It contains invaluable data about pre-Inca and Inca civilizations,(15) as well as detailed descriptions of the drastic Indian population decline in the sixteenth century.(16) It also stands as a metaphor for the meeting of two worlds within an individual mind.

The long argument for separatism, which for the greater part of the manuscript remains oblique and intertwined with innumerable other topics, has often been described as an outline for Utopia. Trying to differentiate between ideology and utopia, Karl Mannheim writes:

> Every period in history contained ideas transcending the existing order, but these did not function as utopias, they were rather the appropriate ideologies of this stage of existence as long as they were "organically" and harmoniously

> integrated into the world view characteristic of the
> period....Not until certain groups embodied these
> wish images into their actual conduct, and tried to
> realize them, did these ideologies become
> utopias.(17)

With this in mind and in anticipation of Poma's arguments for
"good government" that is to say "Christian government," it
would seem that Poma's manuscript constitutes a set of ideological propositions not so "harmoniously" integrated into the
"characteristic world view of the period" (European), even
though they were expounded as the rationale for the
domination of the newly-discovered inhabitants of the New
World. The existing ideologies (Andean as well as European)
had not anticipated reality; and, during Poma's time, they
were contorted in order to absorb the shock of reality.
Furthermore, if we take European "Christian" ideology to be
the characteristic world view of the dominant group, and if we
see Huaman Poma as an individual member of the vanquished
group attempting to turn this ideology into actual behavior,
Manheim's differentiating definition is not helpful. To think in
Manheim's terms, one would have to hold that the ideology of
the Spanish conqueror and colonizer in the sixteenth century
was uniform, when, in fact, the Crown, the missionary orders,
and the colonizers were often at odds as to their understanding of the goals and the meaning of Spanish endeavour
and behavior in the New World. One would also have to
assume that the dominant class and the vanquished Indians
already formed one single social organism. To complicate the
matter further, it is not known to what extent Poma's wish-
image of an ethnic separate state was something the rest of his
group, which was not monolithic either, was prepared, ideologically or practically, to turn into actual behavior. Therefore we must view Poma's ideological appeals and blueprint for
the future outside restricting categories, such as ideol-
ogy/dormant praxis and utopia/activated ideological praxis.
   In assessing the impact that the New World had on the
Old, it appears certain that Thomas More's critique of un-
restrained economic individualism and inclination for communal
property rights were inspired by what he had read about
Indian societies in Vespucci's letters.(18) It is perhaps because Huaman Poma's blueprint for the future shares this
feature with More's insular society that it has been so readily
labeled "utopian." There is, however, a very significant
difference in the dreams of these two contemporaries. Huaman
Poma was using his own historical past, a concrete experience
albeit idealized, as a model for a future close at hand; More's
reverie was motivated by a distant and imperfectly-known
human order. Because Huaman Poma's model was part of his
own experience, his blueprint was not for some far-off future

time, nor was it a dubious experiment. His separate state could have happened right then and there. All that was necessary was to sever the ties to the Spanish world, and keep the new space hermetically sealed from the outside. Then the task of restoration - not experimentation - could have begun.(19) The effects of the Spanish invasion could have been absorbed by the Andean society as a severe pruning from which the trunk of the tree could have recovered.

The functional opposition in Poma's mind, a typical Renaissance opposition but also a very concrete one in his experience, was between the Spanish towns and the Indian communities. For Poma, the task at hand was to accept the conquest and cut losses, leaving the towns and cities to the Spaniards with their black slaves and their mestizo broods. The Indians could go back to their villages and fields, where they could start to regroup according to their pre-Inca ethnic divisions.(20)

Like most Indian or mestizo writers of his time, Huaman Poma had experienced a complete loss of power and status.(21) In this sense, he writes from the margins of established power, yet he does not write against authority or against the forms of repression that civilization entails, as Charles Fourier does at the end of the eighteenth century in France.(22) Were these two dreamers of a new order to meet, they would find very little common ground. Huaman Poma's moral sensitivity knows no bounds; his capacity for ethical outrage is never exhausted; and he expects his "Christian reader" to agree with him. Damned be the reader who finds himself unable to decry one more flogging, rape, decapitation, or dispossession. He is obsessed by his desperate sense of loss and his urgency to restore the world before it is too late. In Poma's eyes, Fourier and his phalanxes of pleasure-seeking individuals would probably deserve to be cast in the sea, along with the avaricious corregidor, the voracious judge, and the sensual priest. These people had come to America to corrupt a just and uncontaminated order. They set the world upside down (el mundo al reves), and, in a way, they fulfilled Christian hell where, "habra hambre, y sed y llanto y crugir de dientes y gusanos y escorpiones" ["there will be hunger, thirst, tears and gnashing of teeth, worms and scorpions"] (folio 944). For Poma the moralist, a cult of the individual's senses, preferences, and emotions would only amount to further perversion.

Before proceeding to a description of the organization of the Indian separate state under Spanish rule, the ideological basis for Huaman Poma's gambit should be examined, for it determines the parameters of the dreamer's imagination.(23)

A sense of duality pervades all key aspects of the text. The writer is at least bilingual. The manuscript is both written and drawn for "readers" who can read abstract characters and for others who read pictures. It encompasses a historical reflexion and a blueprint for the future. His discourse posits, further, two other types of readers, the Christian reader of the published manuscript (folio 7) - the public - and the Christian reader - the King - of the unpublished text.

Roughly the first part of the text is addressed to Philip II (dead by 1598), and the second supposes Philip III as its reader. There can be no doubt, as unthinkable as it may seem, that Poma fully expected the King to be his first reader, to rule on his proposals, and to order the publication of his work. His new authorial persona and soaring pride allows Huaman Poma to imagine a scene in which he holds forth in dialogue with the King. Either of the Philips would ask him, as they would of their most trusted advisers, such as the Duke of Alba with whom he compares himself, for his council on how to put an end to the brutal ravagins of the Spanish petty bureaucrats and the depopulation of Peru.

On what grounds did Huaman Poma base his pretensions? How could a vanquished man persuade the King to set up a separate realm exclusively for Indians, when the New World was already teeming with mestizos, mulattoes, blacks, zambos, and whites? The answer is very complex, but at least part of it entails Huaman Poma's reading or misreading of ideological struggle as the most important determinant of his time.

Confidence in the power of the word as metaphor of the world would appear to have motivated Poma. Although he argues without using linear, explicit logic and prefers the accumulation of data, what he finally constructs is a vast net of allusions. The power of his descriptive material, as well as his many asides, reaches full meaning if one does not forget that the context for his writing is the theological-political issues that the discovery of the Indian raised in Europe. This Indian writer was not only keenly aware of the fact that one had to engage in religious discourse to settle political problems, but he also recognized them as indistinguishable from one another. Paramount in his mind was the rationale given to justify war on the Indians and the conquest itself - evangelization. Thus he sought, with naive sincerity or with great cunning, one cannot tell, the use of the same weapons that had declared him and his vanquished race to be irresponsible children.(24) Turning the aim of the weapons around, he could show that the Spaniards were in fact bad Christians; sensual, deceiving, uncharitable, greedy, etc., and thus had no right to rule the land, much less the Indians.(25) Questioning the legitimacy of the Spanish conquest made his work not only subversive, along with the works of many Spaniards who had posed the same question, but probably also heretical because it came from an Indian, an idolatrous savage.

Throughout his repetitious and tiresome description of sadistic Spanish abuses, he tells the King that his government

is inept. The King is informed of his failure to keep up his
part of the bargain with the Indian peoples: land was to be
exchanged for souls. Both Philips are reminded that they are
not sending evangelizing priests and encomenderos to their
subjects in America. Rather, they are unleashing a pack of
"rats, cats, lions, and vipers" (folio 704) on the innocent
flesh of a faithful and excellent labor force. The comparison
of the Spaniards to carniverous fauna carries greater political
than literary impact. Their animalization stresses the "wild"
behavior of the "civilizing" masters, and Poma thus places a
direct challenge to the "spiritual" rationale that supported the
ideology of exploitation and domination. The Indians, pure
"natural" flesh, are capable of two of the highest human
values in Poma's eyes: work and organized society. The
Spaniards, in contrast, live off the labor of others, and cannot even organize the running of the Empire.

He has just scored a major ideological point. Yet he
knows from observing the Spaniards with whom he comes in
contact that the ethical part of their ideology does not motivate
most of their behavior, otherwise they would not be flogging
women who are one egg short in their tribute. So he aims for
the King's pocketbook, warning him of the disastrous consequences on his imperial economy should the native population
(labor force) be weakened to the point of extinction. The
king might listen to those who forecast doom for his soul and
his gold, but surely he would heed someone capable of
stemming disaster and guaranteeing a continuous flow of gold.

Poma imitates the Spanish and astutely placates the In-
quisition by making the reforma of souls the ostensible purpose
of his writing. The moral intent of his criticism will blunt the
dangerous political thrust of his examples and lamentations.

Ironically, it is at this juncture of his writing that the
blueprint for the future starts to become history. Besides
Christianity, universal reading and writing are the only
Spanish cultural tools that he is willing to retain (folio 792).
Everything else, except perhaps scissors, must be returned
from whence it came. For Poma, the best order is when
things and people remain where fate placed them originally: "el
espanol a Espana y el Negro a Guinea."

However sadistic (folios 566-591) and devastating Spanish
rule was demonstrated to be, the possibility of anything other
than reform was almost unthinkable. With the circulation of
the Breve Historia de la Destruccion de las Indias in 1542, Las
Casas had already convinced many of his contemporaries of the
Spaniards' moral unfitness for colonial rule. The Dominican
had even advanced the temerarious notion that the people who
were entitled to rule were the mestizos. Their fathers had
conquered the land and their mothers had inherited it. The
Crown's response was to enact more laws to protect the
Indians and to contain the restless, ambitious, and rebellious
mestizos.

In view of this mind set, what else could a man trying to claim the right of the Indians to rule themselves argue? He must persuade his Christian Reader, his master, that he is an equal human being.(26) Poma argues successfully that his fellow Indian is not just a human being by virtue of theological reasoning, but a human being by virtue of the history of his nation, which makes him at least equal to the task of ruling the land and the people. Scandalous, given European ethnocentrism? Yes. Impossible? Huaman Poma thought not at the time he began to write.

Consequently, Huaman Poma starts his long equalization argument with an assault on Time. Fully aware that the narrative composite of the Bible is the mechanism by which the Spaniards reckon time and the political legitimization of the events in it, Poma seeks the soft spots upon which he can graft Indian Time(27) into the single flow of Christian Time. His pressing need is to show Indians, and especially his ethnic group, the Yarovilcas, to be the descendants of Adam and Eve.(28) The flood seems to him, as it had to many Spanish missionaries and theologians,(29) to be an event plagued with enough confusion about who and how many were saved to admit the theory of a third age of creation, in which some of Noah's descendants were brought to populate the New World by God Himself. Here Poma follows the thought of his time, (both European and Indian) which regarded the idea of a single creation as the only possible one. This notion has continued to dominate European thought despite most modern and scientific expression, such as the theory of evolution and the Bering Strait migration of "Indians" to this hemisphere.

More concerned with the concrete mechanics of reproduction than with the Bible, Poma calculates how fast the land could have been populated. His preoccupation with population growth and decline is no mere intellectual indulgence. Some earlier commentators have said that he exhibits the peculiar fascination with numbers typical of the statistically-minded Incas. This may well be true, but it cannot be forgotten that he wants an Indian State for the express purpose of fostering the reproduction of Indians whose population decline had become an obsessive phrase ("se despueblan las Indias") in the minds of his contemporaries, Indians and Spanish alike. It is estimated that, between 1519 and 1605, the population in central Mexico declined by 95 percent; and, in Peru, between 1572 and 1620, by 50 percent. During the first decades of the conquest, the population of the coast of Peru also experienced a decline of 95 percent.(30)

Population growth was literally a game of life and death for his kin and kind at the moment of his writing. Here, as in other topos of his discourse, the concrete is welded to political ideology, and it, in turn, becomes inseparable from religious or cosmological considerations. Poma is keenly aware that the question of the original couple's descent lies at the doorstep of the great tabu of incest. The Incas' custom of marrying their sisters had been used to declare them immoral and unfit to rule, and thus deserving of Spanish subjugation. By resorting once more to confusion, he sees the avenue out of the zone of danger. He proposes that, like Adam and Eve, the founders of the third age in the New World must have lived very long lives and borne many sets of twins. There would have been so many people of mating age within such a short time that it would have become impossible to keep track of everyone's relations. And yet, when pages later he speaks of the Inca's claim to divide origin as Children of the Sun, he ruthlessly demolishes such pretentions by throwing the incest accusation in their faces. For Poma, the Inca's divine origins are nothing but a fraud; and what is more, Manco Capac was the fatherless creation of an ambitious mother-witch, who married her own son and then proceeded to fabricate the whole story of direct divine descent (folio 51).

If the charge of incest is dispelled from his Yarovilca ancestors in at least as muddled a manner as the Bible's, the question of human rights as the exclusive corollary to Christianity is not. The "discovery" of the New World had thrown most European notions of human nature - neither divine nor animal - into a crisis.(31) Contemporary theories on the right to make war and to take the spoils of conquest, as well as the economic, political, and social rights of the in- dividual subject of the state, had to be reexamined in the light of a new presence - the Indian. Huaman Poma's mind seems steeped in the debate that followed the publication of Las Casas' Destruction of the Indies, especially the one between Sepulveda and Vitoria. He must have had the access to the arguments on both sides. Of course, he saw and recorded the effects the dispute had on the daily life of his fellow man. The Indian's humanity loses ground with the passing of every day of Spanish rule, a rule that increasingly sees him as simply a body devoid of human rights or "spirit." Poma's gaze on this landscape of suffering and death is not exclusively moral; he sees dashed about him ("todo en el suelo")(folio 1024), with the dying of bodies, the broken families, in short the disappearance of a culture, the old hopes of the Indian nobility. Huaman's relatives had consoled themselves with the idea of superimposing the new crede onto the old cosmos, as the great price of continuity.

He next shows that, although just and moral government is the only justification for the existence of the state and the exercise of power, Christians have by no means a monopoly on it. Quite to the contrary, history - in the Old and the New World - allows him to prove that pagan rulers had been just and loved by their subjects to a greater degree than many a ruler who claims to govern in the name of the Christian Spanish King.

Although a great part of the book is dedicated to a recollection of the Inca social, political, and economic systems, a model system in Poma's mind, he claims that the foundations for it were put down during the times of the Yarovilcas. In a constant oscillation of feeling, he exhibits both the depths of disdain and the heights of admiration for the Incas. They represent to him what Indians are capable of accomplishing. He thus proceeds to make the case that they were just rulers, even though they were heathen, and even though they conquered and ruled over his male ancestors.

In another one of his calculations, he figures that Christ was born the same year as Julius Ceasar was born in Rome and Sinchi Roca in Cuzco, the two cosmological centers of the clashing empires. The thrust of his argument here has to do with just imperial expansion. Conquest and Empire found their justification, and still do, in their civilizing mission, now called development. For Huaman, the Roman Empire was no greater a civilizing force than the Inca empire had been, and both of these were no less virtuous than the Spanish Christian Empire itself. As if this were not enough, Poma then goes on to remind his readers that the Spaniards had lived under Roman rule for a very long time, and nobody faulted them for their previous obediance to pagan rule. Only when Santiago the Apostle took the word to them did they become Christian.(32) Therefore, the Spaniards are converts themselves, not really born to Christianity, not really such "old" Christians as they make themselves out to be. The holy city of Rome could preside over the Indians in the same way it presides over Spain. It is thus not inconceivable that the Indians could duplicate the faithful conversion of the Spaniards and become great defenders of the faith themselves, or saints, theologians, religious artists, all that human beings are capable of becoming. Proof can be readily found in the saintly life of his half-brother, Martin de Ayala, or in the writing of such pious books as the Primer Nueva Cronica.

The Yarovilcas' daring does not stop here. Good government requires appropriate delegation of authority, not mere lip service to a politico-religious doctrine. Christ himself gave the first and best example. He delegated His authority to St. Peter, and passed it down to the Popes in Rome. At this point in his argument, Huaman Poma invokes a pontifical order of the world by embarking on the most tedious and obscure recitation of the names and dates of the Popes, intertwined with the Inca line of descent. Some of its meaning becomes clear if one bears his equalizing quest in mind. In the flow of Christian-Pontifical time, there have been many lineages of rulers, all beholden to Rome for legitimization. Poma plunges to the heart of the matter when he gently and very obliquely reminds the King of Spain that his authority is tenable only under the Doctrine of Divine Rule. Christ left Peter; Peter left the Popes; the Popes authorize kings; kings authorize viceroys, and so on <u>ad infinitum</u>. A Yarovilca nobleman can be the King's second person, in the New World, as well as the bridge to a future separate Indian state.

The King's office has once more come through unscathed, even though the administration of justice that flows from it is under serious attack. The question is not whether Spain should have an empire in the New World, but rather, who should rule in the name of the chain: King   pope   Christ. Having shown the bureaucratic incompetence and moral unfitness of the Spaniards, Huaman Poma can see only one other logical choice - the Indians. They had done quite well without the benefit of Christianity, and, therefore, they could only be expected to do that much better with the gift of the new light.

The logical case, then, for separate Indian rule would seem to be closed. They were rational human beings, newly-introduced to Christianity, and, above all, they were historical, not natural. They had a place in time; this entitled them to continue to exist in the flow of Christian/Historical Time.

Unfortunately for Huaman Poma, the greatest <u>natural</u> enemy of all his ideological labor has yet to be disposed of - the <u>mestizo</u>. Nowhere does Huaman Poma make any effort to disguise his hatred for the <u>mestizo</u>. Although he does not mount a moral critique as he does of the Spaniards, his physical revulsion is often what informs his charges of the <u>mestizos'</u> laziness, shiftlessness, sensuality, and arrogance. Only zambos, the offspring of blacks and Indians are deserving of equal loathing. Poma is totally alienated from these people. Purity of blood and spotless descent are all-important to Poma; so much so that his unmitigated disgust for the zambo, the <u>mestizo</u> and the mulatto can be turned into unexpected pity and compassion for the black slave, who is "human too."

Central and overwhelming to his mind is the part <u>mestizaje</u> plays in eroding Indian culture. The image of the <u>mestizo</u> touches a vulnerable spot in all levels of Poma's consciousness, from the physical to the moral. <u>Mestizaje</u> means that Indian women will bear children whose <u>physical</u> being cannot perpetuate the material being of the Indian men. The males of a staunch patriarchal culture will thus be cursed with barren lives. Poma tells of many a husband who has come back from the <u>mita</u> (forced labor tribute) to find his house full of <u>mestizo</u> babies. The man abandons his home and village, known in order not to give vent to his disgust, fear, by killing the babies of the conqueror in his woman ("por no matarlos"). The normal narcissistic love of the parent for the child, the ego love of the ethnic group for itself is negated by <u>mestizaje</u>. The threat to self-continuity, to self-differentiation, the fear of racial extinction and alienation is more than Huaman Poma and his fellow male Indians can bear.

Poma's own father must have faced this trauma. Poma's "dear" half-brother, Martin de Ayala, was a mestizo. The rape, seduction, or willing participation of his own mother in the birth of a mestizo could constitute the grounds for Poma's psychological and physical revulsion. What is more, in a rare personal note, he confesses that "mira cristiano, a mi todo se me ha hecho, hasta quererme quitar mi mujer un fraile mercedario ... pretenden que fueran los indios bobos, asnos, para acabar de quitarle cuanto tiene, hacienda, mujer, hija" ["Look Christian, everything has been done to me, even to the point where a meredarean priest wanted to take my wife away from me. They think that the Indians are dumb, stupid, so that they can take all his possessions from him; land, wife, daughter"] (folio 916).

Mestizaje also means, by and large, the group's loss of control over the reproductive and kinship system of Indian society. Huaman Poma knows that no law protecting the Indians can have any effect whatsoever over the intractable destruction of mestizaje.

From the data that he records it would seem that the women do not share his revulsion at the notion of sexual and cultural intercourse.(33) Although some, the good ones in Poma's eyes, felt so ashamed and alienated after being raped by a priest or corregidor that they ran way and were never heard from again; others were not horrified by the idea of becoming the concubines of Spaniards or black men. Huaman comments, "Y se acaban los indios por no tener mujeres y porque todas las mujeres se van detras de los/espanoles" ["And the Indians face extinction because they have no women, because the women run away in pursuit of the Spaniards."] (folio 1018). Worried that this new freedom in mating has affected the Indians because it has "desatado tanta lujuria entre los indios" ["unleashed such sensual desire among the Indians"] (folio 888), and concerned with the depopulation of Indian towns, Huaman Poma insults the women who are leaving for the cities with the Spaniards. "Las mujeres salen, se ausentan salen de noche, se hacen bellacas, putas" ["The women leave their homes, they go out at night, they become fools and whores"] (folio 880). For him, these women are all traitors and whores. He cannot see any other motivation. However, as he describes the life of the ideal woman in pre-Hispanic times, it would seem that many of those who left sought a refuge from the life of endless toil and submission to male authority in the house, in the field, and in every other sphere of life.

Work is the other point of contention Poma has with the mestizos. Although his indignation burns with implacable fury when the Spaniards do not pay the Indians for their work, the fact that the mestizo is not obligated to perform the same forced labor is unbearable for Poma. It is equivalent of the world upside down, hell itself. If the mestizos have no labor obligations, let them be barred from the Indian villages. Let them join the world of the Spaniards, with their mulattoes and zambos. Or better yet, deport them to Chile, cast them into the sea, but keep them away from Poma's sight; like the cuckhold of the Spanish theater, he wants to kill them himself.

Miscegenation not only involves the sin of a priest against God and society, robs the virginity and decency of Indian women, and produces the cursed, rebellious Mestizo, but, above all, it weakens the labor force of the Indian communities; the women leave and their offspring are not subject to Indian labor systems and tribute. The mestizo is a plague almost as ruinous as the Spaniard himself.(34)

Worse yet, the plague is on the King himself; without Indians, there would be no skilled labor:

se ha de perder la tierra porque ellos (espanoles y mestizos) han causado gran dano y pleitos y perdiciones. Se perdera la tierra y quedara solitario y despoblado el reino y quedara muy pobre el rey por causa del dicho correigidor y demas espanoles que roban a los indios sus haciendas, casa, sementeras, pastos, y sus mujeres, por asi casadas y doncellas, todas paren ya mestizos y cholos, hay clerigo que tiene ya veinte hijos y no hay remedio. [The land will grow sterile because they have caused great damage and litigation and losses. The land will grow foul and the kingdom will become solitary and depopulated and the king shall grow very poor and all because of the corregidor and the said Spaniards who steal from the Indians house and fields, all manner of possessions, and women; whether they be married or virgins, they all bear mestizos and cholos; there are priests who have already fathered 20 children and there is no stopping any of these.] (folio 446)

An Indian state would consequently be dedicated to the three items that would satisfy the King's highest ideological and economic interest: it would produce loyal Christian subjects, goods destined to satisfy the survival needs of the labor force and the surplus needs of the state. Despite Las Casas' argument in favor of the inheritance rights of the mestizos, Poma makes it clear that the only people fit to rule and capable of "buen gobierno" are the Indians. Mestizos would be the least capable, for they have no history and no cosmos on which to rely for a model.

Which Indians will be capable of delivering the promises just made to the King? Because Poma's blueprint for the future Indian state is modeled on the past, he envisions the

surviving and historically-reflective Indian nobility as the ones
who will carry on the traditions of good government. The old
remember, and they also embody a series of negations basic to
the administration of good government.(35) Old men no longer
harbor a desire for personal pleasure or acquisition of power;
they do not suffer the lust of younger men; they do not covet
an excess of material goods because, in a society without
private property, there is no question of inheritance; and they
are not moved by political ambition. Worldly honor and the
glory of power is no longer a temptation for those so close to
the kingdom of God. The shortness of their lives, the
proximity of death, compels them to ethical behavior. God
forbid the follies and the experimental desires of youth!

The conservative profile of Poma's vision prefers the
elderly. If he proposes sweeping change in the present, it is
to stem the chaos unleashed in Peru by the conquest. Poma,
like other dreamers of a perfect society, proposes an ultimate
stage of complete stability marked by its purity, coherence,
unity, and lack of contradictions. A mixture of categories, an
ambiguity of positions, and pluralities act as destabilizers in
Poma's scheme. Singleness, separation, differentiation, and
classification foster order, knowledge, planning, and predict-
ability. Every object, every task, every act, and every
office, must be clearly distinguished from every other to avoid
confusion and error. Thus, he would have people dressed in
different colors and ornaments to signal unequivocally their
occupations, stations, regional origins, and responsibilities.
He could then take pleasure in the intellectual delight of
order: "Que bien se ve cada uno en su traje!" (folio 797).

In an anticipation of modern anthropology, division of
labor and kinship constitute for Poma the fundamental
principles of human organization. In the social contract,
struck between the single member of the community - I am
staying away from the term "individual" because I don't believe
that Poma defined it in the same way the European has over
the last two hundred years - and the state, the latter
guarantees the universal right and obligation to work and to
procreate. For Poma, all human relations are cast in terms of
work. Sex, physical capacity, and skills would be, in mimesis
of the Inca order, the three criteria for the assignation of
work. Children would begin to work as soon as they could
spend significant time away from their mothers. Before the
age of five, when they start catching small birds for feathers,
they could sweep, bring firewood, and help to card wool.
Poma delights in describing how each member of the community
would work, and therefore exist socially, from the age of three
until death. Poma praises the Incas because they gave work
and mates to even those born with birth defects. Often, the
hunchback, the deaf, or even the blind became the best
weavers and potters in the community. They also bore healthy

children.   Under Spanish rule the old and the sick asphyxiate
the towns with their useless bodies and outstretched hands,
attempting to consume what they can no longer produce.
Destruction of the family as a result of the introduction
of new modes of production and reproduction, Poma's bitterest
complaint against the Spanish administration.(36)   Emotional
comfort, a sense of self-respect, love, and all other "spiritual"
values for which the family is idealized cannot be disentangled
from his view of the family as the basic unit of procreation
and production.(37)   Because the family works primarily for
its needs, it is allowed a few items of private property, such
as household utensils and domestic animals.   The surplus
produced by work inside and outside the household, whether it
be textiles or eggs, sustains the state.   In a non-monetary
economy, state officials are paid in goods destined for consumption rather than accumulation, and especially not destined
for the Spaniards wasteful consumption in unnecessary ban-
quets and ornate clothing.   The role of the state would be
minimal, and thus not expensive.   There would never be
"comenderos (que) gastan largamente como no les cuesta su
trabajo, ni sudor, sino que pide a los pobres indios" ["These
comenderos spend lavishly because it is not the product of
their work or their sweat, but what they take from the poor
Indians'] (folio 559).   And the King would be given his tribute
in labor, and in goods - silver, coca, cattle and of course
gold, to do with the latter as he pleased.   The conversion of
the goods into uses and values outside of the Indian economy
did not concern him, as long as the Spaniards kept their
wicked system to themselves.
In this world of work, the state would be comparable to a
wart on the smooth epidermis of a giant body of laborers.
The state was to be an invisible presence in charge of overseeing the functioning of a society in a steady-state.   Slow
adaptation to unexpected breakdowns of the perfect machine is
the most Poma's consciousness can tolerate; there is nothing
more abhorrent to him, save the mestizos, than the notion of
rapid change or experimentations, or change in one's station in
life at the expense of the work of others.(38)   In one of his
many imagined scenes, he ridicules the pauper Spanish family
that fancies riches for its brood in the New World:

What the Spanish Christians who have many
children imagine is all gold and silver.   Husband
and wife spend their days and nights thinking.
The husband tells the wife:

"You know I am always thinking that all our
boys should study for the priesthood."

The wife answers:

"How well conceived and said my lord and
husband, for God has given us these many children
in order to enrich us. Yago will be a cleric [yagito
sera cleriguito] and so will Francis. This way they
can earn [ganar] money and send us Indians to
serve us, send us money and gifts: porridge,
chickens, eggs, fruit, corn, potatoes, and even the
greens the Indians eat. It would be a good thing
for our Martin to be a Dominican and for Gonzalo to
be a Mercedarian. But it would not be a good
thing for either one to join the Franciscan or the
Jesuits, because the ones who join those orders
forget their parents and stay poor and become
saints and make no money.(folio 546)

In order to keep the Mercedarians and the other priests
at home, and for the separate Indian state to become a reality,
the second stage of the utopia must take place in writing.
The King must decree its reality, and a return to the past will
begin with the return of the land to its original owners. Poma
writes:

Es muy justo que se vuelva y restituya las dichas
tierras y corrales y pastos que se vendieron en
nombre de su majestad, porque de bajo de con-
ciencia no se le puede quitarsela a los naturales
lexitimos proprietarios de las tierras....Despues que
se les vuelva a los Indios e Indias les valdra muy
mucho a su majestad"["It is only just that the lands
and fields should be restored to the Indians, because in good conscience these lands which were
sold under your majesty's order cannot really be
taken away from the Indians, the only legitimate
owners of the lands....After they are returned to
the Indians, the lands will be worth a great deal
more to your majesty"]. (folio 536)

He is not unaware of the impossible web of complications that
would arise with the return of communal property, especially
after the initial dispersal of Indians because of war and the
encomienda. Therefore, land transfer would go back to the
time of his grandfather, Tupac Inca Yupanqui

y si fuere o comun sementera o pastos de los pueb-
los de quien fuere justo titulo dese abinicio y desde
Topa Inca Yupanqui, ...y a los indios que no fuere
heredero se lo arriende y paguen un tanto al dicho
dueno [and if the land were communal land or
forest give it back to whoever held it under the
reign of Topa Inca Yupanqui ... and the Indians

who would thus receive nothing, should have a right to rent the land and pay the owners]. (folio 536)

No matter how attractive or how necessary the separate Indian state might have seemed to the King, abrogation of the rights of conquest was a politically-impossible card to play. The Crown had enough trouble controlling its Spanish subjects in the New World to risk, even on paper, the economic and political autonomy of the Indians. Even though Poma dangled the promise of greater surpluses for the Crown, let alone more and better Christian souls, the forces that shaped the Spanish colonial world, often in great disparity with the Crown's public wishes, could not be controlled by an ideological appeal. El Primer Nueva Cronica, aside from rescuing a cultural legacy from oblivion, convincingly proposes a separate ethnic state within the ideological parameters of the conquering culture. Poma's greatest failure, one no greater than that of many of his contemporaries who sought similar changes, was to believe that history could be changed by the appeal of one Prince ("que soy su principe y protector" [folio 981]) to another, no matter how absolute the power of that King or Prince. Although Poma understood the functioning of society as an organic process, he did not accord drastic political change a similar attribute. A book could be written on the reasons for the failure of his dream. A glimpse of the impossibility of his dream begins to hound him as he writes the last one hundred pages of his manuscript. He defends his fellow Indians as their Prince must, even if the new masters refuse to hear his complaints: "y asi escribo esta historia para que sea memoria y se ponga en el archivo de la justicia" ["and thus I write this history so that it will serve as a memory and be placed in the archives of justice"] (folio 981). With this sentence, he begins to separate his work and his dreams from the rest of the world.

When Huaman Poma asks how an ethnic and cultural entity can endure, he is asking a crucial historical question. Further, when he cites overwork and race mixture as the principal dangers to his culture's endurance, he perceived most accurately the desperate moment the Indians of Peru were living.

Woodrow Wilson Borah's analysis of the depopulation process of Mexico spells out today what Huaman Poma was trying to articulate in Peru at the end of the sixteenth century:

The sharp and continued decrease of Mexico's Indians from the Conquest until the beginning of the eighteenth century must be accounted one of the most important factors in Mexican history. Had

the original populations of central Mexico borne the
impact of the conquest with little demographic loss,
there could have been scant room for their conquerors except as administrators and receivers of
tribute. Mexico today would be an Indian area from
which, in the process of achieving independence
from Spain, a white upper stratum holding itself
apart like the British in India, could easily, have
been expelled.(39)

Poma's dream was rooted in reality, and it could have
come about if his worst fears -depopulation and mestizaje - had
not galloped ahead of his high hopes.

NOTES

1. For the question of disease as a formidable ally of the
    Spaniards, see Alfred W. Crosby, The Columbia Exchange:
    Biological and Cultural Consequences of 1492   (Westport,
    Ct.: Greenwood Press, 1972).   On the question of con-
    quest and armies: "The army that captured Tenochtlitlan
    was really an army of Indians captained by a few Span-
    iards" says Lewis Hanke (ed.), History of Latin American
    Civilization, Sources and Interpretations, vol. 1 (Boston:
    Little Brown and Company, 1973), p. 168. For the case
    of Peru, see Waldemar Espinosa Soriano, Los Huancas,
    Aliados de los conquistadores; Tres informaciones ineditas
    sobre la participacion indigena en la conquista del Peru,
    1558-60-1561 (Huancayo: Universidad Nacional del Centro,
    1971).
2. "Cuarenta anos en que la penetracion hispanica en Sud
    America tropezaba con una obstinada resistencia en
    Vilcabamba y el grupo seguia manteniendo la esperanza de
    recobrar la tierra," writes Hector Lopez Martinez in
    Rebeliones de Mestizos Y Otros temas quinientistas (Lima:
    1972), p. 143.
3. For further information on the ethnic divisions that
    weakened the Inca empire at the time of the conquest, see
    Waldemar Espinosa Soriano, La destruccion del imperio de
    los Incas: La Rivalidad Politica y Senorial de los Cura-
    cazgos Andinos (Lima: Instituto Nacional de Investigacion
    y Desarrollo de la Educacion, Ediciones Retablo de Papel,
    1973).
4. See Lopez Martinez, Rebeliones de Mestizos, p. 155.
5. "As recently as 1848 the descendants of the ancient Maya,
    after centuries of subjugation, fought their way across
    the peninsula of Yucatan and came within a hair's breadth
    of driving their white masters into the sea," writes Nelson

Reed, The Caste War of Yucatan (Palo Alto, Cal.: University of Stanford Press, 1964), p. vii.

6. See Jose Maria Arguedas, Formacion de una cultura Nacional Indoamericana, Seleccion y prologo de Angel Rama (Mexico: Siglo XXI, 1975), pp. 173-182.

7. For a discussion of the classic Andean cosmic temporal arrangement into four eschatological ages, see Nathan Wachtel, Sociedad e ideologia, ensayos de Historia y antropologia Andinas (Lima: Instituto de Estudios Peruanos, 1973), pp. 190-91.

8. Recent studies of folk belief in Peru show that a commonly-held myth by the Quecha-speaking people of Peru holds that the head of the last Inca, severed from the body by the Spaniards in 1532, remains alive. It is buried someplace near Cuzco, the former center of the Andean Cosmos. The body has been growing back over time and, when it is complete, the present masters of the land will be expelled and the Indians will again have diminion over their land. At the core of this skeleton apocalyptic myth reside two items of historical desideratum: (1) restoration of a native, racially homogeneous realm and (2) expulsion of the outsiders. Fulfillment depends solely on the magic growth the body of the Inca máy be able to accomplish, and it does not require any behavior modification on the part of the peasants who hold the myth.

9. Christopher Dilke, trans., Letter to a King: A Peruvian Chief's Account of Life Under the Incas and Under Spanish Rule (New York: E.P. Dutton, 1978). From the account contained in the manuscript, it would seem that Poma wrote it between 1583 and 1613. Wachtel argues that Poma began copying his chronicle in 1612 and finished it by 1615 (Sociedad e ideologia, p. 168)."

10. See, for example, "Juicio critico de R. Pietschman" in the appendix to Julio C. Tello, Las Primeras Edades del Peru por Guaman Poma (Lima: 1939), p. 84. See Raul Porras Barrenechea, El cronista indio Felipe Huaman Poma de Ayala (Lima: Ed. Lumen, 1948), p. 7.

11. The existence among the Franciscan missionaries of Mexico of a millenarian realm inherited through St. Francis of Assissi from Joachim of Floris is amply discussed in Jacques Lafaye, Quetzalcoatle and Guadalupe, the Formation of Mexican National Consciousness, 1531-1813 (University of Chicago Press, 1976), pp. 30-31. Lafaye also discusses (p. 33) Friar Vasco de Quiroga's utopian experiment in Michoacan with the Tarascan Indians. For further details on the Franciscan experiment, see John L. Phelan, The Millenial Kingdom of the Franciscans in the New World (Berkeley: University of California Press, 1958).

12. The manuscript was found in 1908 by R. Pietschman in the Royal Library of Copenhagen. I have used the printed edition transcribed and annotated by Arthur Posnansky, published in La Paz in 1944. All folio references are made to this transcription.

13. Wachtel has shown how his seemingly confused temporal sequences of the world's time flow, from its creation to the present, obey Andean space and time categories. In fact, Poma manages to graft Christian time and space into the Andean cuatripartite divisions of time and space (pacha), (Sociedad e ideologia, pp. 202-26). Yet, there is also a counter flow in his thought, and it would graft Indian time and the Indian cosmos into the expanding European imperial culture.

14. It seems, from his constant laudatory remarks about him, that his half brother, the hermit Martin de Ayala, instructed him in matters of the Catholic faith. His other main source is probably the preaching missionaries. As he roamed through Spanish towns and Indian villages, Poma heard many a sermon and many a Mass. As illiterates today take their daily dose of the issues of their time in television or radio, Poma seems caught up in the sheer fascination of the word as metaphor in a totally new world. Sermons stand out in his mind with poignant clarity, and, as he remembers them, he can still rage at the misunderstanding of his culture that passed for evangelization and eradication of idolatry.

15. The reconstruction of the ceque system of Cuzco by R.T. Zuidema in The Ceque System of Cuzco: The Social Organization of the Capital of the Inca (1964), and Wachtel's own revision of Zuidema's thesis, Sociedad e ideologia, pp. 23-58, both make ample and brilliant use of the data available in Poma's manuscript.

16. There is no equivalent in the historiography of Peru for Charles Gibson, The Aztecs under Spanish Rule: A History of the Indians of the Valley of Mexico, 1519-1580 (Palo Alto, Cal.: Stanford University Press, 1964), but his assertion that "Indian society seemed headed for extinction in the late 16th" is only too emphatically addressed in the pages of the Nueva Cronica, for Huaman Poma tells us that "A donde habia en la visita general cien indios tributarios no hay diez" (folio 931) Hanke, History of Latin American Civilization, p. 155.

17. Karl Manheim, Ideology and Utopia (New York, 1936), pp. 173-74.

18. See Arthur J. Slavin, "The American Principle from More to Locke," in Fredi Chiappelli (ed.), First Images of America, vol. 1 (Los Angeles: University of California Press, 1976), pp. 142-47.

19. Poma reasons with the King that "que es muy justo y servicio de Dios y su magestad de que los espanoles no se puede poblar junto con los Indios en las cuidades ni en las villas, aldeas, ni vaya a morar ningun espanol ni eslanola ni mestizo ni zambahijo ni cholo ... que los Indios se hacen bellacos y borrachos, jugadores perezosos, la drones, cimarrones. Viviendo con ellos se alzaran y se haran traidores" (folio 543).

20. In this respect, Poma goes much further than Philip II's cedula of 1578 which forbade blacks, mulattoes and mestizos, but not Spaniards, from being in the company of Indians in order to prevent the corruption of the "naturales." Although segregation was established by law, it was never actually obeyed, and Poma is aware of both the law and its ineffective application. See Charles Gibson (ed.), The Spanish Tradition in America (New York: Harper and Row, 1968), pp. 135-36.

21. "Sean mestizos o indios ... un hecho innegable surge de la historia de sus vidas: su facraso social. ...Cada uno en su orbita, fue arrojado de la posicion a la que habria podido pretender pos su nacimiento" writes Nicole Giron de Villasenor in Peru: Cronistas Indios y Mestizos en el siglo XVI (Mexico: SepSetenta, 1975), p. 98.

22. Charles Fourier, Design for Utopia, Selected Writings of Charles Fourier (New York: Schocken Books, 1971).

23. I am using the term dream in the sense that Gaston Bachelard has given it in The Poetics of Space, trans. Etienne Gibson, (Boston: Beacon Press, 1969), pp. 3-38.

24. A comparison with the ideological appeals of the black movement in the United States, especially under Martin Luther King, could yield many illuminating comparisons and differences, but there is no space for it here.

25. Giron de Villasenor points out that "obra civilizadora de los espanoles es menos brillante que la de los Incas para el Inca Garcilaso y tambien menos brillante que la de los Yarovilcas para Huaman Poma," (Peru, p. 131).

26. Although Hayden White shows the function of the theme of the noble savage in the eighteenth century to be fetishistic, it would not be anachronistic to extend his analysis to the Crown's laws designed to protect the so-called "naturales." See Hayden White, "The Noble Savage: Theme as Fetish," in Slavin, pp. 121-135.

27. Here I differ from Wachtel, in that I believe Poma's political thrust is to find a place for the Indian in the European cosmos, more than to invert the operation. Wachtel shows with his analysis of Poma's "mapa mundi" what Poma's geographical categories permit him to do is to integrate the King of Spain and the Pope in the Andean Cosmos of the four corners and the high and low.

28. In this regard he is, of course, not original. But it is not his originality that concerns me, for what I am trying to show is his deftness in adapting the complex of Euro-

pean Renaissance thought to his personal and ethnic
political needs.

29. See Lafaye, Quetzalcoatle and Guadalupe, pp. 30-50.
30. See Nicolas Sanchex-Albornoz, The Population of Latin
     America, a History, Trans. by W.A.R. Richardson (Los
     Angeles, 1974), pp. 22-85.
31. For recent discussion of this crisis and the many solutions
     that it were proposed for see Lafaye, Quetzalcoatle and
     Guadalupe, pp. 30-50.
32. Not content with having lowered the Spaniards to the
     level of heathens, he posits the notion, popular at the
     time with some friars, that St. Bartholomew had come to
     Peru at the time of Sinchi Roca and preached the
     Christian faith. It later grew very relaxed, but it ex-
     plained the "coincidences" between Christian belief and
     Indian notions of a creator, the holy spirits, after-death,
     good and evil, etc. Friar Antonio de la Calancha (1539)
     was the main proponent of this view. See Lafaye
     Quetzalcoatle and Guadalupe, p. 46.
33. Besides the common rape of Indian women, the Spaniards
     often fathered children in the women they received as
     gifts from Indian caciques eager to consolidate alliances.
     Many a common Spanish soldier was married to Indian
     women of high birth in keeping with the king's policy of
     assigning Indian lands to Spaniards as legally as possible.
     Many Indian women whose tribute of labor meant going
     into service in the house of Spanish priests ended up as
     concubines. It is also possible that Indian women hoped
     that, by having children from the new masters, they
     could spare their offspring from servitude and make them
     more acceptable to the new society, a new society that
     quickly became racist. See Magnus Morner, Race Mixture
     in the History of Latin America (Boston: Little, Brown,
     1967).
34. Ironically, the king's high officials had no use for the
     mestizo either. He was thought to be contentious, rebel-
     lious, half-educated, pretentious, and above all, fast
     growing. Letters to the king abound with forecasts of
     imminent rebellion and recommendations that Spaniards,
     mestizos and blacks should be deported. See James
     Lockhart, "Letters and Peoples to Spain" in Slavin, pp.
     783-796.
35. Alfred Metraux's thesis that the Incas "combined the most
     absolute kind of despotism with the greatest tolerance
     toward the social and political order of its subject
     peoples" could also describe Poma's blueprint for the
     future. See "The Inca Empire: Despotism or Socialism,"
     in Hanke, History of Latin American Civilization, p. 81.
36. In Poma's effort to compare the decline of the Indian
     present, as the result of the impact of Christian culture,
     to the stability of the past and future, one finds an

amazing number of coincidences with the reasons given by the Indians of New Spain for their own decline at about the same time. The Spanish Crown had ordered a cosmographic questionnaire to be carried out to find out why the Indians enjoyed greater longevity before the arrival of the Spanish. The general thrust of the answers, like that of Poma's arguments, assert the superiority of Indian culture. Austerity of dress, food, housing, and sex are cited as reasons for better health. Better herb doctors, monthly food and sexual abstinence, and sex later in life are seen in Mexico as causes of better health and longer lives. Another point of coincidence is the question of work. While in New Spain there was a divided opinion as to whether the Indians were doing more or less work under the Spanish than under Aztec rule, in Poma one finds a monolithic position in denouncing the overwork of the <u>mita</u> and <u>ecomienda</u> system. Yet this is accompanied by a regret. Many displaced Indians find themselves roaming around towns and villages, idling away at <u>tambos</u> and pubs. Unable to find work, they end their lives sadly, lonely and sooner than they should. Finally, George Kubler writes that "in Colonial life, when physical labor without ceremonial adornment was forced on the Indians, they became so to speak psychologically unemployed." (see Hanke, <u>History of Latin American Civilization</u>, p. 182). In both cases the absence of order and pattern to the life of the Indian is stressed and is blamed on the chaos the Spaniards had instituted.

37. Whether Poma had any knowledge of Plato's <u>Republic</u> can be of interest only for comparative purposes and not for intellectual philiation. Poma is using the Andean past as his model of the future, and I dare say that if he heard of the many Utopian ideas floating around at the time, many of which had the New World as their inspiration, he must have felt elated and confirmed in his belief in the possibility of "good government." That Plato wanted to do away with the family because he felt that the state could do a better job of indoctrination into the ideals of the republic is of little relevance to our judgment of Poma's blueprint.

38. Even though both the Inca and the Spanish societies are clearly and firmly hierarchically-oriented and Poma has no use for the common Spanish soldier who wants to be treated as if he were a lord, his observations here are centered on the question of labor ownership.

39. Hanke, <u>History of Latin American Civilization</u>, p. 167.

17 The Politics of Unanticipated Trickle: Penetration, Permeation, and Absorption in Peru

Bernard E. Segal

Ethnic autonomy does not flourish in Latin America, despite important differences in both the culture and the physical appearance of the peoples who make up the population of most of the countries in the region. From the beginning of the history of European discovery and conquest of Latin America, a system of domination and subordination was established that has persisted; in some places, it has not yet disappeared. Indeed, as in so many of the government coups of more recent times, the Latin American wars of independence changed the personnel who did the dominating, but not their character or the system of control. The system was even extended during the latter part of the nineteenth and early part of the twentieth centuries when Latin America was brought into the world market. Foreigners helped prop up archaic political and managerial arrangements so that they and local elites could make greater profits from Latin America's food, fiber, and ores. The system was occasionally rocked quite hard, as in Mexico after the Revolution of 1910-20 or in Bolivia's Revolution in 1952, but it was re-established in new, more "modern" hands. And again, newly-established freeholders were choked for lack of credit and market facilities while government help and subsidies went to commercially-successful agricultural operators.

Everywhere but in Cuba, present sociopolitical arrangements still struggle with a heritage of stratification systems established and consolidated during the Latin conquests and their aftermath. Those systems allowed little possibility of considering the rights of private persons. Instead, they reenforced and rationalized through a sacred standard that tried to mitigate harshness by insisting in its nobler moments on the ultimate brotherliness of souls, but which, at the same time, assured the privileged by providing

them with a theodicy of good fortune. Conquistadores did
more than conquer. They penetrated, extended, and institutionalized.

Thus, in most of Latin America, a small elite sector of the
dominant white minority, whether one that had conquered
Indians or imported black slaves, was able to maintain advantages flowing from ethnic group differences. Minority
control of the land and the non-white people who work it
remains the core institution in many different nations.

Here, for example, is how Joseph Kahl recapitulates and
summarizes some of Gonzalez Casanova's views of internal
colonialism in Mexico:

> In the poorer agricultural zones of the country, the
> local inhabitants do the heavy work, but out-
> siders - mestizos or latinos rather than indios -
> control commerce and credit and collect the profits.
> Capital is drained out; so is talent, for the suc-
> cessful indios often changed their clothes and
> language and become imestizes themselves, but the
> community remains poor and backward. And it
> remains politically impotent; the people are not
> organized into unions or pressure groups...The
> statistics on government investment show that funds
> tend to flow to the advanced regions in response to
> effective demand, instead of flowing to the poorest
> regions to help them move forward (p. 85).

Peru is a particularly interesting case in this light because of its large size, the territorial concentration of its
Indian population, and its stark retention of well-established
patterns of domination and subordination until quite recent
times, when some were shaken and others modified. Still more
recently a military regime attempted to carry forward the
process of change. However, this was done by capping,
co-opting, and managing it from a top and center that, despite
their non-traditional composition, are nearly as insulated as
their predecessors from local or regional wellsprings and bases
of autonomous thrust.

Peru has frequently struck observers as being two distinct nations, a dual society with two major sectors sharply
and consistently variant on the major dimensions of almost any
conceivable list of rank differentiation: language and literacy,
culture, wealth, education, occupation, political participation,
legal access, and influence. The derivatives of these differences affect nutrition, morbidity, infant mortality, and life ex-
pectancy. Parallel to the high and low distributions on each
item are territory and ethnicity; so-called "racial" categories in
Peru have little about them stemming from biological or genetic
differences, even as purported explanations of stereotypes

(Fuenzalida and Mayer; Van den Berghe and Primov). Coastal
Peru, wealthier and more advanced, tends more toward whiteness, but with a considerable mestizo admixture. It has been
dominant since the Spanish conquest, even though it has been
a demographic minority until quite recently. Sierra, or highland Peru, which has had most of Peru's population throughout
its history, has more Indians and is poorer by far, particularly in the six departments, or provinces, conventionally known
as La Mancha India, the Indian strip or belt.

        Naked force alone, as the single major bulwark of the
Peruvian system, might have served to maintain such a pattern
of rule and distribution of privilege for a rather long period of
time.   Actually, however, the long-term stability of this arrangement was enhanced by a dilution and diffusion of discontent among subordinate group members. That could have
taken place in a number of different ways. For example, Max
Weber points out how, in some rare cases, and obviously at
the sufferance of a dominant group elite that continues to hold
the most important levers of power, all or some of the members
of a subordinate ethnic group, for the sake of a particular
necessary contribution they alone can make, will be allowed
more economic privilege than is available to most members of
the dominant group (in Gerth and Mills). Unusual though
such cases may be, they illustrate with particular clarity how
the provision or extension of advantage to members of subordinate ethnic groups is likely to be more a matter of ex-
pediency than of justice, a necessary accomodation if a system
as a whole is not to be threatened with disintegration.

        Peru, like other countries of Latin America, has relied on
another less conscious, but equally effective, mode of accomodation, one that emerged as the unanticipated consequence
of more spontaneous forms of interaction and of social changes
that were consciously introduced, but with quite other
purposes in mind. Early and easy miscegenation between
Spanish conquerors and vanquished Indians gave rise to an
interstitial group, the mestizos. Their presence provided a
means of limited mobility for the Indians, and of indirect
control for the whites or criollos. Originally, criollos were
Spanish Peruvians native to Peru, with the additional connotation of a hint or presumption of some racial intermixture
among them; then the term was extended to include anyone
well enough off, and sufficiently cultured, to live the Hispanic
life-style while associating mostly with Hispanics; by a final
and more modern definition, the name applies to any non-
Indian resident of coastal Peru, or to the culture of that
region as a whole. Entrance into the mestizo group has been
limited, but it has never been tightly closed, or as dependent
on strict lines of descent as on cultural shift and adaptation.
Being or becoming a mestizo, a way of avoiding the restrictions and opprobrium characteristically associated with

being defined as Indian, is a process as old as post-Columbian Peru itself. It continues to occur, still more without than with conscious direction, even though contemporary programs such as agrarian and educational reforms show state involvement and calculation in the formal processes of incorporation and ac-comodation. These processes, however, are by no means always carried out without biases resting on well established conventional assumptions about differences between Indians and other kinds of people.

In today's Peru, the poorest regions are unable to generate much profit, no matter how tightly they are squeezed (Van den Berghe and Primov). Indeed, their poverty appears to have been one of the reasons for the reformist military coup of 1968; the people who controlled the Sierrra were unable to continue converting that control into equivalent influence over the central government. In addition, there is no doubt that labor-management relations, decisions about the use of other production factors, and definitions of ethnic status have all been different in those areas where production was better attuned to market forces. The consequences of economic change have so altered Peru's social structure that it offers myriad examples of sectors of its Indian group that are now ethclasses, and of ethclasses that have been transformed to class sectors per se. The idea that there are just two Perus is too simple; there are many (Fuenzalida and Mayer). Yet the shift in reference from ethnicity to class elsewhere in Peru has helped to highlight further the insolation of the bottommost group, a third of Peru, the Indians still overwhelmingly con-centrated in the Mancha India.

Mexico, where Gonzalez Casanova first fruitfully used the model of internal colonialism to study a Latin American case, passed through a major revolution over two generations ago. Nevertheless, the subsequent overhaul of its social system was insufficient to do away with some of the most entrenched aspects of the link between class and ethnicity. Peru's "revolution" began with the coup of 1968, and there were strong indications that it would go no further after a change in military junta leadership took place in 1975. In any case, Peru's reforms have not been operational as long as Mexico's, nor has Peru had the resources available to carry them through. With a great proportion of its population still almost isolated and undermobilized, Peru has an enormous task in the years ahead. If the class-ethnicity tie remains significant in Mexico nearly 60 years after the end of a revolutionary war, it is obvious that it should remain more significant still in Peru.

Nevertheless, the relation between ethnicity and class in Peru has never been constant. Instead, it has been subject to shifts and changes. Some have been swift and dramatic; others have been slower, pregnant with possibilities un-delivered until long gestation periods had passed. An exam-

ination of the character and many facets of that relation is
essential for understanding why separatism has had so little
scope in Peru.

There is a quote of Max Weber's that should be better
known among American sociologists who treat "status" as if it
were a naturally occurring pristine phenomenon:

> The development of status is essentially a question
> of stratification resting upon usurpation. Such
> usurpation is the normal origin of almost all status
> honor. But the road from this purely conventional
> situation to legal privilege, positive or negative, is
> easily traveled as soon as a certain stratification of
> the social order has been lived in and has achieved
> stability by virtue of a stable distribution of
> economic power (Gerth and Mills, p. 188).

Peru is a crystalline example of how short that road was
in Latin America. Within scarcely 50 years of conquest, the
Spaniards had established a system of social classes that
rested upon their control of the economic sector in general,
and the agrarian sector in particular. Scholars may argue
whether this feudal system was purer in its original Spanish
form or in its transplanted Latin American form. Although
details are important to specialists, what matters here is that
certain key aspects of a feudal sort of social organization and
world view helped establish modes and justifications of control
so strong that their effects are still being felt more than 400
years later. The most frequently cited characteristics of the
system are almost a litany: paternalistic authoritarianism,
organicistic social ethics, particularistic status relations,
aristocratic honor. Resting on the pedestal of grossly unequal
land distribution, the whole was crowned by a near-ethereal
sacred aura that could make men's material interests seem less
than earthbound, more than venal.

Originally, racial differences were grafted onto that base.
The conquerors were Caucasian; the conquered, Indian. In
order to safeguard the unique rights and privileges of each,
Church and Crown made consistent attempts to define the two
groups as legally different; but there was never much doubt
that the Spaniards were dominant, while the Indians - although
held by the Church to have souls - were, in practice, not
much more than a human resource, a labor supply without
which the control of economic resources, chiefly land and
mines, would not have meant much. There was similarly not
much doubt that rules meant to protect the Indians from the
rapacity and greed of their new rulers were honored more in
the breach than in fact.

A relative handful of Spaniards ruled a much larger
Indian population. Reasonable estimates are that the Indian

population of Peru was as high as between six and ten million
people at the time of the conquest; this was cut by between a
half and three-quarters in the next century (Mormer, pp.
12, 31-2; Van den Berghe and Primov, p. 37). In Spanish
America, the Indians weren't slaughtered in warfare; they died
from overwork, especially in the mines, and from epidemics of
new diseases brought them by the conquerors. It would have
been absurd for the Spaniards, who, by 1600, were still less
than 5 percent of the population in Peru, deliberately to kill
off a labor supply upon which they were so dependent. In
fact, Indian population decline helped bring on a serious
economic depression in the seventeenth century. Population
loss and depression, in turn, probably led to the spread of the
hacienda system (Lockhart). In any case, whether or not
demographic and economic decline were among the causes, both
Crown and former Indian land became an important source of
state revenue, offered for sale in enormous tracts to the
relatively few members of the small ruling group who were in a
position to buy it. Once the land was in private hands, it
was hoped that it would be utilized more effectively, though
more effective land utilization presupposed as well a more
effective use of the cheap available labor. Along the coast,
where the land was best and Indian labor in shortest supply,
black slaves helped fill the gap. (The history of blacks in
Peru is worth serious attention, as is that of the Chinese
coolies who replaced many of them after the mid-nineteenth
Century when slavery had been abolished and coastal agriculture began to expand. Unfortunately, there is only room
here enough to consider the largest groups in Peru's shifting
ethnic mosaic.)

While the Indian population was falling and withdrawing to
the Sierra, newer population groups were being formed.
Foremost among these were mestizos, the outcome of miscegenation that had apparently begun as soon as Pizarro and
his crew reached shore. There were no legal restrictions on
inter-marriage between Spaniards and Indians, and the first
mestizos, offspring of legitimate unions, were apparently
counted and accepted as Spaniards. However, before long,
and particularly as women began to arrive from Spain, it
became the customary normal presumption - evidently reflecting
the facts of the matter to some unknown extent - that mestizos
were illegitimate and, therefore, not entitled to membership in
the Spaniards' superior group (Morner).

In one sense, the distinction between Spaniard and
mestizo represented greater social distance and a hardening of
caste lines between Spaniards and Indians; mestizos carried
out mostly interstitial, middle-rank tasks that Spaniards didn't
want, and that Indians weren't allowed or prepared to do.
Mestizos were foremen, artisans, dealers in petty commerce,
clearly products of the Hispanic rather than the Indian am-

biance.   Peru thus seemed to be composed of three castes,
which corresponded - but only in broad outline and not in
precise detail - to three different classes: Spaniards were at
the top; mestizos were in what passed for a nascent working,
or middle, sector; and Indians were at the bottom, further
away from the previous two than they were from each other,
despite a legal standing that ostensibly gave them more extensive and better-protected rights than mestizos.   (There
was, of course, a fourth - and lowest - caste, the black
slaves.   Some of their descendants, still identifiably black,
continue to live in Peru as a very small minority population.

Socially not as legally privileged as the Indians, and with
a syncretic culture and life-style critically dependent on the
Spaniards who disparaged and disdained them, mestizos closely
approximated what Weber called a "pariah people."   They lived
in a "diaspora," strictly segregated from all personal intercourse except that of an unavoidable sort, their situation
legally precarious.   "These people," Weber adds, "form
communities, acquire specific occupational traditions or handi-
crafts or other arts, and cultivate a belief in their ethnic
community" (Gerth and Mills, 1964: p. 189).   Except for the
last characteristic, Weber's definition holds; but the exception
is quite important.   In one fundamental respect, neither
Peruvian mestizos nor Peruvian Indians were like Jews, the
group Weber had in mind as a concrete example of his case.
On the contrary, in Peru no belief in ethnic community was
ever concretized, reenforced, and maintained by a unique
faith; the spiritual quest of a militant Church was a major
impetus and instrument of Spanish political domination and
cultural expansion.   The success of the religious effort could
be measured directly in numbers of baptisms.   It could be
measured indirectly, but equally accurately, by its weakening
of possible ideational bases of local autonomy.   By either
measure, the Church's penetration was extraordinarily
effective.

In addition, the white and Indian poles of the caste-estate
pattern were at their margins phylogenetically indistinct from
the mestizos, who may have increased the distance between the
other two groups, but who bridged it as well.   As early as
the end of the eighteenth century, the Spanish laws of the
castas were in a shambles (Morner).   It was evident by then
that cultural factors and social accomplishments could modify
racial assignments.   With its allowances for shifting, ab-
sorbing, and upgrading, the system of racial categorization
was giving way to an ethnic one that had already drained off
some discontent, and would continue to do so up to the
present.   Moreover, although the white or Spanish group was
and would for long remain dominant, it was already a group
with a considerable racial admixture.   It was quite unlikely,
therefore, that any purported "racial purity" could be made a

criterion for acceptance within it. Peninsular Spaniards, it is true, were likely to disparage the racial mixture apparent among criollos, but the conflict between these two groups was far less marked in Peru than elsewhere in Latin America, evidently because Peruvian criollos had less to gain from independence from Spain than did their counterparts in other areas. Thus, although lightness or whiteness might have been preferred, in a society where kinship was known and emphasized among the upper strata, signs of racial admixture could be easily overridden by the length and extent of one's membership in a family already known to belong to the inner circles.

Lower in the status order, where elitist selection criteria were harder to maintain, assimilative bleaching was an important safety valve mitigating the effects of what otherwise would have been categorical exclusion. For mestizos, there were favors to be had from patron-client relations that were simply unavailable to Indians. Except for a few chiefs who served the Spaniards as instruments of indirect rule, and even most of them were absorbed over time, Indians so lacked the minimum essential cultural skills - most notably language and "style" - that they could occupy only the most subordinate and tightly-controlled positions in the Hispanic world. Mestizos, however, shared with the Spaniards and criollos that knowledge and implicit sharing of ideas and activity patterns that makes rapid and easy communication possible between peoples, even when it rests more on mutual suspicion than on trust.

In fact, a great majority of the Indians living in the Andean regions, where Spanish control but not the Spanish way of life had penetrated, were less involved in the day-to-day operation of the Hispanic world than mestizos were. Nevertheless, some Indians were more likely to feel the press of acculturation, and to sense the limited advantages that could flow from it. Then, as now, if the acculturation were sufficient, and the need or advantage of undergoing it clear enough, Indians were able to move into the mestizo group, just as mestizos could, in much smaller numbers, get to be criollos. Yet the process was not automatic, for mobility channels were narrow, and even some of the Indians who were assumed to be acculturated clearly felt that their best interest lay in the other direction. Karen Spalding (1972, p. 65) puts it as follows:

Colonial urban society is commonly regarded as a European society, despite the recognized importance of Indian migration to the cities and the growth of substantial native urban population. Indian residents of the cities, it is suggested, were "acculturated," adopting Spanish habits and attitudes. This conclusion is supported by a great deal of evidence. Despite legal provisions to the contrary, Indian and Spanish populations in the urban areas were increasingly intermingled in the course of the colonial period. Despite this evidence, I find myself somewhat skeptical about the assumption that the Indian migrants to Lima exchanged their culture for that of the Europeans. The participation and in many cases the active leadership of urban Indians in Lima in [eighteenth century] native rebellions suggests that many among this group, despite their external similarity to their European urban neighbors, regarded themselves as Indian, a category different from and increasingly in opposition to the Europeans.

Yet those rebellions had the same outcome as preceding ones: the Indians lost them all. With each loss, their chances for competing with European culture bearers became reduced to relying on the terms the Europeans would allow: they had to settle for measured acculturation and gradual absorption, their pace kept slow by their isolation and their tight subjection, often directly administered by mestizos in locations distant from Lima, the seat of power and the center of Hispanic culture. The mass of Indians were, and remained, peons or subsistence farmers, illiterate, monolingual in their native tongue, and without any ties of their own to a market economy or the material and symbolic instruments of its commerce.

At the dawn of Peruvian independence, "whites" were at the top of Peru's stratification system, mestizos were in the center in a more muddled mosaic, and Indians were at the bottom. Although congruence along the major dimensions of status was no more than a chimera through most of the system, it was clear enough among a small pinnacle of bureaucratic-colonial peninsulares and land-holding criollos. Wealth, prestige, and power were what this group held, what it wanted, and what it had been able to keep. At the much larger bottom, among the Indians who were the overwhelming majority of the population, the congruence was equally clear. Of wealth, prestige, and power, they had little or none. Only pale imitations of them were possible, based on syncretic religious-communal patterns and the slight autonomy that indirect Spanish rule had left to nominally self-sufficient Indian communities.

In the three centuries that passed between conquest and independence, no competing doctrine emerged to challenge the view that conquerors and conquered were two different peoples, governed by different rules, subject to different rights and obligations. Only at independence did Enlightenment challenge the ideas that status determined right, that options and privilege, restriction and prohibition were dependent on rank, and that rank depended upon and reenforced ethnicity. Yet independence and the shift in doctrine had disastrous consequences. It did away with those portions of Spanish law that provided Indians with a special status and helped to insulate them, however tenuously, from the depredations that higher-ranking groups were always ready to visit upon them.

In particular, still more Indian land became available. At first, the process was slow because, in the absence of royal authority, a fissiparous Peru was torn apart for a generation by struggles among regional caudillos. By the middle of the nineteenth century, the political center became more stable, and an economic revival began; based on the export of guano and agricultural products, this was spurred in part by the availability of British capital. Now encroachment could begin again in earnest. By fair means and foul, hacendados grabbed more and more of the land that had been reserved for the Indians under colonial grants. Political consolidation and economic growth at the start of Peru's "era of outward expansion" were accomplished partly at the expense of the Indian population, and the state gave at least tacit approval to the process. A classically liberal conception of property rights, in conjunction with an assumption of equal legal status for everyone that was more rhetorical than actual, provided a thin cosmetic cover for what was actually an almost naked play of power by those who were, in fact, much more "equal" than the people they absorbed and displaced. An economic downturn, following Peru's ignominious and overwhelming defeat by Chile in the War of the Pacific, slowed the land takeovers once more. Even so, Alberti believes that, at the end of the nineteenth century, the gap in power, option, and social possibility between Peru's Indians on the one hand, and her white and mestizo population on the other, was greater than at any time before or since (Chaplin).

Yet the social changes that were beginning around the turn of the century planted the seeds of other changes to come, although not all at the same time, or in the same place. For one thing, despite the apparent tightening of the social and cultural line between Indians and mestizos, the mestizo population grew so quickly all through the nineteenth century that it was evident the increase owed more to upgrading by acculturation than to interbreeding. That process continued and quickened, but not because urbanism and its signs of "modernity" - communication made easier by new transport facilities, a spread of commerce accompanied by growing numbers of private and public bureaucrats, an expansion of formal education for training new recruits to the new middle sectors - were reaching out to the countryside. On the contrary, although Lima had ruled Peru since the conquest, by 1900 the country had already begun the process that would

lead to its ultimately becoming demographically, as well as
administratively, hydrocephalic. Lima's slums were starting to
grow with new migrants from the rural areas. Then, as now,
urban residence meant Hispanization and a shift in ethnic
status, whether self-perceived or assigned by others. Meanwhile, increasing land hunger, caused both by hacendado
encroachment and their own population increase, pushed most
Indians further back and higher up in the Sierra. Otherwise,
those parts of the rural hinterland where the Indian population
was concentrated were hardly touched. The twentieth century
would not effectively reach them until 50 or 60 years after it
had begun.

Peru's indigenous movement that protested the treatment
of the Indians and insisted that the country's heritage was
multicultural was led not by Indians, but by reformist political
figures and the urban intelligentsia on the coast. As early as
1919, the official name for Indians became the more euphemistic
indigenas, and legislation gave formal recognition to the local
Indian groupings, thenceforth known as comunidades indigenas.
An Instituto Indigenista was also created in the Ministry of
Labor and Communities, although, according to Cotler, it had
only one translator of Quechua and Aymara in 1966. Since
then, official designations have gone further still. When, on
the Dia del Indio (sic!), President Velasco announced the
agrarian reform law of 1969, he followed the practice introduced in Bolivia after the revolution of 1952 by declaring
that the former Indians and erstwhile indigenas were henceforth campesinos.

Official designations aside, Richard Patch wrote on
language as a distinguishing feature of Indians and mestizos:

> It would require a monograph to discuss what
> various authorities have meant by Indian and
> mestizo, but the simplest and most meaningful
> criterion is language. It is in this sense that I am
> using the term here: Indian meaning those who
> speak native languages, and mestizo, those who
> speak Spanish by preference (p. 26).

It seems simple enough, yet it isn't. Is Spanish spoken with
an accent or not? Is it spoken by preference at home or at
work? Is the reference point Lima or the Mancha India? In
short, how much Spanish is enough to make someone who was
born an Indian into a mestizo? Complicating the matter still
further is the rapidly growing interstitial category, cholos,
who fall between the Indians and mestizos. Although cholos
display some Indian cultural characteristics, they speak
Spanish, reside in urban areas, work at blue-collar jobs,
dress in Western trousers, wear their hair short, and have an
assertive attitude. Boundary limits on cholos are as vague as

those for the other two or three ethclass categories - two if
just Indians and mestizos are counted, and three if mestizos
who are well enough off for a period of time can be considered
"white," a distinction that probably matters less than it used
to since the revolution of 1968 was led by predominantly
mestizo military officers. Van den Berghe and Primov, and
Fuenzalida and Mayer - whose strictures are less explicit -
have decided not to use the term cholo at all, claiming that
people do not use it of themselves, and that in too many
instances a mestizo in a rather isolated Sierra village would be
a cholo in Lima. By the same token, however, there are
hardly any Indians in Lima because the Indians who go there
are not likely to remain Indians for very long. Higher-
ranking people - mestizos, criollos, blancos - consider them
cholos, but many of these reputational cholos think of themselves as mestizos.

       To continue in this vein would run the risk of writing
that monograph that Patch, perhaps wisely, decided to leave
on the back burner. Some summary is possible, however.
Evident since the turn of the century is the fact that additional penetration and incorporation of Indians by the
Hispanic center has been occurring at an accelerating pace.
The initial impetus for these processes has been economic,
although not always planned; planned political responses to the
changes have tended to come later. Both economic and
political changes have weakened ethnic distinctions, but these
effects have taken longer to reach the Mancha India than any
other part of Peru; and their impact is still less there than it
is elsewhere. In general, the more Hispanic an area, the
smaller the proportion of people who display Indian culture in
unadulterated form; however, in the Sierra, cultural differences that would strike a more Hispanic observer as quite
small, perhaps even meaningless, are sufficient to mark a shift
in ethnic status from Indian to cholo or mestizo. In simpler
language, there aren't many Indians on the Peruvian coast,
but Peru, as seen from the coast, appears to have more Indians than when it's seen from the Sierra. Class relations
tend to supplant ethnic relations on the coast; but, although
ethnic distinctions have also been blurred and moderated in
the Sierra, by no means have they lost either their objective
or their subjective significance. Being an Indian there still
means being cut off from cultural and economic resources
essential for any effective competitive participation in the
Hispanic world.

       Nevertheless, because processes of penetration and in-
corporation have taken place at different rates in different
parts of Peru, they have divided what was once a common
subordinate mass into a complex set of groups with different
attitudes, interests, and kinds and amounts of influence.
Clearly, more is involved than a general shift in subjective

status occasioned by a secular trend toward structural
mobility. In various small worlds of work and residence,
specific contextual elements and situational concerns not only
dominate daily life, but affect the sorts of demands that are -
and can be - made concerning the larger worlds of the national
economic and political systems. Solidarity there may be, but it
is often local or regional, with limited specific aims. The
center's continuing ability to maintain itself, despite significant
transformation in the composition of its core elites, and its
capacity to go on regulating through positive and negative
sanction, even after having been shaken by displays of force
by outside power contenders, reflect how Peruvian social
change has proceeded through phased segmental incorporation
rather than through sweeping fundamental structural shifts.
Segmental incorporation has diluted closure and weakened
solidarism. However, it has also caused general class consciousness and widespread ethnic separatist consciousness to
continue as ideological visions and rhetorical themes.
    In its modern form, the story of segmental incorporation
and penetration begins with two primary products that Peru
had and that the world, especially the United States, wanted:
one was sugar, grown on the northern coast; the other was
copper, dug out of the mountain rock of the central Sierra.
Sugar and copper production helped American firms and their
financial backers and intermediaries to gain dominance over the
Peruvian economy, changed the character of Peruvian local and
national elites, wiped out local smallholders and entire Indian
communities, created proletarians of serfs, provided locuses of
membership and support for Peru's most important union organizations for more than 40 years. All these developments,
in turn, helped to create and sustain APRA, the longest-
lasting and most effective mass political association Peru has
ever had, although it was never allowed to govern.
    The effects of sugar production were apparent first. The
older of the two industries, it developed in an area that was
economically advanced. The sugar export trade began early.
Until the abolition of slavery in 1849, the plantations were
worked by blacks, then, by Chinese coolies. Financed by
foreign capital, the industry underwent major growth after
World War I. Holdings were expanded and consolidated in
what were increasingly becoming industrialized and capital-
intensive plantations that depended on Indian migrants from
the Sierra for labor. The early recruits were "hooked ones"
(enganchados); they were given cash advances on wages
before leaving their homes, only to discover later that their
pay was too low, and their expenses at company stores too
high to ever get out of debt. By about 1940, however, increases in the Indian population and land scarcity began
prompting considerable voluntary migration, providing the
plantations with a closer and more permanent labor supply.

Indeed, by 1960, there was a labor surplus already resident
on the major plantations because "commercially oriented
haciendas need[ed] fewer and fewer workers as technology
advance[d], [and] scarce permanent jobs are not given up by
their holders lightly to make room for newcomers" (Goodsell,
p. 208).

At Paramonga, one of W.R. Grace's major holdings, "... a
study conducted in 1958 showed that 56 percent of community
residents were born off the hacienda, and that 34 percent
came from the Department of Ancash" (Goodsell, pp. 208-209),
one of the six Departments of the Mancha India. Paramonga's
population, swelled by migration, had grown from 4,985 in 1940
to more than 18,000 in 1960, before leveling at 22,000 in 1968.
The growth was not surprising. After all, "although wages
averaged only 40 cents a day for field workers at Paramonga
when [anthropologist Richard] Patch visited it in 1959, the
sugar workers represented something of a labor aristocracy in
Peru and earned more than twice as much as workers on
coastal cotton estates" (Paige, p. 145).

Paramonga illustrates a more general process that has
been accelerating since 1940: the land-hungry have migrated
from Sierra to the coast; and, with that migration, there has
been a class transformation from peasant to unskilled wage
laborer, and an ethnic transformation from Indian to cholo.

> According to Richard Patch, the Indians arriving at
> Paramonga... attempt deliberately to rise to what is
> perceived as a superior social class, that of the
> acriollados. After arriving at this intermediate
> level, Patch continues, an effort is made to reach
> the next highest class, the criollo or
> mestizo.....Seldom, Patch believes, is criollo or
> mestizo status actually achieved by the Paramonga
> worker who has come to the hacienda as a young
> Indian. But, he says, "the children of the
> acriollado group will normally be considered
> mestizos" (Goodsell, p. 209).

The status shifts weaken subjective ethnic solidarism.
They also represent a departure from objective ties that might
have bound migrants to the life styles and interests of their
home communities; "ties to the land, particularly the association with land ownership in the Sierra, are increasingly
tenuous on most plantations" (Paige, p. 147). In addition,
ex-migrants or their children with good jobs could hardly
welcome newcomers whose greater need allowed management to
use them in a way that discouraged the development of common
interests and aims beyond the plantation. "Migratory workers
with close ties to Sierra peasant communities had traditionally
been used as strikebreakers," Paige continues, adding, how-

ever, that "with the increasing dependence of the plantations on wage labor, this source of division has been largely eliminated." It was eliminated on the plantation itself, but not outside; there was a sharp division between the relative few with secure plantation jobs and those without them, large numbers of migratory, temporary workers. They would gladly have shared, but could not, in the higher wages available on the plantations. They would now gladly share, but cannot, in the still higher wages available on the nationalized sugar co-operatives that the 1969 Agrarian Reform law created out of the old plantations.

Can the sugar industry serve as a microcosmic example of other processes in Peru? Evidently it can, because so many similar phenomena have occurred in other sectors. For example, Chaplin (1976) points out how blue-collar industrial workers, relatively protected and relatively privileged, are quite moderate, far more concerned with their own job security and wages than with general structural change. Writing of the barriadas, the squatter settlements ringing Lima that hold at least a quarter of the capital area's metropolitan population, David Collier notes how their residents are especially concerned with local issues such as land titles and the provision of municipal services. Various governments have easily used these residents as sources of clientelistic support. Another observer has noted: "...demand aggregation by ideologically leftist parties or by strong political organizations acting independently of political parties and using either the electoral process or tactics of limited violence (might be expected to occur, and yet) ...neither of these forms of behavior exists in the Lima barriadas to any great degree" (Chaplin, p. 168).

As for possible ethnic solidarity and action, barriadas have different characteristics:

Some barriadas are slums.... Many, but not all, of the people living there have come directly from the Sierra. They still speak Quechua and have not been assimilated into the Spanish culture of the Lima coastal region....Markedly different....are barriadas...formed by invasion by people who first had acquired job security and then wanted land to assure themselves a permanent home....People instrumental in an invasion...probably have succeeded in their assimilation efforts. They are now mestizos, unlike the Indians from the Sierra who settle in a slum barriada immediately upon arriving in the city (Chaplin, pp. 170-71).

Rural transformations in the sugar industry and urban transformations in the barriadas created a new working class, but divided that class by making some more privileged than

others. Both also diluted ethnic ties, as gradual assimilation
led to shifts of interest more congruent with immediate situations. Both also led to cross-class and cross-ethnic ties in
mass parties. Party impact was thereby strengthened, but the
possibility of particularistic militance was weakened. In addition, because the parties had strong regional bases, they
introduced another source of division by making it more difficult for general social movements to cover the whole nation.
       The case of APRA is illustrative of these points. Formed
in the late 1920s out of the new working classes and the old
middle sectors who had lost their stake in the economic system
as a result of the expansion and consolidation of the sugar
haciendas, APRA has been Peru's major mass party for more
than a generation. Although never allowed to rule, in large
measure because it was an anathema to the military, APRA
became more moderate with the years, a nearly classic case of
a once-radical Latin American party shifting its emphases to
correspond to the gradually rising status of its constituency.
Indigenous in its rhetoric, it was so coastal in practice, so
electoral in orientation that it was quite left behind in the
southern Sierra when a major rural awakening began in the
1960s. Neither APRA as a whole nor the already accultured
sugar workers on the great coastal haciendas gave their
support to agrarian reform or to the Sierran rural insurgents
who were trying to carry it out (Handleman, p. 36).
       How important was the effort? Handleman responds
crisply and simply: "The land invasion movement of the early
1960s was unquestionably Peru's most significant rural
mobilization in modern times" (Handleman, p. 7). Space
limitations preclude full treatment here, for the movement had
somewhat different sources and outcomes in different areas. It
must suffice to point out that in the central Sierra where it
went further than in the south, it was led by members of
Indian communities rather than by serfs resident on traditional
haciendas, and that it was the indirect outcome of the exploitation of copper. Beginning in 1915, with the formation of
what ultimately became Peru's largest single enterprise and
employer, the Cerro de Pasco Corporation, copper in the
mountains played a role that was similar, but not identical, to
the one that sugar played on the coast.
       Some direct parallels are evident: the financing was
foreign; local elites were at first displaced, and then those
who remained or entered the area anew became commercial,
rather than traditional, hacendados; and the first laborers at
Cerro were enganchados who would later become unionized,
proletarianized, and accultured - but only partially. A very
important difference between sugar and copper was that copper
was produced in an Indian area. Much more of the copper
labor force was temporary and migratory, returning to live in
the Indian communities from which it had come. Thus, al-

though there was considerable labor militance, it had limited
aims. Whereas in the sugar industry a permanent labor force
gradually came to depend on the labor policies and general
prosperity of the plantations, laborers in the central Sierra
maintained a primary interest in their communities of origin
rather than in the communities where they were temporary
residents.

> "Collective bargaining is spirited and strikes quite
> frequent; wage increases and other benefits are
> won frequently, and by Peruvian standards the
> workers of these companies are well paid. Yet this
> does not mean the unions were effective political-
> ly.... Furthermore - and this is perhaps the most
> important point here - the union leaders take little
> interest in community issues. Their concern is the
> type of question that is most tangibly meaningful to
> memberships: wage rates, work schedules, dis-
> missals, and such inconveniences as time clocks
> (Goodsell, pp. 184-85).

Even so, these miners and refinery operatives were
"always more militant than the average peasant villager. It is
likely that the miners carried their new militancy and class
consciousness back to their native villages when they returned
home" Handleman, p. 51). Home for them, however, was not
the haciendas where they would have sharecropped as serfs
(colonos) under rigid near-feudal restrictions. Instead, they
were comuneros, residents of comunidades indigenas. Such
communities, despite their name, tended to get that official
designation, along with certain associated rights, only after
they had lost many of their Indian characteristics.
   Thus, the forces that promoted acculturation at work
were reflected in the changing character of local areas.
Furthermore, those same forces were also responsible for a
spreading encroachment and takeover of community lands; the
Central Sierra was "the area of the most extensive com-
mercialization and the most widespread land expropriations
during the twentieth century" (Paige, p. 189). In particular,
Cerro became the largest landholder and sheep breeder in the
area. Its success on the land, quite aside from its success
with the ore it was drawing from it, encouraged others to open
ranches in the area, further encroaching on indigenous communities' lands. Those communities that were left withdrew to
higher and higher areas, turning from agriculture to
pastoralism. A final irony, however, was that community wool
became a cash crop, and comuneros were drawn into the
market economy because Cerro's needs had brought transportation to the area.
   The combination was a tinder box awaiting a spark:

partially accultured communities capable of autonomous organization, familiar with national politics, resentful of recent
encroachment, aware of how possessing more land would lead
to earning more money, supplied with ideas and leadership
from mobilized ex-miners and refinery workers, strongly tied
to APRA's rural federation, FENCAP, witness to a few successful land invasions already carried out in the area, and
aware of the need for agrarian reform. The spark came from
a successful peasant movement in Cuzco's La Convencion Valley
between 1958 and 1963, and the promise it exacted from
presidential candidate Belaunde that he would support and
carry out an agrarian reform if he were elected. Thus, in the
Central Sierra, the first invasion occurred in January 1960.

> Invasions continued on a small scale in Pasco and
> neighboring Junin between 1960 and 1963....after
> July 1963... the comunero movement exploded into a
> massive series of invasions ...rapidly spreading
> throughout the central Sierra. At its peak the
> movement involved invasions by over a hundred
> distinct communities and may have involved as many
> as 300,000 individuals... in a widening circle of
> activity spreading outward from the initial centers
> of unrest in the central provinces of Junin and
> Paso (Paige, p. 185).

Was the movement separatist? Was it even consciously,
assertively ethnic? The answer to both questions is clearly
and resoundingly negative.

> The peasants took pains to demonstrate their piety
> and patriotism, frequently holding religious services
> on invaded haciendas and prominently displaying
> the Peruvian flag....The comunero invasions...
> were almost completely devoid of references to
> Indian cultural identity and instead focused ex-
> clusively on land rights....In fact, the Peruvian
> indigenous communities were neither indigenous nor
> communal, and despite vestigial remnants of Incan
> language and culture, had been submerged in the
> Sierra peasant class and left with little or no
> autonomous political or social identity (Paige, p.
> 186).

Autonomy's growth in the central Sierra had been watered
more by external freshets than by internal springs. Mobilization struck among the more acculturated, its form depending
upon and reflecting contemporary class conflicts more than
ancient ethnic tensions. It was another indication that to
speak of market-oriented, shoe-wearing, semi-literate Spanish-

speaking Indians in Peru is to speak of a category that doesn't exist.

The moment might have led to separatism if the movement had spread to the southern Sierra, to the heartland of the Mancha India, but the moment passed. In the Central Sierra, "by the end of 1963 the number of invasions dwindled simply because most mobilized villagers were in de facto control of disputed lands, or expected to receive them from the government in the near future" (Handleman, p. 123). "Of the one hundred thousand families which Belaunde claimed had benefited by the 1964 agrarian reform, more than seventy thousand received their land by virtue of de facto occupation of lands, which the law in effect legitimized." (Bourque and Palmer, p. 197). Not all these lands were in Junin and Pasco; others were in the southern Cuzco, in the rather isolated La Convencion Valley that is on the other side of the Andes from the Sierra, in the region known as the Selva. The military easily put down any further uprisings in the rest of Cuzco, the mass of Cuzco, the Mancha India Cuzco. The army's task made easier by still another internal division among the population:

> One of the critical failures of the Cuzco peasant federations was their inability to institutionalize their organizations. Their attempts to establish a national organization similar to [APRA's] FENCAP failed, in part because they never enjoyed enough support from a powerful political group at the center after their split with the Communist Cuzco Federation of Workers. [While the alliance lasted, it was one of very few examples in all of Peru of genuine co-operation between the poor and working class sectors of rural and urban areas.] When the national system turned to repression of the land invasions, the peasants found themselves encapsulated....The split between the Cuzco Federation of Workers and the Campesino Federations occurred primarily because the peasants were not anxious to support a sustained radical movement. Whereas they were willing to co-ordinate their efforts and take considerable risks for clearly defined short-term goals, once these goals had been achieved they were not willing to expand their activities into a movement which challenged the basic framework of the society (Bourque and Palmer, pp. 199-200).

The moment passed, and a new one came, but the old beat goes on. Since 1969, far more extensive agrarian reform has been carried out by Peru's military government, which has

made more land grants in developed than in marginal areas.
The government possesses neither land nor finances enough to
find adequate placement for hundreds of thousands of families
in the Mancha India. Mestizo landholders and administrators
have been replaced by other mestizos who are government
officials and technocrats. It has carried further the process
begun under Belaunde of dismantling traditional forms of
leadership and organization in the comunidades, but it has not
resolved serious difficulties in reconciling the competing claims
of comuneros and colonos for the same ex-hacienda land. It
has co-opted and pre-empted, while managing a top-down
system designed to keep protests local, controlled, and subject
to incorporation. Finally, it has used an evidently sincere but
poorly administered understaffed, and underfinanced set of
educational reforms - ostensibly designed to legitimate bilingual and bi-cultural training and socialization, including
making Quechua an official language - to help place part of
a swollen lower-middle class in government jobs, to buy off
discontent among marginal sectors hopeful that their children
might prosper, and to Hispanicize further. Before 1968,
literacy requirements kept Peru's Indians disfranchised. Since
then, there have been no national elections in Peru, and
government remains as much as a criollo-mestizo monopoly as
ever. (Since this paper was written, there have been elections for a Constitutional Assembly to draft the document
under which Peru will be governed as soon as the junta hands
over control to civilians, probably within a year or two.
APRA, led by its venerable founder, the 83-year-old Haya de
la Torre, won a majority of Assembly seats. Parties furthest
to the left were "discouraged" from participating in the electoral contest.) And "agrarian reform, while making peasants
nominal owners of the land, has not substantially changed the
economic dependence of the Indians on the mestizo-dominated
urban economy" (Van den Berghe, 1974, p. 126).

A moment passes, a beat goes on, and separatism
slumbers, victim of an internally-divided population, of in-
efficient but effective central control, of co-opted prospective
leadership, of regionalism and localism, of 400 years of a
dominant Western presence and heritage, and now, among
young and clamorous but powerless universitarians, of a
competing world view and ideology holding that it is only an
Eastern method that could definitely overcome that presence,
that heritage. There is no agreement among them, however,
on which Eastern method to use. Should it be Lenin's, or
Trotsky's, or Mao's? In any case, it is ironic that the ideas
from the East are imported too. Are there better hopes now
than in the days of Mariategui, Peru's seminal radical-
indigenous thinker of the 1920s, that there will emerge a way,
true and genuine, to make a single nation of the many Perus?
In 1968, the prospects seemed bright. Still, just in sheer

economic terms, Peru's revolution has been expensive. Debts
are now due to foreign creditors. The IMF demands an
austerity program that falls, as austerity programs usually do,
on the majority, on the poor and the powerless. The once
bright prospects of 1968 glitter much less a decade later.

Separatism expresses discontent over exclusion from
access to, or control over, resources and instruments governing the allocation of material and privilege in a given
society. Like a class movement, with which it may be associated, it depends upon the solidarism of the excluded
group's members; the weight of their numbers, and whatever
other resources they may have – such as unique skills or the
occupation of a given space or territory – demonstrate their
capacity to disrupt or change established authority. However,
while most class movements tend to seek control over a larger
society or to find more satisfying incorporation within it,
separatism seeks distance. Class-based movements also tend to
emphasize discontents stemming from unequal economic outcomes; although separatist movements may also do so, it is not
their primary concern. Instead, their central aim is autonomy.
Harold Isaacs phrases it succinctly by saying that separatists
seek the establishment of a nation of their own on lands of
their own. In such a nation, presumably, separatists would
either be free to arrange the sort of economic system they
would like to have, or to contest among themselves to determine what sort of economic arrangements would emerge.

Established authority resists class-based movements that
threaten the basis on which exclusion from privilege rests. It
similarly resists separatism, particularly if the group seeking
distance and autonomy has been responsible for producing an
expropriatable surplus that makes greater privilege possible
for some than for others. Even if that were not the case,
authority would still resist separatism, for any successful
separatist movement both diminishes the whole of the society
and threatens the capacity of its center to maintain integration
among the remainder. Successful separatism demonstrates the
center's weakness, its inability to generate general loyalty and
satisfaction, and its failure to maintain obedience.

A number of necessary conditions must coalesce for a
successful separatist movement to occur: the solidarism of the
group desiring to separate is one of them; its mobilization,
another; the absence of any alternative possibility of satisfactory inclusion of incorporation, a third. All are relative,
and they depend on one another, as well as on external
circumstances. The ease of mobilization and organization
within a separatist group may depend partly, for example, on
how well a society honors its claims to being free and open, or
its reluctance to rely on force to quell dissent. Alternatively,
a society with a resolute elite in control of effective central
mechanisms of social control might rely on force as a matter of

course. Some repression through force could create martyrs, spread hostility, and lead to a surge of heroism. Enough force applied without scruple could set a movement back for years, if not wipe it out entirely - particularly in combination with techniques of co-optation or inclusion.

In Peru, exclusivist central control institutions linked with processes of inclusion have kept solidary separatist consciousness from arising and spreading. Inclusion has never been more than partial, and it probably would not have been sufficient to diminish a separatist thrust if the central controlling institutions, resting in the stratification and political systems, had not been so strong. Moreover, the inclusion that did take place was less often the product of conscious design than an unintended and often undesired outcome of changed patterns of control shifting as a consequence of changed economic arrangements.

Thus, although it is too simple to call Peru a dual society, or two separate nations, it has always been, and remains, a country marked by harsh class divisions that are reenforced by ethnic stratification. Despite conditions like these, Peru has not had a significant separatist movement since 1780, and there are doubts about whether that one was separatist. Other, smaller Indian revolts occurred earlier and later, but were all put down. Not until the 1960s did a set of peasant autonomous movements accomplish major structural changes in the highland agrarian sector, but, by then, they were led and carried out by people who desired social justice within Peruvian society, not separation from it. Their accomplishment, in any case, served as prelude and partial cause for the reformist thrust of the military regime that has ruled Peru since 1968. The movements major achievement was to put a definitive end to the power of the landholding oligarchies, Peruvian and foreign on the coast and wholly Peruvian in the Sierra, in effect Peru's ruling classes for generation upon generation. The military still controls the government, and may do so indefinitely, but it has been far less reformist since 1975 than it was before.

It is too early to know how much a partial roll-back of recent hard-won changes might provoke the sort of disappointment and anger that could ultimately lead to still greater transformations in the distribution and control of access, privilege, and resources. Any assessment of that possibility must be tempered by knowledge of the past. It bears repeating how old Peru is, how rapidly Spanish control was established there, and how long it lasted. Much of the "traditional" political and social structure of Peru was still in place four centuries later, despite the fact that signs of its breakdown began to appear as long as 50 years ago. Moreover, as an independent country for nearly 150 years, Peru has seen many of its central controlling groups profit from their practice in struggles of crisis management, particularly because the state was so often so weak. It is less weak now, and its greater strength almost surely means that present prospects for separatism are far weaker in Peru than in states that have become nations during the second half of this century. Peru's colonial heritage is part of its national heritage. There are no outside colonialists to overthrow, no power vacuums to be left by their disappearance.

Through most of Peruvian history, the majority of the people were so cut off from effective influence and participation that the post-1968 reforms seemed long overdue to most observers, and insufficient to many others when they finally arrived. Most Peruvians, so long impotent, more often accomodationist, compromising, and long-suffering than angry and effectively militant, may have neither choice nor inclination to do more than wait once again. There is little for them to rely on other than local resistance and pressure, to try to speed and take advantage of the long-term tendencies toward a more open and equitable society that economic modernization and increased political rationality can, but often do not, trail in their wake. It has been said that they also serve who stand and wait. Does time stand at their shoulders waiting to serve them better when their own waiting time is over?

BIBLIOGRAPHY

Bourque, Susan C. and David Scott Palmer. "Transforming the Rural Sector: Government Policy and Peasant Response." In A. Lowenthal (ed.). The Peruvian Experiment. Princeton: Princeton University Press, 1975. Pp. 179-219.

Chaplin, David. "Blue-Collar Workers in Peru," pp. 205 - 221. In D. Chaplin, (ed.). Peruvian Nationalism: a Corporatist Revolution. New Brunswick, N.J.: Transaction, Inc., 1976. Pp. 205-221.

Collier, David. "The Politics of Squatter Settlement in Peru." In D. Chaplin (ed.). Peruvian Nationalism, pp. 205 - 221.

Cotler, Julio. "The Mechanics of Internal Domination and Social Change in Peru." In D. Chaplin (ed.). Peruvian Nationalism.

Fuenzalida, V., Fernando and Enrique Mayer. El Peru de las tres razas. New York: United Nations Institute for Professional Development and Investigations, 1974.

Gerth, Hans and E. Wright Mills (eds.). From Max Weber. Essays in Sociology. New York: Oxford University Press, 1946.

Goodsell, Charles, T. American Corporations and Peruvian Politics. Cambridge: Harvard University Press, 1974.

Handelman, Howard. Struggle in the Andes. Austin: University of Texas Press, 1975.

Kahl, Joseph. Modernization, Exploitation, and Dependency in Latin America: Germani, Gonzalez Casanoya, and Cardoso. New Brunswick, N.J.: Transaction, Inc., 1976.

Lockhart, James. "The Social History of Colonial Spanish America: Evolution and Potential." Latin American Research Review 7 (1972): 6-46.

Morner, Magnus. Race Mixture in the History of Latin America. Boston: Little, Brown, 1967.

Paige, Jeffrey M. Agrarian Revolution: Social Movements and Export Agriculture in the Undeveloped World. New York: Free Press, 1975.

Patch, Richard W. "A note on Bolivia and Peru." American University Field Staff Reports, West Coast South America Series 12, no. 2, 1965.

Powell, Sandra. "Political Participation in the Barriadas," in D. Chaplin (ed.), Peruvian Nationalism, pp. 150-172.

Spalding, Karen. "The Colonial Indian: Past and Future Research Perspectives." Latin American Research Review 7 (1972): 47-76.

Van den Berghe, Pierre "Introduction" and "The Use of Ethnic Terms in the Peruvian Social Science Literature." International Journal of Comparative Sociology 15 (1974): 121-142.

Van den Berge, Pierre and George Primov. Inequality in the Peruvian Andes: Class and Ethnicity in Cuzco. Columbia: University of Missouri Press, 1977.

18 Autonomy Movements in India

Howard L. Erdman

"...there are forces in our society which tend to undermine unity and hamper national integration. We cannot ignore tham; they cannot be wished away."

Report of the Committee on
Emotional Integration,
Ministry of Education,
Government of India, 1962.

INTRODUCTION

True to its reputation or diversity, India has been confronted by a wide variety of autonomy movements. Virtually every dimension of India's diversity has at one time or another been brought into play, as religious, tribal, and linguistic cultural groups have become involved in the process.(1)

Some movements have been explicitly secessionist. These have been troublesome in principle, challenging the legitimate integrity of the Union of India, even when there has been reason to doubt the commitment of the movements' leaders to full separation. They have also been troublesome in practice, testing the political, and in some instances the military, capabilities of the regime. Non-secessionist demands for territorial redistribution of powers within the Union have been more numerous. Although these have not directly challenged the legitimacy of the Union, they have, in some instances, severely tested regime capabilities.

In both areas, the regime has met all such tests, in the

obvious yet important sense that India has remained intact and without debilitating domestic strife, and there is no compelling evidence to suggest that the Union is now in jeopardy. This judgment is not uniformly shared, and there is surely no reason for complacency, as India's leaders are themselves aware. Yet, in view of widely-heard predictions of balkanization, a bit of guarded optimism is entirely appropriate here. There is, of course, a difference between guarded optimism and wishful thinking.

THE BENEFITS OF PARTITION

An important reason for India's success in maintaining unity following independence in August 1947 is an event normally considered a major tragedy in human terms, and a major failure in state formation: the partition of India upon the departure of the British. The formation of Pakistan, with its attendant massive migration of peoples and communal slaughter, helped the truncated India in two, related respects. One is quite obvious, the other is more obscure and generally overlooked by non-Indian commentators.

First, partition removed many of the Muslims who were skeptical of their ability to live as first class citizens in a State whose population was overwhelmingly Hindu. As is abundantly clear from the painfully complex constitutional proposals of the early 1940s, an undivided India could have been purchased only at the price of a very weak central government. Provinces within India would have retained great autonomy and, under some proposals, they would have had the right to opt out of the Union altogether. A virtually-guaranteed threat of secession would thus have been built into the regime. Few doubt that a Pakistan would have come to pass in relatively short order.

Second, and less obvious, is the fact that a Muslim-required weak center would have encouraged political fragmentation in other respects as well. For example, under the British, more than five hundred "princely states" rule by (maha)rajas were preserved, albeit with attenuated powers, right up to independence. Reluctant to associate themselves with an all-India federation proposed in the Government of India Act of 1935, the princes cherished their considerable autonomy. They would have liked nothing more than a very weak center under which they, like the Muslim majority provinces, would have had great autonomy and, perhaps, the right to secede. Similar considerations would have also applied to virtually any territorially-based group concerned about its standing in a united India.

Partition removed the most intractable of the existing

problems and enabled India's leaders to opt for a more formidable center than would otherwise have been possible. It
also enabled that center to deal more forcefully with the
princes, some of whom literally declared their intention to
remain independent following the departure of the British.
The so-called "integration of the Indian [princely] states" was
a major, if usually neglected, stage in state formation in India.
Even the "Bismarck of India," Sardar Patel, would have found
the going very rough within an undivided India. The
stronger center would also be in better position to deal with
any future challenges to the integrity of the Union.(2)

RELIGIOUS DIVERSITY

The creation of Pakistan by no means eliminated religion
as a basis for autonomy movements. While overwhelmingly
Hindu, India contains a Muslim minority of about 10 percent,
or over 60 million people. Of other religious groups, the far
less numerous Sikhs are of greatest importance.
Most of the autonomy-minded Muslim leadership went to
Pakistan, thus "decapitating" the community that remained in
India. Further, many of the remaining Muslims were somewhat
intimidated, reluctant to assert themselves lest they be
charged with anti-Indian sentiment. Even so, there has been
considerable Muslim-oriented activity, and the possibility of a
resurgent Islam with extra-territorial links cannot be ruled
out.
Freedom of worship, and respect and support for Muslim
religious shrines and schools are formally granted by the
Constitution. A major issue is the status of the Urdu language as an official language of government business in those
states, especially in northern India, where Muslims are
numerous. Given the geographic spread of the Muslim
population, however, such concerns are devoid of a significant
territorial basis. However, within states in the Union, areas
of Muslim density can affect political subdivisions. Thus, as a
payoff for involvement in an electoral alliance in the state of
Kerala, Muslims were rewarded with a redemarcation of district
boundaries, enhancing the specifically Muslim character of an
already predominantly Muslim administrative unit.
Far more problematical, and potentially ominous for the
regime is the northern state of Kashmir. Overwhelmingly
Muslim, Kashmir, prior to independence, had been a princely
state, governed by a Hindu maharaja. Disposed to remain
independent, the ruler initially declined to join either successor State, but quickly joined India - as he was legally
entitled to do - as invading forces from Pakistan moved toward
his capital. India accepted his accession, dispatched troops

which turned back the invaders, and settled for a cease-fire
that left part of Kashmir under Pakistani control. However,
with parition based on religion, with Kashmir overwhelmingly
Muslim and contiguous to Pakistan, and with then Prime
Minister Nehru's aversion to a final settlement based solely on
the ruler's personal decision, there was considerable support
for a plebiscite to determine the wishes of the population of
Kashmir. No such plebiscite has been held. India considers
Kashmir legitimately part of the Union.

A wide variety of carrots and sticks has been employed
by the regime to keep Kashmir quietly within the Union. It
has a special constitutional status within India in that it does
not automatically come under certain parliamentary enactments;
and special attention has been paid to development measures.
Very significant is the fact that Kashmir's activities have been
closely monitored by other Indians. Kashmir is being kept
very much for the Kashmiris, in an obvious effort to minimize
potential conflict between the local population and other
Indians who might want to establish businesses or settle there.
The electoral process has been more carefully circumscribed
than elsewhere in India; and there is a massive military
presence. The "lion of Kashmir," Sheikh Abdullah, was under
house arrest for over a decade because of his commitment to
some sort of plebiscite.

With all of this, Kashmir stands somewhat "exposed." It
is vulnerable to activities by Pakistan, shares a border with
the Peoples' Republic of China, and is close to the USSR. If
only for these reasons, it is of more than passing interest to
the U.S.A. Kashmir, despite India's best efforts, will test the
integrity of the Union.

India's numerically small Sikh population has also been
involved in autonomy movements. Heavily concentrated in the
northwestern state of the Punjab, the proud, militant Sikhs
have long cherished local control over their destiny. Along
with the Muslims and some other groups, the Sikhs were accorded special representation by the British; and some militant
Sikh leaders intermittently talked of an entirely independent
Sikh homeland - Sikhistan. After independence, the Sikhs
were a large minority in the state of the Punjab; and some of
their leadership agitated for the creation of a new state in
which they would constitute a majority. The demand was not
put forth on religious grounds, however; rather, the Sikhs
somewhat speciously argued in terms of the distinctiveness of
their local language, Punjabi, and script, Gurmukhi which
they used. In this form, the religiously-based Sikh claim
sought to be subsumed under the heading of the linguistic
reorganization of India's states. Most Indian leaders contended
that the demands were religious rather than linguistic, that
whatever problems existed in the region would not be settled
by the creation of a de facto Sikh majority state, and that the

demand should, therefore, be rejected; and so it was. However, continued Sikh agitation, including periodic fasts, led to the creation of such a state in 1966, thereby satisfying the aspirations of the vast majority of the Sikhs, who comprise about 55 percent of the new Punjab. In view of the continuing "mixed" character of the state's population, it would be premature to assume that this particular matter is settled.(3)

India's Christians, although more numerous than the Sikhs, have not yet been associated with any significant autonomy movements, save where relatively isolated tribal populations, occasionally with missionary support have sought to preserve or enhance their autonomy. Most notable among these are the Nagas. In the southwest state of Kerala, however, where Christians constitute about 30 percent of the population, some pressures for territorial readjustments might well arise.

TRIBAL GROUPS

India's population contains a sizeable number of tribal peoples, most of them living in relatively compact hinterland regions and possessing their own distinct languages and cultural patterns. Many of them have been involved in autonomy movements, both secessionist and non-secessionist.

Most notable among the former are the Nagas, who occupy sensitive border areas in northeast India. Resisting post-independence efforts to integrate them more fully into the public life of plains-dominated Assam, some Nagas have carried on bitter guerrilla warfare, with an underground government in the tribal hills and a government-in-exile in London. Largely because of their location, they were able to receive external aid from diverse quarters, including some from the P.R.C. The Nagas political and military demands on the regime have been great. The creation of a separate Naga state in 1963 gave the tribe greater control of its own destiny and reconciled, at least temporarily, most of those who were autonomy-minded. Related policies, such as the requirement that the Naga tribal council must explicitly approve the transfer of Naga land to non-Nagas, have further sought to diminish friction-producing interaction with non-Nagas. Some of the Nagas remain resolutely separatist, however, and carry on intermittent guerrilla warfare. Were it not for the exposed border position and some external interference, the regime would have had a far easier time of it; but precisely because of these factors, and the general fluidity of the multi-cultural situation in the northeast, continuing challenges may be expected.

Other tribal groups have also agitated for greater auton-

omy within the Union. Some, in the same uplands border
region where the Nagas live, have been given separate political
identity as part of a comprehensive effort to stabilize the
political situation in the northeast. For example, a special
Union-protected territory was accorded the Mizo tribes in 1972.
Other tribal groups that have agitated for great autonomy have
thus far had their demands for separate state rejected. Most
notable among these is a movement representing a number of
diverse tribes in the eastern state of Bihar and in part of
Orissa that for a time pressed its demands through its own
political party, the Jharkand party. Although separate state-
hood was not conceded, conciliatory policies have been adopted
to respond to some Jharkand demands.

Other groups have advanced, and will no doubt continue
to advance, autonomy demands, especially as they become more
extensively involved in the larger Indian economy on a sustained basis. Both under the British and after 1947, the civil
administration in tribal areas was dominated by educated non-
tribals. "Outsiders" are, by and large, far better prepared to
exploit natural resources and develop industry than are the
tribals themselves, which has been a major factor in the
position of the tribes in India. Although many more tribals
are now equipped to govern themselves within the new political
framework and are better equipped to participate in the wider
economy, they are still in the process of catching up and may,
in any event, question whether they want to undergo the
steady erosion of distinctive tribal life styles through such
wider involvement. As in other cases, it would be foolish to
think that this matter is settled.(4)

LINGUISTIC-CULTURAL DIVERSITY

India's linguistic-cultural diversity has regularly been
identified as a major challenge to the integrity of the Union.
Indeed, following partition, the merchants of gloom, and there
has certainly been no shortage of them among India-watchers,
were convinced that this was the rock upon which the Indian
ship of state would break up. India's leaders were naturally
more sanguine, but they know better than anyone that this
will be a continuing challenge, even if balkanization is
averted.

While the leaders of the Indian National Congress were
belaboring the British for encouraging divisiveness among the
various groups to the detriment of unity, they were also
belaboring them for failing to use linguistic-cultural boundaries
as the basis for internal political subdivisions. Obviously
confident that "linguistic states" were compatible with long-
term unity, the INC reorganized itself along these lines during

the 1920s and promised linguistic states after independence.
        As independence neared, however, the INC leadership
retreated from the principle of linguistic states. Citing a
variety of factors, such as economic and administrative
viability, that would have to be weighed in the balance, the
leaders made it abundantly clear that a major concern was the
threat to unity. The situation was reviewed in the 1950s:

> The language and culture of an area have an un-
> doubted importance as they represent a pattern of
> living in that area. In considering a reorganization
> of States, however, there are other important
> factors which have also to be borne in mind. The
> first essential consideration in the preservation and
> strengthening of the unity and security of India...
> India has embarked upon a great ordered plan for
> her economic, cultural and moral progress.
> Changes which interfere with the successful
> prosecution of such a national plan would be
> harmful to the national interest.(5)

        However, the damage had been done: Having suggested
that a separate Telugu-speaking state might be constituted,
without generally accepting the linguistic principle, the government was forced to concede in the aftermath of fasts and
riots. And once Telugu-speaking Andhra was created, the
rest was only a matter of time. With the exception of Bombay
and the Punjab, states were reorganized according to the
linguistic principle in 1956. In the face of continuing
agitations, the GOI divided Bombay in 1960, and the Punjab in
1966. India's states are now, for all practical purposes, based
on the linguistic principle.
        These who subscribed to the balkanization thesis ob-
viously did not expect matters to end with the formation of
linguistic states. Themselves creatures of parochialism, or
what Indians term "fissiparous tendencies," linguistic states
were expected to intensify local chauvinism further and to
contribute, willy-nilly, to the eventual break-up of the union,
even if secession was not a part of some states' original
programs, and even if others were determined to keep the
Union in tact. The argument runs as follows:
        First, each of India's linguistic groups has an associated
literature, and culture that is a source of pride and a basis
for mobilizing people in a variety of ways.
        Second, it is held that not only are there such dif-
ferences among Indians, but these differences often have an
antagonistic historical dimension. For example, one cultural
group's real or imaginary Golden Age often includes domination
over another group of Indians.

Third, as education in the regional language proceeds apace, parochial themes will predominate, reviving - if they were ever dormant - such historical antagonisms. "Already in the schools of some of the States, songs exalting the regional idea have been introduced into text books. History books taught in lower classes have disclosed a marked tendency to exaggerate the past achievements of the dominant linguistic groups. These inevitable tendencies in language based States will unavoidably weaken our sense of national unity."(6) Thus, even if done without malice afterthought, any linguistic minorities or visitors would be made to feel uncomfortable or unwelcome. To the extent that people knew only their own regional language, they would be literally unable to communicate with other Indians.

Fourth, whatever tendencies toward parochialism exist on such a basis, they will be exploited and intensified under conditions of economic scarcity and democratic politics. In the clamor for scarce resources, including jobs, outsiders, even if they are not identified as exploiters, become vulnerable and are prime targets for exclusion in favor of "sons of the soil." In the clamor to get elected, local politicians will at their own peril ignore such sentiment; rather, so the argument goes, they will have ample temptation to whip up a storm of localism, because that is the "language" in which the voting public is inclined to think.

Fifth, as such movements gain momentum, however unevenly, across India, they will exacerbate interstate tensions and invite reprisals in other parts of the country, making each linguistic state more and more insular and contentious vis-a-vis the rest.

Sixth, it is held that the Indian National Congress and the Indian Administrative Service, the two great civilian political instruments which served India so well after independence are themselves being fragmented and will be unable to perform their integrative roles, as in the past. The result will be balkanization, a military regime.(7)

Throughout the 1950s and 1960s, the major source of concern was the southern Indian state of Madras. There, prior to independence, the Dravidian Federation (D.K.) articulated an ideology that held there were two races in India, the Aryans of the north and the Dravidians of the south. The D.K. further contended that classical Hinduism was imposed in imperialistic fashion on the south by Aryan brahmans, and that, as long as the Dravidians remained subject to the GOI, they would at best be neglected, at worst exploited. It recommended resolute anti-northernism, which would include anti-brahman and anti-orthodox Hindu elements, with the eventual aim of secession - the formation of Dravidistan or Dravida Nadu. An extreme minority routinely burned Indian flags and copies of the Constitution, opposed Hindi as the official Union language and its study in local schools, burned copies of Hinduism's sacred scriptures, and even advocated the killing of brahmans. It was a very small minority, however.

Much of this ideology, somewhat tamed, was carried forth by the more notable and successful political offshoot of the D.K., the D.M.K. (Dravidian Progressive Federation). The D.M.K. was explicitly secessionist, although many doubted the commitment to secession; they pointed to the party's view that the entire Dravidian south would have to secede, not just the state of Madras where the D.M.K.'s strength was confined. Even so, there was considerable fear that the D.M.K., emphasizing northern Indian exploitation, would seek to take Madras out of the Union.

The results were far short of another Biafra, despite considerable agitation, sometimes violent, in opposition to the use of Hindi as the official language of the Union government, the symbol par excellence of northern domination. Largely as a result of determined southern Indian opposition, English remains as an associate official Union language, although the original constitutional requirement called for English to be replaced by Hindi in 1965.

Beyond this the D.M.K.'s record points in the direction of accomodation rather than secession. For example, it was thought that the D.M.K. might exploit an international crisis to take Madras out of the Union; instead, it supported India in the 1962 border war with China, saying, in effect, that secession could wait. Subsequently, the D.M.K. lost its pre-1962 zeal, in part because of a constitutional amendment banning secessionist appeals - an amendment which, many held, was welcomed by the D.M.K. Madras became Tamil Nadu - the land or place of the Tamils - after the D.M.K.'s accession to power in 1967. Instruction in Hindi, the official-language-to-be, was drastically curtailed, and state and party flags were to be flown above or on a level equal with the Union flag; but no effort to secede was made, nor is there one in the offing. The GOI has, thus far, been able to accomodate the D.M.K., the most explicitly linguistic-cultural, anti-center political movement in India.

The continuing potential for disaffection is acknowledged, however. When the Peoples' Party (Janata), led by Morarji Desai, routed Indira Gandhi's Congress Party in elections in March 1977, it secured its comfortable parliamentary majority at the center solely on the basis of northern votes; it has virtually no parliamentary support from any of the southern states, and does not control any of the state governments. Thus superficially a northern party, containing many people who had advocated a swift changeover to Hindi as the official language, Janata, through Desai, explicitly reassured the south that it would not be orphaned, let alone exploited.(8) It would, however, be foolhardy to think that the south - Tamil Nadu in particular - will not be heard from again; and there will be no shortage of local politicians who will raise the charge of neglect or discrimination, especially if the Hindi issue bulks large again.

Although the eastern state of Bengal has not received the attention devoted to Tamil Nadu, the regime has good cause for concern in that area. Bengalis have long been proud of their regional culture, and, through the locally-powerful, Marxist-oriented Communist Party of India, they have found vocal champions for greater autonomy within the Union. With their Bengali counterparts to the east separating themselves from Pakistan to form Bangladesh, some of India's Bengalis no doubt considered what independence might mean to them, possibly a reunited Bengal. The CPI has intermittently been involved in Bengal ministries; it now dominates state politics, and gives evidence of becoming more strident in its demands for greater autonomy from a center controlled by a different political party. Important in itself, a serious secessionist effort among Bengalis would have massive repercussions: as a glance at the map of India will show, India's only present land link with its volatile northeastern states is a narrow corridor in Bengal.

Short of explicitly secessionist movements, there will be enough autonomy and "sons of the soil" movements to keep any regime in New Delhi quite busy. Because of its virulence, the most notable among "sons of the soil" groups is the Shiv Sena in and around Bombay city. A group dedicated to keeping the state of Maharashtra for the Masharashtrians, the Shiv Sena has directed much of its energy toward harassing, intimidating, physically abusing, and occasionally murdering non-Maharashtrians, especially southern Indians, of whom there are sizable numbers in the Bombay city labor force. Nevertheless, unless such movements multiply and intensify across a wide part of India, they are no short-run threat to the integrity of the Union, however much they disturb the peace and the principles of the ardent nationalist.(9)

While such movements are not being taken lightly, the regime still has a great deal going for it in its efforts to mitigate their effects. Apart from its own political skill, the regime can certainly count on, and take advantage of, some forces which run counter to linguistic-cultural fragmentation.

For one thing, in many of the present linguistic states there are movements for further subdivision; groups in one region complain of neglect at the hands of those who dominate the state government. Such movements, which would include certain tribal groups, may not augur well for peace and quiet on the reorganization front, but they do serve to mitigate the impact of strictly linguistic-cultural movements. And it could very plausibly be argued, despite the regime's understandable reluctance to be redrawing state boundaries constantly, that the Union would be more stable with 30 or more states than with fewer, larger, more potentially viable ones.

A second factor concerns non-geographically based groups in existing states. Thus, for example, it is not at all clear to what extent untouchables in Bombay city identify with the Shiv Sena and its campaign to secure "Maharashtra for the Maharashtrians." For some purposes, the local untouchables identify with the "Dalit Panthers," a Bombay-based group of militant untouchables, and with untouchable groups outside of the state. There are other interests that dimininish the impact of the linguistic-cultural forces by looking both "below" and "above" the level of the linguistic state. And one place many groups in India regularly look is to the government at the center. Apart from any political skills which the center may have, and they are considerable, there are interests which clearly cut across those associated with regional languages and cultures. Quite apart from considerations of patriotism, Indians committed to the maintenance of the Union simply do not, and will not, want to become embroiled with monolithic linguistic-cultural formations forever moving away from the center. They take pride in India's achievements, have an ever-extending network of economic interdependencies, and fear outside domination if they should secede.

WHAT LIES IN STORE?

India's post-1947 efforts to maintain unity have obviously been successful in the sense that even those movements that have been explicitly secessionist have not led to fragmentation. Dealing with the Nagas has been vexing and costly, and has involved the use of the military means. However, the creation of Nagaland has satisfied many and, barring extensive external intervention, regime resources should be adequate to deal with those who are unreconciled to autonomy within the Indian union. The D.M.K. movement, even at its most explicitly secessionist peak, was not the immediate threat that many had feared. The party itself has now split. (Hindsight is wonderful!) Sikhistan was, in the vernacular, a "non-starter." It must be emphasized, however, that a major reason for India's ability to contain such pressures was the stronger center that partition made possible.

Many factors, obviously, will affect India's continued ability to maintain its unity, just as many factors will affect the extent and character of the autonomy movements with which the regime will have to deal.

Direct and Indirect "Confrontations Among Groups

Autonomy demands will continue to be caused by <u>interaction</u> among the diverse groups which comprise India's population. Where groups are relatively free of penetration by outsiders, policies which limit competitive interaction will diiminish inter-group tensions and, thereby some of the autonomy demands. That India's leaders are sensitive to this is clear from the Kashmir situation. Where interaction is already a fact of life, one may anticipate that "sons of the soil" movements, including tribal ones will cause friction as they attempt to reduce undesired interaction by favoring locals to the exclusion of outsiders.

However, interaction of a more remote nature may be necessary to preserve the Union. Even if local affairs are dominated by "sons of the soil," trouble will arise if there is a feeling of consistent neglect or exploitation vis-a-vis the center. Political representation and expenditures for development must be perceived as relatively just if states such as Tamil Nadu are to feel comfortable within the Union, even if every major activity within the state's boundaries is carried on by "sons of the soil." That India's leaders are sensitive to this is clear from the speed with which Prime Minister Desai sought to reassure the four southern states that, despite being governed by parties other than the Janata, which controls the center, they would not be stepchildren within the Union.

External Factors and Geopolitical Considerations

In the above summaries, I have noted and stressed the importance of location and the opportunity for external influence as significant factors in the extent and character of autonomy demands. An autonomy-minded tribal group embedded in central India is, other things being equal, far less a challenge to the regime than one located on a border, especially if that border is fluid and open to external influences; the Nagas and Mizos are examples of this. Similarly, an overwhelmingly Muslim state in central India would not be as vulnerable as one contiguous to Pakistan and other countries that might choose to subvert the Indian regime. For related reasons, a lower level of pressure in Bengal could do far more harm to the unity of India than a higher level of pressure in Tamil Nadu because of Bengal's border position and its control of the sole land corridor to the northeastern region, itself troubled and periodically tumultuous. India, for precisely these reasons, is taking special care to maintain stability and security in these areas.

By the same token, however, prospective relations with adjacent regimes will be a factor in pressing for secession: there is little evidence, now, for example, that many Kashmiri Muslims want any part of the political turbulence of Pakistan; and, although the consequences of the new regime in Afghan-

istan are by no means clear, it is unlikely that they will be
beneficial to India, or even to any secession-minded Kashmiris.

Scope Considerations

Obviously, the capabilities of the regime would be more
sorely taxed by several major challenges coming simultaneously
than by a few localized ones, although even one major challenge could be very demanding. Given the extent of India,
and the unevenness of development within it, major, simultaneous autonomy movements are unlikely in the absence of
coordinated external efforts or regime policies that are narrowly focused, most likely on an aggressively Hindi-Hindu
chauvinistic basis. Neither seems likely at present, and the
incumbent government is abundantly aware of the fact that it
must reassure parts of the Union where it has no significant
political representation.

CONCLUSION

India's founding fathers devised a constitution for a
federal democracy. Thus far India's abundant diversity has
been contained within that framework, owing in no small part
to the accomodative approach of a time-tested political elite:
Kashmir has received very special consideration in a variety of
ways; tribals have in many cases been given their own states
of territories, and linguistic states have been conceded.
Policies have reflected great sensitivity to these elements of
Indian society. Hindu private law was codified in the 1950s.
Islamic law was not. Naga territory may not be alienated to
non-Nagas without the sanction of the tribal council. The
constitution provides for guaranteed representation for tribals
through "reserved seats," which are also provided for the
untouchables; and the President of the Union may appoint
members to parliament to represent interests not otherwise
represented, Anglo-Indians, for example. The official language question has been handled quite pragmatically. Where
accomodation has seemed inappropriate or has failed, the
regime has availed itself of constitutionally-provided powers,
including those for "President's rule," under which a state
may be governed by the center for specified periods of time,
and for outright emergency rule. By all accounts, India's
record has been admirable, given the enormity of the problems
confronting it. Her seasoned political leaders are not likely to
embark on policies which would alienate large segments of the
population simultaneously; and they should, moreover, be able
to cope with autonomy-oriented movements as they continue to
manifest themselves.

NOTES

1. For a general, politically oriented survey, see Robert L. Hardgrave, Jr., India: Government and Politics in a Developing Nation (2nd ed., New York: Harcourt, Brace, Jovanovich, 1975), chaps. 4 and 5, and the parts of chapter 6 that deal with autonomy-oriented political parties.
2. These points are developed in V.V. Nagarkar, Genesis of Pakistan (Bombay: Allied Publishers, 1975); V.P. Menon, The Story of the Integration of the Indian States (Bombay: Orient Longmans, 1956); and idem, The Transfer of Power in India (Bombay: Orient Longmans, 1957). S.M. Lipset, The First New Nation (New York: Basic Books, 1963), speculates that political life in the U.S. might well have been different had Royalists not been able to migrate to Canada in 1776, thus eliminating them as sources of instability in the fledgling republic.
3. For a group of Muslims in the south, see Roland E. Miller, Mappila Muslims of Kerala (Bombay: Orient Longmans, 1976); for Kashmir, see Josef Korbel, Danger in Kashmir (Princeton: Princeton University Press, 1966); for the Sikhs, see Baldev Raj Nayar, Minority Politics in the Punjab (Princeton: Princeton University Press, 1966).
4. For the Nagas, see Y.D. Gundevia, War and Peace in Nagaland (Dehra Dun: Palit and Palit, 1975). For more general coverage (including the Nagas), see Hardgrave, India; Myron Weiner, The Politics of Scarcity (Chicago: University of Chicago Press, 1962), chap. 3, "Community Associations"; and the chapter by Furer-Haimendorf in Philip Mason (ed.), India and Ceylon: Unity and Diversity (London: Oxford University Press, 1967).
5. From a Ministry of Home Affairs Resolution, December 1963, reproduced in Report of the States Reorganization Commission 1955, p. 264.
6. Ibid., p. 39.
7. For the balkanization thesis, see Selig Herrison, India: The Most Dangerous Decades (Princeton: Princeton University Press, 1960). For the D.M.K., etc., see Hardgrave, India.
8. Prime Minister Desai concluded his April 4, 1977 inaugural broadcast to the nation with the words: "Whatever geographical distribution of seats won by the Janata party, the people of the South should have absolutely no fear that their interests will be overlooked. This is a national government, and no region or segment of the population has reason to feel orphaned; and I am sure that in the course of time they will realize that their fears, if any, were groundless and that their legitimate aspirations are

fulfilled.   Nor need state governments formed by other
parties worry about lack of cooperation from the center."
9.   For the Shiv Sena and D.M.K., see Hargrave, India, and
the sources cited there.

SELECTED BIBLIOGRAPHY

Desai, Morarji.   Indian Unity: From Dream to Reality.   New
Delhi: Government of India, 1964.

Gundevia, Y.D.   War and Peace in Nagaland.   Dehra Dun:
Palit and Palit, 1975.

Hardgrave, Robert L., Jr.   India: Government and Politics
in a Developing Nation.   2nd ed. New York: Harcourt Brace
Jovanovich, 1975.

Harrison, Selig.   India: The Most Dangerous Decades.   Princeton: Princeton University Press, 1960.

Korbel, Josef.   Danger in Kashmir.   Princeton: Princeton
University Press, 1966.

Mason, Philip (ed.).   India and Ceylon: Unity and Diversity.
London: Oxford University Press, 1967.

Menon, V.P. The Story of the Integration of the Indian States.
Bombay: Orient Longmans, 1956.

_____.   The Transfer of Power in India.   Bombay: Orient
Longmans, 1957.

Miller, Roland E.   Mappila Muslims of Kerala.   Bombay: Orient
Longmans, 1976.

Nayar, Baldev Raj.   Minority Politics in the Punjab.   Princeton: Princeton University Press, 1966.

Nagarkar, V.V.   Genesis of Pakistan.   Bombay: Allied Publishers, 1975.

Schermerhorn, R.A.   Ethnic Plurality in India.   Tucson: University of Arizona Press, 1978.

Weiner, Myron   The Politics of Scarcity.   Chicago: University
of Chicago Press, 1962.   See Ch. 3, "Community Associations."

Government of India.   Report of the Official Language Commission.   New Delhi, 1956.

_____.   Report of the States Reorganization Commission.
New Delhi, 1955.

_____.   Report of the Committee on Emotional Integration.
New Delhi, 1962.

V
Autonomy in Perspective

Introduction

The last part of this volume attempts to place ethnicity and
ethnic autonomy, particularly separatism, in international
perspective. Sterling, a leading authority on international
relations, argues that "ethnic separatism, wherever it appears,
is a political movement whose purpose is the parting of
peoples. In all cases, it is directed against prevailing
domestic political arrangements, and aspires to a greater
measure of self-government for the ethnic group it represents.
Just as soon as separatist discontent surfaces, an affected
state becomes relatively weaker than surrounding states, and
absolutely weaker than states whose internal unity is intact.
In all cases - and at all stages - separatism affects state
power."
    Finally, the McCords are concerned with ethnicity and
separatism from a socio-historical perspective. In addition,
they undertake the difficult task of attempting to place most of
the above contributions in a framework whereby they can be
assessed with respect to their strengths and weaknesses.

19 Ethnic Separatism in the International System
Richard W. Sterling

Ethnic separatism, wherever it appears, is a political movement whose purpose is the parting of peoples (all further references to separatism should be taken to mean ethnic separatism, unless otherwise specified). Hence, it is a phenomenon that necessarily straddles the boundary between domestic and international politics. The separatist ethnic movement is, in all cases, directed against prevailing domestic political arrangements. In all cases, too, it aspires to a greater measure of self-government for the ethnic group it seeks to represent. In very many of these cases, the goal of separatism is to form a new sovereignty, to introduce a new actor into the international system. The system itself will undergo greater or lesser change as a consequence of the new member's presence.

Moreover, the international behavior of the remainder state, diminished by secession, will be significantly altered. Its role and weight in the international system will change from what it was when the separating society was still part of its domain. Thus, when separatism succeeds in achieving independence, a new actor is added to international politics, and an established actor is no longer able to follow accustomed policies.

These kinds of changes or prospective changes, in turn, cause other members of the international system to recalculate their interests. Separatist movements, whether incipient or full-blown, invite the attention of other international actors to the degree they perceive their interests to be affected. A new presence on the international scene, and the altered status of one previously established, will unavoidably alter regional or global relations of power and weakness.

The actual achievement of sovereignty by the separatist movement is by no means the necessary condition for effecting an internationalization of what were once domestic issues. Just as soon as separatist discontent surfaces, an affected state becomes relatively weaker than surrounding states, and absolutely weaker than states whose internal unity is intact. In all cases - and at all stages - separatism affects state power. It follows that separatism must also affect both the structure and process of international politics.

In consonance with these observations, the present inquiry examines separatism as a phenomenon in the global system. It considers the impact of separatist movements on the general conduct of international relations and on specific foreign policies. Because it deals with a number of different separatist movements around the world, this essay also seeks to make a contribution to a comparative evaluation of separatist movements by distinguishing some elements common to all such movements from elements unique to particular movements. Finally, but first in order of analysis, it explores the relationship of separatism to nationalism, because in the main, it is nationalism that has shaped the politics of separation in the modern world.

In the ancient world, Moses might well claim title to being the first separatist leader of record. The story of Exodus bore all the earmarks of modern separatist dynamics: ethnic, religious, class, and cultural conflict led to the persecution of ethnic minority by ethnic majority. However, the flight of the Jews from Egypt, as well as their subsequent dispersions, are exceptional in the annals of ancient history. The rule was one of heterogeneous groups living over long periods of time in close proximity to one another in both urban and rural settings.

Differences in language, culture, and religion within the city's walls, or in the adjacent countryside, meant that the diverse groups lived side-by-side as separate communities. The social pattern was one of a neighborhood of tribes, clans, or cults. Like any other set of intergroup relations, it was a pattern marked by hostility and indifference as well as collaboration and alliance. But the persistence of diversity in close quarters was accepted as a given; geographical separation was not perceived as a live option.

Nor was political independence. In most areas, the ruling power was in the hands of military, landlord, or merchant elites whose members were usually themselves of diverse origin. It was their interest to impose law, order, and taxes on urban or rural units as a whole, and not to represent one or another group within the governmental unit. Their contacts with the varied communities within the realm were indirect; they taxed and ruled through the agency of the several community leaders. These ancient governing practices continually reenforced the assumption that diversity of communities and leadership was an immutable feature of the political landscape.

Like others before and after, the Romans took over these multicultural microcosms virtually intact and used them to build the macrocosm of empire. Compliant provincial leaders became Roman citizens and thus part of the governing elite. But the peoples of the provinces remained largely the same in their inherited diversities as well as in their inherited status of political subordination. The only obvious change for the governed of the Roman Empire was a change of governors. The distribution of power between elite and mass remained constant.

Rome's inheritors in medieval Europe and the world of Islam perpetuated the transmitted patterns of social structure, cultural diversity, and elite rule. The millet system of the Ottoman Empire was a notable exemplar. With latter day exceptions, such as the Armenian persecutions, peoples of the Empire were left largely undisturbed, save for a head tax imposed on the various communities and collected by the community authorities. Just as in Medieval Europe, the majority of people under the Ottomans shared the one common bond of religion. Their otherwise divergent communal allegiances based on kinship, culture, or language were of little importance in the political scheme of things.

The multicultural politics of the Islamic tradition remain a powerful force in the contemporary Middle East. They are, indeed, still locked in combat with the new forces of nationalism and provide an essential part of the explanation for the ferocity of political conflict in the region. These observations apply with equal force to contemporary Africa and, to a lesser extent, to Asia and Latin America. That is to say, almost all countries of the Third World continue to exhibit the traditional pattern of a diversity of cultural groups with separate senses of identity but governed collectively with more or less effectiveness and coercion by minority elites.

The great breakaway from what was until then the universal tradition of government took place in eighteenth century Europe. Among leaders and in public sentiment, the idea of homogeneous nations began to gain adherents and then to replace the collection of heterogeneous cultural groups as the accepted unit of government and political allegiance. The national model gained its force from historical trends that had already amalgamated many smaller linguistic, cultural, and ethnic communities into larger groupings. But the decisive appeal of nationalism was not so much its conversion of microethnicity into macroethnicity; it was, instead, nationalism's ideological break with elite rule and its championship of the mass society.

Whether culturally homogeneous or heterogeneous, the mass in the elite state lacked power and so remained politically undifferentiated. Whether majority or minority in terms of race, ethnicity, or language, the mass was politically inert.

Nationalism initiated a revolutionary change: it began to energize the mass. The central tenet of nationalism was that political participation is the birthright of all who belong to the nation. With one doctrinal stroke, nationalism declared war on the elite rule of the traditional state, and the ideological connection between nationalism and democracy was born. From the beginning, modern nationalism and modern democracy became sometime allies; both aimed to break the monopoly of the traditional ruling classes. But it was only an alliance and not an identity of purpose.

The formal platform of democracy was power to the people. The formal platform of nationalism was power to the nation. The difference between the democratic and the nationalist doctrines was the distinction between a demand for an end to elite rule everywhere and a demand for an end to elite rule in a single society defined in terms of territory, ethnicity, language, historical association, and other discrete characteristics. In short, nationalism championed the transfer of power from the elite governors not to the people in general but to a specific ethnic mass.

Up to a point, nationalism and democracy reenforced one another in the highly complex process that jointly produced mass power. The process obviously involved much more than pioneering the long road from the equality doctrines of 1776 and the 1789 to the achievement of universal suffrage in the twentieth century West. Essential to its forward movement was the growth of entrepreneurial activity, capital accumulation, and then free labor and labor organization. This energizing of capital and labor, in turn, was the indispensable forerunner of mass production and mass consumption. The final element basic to the process was the continual expansion of access to education.

The transfer of power from elite to mass under the double aegis of nationalism and democracy enormously extended the reach of the political community. However, because nationalism was the stronger force, it rigidified the boundaries between those who belonged to the enlarged community and those who did not. The old barrier between elite and mass was replaced by a new barrier between ethnic majorities and ethnic minorities. The nationalisms of the United States and of all the major nations of Europe - England, France, Germany, Russia, Italy, and Spain - were nationalisms of the majority populations. The ethnic minorities lost their traditional status as an accepted part of an otherwise politically undifferentiated mass and became appendages to the new ruling majorities. Without exception, the ethnic majorities attempted to impose their cultural values on the ethnic minorities within the new national jurisdictions.

The only defense against the new power of the national majority was to make the minority as powerful as possible.

Several strategies were available to achieve this objective: internal alliances, internal development, external alliances, and secession. Each specific case of minority political action has exhibited a unique combination of these strategies and, of course, variations on the strategic themes.

The internal alliance strategy is the oldest expedient of minorities. It seeks to capitalize on divisions within the majority group by contracting to throw political support to one or another of the mainstream contenders in return for concession to minority, or minority elite, demands. But prior to the mass state, it was a private game played by minority elites and the governors of elite states. With the coming of the mass state, the game became public; ethnic numbers and bloc votes gradually came to be the chief instruments of persuasion.

Although this strategy has often registered successes, its limitations are evident. Majority politicians can also play the balance-of-power game by initiating policies aimed at dividing ethnic leadership and bloc votes and by reducing minority influence through the manipulation of electoral districting. If there is more than one ethnic minority, majority balance-of-power techniques take the form of playing off one against another. Above all, the majority players in the internal alliances attempt to restrict the minority to a static role and ephemeral gains, thereby perpetuating their own superior position.

The internal development strategy seeks to bring the minority population to a level that is at least even with the majority in terms of wealth and education in order to improve the minority's living conditions and its political bargaining position. The history of the United States, in particular, offers abundant evidence to show that minority development strategy can succeed only if the majority is disposed to accept a long-term redistribution of power. The firmness of that disposition is still in the testing stage. It is also still hobbled by the contradiction between the concept of assimilation and the concept of autonomous cultural development.

Still, if the internal development strategy succeeds, minorities in the United States (and elsewhere) will be able to address the issue of assimilation or autonomy from a more advantageous power position, and with a greater degree of cultural self-awareness and self-confidence. What is not in doubt is the impact of nationalism, democracy, and mass society in the countries of the West; ethnic minorities, wherever they may be, now demand the same instruments of mass power enjoyed by ethnic majorities.

Obviously, these instruments cannot be used to alter ethnic ratios, but they can be used to combat ethnic discrimination. Slowly and unevenly, rising levels of wealth and education erode the class and status aspects of social bias against minorities, just as they previously breached the non-

ethnic class line that divided traditional elites and masses.
The strategy of internal development among minorities is, in
fact, a reenactment of the process of (majority) national internal development. Its goal is also the same: the egalitarian
proposition that there should be no second class citizens.

Thus, mass nationalism among majorities spawned mass
nationalism among minorities. Traditionally inert and politically
faceless during the long ascendancy of the elite state, ethnic
majorities and minorities subsequently divided into distinct
political blocs. The characteristic response of the minority to
this division was the conviction that it had traded the tyranny
of an elite for the far more pervasive tyranny of the majority.
The characteristic response of the majority was to doubt the
value and loyalty of the minority to the nation. Where internal
strategies were perceived as inadequate to resolve the conflict, minorities typically turned to external strategies.

Ethnic minorities may strive to amalgamate with fellow
ethnics beyond the national border. Poland is a classic
example; for nearly two centuries, it was divided into three
parts by Austria, Prussia, and Russia. Or ethnic minorities
may seek external protectors with whom they may or may not
have ethnic bonds. Tsarist Russia displayed an avid, though
sporadic, interest in playing the role of protector not only to
the Slavic populations in the Turkish and Austrian empires,
but also to the Greek and Armenian populations under Ottoman
rule. The Russian protector role in turn, was intimately
linked to Russian aspirations for imperial expansion and thus
to the dynamics of international power rivalry.

The Russian example can serve to illustrate a general
proposition: ethnic minorities that pursue external strategies
are engaged in enterprises carrying high risks of violence.
The state facing secession resists the severance. Even if the
minority is deemed undesirable and disloyal, its departure
means a decline in mass power and levels of production, plus
losses in territory, strategic boundaries, buffer zones, and
other components of the physical security of the state. The
argument of reason, that these losses might be outweighed by
the consolidation of a national society unburdened by a dissatisfied minority within its borders, has usually gone un-
heeded. Reason is further disconcerted by the behavior of
rival states, which are typically less interested in any given
separatist cause than in the dividends it might yield for their
own power interests.

Separation unavoidably involves the redistribution of
sovereignty and the relocation of national boundaries. It
follows that the international power structure will undergo
alterations, although the ultimate losers and beneficiaries are
not always immediately obvious. In any case, separatist
demands, both singly and cumulatively, created a new international fault line in the world of nations, and particularly in
the European political system where nationalism originated.

Indeed, separatist politics were the catalysts, although not the root causes, of both World Wars. The Austrian Archduke was assassinated at Sarajevo by members of the South Slav nationalist movement, whose objectives had long been supported by Russia, and whose purpose was secession from Austria-Hungary and unification with Serbia. In the west, the determination of France to retrieve French Lorraine as well as ethnically-German Alsace, thereby undoing the Prussian conquest of 1870, was a basic and intractable issue in the Franco-German emnity that exploded in 1914.

Ethnic minority issues played an even greater role in the outbreak of World War II. Mussolini's irredentist claims against France for Corsica, Savoy, Nice, and even Tunisia, were both tenuous in their ethnic rationale and secondary in their international importance. It was German ethnics beyond the borders of Hitler's Reich who became the triggers of war and peace in Europe. The mounting power of the Nazis was matched by the growing stridency of their ethnic-nationalist demands. The result was the fatal 18-month sequence of events that led to war: the annexation of Austria, the Munich agreement to cede the German-majority areas of Czechoslovakia to Germany, and Hitler's attack on Poland, ostensibly to reclaim German Danzig and the not-so-German Polish Corridor.

Almost all of the ethnic issues enmeshed in the causes and consequences of both World Wars involved the transfer of sovereignty. Minorities demanding new national sovereignties of their own established Poland, Czechoslovakia, Finland, the three Baltic states, the Ottoman-ruled Arab states, and, briefly, the Ukraine. Other minorities demanded unification with an existing ethnically-related sovereign state - Yugoslavia, Romania, Italy, France, Belgium, Denmark and, in the 1930s, Germany. Whatever the category of sovereignty transfers, they were bitterly resisted by the states that they would diminish. Minorities were yielded up only by losers in war, or by weak states confronted with an overwhelming military threat.

Since World War II ethnic separatist issues in Europe have undergone significant change, particularly in Western Europe. On the one hand, ethnic minorities that have been long quiescent or only sporadically activist have emerged as new centers of autonomist or separatist aspirations. Some of these centers are located in Northern Ireland, Scotland, and Wales, and among the Flemings in Belgium, the Bretons in France, and the Basques and Catalonians in Spain. (Flemings now outnumber Walloons in Belgium, but historically they have been the economic, political, and social underdogs.) On the other hand, the governments of the states in which they are located are displaying greater tolerance toward autonomist demands - providing they are not militantly separatist.

In part, this tolerance, can be attributed to new appraisals of sovereignty and power. The traditional assets of national power were calculated as far as possible in terms of a self-sufficient sovereignty. Ideally, they would include a spacious territorial base and abundant natural resources, a numerous and economically productive population, a large military force and defensible frontiers, and, when necessary, reliable allies. In contemporary Western Europe among the ensemble of security considerations only economic productivity and alliances have increased in importance; the value of the other security factors has diminished.

What is more, both economic production and alliances have become institutionally transnational. Military security depends far more on long term stable alliance systems and far less on a self-contained defense of national territory. Economic productivity is irrevocably tied to the successful functioning of transnational economic organizations and to the international economy as a whole. In sum, survival and prosperity for Western European countries require guarantees beyond what the national territorial base and the people who inhabit it can offer.

In these circumstances, demands for the autonomy of ethnic minorities no longer seem so threatening. If outright separation is hardly a palatable proposition to the governments concerned, there are no bans on (non-violent) separatist political activity. This also holds true in the United States and, most dramatically, in Canada where a separatist regime governs the province of Quebec. In both Western Europe and North America, then, the old nationalist tendency to keep a tight rein on minorities in the name of security has given way to more forthcoming approaches. Diversity of ethnic cultures and the practice of ethnic politics have achieved a legitimacy that would have been unthinkable between 1789 and 1945, when European and European-style nationalism was in its heyday.

The situation in communist Europe is obviously quite different. Majority-minority ethnic relationships are tightly bound to the general rules governing totalitarian states. Like traditional prenational regimes the mass, whether ethnic majority or minority, has no effective political, economic, or social franchise. Moreover, official doctrine requires that ethnic identity must be subordinated to ideological loyalty. The official objective is to replace the old ethnic man with the new Soviet or communist man.

Nevertheless, the communist regimes have felt it necessary on occasion to pay lip service - and sometimes a bit more than that - to the ethnic principle. After all, the Soviet lid was clamped down after both World Wars at times, when a multitude of nationalisms had already reached a stage of rapid growth; curbing them was not an easy task. From an initial position of weakness, Lenin was forced to respond to the nationalist ferment with the un-Marxist doctrine of national self-determination. It was left to Stalin, first as Commissar of Nationalities and later as Lenin's successor, to reverse direction and purge ethnicity of its political content.

Stalin's denationalization policies permitted only a single and crucial exception: the majority nationalism of the Great Russians. Thus the pattern of dominance by the ethnic majority in Western nationalism was reproduced under the auspices of the Marxist state. The privileged position of the Great Russians, the Russian language, and Russian cultural norms has, in truth, kept alive and frequently enough sharpened the ethnic animosities inherited by the Soviet regime from its Tsarist predecessors.

Yet the Soviet lid remains firmly in place. The number of Jews permitted to emigrate represent only a miniscule fraction of the Soviet-Jewish community. Heroic acts of resistance to tyranny by individual Jews suffer the same fate as similar acts by non-Jews: harsh punishment and a thick screen of censorship and threat isolate them from both their own ethnic groups and from the Soviet mass at large.

Although the rights of over 100 ethnic groups in the Soviet Union are recognized constitutionally or in legislation, they are exercised at the will of the central regime, and none extend to contesting Great Russian dominance or policies of the Communist Party. The political muzzling of Soviet ethnic groups is only part of the whole: the political repression that blankets the entire Soviet population. The party elite rules without contest. With some modifications, then, the Soviet regime duplicates the governing features of the traditional pre-national elite state. The modifications derive from the fact that the Soviets have already passed through most of the stages characteristic of the nation-building process: industrial-ization, urbanization, and mass education. In order to manage the more complex mass, the elite has had to expand in num-bers and to elaborate its functions and controls to a degree unimaginable in traditionally-governed societies.

To create a mass society and nonetheless deny it the franchise in all key respects of public life is an exercise which necessarily requires an extraordinary concentration of power in the elite. As long as these central features prevail in the governing of the Soviet Union and most of Communist Europe, ethnic minorities can expect little progress toward greater autonomy -- and none at all insofar as they may harbor separatist aspirations.

In the Third World, the pre-national elite state is almost everywhere the governing political form. Almost nowhere is the mass society at even an early stage of development. Moreover, a majority of Third World states exhibits an ethnic heterogeneity more extreme than any of the developed nations except for the Soviet Union and, in a special sense, the United States.(1)   Finally, the boundaries of most Third

World states, and thus their ethnic composition, were fixed by
imperial fiat.   Considerations such as tribal, ethnic, or
religious bonds among the populace and regional geographic or
economic coherence were wholly subordinate in the building of
imperial political units.

To list these characteristics of Third World states and to
record that they interact and reenforce one another is to
stress the extraordinary obstacles that impede the development
of nationalism and the mass society along the lines of either
the Western or Soviet models.   At the same time, the distance
to be covered between national aspirations and realization of
national goals does much to explain why separatist movements
have not yet been as frequent and explosive a problem as one
might have otherwise anticipated given the vast diversity of
ethnic groups living in geographic intimacy.

Since their various dates of independence, Third World
countries have, with few exceptions, maintained their
boundaries intact.   The principal and most fateful exception
was India, which had to agree to the separation of Pakistan as
a condition of its own independence.   The policies of both
governments sought to carry out a peaceful partition.   Instead, panic and ancient religious fears and animosities made it
the bloodiest of separatist struggles.   Communal rioting and
microwarfare took an appalling toll, with estimates running
into millions of dead.   The subsequent partition of Pakistan in
1971 and the emergence of Bangladesh generated millions of
refugees, but the number of casualties was small compared to
the blood-letting of 1947.   The other major separatist movement
in Asia resulted in the secession of Singapore from Malaysia
with a minimum of violence.

In contrast to Asia, all the former colonial countries in
Africa still maintain the boundaries they were endowed with at
the time they gained their independence.   The Ibos of Nigeria
almost established the new sovereignty of Biafra, but the
Nigerian central government was able to prevent secession
after a bitter war.   Zaire, often with western help, has successfully beaten back numerous secession attempts, particularly
in the province of Shaba (Katanga).   Ethiopia has so far
maintained its military control over Eritreans and Somalis, as
well as other groups.   Sudan's long civil war between the
Arab north and the black south has given way to a tenuous
coexistence.   Numerous internal, tribal, and ethnic-linguistic
divisions in other African countries have been contested
primarily within the boundaries of the affected states.   The
terrible massacres that engulfed both Ruanda and Burundi are
exceptions, in part because the same two ethnic groups make
up the populations of both states.

Latin America concludes this brief survey of ethnic
division in Third World countries.   There, the centuries-old
white-mestizo oppression of Indians, who constitute the major-

ity of the population in many countries, continues with very few overt confrontations between the two groups. Both national boundaries and boundaries between elite and mass have remained rigid and stable to a remarkable degree.

A graphic overview of the world's ethnic divisions appears in Fig. 19.1. Its most salient feature is the contrast between the relative homogeneity of European and Western states generally and the number of multi-ethnic states in the Third World. In Africa, only six of 50 states are either nearly homogeneous, or populated by a single dominant group. In Latin America, the figures are eight of 21; in Asia, 22 of 36.

The potential for further ethnic strife and separatist movements is obviously great. Indeed, along with the necessity for development, internal ethnic divisions will constitute the major challenge to the viability of the great majority of Third World societies. Moreover, development and ethnicity are organically joined. Should one or more ethnic groups lag behind in the development process in any given country, they will sooner or later constitute a drag on the general momentum of development. Regional and ethnic disparities in productivity and education will mean regional and ethnic disparities in power. Power disparities, in turn, will stimulate the proclivities of the more powerful to dominate the less powerful, thus accentuating the unevenness of development.

These dynamics run an obvious parallel to those that have marked the history of Western nationalism. However, they will evolve in contexts much less favorable for development and internal and external peace. In most Third World countries, nationalism cannot be majoritarian because there are only ethnic elites and pluralities rather than majorities. Majoritarian nationalism has, through most of its history, a poor record concerning the human rights of minorities. The number of minority dissidents and those left behind in the development process will be far greater than was true in the Western experience. In these circumstances, bitter and indecisive conflict must be the prognosis rather than the achievement of a national state resting on at least near-consensus.

To the extent that any state grows in the direction of the mass society it will attract closer attention from outside powers. The increase of wealth and productivity, and of political and military power, will make it a more desirable ally - or a more dangerous enemy. Whenever such a state is deeply divided between those who benefit from the growth and those who do not, the division offers opportunities for exploitation by neighboring or distant states. Western, Soviet, Chinese, and Cuban undertakings since 1945 and 1960 have been fewer than they might have been considering the ethnic fragility of Third World countries. Nevertheless, as some of these coun-

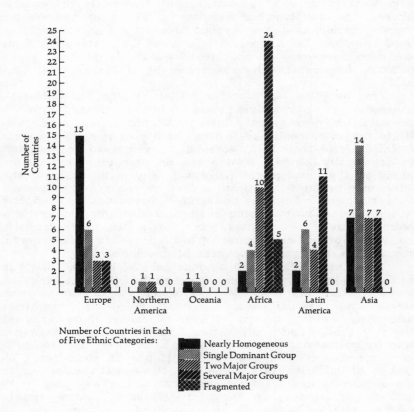

Number of Countries in Each
of Five Ethnic Categories:

- Nearly Homogeneous
- Single Dominant Group
- Two Major Groups
- Several Major Groups
- Fragmented

*In some cases linguistic or religious groupings provide the basis for classification.

Fig. 19.1. Ethnic composition by continent: number of countries in each of five ethnic categories (total number of countries is 134).

tries grow in power, both their viability and vulnerability will become of greater political moment. Then they could become, as European minorities have been in the past, major international danger zones.

Adherence to Western or Soviet models of nationalism can only produce growing internal and external perils for the ethnically-diverse Third World countries. A nationalism pre-occupied with building a homogeneous state must fail in societies where heterogeneity is the basic fact with which the state must content. Only a policy that promotes equality in politics and development opportunity for all ethnic groups can avoid the internal dimensions which must lead to separatist activity and foreign intervention.

History and present circumstances make clear that policies of equality are difficult to implement; they must cope with determined opposition from groups who believe they will profit from discrimination. But poor and weak countries that aspire to development and the wealth and power it produces need to recognize that inclusion of all sectors of their populations in the development process hastens and safeguards its evolution. Development sets hard enough tasks in mobilizing resources; squandering them in domestic strife or foreign wars can only delay or negate development's promise.

Separatism emerges when a portion of the population of a state seeks another political home from the one in which it finds itself. Its motive is almost invariably the conviction that the population involved is the victim of discrimination. No discrimination, no separation is a guideline applicable to underdeveloped and developed states alike. Power, wealth, and unity together with those still more desirable values of freedom and justice, are most completely attained in societies where all citizens feel themselves to be at home.

NOTE

1. See Richard W. Sterling, Macropolitics: International Relations in a Global Society (New York: Alfred A. Knopf, 1974), chap. 7 and Appendixes D and E.

20 Ethnic Autonomy: A Socio-Historical Synthesis

Arline McCord
William McCord

Paradoxes and irony plague our age. On the one hand, as Arnold Toynbee once commented, "Our century will be chiefly remembered by future generations as an age in which human society dared to think of the welfare of the whole human race" (Toynbee, intro.). Many aspects of our era support this belief: the United Nations was created, a second stumbling attempt at world unity; the EEC and NATO have erased the previously separatist national boundaries which threw Europe into turmoil; an international Marxist movement, dedicated in theory to the building of a united socialist world has emerged; and large business corporations ignore the limits of national boundaries. Further, we have ushered in an age in which the tri-lateral nations, overcoming their earlier hostilities, have now reached an uneasy detente with both Russia and China. An optimistic prophet would declare, with substantial reason, that the entire world is headed toward unity.

Yet, just as unity is in evidence, so are separatist movements blossoming prolificly. Beginning in the nineteenth century, nationalism - one variety of separatism - destroyed the British, French, Dutch, Belgium, and Austro-Hungarian empires. New nations - ranging from Yugoslavia to Hungary, Somalia to Kenya, Ghana to Indonesia - dot the world's map. Within these new nations, as well as the old, separatist movements - the Basques in Spain, Sumatrans in Indonesia, Ashanti in Ghana, - have gained strength at the point where old boundaries and antagonisms have collapsed.

This is, perhaps, the supreme paradox of the twentieth century: as the people of the globe move economically, politically, and culturally towards the creation of a more unitary world, different lines of commitment are drawn based on difference in power, religion, language, or race; and these

426

give rise to a cry for separatism. Opposite tendencies appear to be moving together.

The various separatists are potentially, or actually, violent: in Northern Ireland, people are killed regularly as a result of bombings; in France, the Bretons blew up a section of the Versailles Palace; in Ethiopia, Somalias and Eritreans fight doggedly to maintain their identity against Ethiopian forces. Yet, as the authors of this book make clear, the reaons behind separatist revolts and the claims they advance are often fragile, if not imaginary. Social scientific explanation, then, of the causes and the course of a particular event is obscure.

THE MYTHICAL BASE OF SEPARATISM

Any separatist movement bases itself ultimately upon a sense of ethnic identity. Clearly, however, the objective foundation of many of the groups has its origins in the myths, superstitions, and stereotypes created by leaders of the group, or by their opposition. For a separatist movement to emerge, people must first be convinced that they share something in common against an enemy. This is the subjective basis of the social movement. Objective differences in power, status, religion, ethnicity, or other factors may have little to do with the development of a subjective conviction.

A few examples can be given: In the nineteenth century, Theodore Herzl created political Zionism, or the belief that Jews should return to Palestine and the land. Shrewdly, he recognized that the invention of a flag to serve as a symbol would be one way to mobilize his people. In the twentieth century, a uniquely black literature - written in English - has emerged to galvanize American blacks into a recognition of their identity (Cook, Chapter 4). In the Southwest and California, artificial techniques have been used to create the label "Chicano" (Kleitz, Chapter 6); and even the pachucos, who were mere gang delinquents, have now been idolized as heralding a new age. On the Horn of Africa, the myth of a "Greater Somalia" has apparently failed to overcome basic differences between clans and their demands for grazing land, despite many propaganda efforts (Abate, Chapter 14). And more anciently, Huaman Poma believed in the symbolic efficacy of writing as a way to convince the King of Spain to create a nation of Indians (Castro-Klaren, Chapter 16).

This is not to say that the symbols that are used do not have any social foundation. Success in mobilizing popular support is dependent on touching familiar ground. In creating their various symbols and developing associated myths, some separatists would appear to have confounded reality. French

Canadian separatists, for example, continue their push toward the creation of an independent Quebec, even though their leaders realize that 70 percent of Quebec residents rejected this alternative in a Roper poll (Theriault, Chapter 7). Further, some Spanish Basques vigorously pursue their ideals of separatism, even though 76 percent of the people in the Basque regions cannot speak that particular language.

In Scotland, the nationalists pursue their ideal, although they realize that there are no longer any religious or cultural issues to divide them from the English. They also recognize that many Scotsmen reject the concept that the newly-discovered North Sea oil belongs to them exclusively (Furniss, Chapter 9). Indeed, they face the shocking possibility that the people of the Shetland Islands, under which most of the oil flows, might, in turn, declare themselves independent of Scotland.

Conversely, in some regions that would appear to be wide open to a separatist movement, such activity has not taken hold. In Latin America, differences in culture, forms of religion, language, and ethnic identity provide a fertile breeding ground for separatist movements. However, they have not appeared (Segal, Chapter 17). Instead, isolated Indian groups vainly hope that the resurrected body of one of their leaders may eventually reestablish their power against the Spaniards.

Thus, the success or failure of a separatist movement to develop and grow depends upon whether the leaders can invent and communicate a series of acceptable symbols, ideologies, and myths, as well as strategies to counter their defined enemy. This subjective variable, contingent, in part, upon the style, cleverness, or even charisma of the leaders, appears as a dominant factor in deciding the fate of separatist movements. How can it be measured or predicted?

OBJECTIVE VARIABLES AFFECTING SEPARATIST MOVEMENTS

As Raymond Hall has observed in his introduction, several variables that can be measured by social scientists appear to affect the rise or fall of a separatist movement.

Differential Access to Power

On the most obvious level, differences in power between various groups provide the basis for the origin, the rise, and the fall of a separatist movement. Planned, or unplanned, severe repression of a dissident group erodes the possibility of developing a separatist social movement. Native American Indians suffered from this fate when they were decimated by European diseases and advanced military technology (Dorris, Chapter 5). Although different in language, ideology, religion, and race from their conquerors, Native Americans had little chance, until recent times, to fulfill their indigenous ideals. Similarly, the Spanish in Latin America conquered and isolated the Indian groups that tried to oppose them, and imposed an Hispanic culture that has dominated for 400 years (Castro-Klaren, Chapter 16).

If the dominant group relents and allows, for whatever reason, the partial absorption of a defined subordinate group into the political, or economic life of the center, a separatist movement may well emerge. At what point in the relationship demands for independence by the subordinated group are made remains unspecifiable. On the one hand, Scotland garnered great economic advantage from its union with England, although it lost much of its popular culture; but a separatist movement did not develop until the Scots had attained, or actually surpassed, the English in economic power and potential (Furniss, Chapter 9). On the other hand, despite early English efforts to destroy Quebec culture, a separatist movement did not emerge politically until the central government devolved many of its powers upon Quebec. The French in Quebec were allowed to mandate the official language; and, in 1978, Quebec was granted virtual autonomy, with only two exceptions: Canada should remain united, and the rights of the English speaking minority should be preserved (Theriault, Chapter 7).

Language

Few would question the fact that language often plays a paramount, if at times symbolic, role in the emergence and survival of separatist movements (Sagarin and Moneymaker, Chapter 3). Francophones in Quebec seek to assert their power by destroying English language schools; the Flemish in Belgium and, to a lesser degree, in France wish to eliminate French as the dominant language. Bretons desire to revive their original language as a means of opposing the French "invasion"; and Basques flaunt their own language as an alternative to Spanish. Language serves as a clear and meaningful division between people.

Yet, quite often, language plays no more than a symbolic role in the creation and continuance of a separatist movement. Most Basques, as has been noted, cannot speak their language; most Catholics in Northern Ireland do not speak Gaelic fluently; people who assume the Chicano identity in America have abandoned Spanish as their language of their home. At times, some are made to feel ashamed of this fact (Kleitz, Chapter 6).

Language may emerge as an important factor in the distribution of power, as in Quebec, where English has traditionally served as the lingua franca of the business classes. Equally often, language, like a flag, can serve as a symbolic rallying point for people who wish to create or maintain a sense of commonality in order to define themselves and others more clearly.

Religion

Although we live in an age of secularization, religion may serve as a variable that divides people from each other. In Northern Ireland, the Protestant-Catholic division plays a crucial role, although the religious distinctions mirror political, economic, and social factors (Curran, Chapter 8). In Ethiopia, the traditional antagonism between Muslims and Christians adds fire to the conflict (Abate, Chapter 14). And India's division in 1948, represents the classic example of religiosity cleaving a subcontinent into violently antagonistic camps.

As with language differences, however, one cannot assume that religion is the sole or even the major ignitor of separatist conflict in most regions. The French and the Bretons share the same religion, as do the Basques and the Spanish; yet, they are at odds. In Uganda, Protestants rebel against their fellow Protestants' authority in particular districts (Doornbos, Chapter 13).

Economic Divisions

Economic subordination undoubtedly has importance for many separatist movements. France has developed its center, the Paris region, at the expense of various secessionist territories (Beer, Chapter 11). Francophones in Quebec have suffered from economic discrimination (Theriault, Chapter 7), and irredentists in Ethiopia fight primarily over grazing land that they believe has been unjustly taken from them (Abate, Chapter 14).

In spite of these examples, the specific nature of the relationship remains unspecifiable. Economic deprivation in itself does not lead to separatist movements. And it is quite evident that economic progress for a previously-deprived ethnic group may well lead to an increase in separatist sentiment, rather than a decrease (Beer, Chapter 11; Furniss, Chapter 9; Heiberg, Chapter 10). Under some conditions, sober economic considerations, even among a relatively-deprived ethnic group, may lead to the diminution of a separatist sentiment. The Quebecois, for example, seem to lose strength as their adherents realize the potential economic cost of a division from the rest of Canada (Theriault, Chapter 7).

Culture

Culture - as distinct from religion, economic, or language - is most general and difficult to operationalize independently, but it would appear to have a real impact. Presumably, those who use the term in dealing with separatist social movements refer to a situation associated with a holistic common identity that supercedes other divisions. Indeed, some separatist movements flourish despite the fact that their members have little, if anything, in common except some sense of a common culture. The Basques have little unity in terms of religion, territory, language, economics, or race. Yet, they maintain the ideological goal of creating a "Basque nation" (Heiberg, Chapter 10). A vague identification based on historical experiences from centuries past lies at the base of their actions. In Uganda, tribal identifications supercede objective economic, religious, and geographical distinctions (Doornbos, Chapter 13). In Somali, people forget their common language and Muslim religion to fight over tribal rights to grazing land (Abate, Chapter 14).

Geography

Geographical differences - physically-isolated enclaves of people speaking a particular language, or holding a special religion, or adhering to a common cultural identity - have obviously spawned some separatist social movements. Isolated by great deserts, Central Asians, if and when they are relieved of central control from the Russian center, may reignite separatist action (Lindgren, Chapter 12). Quarrels with the center of geographical entity, such as London, sparked the Scottish National Party, which remains at the geographical periphery. After the death of Tito, as he had feared, differences between the "center" of the nation and its mountainous regions, such as Montenegro, may erupt into separatist conflicts.

Except in immediate territorial conflicts, similar to those that exist among the various tribes of Africa, geography in and of itself seems a relatively minor factor in separatist movements. A solution to separatist conflicts, however, may well lie in the geographical separation of antagonistic parties, as Joseph Curran has suggested in the case of Ulster (Curran, Chapter 8).

INADEQUACY OF PREVAILING THEORIES

No single theory or set of variables seems to explain the origins, timing, and course of each of the various separatist movements. Traditional sociological theories offer little insight into the developments of particular situations, the weighting of the different variables as they have evolved through their unique histories, or the entire global phenomenon.

Karl Marx and Frederick Engels assumed that capitalism, and eventually communism, would abolish the importance of ethnic differences. Clearly, capitalism has nothing to do with ethnic problems in the Soviet Union, or for that matter in Uganda or Somalia. Similarly, German sociologist, Max Weber, argued that the advance of bureaucracy and rationality would lead to the disappearance of ethnic, racial, and linguistic factors in modern political life. Yet separatist movements blossom in that most rationalistic of states, France. Similarly, Emile Durkheim (1964) believed that an increasing division of labor would lead to a deemphasis of ethnic loyalties. In fact, events have confounded all of these positions. Nominally socialist societies exhibit signs of ethnic discontent; and a highly "rational" and distinct division of labor makes industrialized, capitalist nations equally subject to separatist social movements.

If classic theories such as Marxism are bankrupt in regard to this form of social movement, structural functionalism as a theory has offered even less toward the understanding of this phenomenon. Writers following this persuasion have largely ignored ethnic divisions and, even when they have dealt with them, have assumed that modernization would lead to the disappearance of separatist sentiments (Parsons). Separatist sentiment and action have not evaporated as some of these theorists would have us predict (Almond and Powell).

Neo-Marxists of the latest variety also do not offer much aid in understanding the phenomenon. Theories of internal colonialism (Gonzales-Cazanova) fail to explain why areas such as Scotland, long dependent on England, failed to develop separatist movements until the region had experienced a rate of economic growth superior to that of the "colonizer." Similarly, theories of dependence, such as those offered by James Wicham, do not explicate the reasons why Somalia, Eritrea, and Soviet Central Asia retain a separate ethnic identity. They have been dependent areas for only short periods. Equally, Michael Hecther's attempt to explain separatist movements by involving theories of internal colonialism and of relative deprivation seem less than convincing when applied to a concrete situation such as France (Beer, Chapter 11).

Even in this book, the various authors offer contradictory

explanations of separatism. Abate argues that such movements arise when economic underdevelopment prevails (Chapter 14). In contrast, Beer suggests that a time of economic progress, albeit, following a time of relative poverty, enhances the chance of success for certain types of separatist movements (Chapter 11). Neither generalization embraces all the many nuances of separatist social movements.

Because of the paucity of contemporary theory to aid in the understanding of social movements, we are left with these alternatives: First, we may plausibly argue that separatist movements are unique, and that any explanation of them must rely upon information of the specific historical circumstances which precede them. It is extremely difficult, if not impossible, to compare the demands of cattle grazers in Somalia, the plight of slave owners in the pre-Civil War South, and the issues that divide Ulster. Can one reasonably compare the complaints of Ashanti separatists, who object to the removal of the golden chairs of their chiefs, with the demands of Scottish nationalists, who wish to retain control of the oil drained from the North Sea? Until social scientists appropriately conceptualize, operationalize, quantify, and replicate the relevant evidence, it is an impossible task.

Second, one may content that certain generalizations apply to all separatist movements despite their particular historical configuration. We can venture a few, admittedly tentative approaches to the problem of separatism. Of necessity, such generalizations must remain at an extremely high level of abstraction and, therefore, must be conditionally specified.

SOME REFLECTIONS ON SEPARATISM

Separatist movements would seem to emerge when one or a combination of eight different variables characterize a particular situation.

First, separatist movements arise when some group has a differential access to power at the political-economic center of the state. The power differential is not complete, however, and one may predict separatist sentiment when the center depends upon the periphery for essential goods, resources, or services. The legitimacy of the central power may be questioned on the basis of that dependency. The Biafran Civil War serves as an example. Ibos in Biafra suffered from violent attacks by the Hausas and the Fulanis who controlled the political center in Nigeria. Further, the discovery of oil in Biafra, and the subsequent profits and tax revenues that flowed to the central government, created a sense of severe injustice among the Ibos. Differences in language, tradition, and religion - Moslim vs. Christian - exacerbated the conflict. Biafrans seceded when it appeared to them that they could no longer tolerate discrimination. The central rulers, the Yorubans, Hausas, and Fulanis, could ill afford a secessionist movement because they would lose the oil revenues of an independent Biafra. Under different economic conditions, it could be argued, they might well have allowed the Ibos to secede. The dependence of the center, however, forced a confrontation that resulted in a bloody civil war.

Second, uneven economic development that encourages the population of some regions to aspire to the affluence enjoyed by others can also play a role in some separatist movements. In Indonesia, Sumatrans envied the economic status of the people of Java; in India, the people of Assam almost left the nation when they suspected that New Delhi was draining their resources; in Quebec, Francophones disliked the supremacy of the English in government and business affairs; and in Pakistan, the people of Bangladesh split the nation when they realized that they were receiving less than their share of the wealth.

Third, a separatist movement may arise if a group that has been only partially assimilated into the mainstream or dominant society finds its traditional culture dying. This may seem contradictory to common sense wisdom, but the fact remains that, in many areas, the erosion of a once-proud culture has inspired, rather than dampened, separatist sentiments. Political nationalism in Scotland, for example, has proceeded hand in hand with the collapse of the original Scottish culture (Furniss, Chapter 9). Similarly, in Quebec, the decline of the church, agriculture, and the traditional family system has entailed the growth of politically-separatist movements (Theriault, Chapter 7). There are a number of alternative explanations for this occurrence. Leadership within a subordinate group, for example, may be threatened by the continued assimilation of the population. As long as the group remains enclosed in an enclave of its own, the leadership does not feel the urgency to restore feelings of unity, upon which their own power is based. Of course, cultural revivalism may be simply a consequence of the realization that inaction will result in the death of the culture. In any instance, revival of a dormant or dying culture may be promoted through political edict regulating language to be spoken, school curriculum, mass media content, military, or even terrorist means.

Fourth, the emergence of a separatist movement requires leadership that can mobilize a population behind the cause. At times, the cause may have its roots in mythic rather than objective reality: the long suppressed Biblical desire among Jews to spend Passover in Jerusalem, or the all-but-forgotten linguistic tradition of the Basques, or the Peruvian Indians' belief that a long dead leader will return to establish Indian rule. It appears to matter little which particular myth is invoked. It becomes valid if it helps separatist leaders instill solidarity among their people.

Fifth, a successful separatist movement must create the belief that the very survival of the group requires a radical solution, and that no other alternative exists. White American Southerners fought The Battle Between the States with that conviction. The current separatist movements in Quebec, Scotland, and Somalia have yet to convince the people that all other alternatives have been exhausted.

Sixth, when a tradition of hatred has been nourished for centuries, and has been complemented by divisive religious, social, economic, political, or ethnic lines, separatism blossoms. In Ulster, both Protestants and Catholics have preserved 400 years of hostility, and have ingrained it into all of their relationships from work to housing, education to marriage. In the face of such enduring hostilities, it is little wonder that each side resorts to violence, beating drums in futile parades and driving the English governmental officials to despair in their attempts to find a lasting, peaceful solution.

Seventh, at an abstract, speculative level, one could hypothesize that the relationship between the direction of economic growth and the legitimacy granted to those in power is positive.

As William Beer suggests in the case of France, an increased level of economic welfare coincides with ethnic protest at the ballot box, while the preservation of a state of "internal colonialism" coincides with violent protest but not with pacific electoral activity (Beer, Chapter 11). The rate of economic growth would seem to conditionally specify the nature of this hypothesized relationship. As economic affluence and expectations increase, rapidly improving economic conditions tend to be associated with violent dissent, while less rapid growth involves more conventional means of political activism. The situation prevails in Uganda (Doornbos, Chapter 15).

Eighth, if a political center arrogates to itself the greatest part of political power, but allows some voices of discontent from ethnic groups, then the probability that a cry for separatism will be raised increases. The Native Americans and American blacks both suffer from severe, but incomplete and ineffectual, repression.

If all of these factors happen to coincide, and are multiplied by genuine religious ethnic, or linguistic differences, there can be little doubt that a separatist movement will arise and, possibly, tear apart the status quo. India has experienced such a fate; Ulster is suffering it today; Yugoslavia may encounter it tomorrow.

RESOLUTIONS OF THE SEPARATIST ISSUE

Historically, societies have responded to the threat of separatism in one of four ways. China and India have absorbed generations of foreigners through complete assimilation. Many states, from the Austro-Hungarian Empire in 1918 to India in 1948, have disintegrated. Other societies, most notably Russia, Israel, and North and South America, have tried, with some degree of success, to obliterate their separatist elements by military conquest or cultural supremacy. A handful of regions, such as France in dealings with the Hugenots or contemporary Ulster in handling the Catholics, may well resort to a policy of exile or redrawing boundaries. Nazi Germany stands alone as a nation that systematically killed off a large proportion of those defined as inferior and foreign.

In the contemporary world, marked as it is by an unmistakable trend toward unity and an equally significant growth in separatist movements, few if any, rational men would dare to predict the exact path which the future will follow.

BIBLIOGRAPHY

Almond, G. and G. Powell. Comparative Politics: A Developmental Approach. Boston: Little, Brown, 1970.

Durkheim, Emile. The Division of Labor in Society. New York: The Free Press, 1964.

Gonzalez-Casanova, H. "Internal Colonialism and Nation Development," Studies in Comparative International Development 1, no. 4 (1970): 27-30.

Hall, Raymond (ed). Ethnic Autonomy. New York: Pergamon Press, 1979.

Marx, Karl and Friederich Engels. The Communist Manifesto. New York: Appleton Century Crofts, 1955.

Parsons, Talcott. The Social System. New York: The Free Press, 1968.

Toynbee, Arnold. A Study of History. New York: MacMillan, 1952.

Weber, Max. Economy and Society. G. Roth and K. Wittich (eds.). New York: The Free Press, 1960.

Index

ETA.
Ethiopia
  and Arab involvement 297–
    299
  attempts to integrate
    Somalis 257, 304–306,
    309–310
  colonial background, 257,
    291–294
  federation with Eritrea,
    296–297
  irredentism in Ogaden
    region 257, 299–310,
    430–431
  Islam-Christian rivalry 288–
    291, 295, 307–308, 309–
    310
  Italian invasion of, 290,
    291–292, 293, 294, 295,
    300
  and Kingdom of Aksum 288,
    309
  military aid 306–307
  Muslim population 284
  nationalism 257
  Orthodox Christianity 286
  and political integration 257
  religion 257, 283, 429–430
  and secession of Eritrea
    257, 294, 336, 422 and
    423
  and Soviet Union 307, 308
  tribes and language 27
  See also Africa, Ethiopian
    separatist movements
Ethiopian separatist movements
  historical background 284–
    288
  secession of Eritrea 295,
    307, 308, 309, 310
  See also Eritrea, Somali
    Republic
Ethnic autonomy
  definition xxi, xxiii
  as developed in urban
    areas xx–xxi
  dissidence and rise of
    movements 9
  implications of xx

intergroup conflict xvii,
    xx, xxi, xxiii, 41–42
  and social environment
    xxvii
  variables used in analysis
    of.
  See also Ethnic behavior,
    Nationalism, Separatism
Ethnic group behavior
  and group homogeneity
    xviii, xix
  identity 3
  and separatism xxiii
  traditions and symbols xx,
    11
  variables used in analysis
    of xxiii, xxvii
  See also Ethnicity, Nation-
    alism, Separatism
Ethnic heterogeneity xvii, xxi,
    255–256
Ethnic movements
  definition 202, 209
  in Latin America 345
  political   210–211
Ethnic separatism
  definition of 413
  dynamics of 414
  politics of 413, 414, 418–
    419
  relationship to nationalism
    414
  and resistance by state
    416, 418–419
  and state power 413–414,
    418–419
  strategies 416–418
Ethnicity
  and adaptability to one's
    environment 14, 15
  definitions of 10, 11, 13,
    14–15, 201–202
  and ethnic boundaries 13–
    14, 15
  and ethnic elites 338, 339
  and formation of new states
    8
  influences on 11–12
  intergroup conflict 12, 41–
    42, 140

About the Contributors

RAYMOND L. HALL - Associate Professor of Sociology at Dartmouth College. He is increasingly concerned with the dynamics of large-scale social change, especially that prompted by social movements. He edited Black Separatism and Social Reality: Rhetoric and Reason, and is the author of Black Separatism in the United States.

YOHANNIS ABATE - Associate Professor of Geography at the University of Maryland, Baltimore County. He teaches geography in the Department of African-American Studies. Born in Ethiopia, his area of specialization is political geography, with special emphasis on Africa.

HOYT S. ALVERSON - Associate Professor and Chairman of the Department of Anthropology at Dartmouth College. He is a cultural anthropologist, with southern Africa being his major comparative interest. His latest book, Mind in the Heart of Darkness, is a study of value and self-identity among the Tswana of southern Africa.

LADUN ANISE - Associate Professor of Political Science at the University of Pittsburgh. He also teaches in the Afro-American Studies Department. Born in Nigeria, much of his written work has centered on political integration in developing countries. His present work focuses attention on economic dimensions of development.

WILLIAM R. BEER - Associate Professor of Sociology at City University of New York (CUNY), Brooklyn College. Beer is a specialist in comparative sociology with special interest in France.

SARA CASTRO-KLAREN - Associate Professor of Comparative Literature at Dartmouth College. Born in Peru, she has published extensively, and was a Woodrow Wilson Fellow in the 1977-78 academic year.

WILLIAM W. COOK - Associate Professor of English and Chairman of the Black Studies Program at Dartmouth College. He has published his own poetry and critical studies of Robert Frost, Walt Whitman, Chinun Achebe, Melvin Tolson, Ishmael Reed, and many others.

JOSEPH M. CURRAN - Professor of History at LeMoyne College in Syracuse, New York. He has published widely on Northern Ireland. His major work, The Birth of the Irish Free State, will be published by the University of Alabama Press.

MARTIN R. DOORNBOS - Senior Lecturer in Political Science at the Institute of Social Studies, the Hague. His major scholarly interest is comparative political movements, with a particular focus on Uganda.

MICHAEL DORRIS - Associate Professor of Anthropology and Chairman of Native American Studies at Dartmouth College. He specializes in cultural anthropology, and is a Guggenheim fellow for the 1978-79 academic year.

HOWARD L. ERDMAN - Professor of Government at Dartmouth College. His area of specialization is international relations, with special emphasis on Indian Politics.

NORMAN FURNISS - Associate Professor of Political Science and Chairman of Western European Studies at the University of Indiana. His special focus is on Scotland. He is co-author of The Case for the Welfare State, published in 1977 by the University of Indiana Press.

MARIANNE HEIBERG - Senior Lecturer in the London School of Economics and Political Science. Her major focus is on comparative political institutions, with Spain as a special interest.

MARIA KLEITZ - An artist and teacher of bi-lingual education in Colorado Springs, Colorado. She firmly believes that intergroup conflict can be mediated through a better understanding and appreciation of different cultures. She has written several children's books, and illustrated many others.

DAVID T. LINDGREN - Associate Professor and Chairman of the Department of Geography and the Urban Studies Program at Dartmouth College. His specialty is remote sensing and political geography. His comparative interest is the Soviet Union.

ARLENE S. McCORD - Associate Professor of Sociology at Hunter College. She is co-author of Black Students on White College Campuses, Urban Social Conflict, Social Stratification, and, with William McCord, Social Problems. Her present research interests include conflict resolution in organizations and educational inequality.

WILLIAM M. McCORD - Professor of Sociology and Chairman of the Sociology Department at the City University of New York (CUNY). He is also Professor of Sociology at the Graduate School and University Center of CUNY. Author of more than 15 books ranging from The Origins of Alcoholism to Mississippi Summer to The Springtime of Freedom (which was nominated for a Pulitzer Prize), he is presently engaged in writing a social history of the impact of major events on the global system in the last 150 years.

JAMES MONEYMAKER - A graduate student in the Department of Sociology at the Graduate School and University Center of the City University of New York (CUNY). His major interest is in the area of comparative linguistic dynamics.

EDWARD SAGARIN - Professor of Sociology at City University of New York (CUNY) and at the Graduate School and University Center of CUNY. He is one of the nation's outstanding symbolic interactionists; he has long been interested in the role of language in ethnic movements for autonomy. He is the author and co-author of several books on a wide range of subjects.

BERNARD E. SEGAL - Professor of Sociology at Dartmouth College. He is the editor of Racial and Ethnic Relations, and author of articles in fields ranging from social psychiatry to Latin American politics. He is currently at work on a book that will compare and contrast various forms of ethnic relations in the Western Hemisphere.

RICHARD W. STERLING - Professor of Government at
    Dartmouth College. He is the author of Ethnics in a
    World of Power and Macropolitics. His major concern
    is the danger inherent in the power imbalance
    between the developed and developing worlds. His
    present research centers around the international
    implications of illegal migration.

GEORGE F. THERIAULT - Professor Emeritus of Sociology
    at Dartmouth College. He has taught sociology for
    40 years. He is a specialist in the social psychology
    of human relations, and an authority on Canadian-
    American relations.

Pergamon Policy Studies